TRANSFORMING
PATRIARCHY

For Joe,
Happy reading!
Stue H.

TRANSFORMING PATRIARCHY

CHINESE FAMILIES *in the* TWENTY-FIRST CENTURY

EDITED BY

Gonçalo Santos

AND

Stevan Harrell

UNIVERSITY OF WASHINGTON PRESS

Seattle and London

The publication of *Transforming Patriarchy* was supported by a grant from the Max Planck Institute for Social Anthropology.

UNIVERSITY OF WASHINGTON PRESS
www.washington.edu/uwpress

LIBRARY OF CONGRESS CATALOGING-IN-PUBLICATION DATA
Names: Santos, Gonçalo D., editor. | Harrell, Stevan, editor.
Title: Transforming patriarchy : Chinese families in the twenty-first century / edited by Gonçalo Santos and Stevan Harrell.
Description: Seattle : University of Washington Press, [2017] | Includes bibliographical references and index.
Identifiers: LCCN 2016013675| ISBN 9780295998978 (hardcover : alk. paper) | ISBN 9780295999821 (pbk. : alk. paper)
Subjects: LCSH: Families—China—History—21st century. | Patriarchy—China. | Kinship—China. | China—Social conditions—21st century.
Classification: LCC HQ684 .T745 2017 | DDC 306.85095109/05—dc23
LC record available at https://lccn.loc.gov/2016013675

CONTENTS

ACKNOWLEDGMENTS

The chapters in this book were first presented in June 2013 at a three-day conference organized at the Max Planck Institute for Social Anthropology in Halle (Saale). We thank Chris Hann, director of the Department "Resilience and Transformation in Eurasia," for making this conference possible through the generous provision of funding and logistic support. We thank also Bettina Mann, Berit Westwood, and Anke Meyer for helping coordinate the conference in Halle and for making it such a pleasure to organize and attend. The conference started in the best possible way with a keynote lecture from Rubie Watson. We would like to thank her for launching the debate and for her sharp-witted comments during the conference. We would also like to thank the discussants Francesca Bray, Janet Carsten, Deborah Davis, Henrike Donner, and Michael Herzfeld for their thought-provoking questions and comments. Michael deserves special thanks for his closing remarks during the conference and for writing a very insightful afterword that we were unable to include in the book for reasons of space. We were also unable to include a highly stimulating essay on female power written by Charles Stafford. We would like to thank him for his contribution and more generally for his unstinting intellectual support. Thanks also to Wu Xiujie and Sara Friedman for their conference papers and their critical input during the conference in Halle. As we progressed toward publication, it became very clear that the work of revision undertaken by all contributors benefited greatly from the lively atmosphere of critical discussion in Halle. We would like to thank everyone who attended the conference for their input.

The writing of the introduction and the final revisions of individual chapters benefited significantly from the close readings of two anonymous reviewers for the University of Washington Press. We thank these reviewers for providing valuable comments and critiques that strengthened the coherence of the volume. Lorri Hagman's support at the University of Washington Press was essential, and we are immensely grateful for her expert guidance throughout the review and publication process. James Wright prepared the index. Lastly we acknowledge our gratitude to Chris Hann and the Max Planck Institute for Social Anthropology for a generous publication subvention.

Gonçalo Santos and Stevan Harrell
September 2015

ACKNOWLEDGMENTS

NOTE ON TRANSCRIPTION

Chinese words are transcribed from standard Chinese in the standard pinyin orthography. A few words in chapter 4 are transcribed from Cantonese in the Yale orthography. Chinese characters are given in the glossary.

TRANSFORMING
PATRIARCHY

INTRODUCTION

STEVAN HARRELL AND GONÇALO SANTOS

A DAUGHTER-IN-LAW in a remote Northern Guangdong village berates her father-in-law for not taking good enough care of her children, and he vows to try harder, because "she's the boss." An elderly couple in rural Liaoning sue their son in a People's Court for the filial support he has not provided, while urban insurance companies sell filial piety plans on the Internet around Mother's Day. A lesbian "fake marries" a gay man to get both families off their backs, but he ends up dominating the "marriage." An ambitious nurse in Nanjing gives up plans for medical school in the United States to marry and have a family, spending nights with her husband at his parents' flat, but all day with her mother nearby. Provincial governments mount aggressive advertising campaigns to recruit sperm donors for infertile couples, while sitting-the-month centers offer spa services along with traditional foods for new mothers in their first postpartum month. In a mountainous county in Zhejiang, almost all brides are pregnant (Liu Fuqin, pers. comm.), while in a similar area in southern Sichuan, a young man tells an ethnographic filmmaker's camera that "of course" people live together before marriage. How else would they know if they can get along (Han et al. 2009)?

Chinese family ideals and practices were subject to significant transformations during the first three-quarters of the twentieth century,[1] especially after the establishment of the People's Republic of China (PRC) in 1949. Writing about the period between the 1950s and 1970s, an earlier generation of anthropologists showed that the Communist attempt to challenge "traditional" gender and generational hierarchies within the family led to significant changes in legal regulations and everyday practices but also contributed to the reinforcement of earlier patriarchal arrangements.[2] Since then, wide-reaching and unprecedented changes have been happening to family and gender relations in the context of the increasingly entangled intersections of private negotiations and public dialogues at various levels in law, state policy, technology, science, and the media. This volume is about the significance of these more recent transformations in the age of market reforms, large-scale industrialization, massive urbanization, and fast-paced globalization.

Noting that there is plenty new under the Chinese sun, sometime in 2011 we decided to convene a conference in June 2013 with the deliberately provocative title "Is Chinese Patriarchy Over?" After three days of intense discussion at the Max Planck Institute for Social Anthropology in Halle (Saale), plus a year of editing and revising chapters, we have reinforced our initial impression that contemporary family processes continue to be shaped by deep-seated gender and generational hierarchies, but these continuities are accompanied by radical transformations that no one would have predicted at the time of William L. Parrish and Martin King Whyte's two classic volumes on Maoist-era families (Parrish and Whyte 1978; Whyte and Parrish 1984) or even a decade later at the time of Deborah Davis and Stevan Harrell's *Chinese Families in the Post-Mao Era* (1993).

The causes of these transformations are many and varied, including rising prosperity, new forms of urban living, increasing transnational ties, growing population mobility, the Birth-Planning Policy,[3] the emergence of new ideas about marriage, gender equality, and conjugal intimacy, and many other aspects of China's spectacular socioeconomic development in the past few decades. Since not all of these factors operate equally in different social contexts, the nature and degree of the changes vary from city to countryside, from region to region, from social class to social class. The chapters in this volume focus on the social, cultural, political, and technological dimensions of this complex multifaceted move away from earlier patriarchal configurations. In contrast to dominant theoretical trends in China studies (see, for example, Barlow 1991, 2004), the present volume does not focus only on macro-level changes in discourses or policies but analyzes such large-scale historical transformations in the context of actual practices and processes of negotiation. This ethnographic focus has led us to develop a model of patriarchy and social change that is sensitive to heterogeneous processes at the local level. The model is based on a definition of patriarchy that includes two axes of inequality (generation and gender), and we show how these two axes interact with each other and with changes in the surrounding environment. This model has a strong spatial component because it is explicitly concerned with linking micro-historical realities to broader historical processes at both

STEVAN HARRELL AND GONÇALO SANTOS

the national and the global level. This model of patriarchy and social change is based on Chinese discourses and experiences, but it can be applied to other contexts. In the concluding section, we show how it represents a challenge to existing Western-centric theorizations based on clear-cut oppositions between private and public and on the concept of the nuclear family.

THE QUESTION AT HAND: IS CHINESE PATRIARCHY OVER?

Both of us began to formulate the ideas for this volume from our empirical observations, in a wide variety of contexts, that Chinese family processes (including the various hierarchies and asymmetries built around differences in gender and generation) were changing at a very fast pace. These changes were not taking place only at the level of hard realities of some sort (i.e., relative economic and political power); they were also having an effect at the level of meanings and values (i.e., what is socially worthy and morally good). We were of course not the only ones to notice. Beginning in the 1990s, a number of publications began to analyze these changes, quite often in light of classic modernization theories. For example, Yunxiang Yan (1997) analyzed the changes in a village in Heilongjiang between the 1970s and the 1990s as symptomatic of a more general process of transformation in Chinese family life: the waning power of the senior generations and the increasing centrality of horizontal conjugal ties. For Yan, the system of kinship and gender relations that had endured in some form since at least the Song neo-Confucian revival, a system that exemplified the ideal of patriarchal structures not only in East Asia but worldwide, was in the process of breaking down, and he conceptualized this rupture as a "triumph of conjugality over patriarchy." Yan saw the emergence of strong conjugal ties as possible only when privacy became a priority and the individual was valorized, and in later works, he extends this thesis to a wider sphere of family (2003) and social relations generally, describing a process he calls, drawing on theorists of globalization such as Ulrich Beck and Anthony Giddens,[4] "the individualization of Chinese society" (2009).[5]

Yan's individualization thesis has merit; certainly personal freedom and self-fulfillment are both widely discussed topics and widely shared goals in today's China. At the same time, no one really claims to agree with Margaret Thatcher's oft-quoted remark, "There is no such thing as society. There are individual men and women, and there are families" (1987). Yan's work has highlighted the broader significance of institutionalized processes of individualization, including negative developments such as the emergence of "uncivic" forms of individualism (Yan 2003, 2009), but his model of social transformation tends to overstate the extent to which individuals have become unmoored from family and other social and cultural ties. Even in the age of the individual, people's lives continue to be shaped by broader social networks, rules, and expectations, and recent literature on Chinese family, marriage, and kinship has attempted to delineate the multiple social platforms and cultural landscapes within which individuals are still expected and motivated to operate.

Davis and Friedman's introduction to their recent volume *Wives, Husbands, and Lovers* (2014) addresses this topic straight on, formulating the thesis that family and gender relations in China are being "deinstitutionalized." The rather rigid social, legal, and ethical norms that have long governed marriage in particular are being replaced by new values of personal fulfillment that allow for much greater individual variation while creating new anxieties about how best to approach and understand marriage.[6] People, they say, are struggling to come to terms with "new sexual mores, the erosion of traditional gender norms, and rising rates of marital infidelity and divorce" (1). People also more readily accept premarital sexuality and cohabitation (16). Davis and Friedman do not make clear whether this dynamic of "deinstitutionalization" is to be followed by "reinstitutionalization" around a new set of norms or by further "deinstitutionalization" and ever greater variation in attitudes toward marriage and sexuality, but they assert that the family, in particular the matrix of intergenerational obligations, is not being deinstitutionalized to anywhere near the same degree: "What is less obvious . . . is the enduring respect for the value of intergenerational reciprocity and lifelong commitments to family ties that extend beyond those between a husband and wife" (26).

This contrast between deinstitutionalized marriage and continually institutionalized intergenerational obligations adds an important qualification to Yan's individualization thesis but is still too simple when we observe closely the great variety of marital and intergenerational relations in China today. Whatever general transformation may be going on, lived local realities are more nuanced, multifaceted, and multidirectional than predicted by the deinstitutionalization model or any other related model of social change postulating a shift from a public to a private ordering of intimate life (Brandtstädter and Santos 2009). In some respects, the magnitude of changes—partly reflected in the opening anecdotes above—seems to signal a brave new world of family practices and intimate relations (premarital cohabitation, pregnant brides, public displays of affection, shrinking families) suggesting the weakening of institutional structures and their replacement by individual strategies, but in other respects, earlier patriarchal norms and procedures seem to prevail (virilocal marriage, women's responsibility for housework, patricentric kin terms). Still other aspects present themselves as paradoxes: a continuing emphasis on filial piety combines with a shift from daughters-in-law to daughters as primary caregivers for the elderly, an increasing emphasis on the value of daughters in the era of the Birth-Planning Policy stands in seeming contradiction to the emergence of increasingly male-biased sex ratios in many rural regions, the growth of an individualistic culture of dating in urban areas goes hand in hand with the continuing ability of the elder generation to influence the decisions of their adult children when it comes to marriage choices.

These and many other seeming paradoxes illustrated by the examples in this book led us to modify our research question. We no longer asked whether classic patriarchal configurations are over, but rather which aspects of these configurations have or have not receded, and in which ways. We were aware that earlier patriarchal configurations had not been completely eradicated as part of the revolutionary changes that characterized China in the Maoist period. What we ask here is how these lingering postrevolutionary patriarchal configurations have been transformed as part of the slower but perhaps more profound changes of the Reform era. Which characteristics of earlier patriarchal configurations have persisted or perhaps even intensified in modified form in the age of economic integration and digital globalization? Even more importantly, *where* have changes occurred faster or more thoroughly, and where has change been slower or more tentative? How have gender and generational relations changed differently in cities and countryside, in different social classes, in one region and another? In order to explore these twin questions of what and where, we first need to define *patriarchy* as we use the term and then trace briefly the history of the concept as it applies to Chinese society.

A BRIEF HISTORY OF THE CONCEPT OF PATRIARCHY

The *Oxford English Dictionary* defines *patriarchy* in several ways, of which two are relevant to contemporary China: "A form of social organization in which the father or oldest male is the head of the family, and descent and relationship are reckoned through the male line; government or rule by a man or men" and "The predominance of men in positions of power and influence in society, with cultural values and norms favouring men. Freq. with pejorative connotation."[7] The first definition prevailed in anthropology from the time of Morgan (1877) and Engels (1884) until the 1970s. For them, the "patriarchal family" was a stage in social evolution between the syndiasmian or pairing family, found in pre-state societies, and the monogamous family, found in modern capitalist societies. They identified the Semitic, South Slavic, and later the Russian families as examples of this stage, characterized, as Engels ([1884] 1972, 31) notes, quoting Morgan (1877, 474), by "the organization of a number of persons, bond and free, into a family, under paternal power, for the purpose of holding lands, and for the care of flocks and herds."

Leaving aside the flocks and herds and adding a few more qualifications, including the provision that women too can be holders of "paternal power," Morgan's description holds remarkably well for the Chinese family in the late imperial and Republican periods. Its most salient characteristics were patrilineal descent and inheritance, patrilocal residence, strong parental authority, and the power of the senior generation (particularly but not exclusively senior males) reinforced by state law and property ownership.

As part of his "lifelong dialogue with the ghost of Marx," Max Weber (1978) refined the understanding of patriarchy in this first sense, describing *Patriarchalismus* as a structure of domination in which the control exercised by the male head of the household (or his representative) was unbound by any restrictions other than tradition. For Weber, the patriarchal family included members not related by blood, and took on the character of an enterprise. Women could have power in these corporate enterprises, but their power tended to be restricted to the sphere of the household—based on reproduction (mother-and-child ties) and on economic factors associated with producing and processing the goods necessary for survival. This structure of domination was not just circumscribed to the realm of the family but also provided a model for power relationships beyond the domestic sphere and was reinforced by those extra-domestic power relationships. The relation between a monarch and his subjects was often depicted in terms akin to the relation between a patriarch and his or her subjects. Weber described this model of "traditional authority" with materials from ancient Rome, but imperial China could also be used to illustrate the ways in which the elder generation's control of productive property, patrilocal marital residence, strict regulations of filial piety and respect for the elder generations, and an ideology of male superiority combined to assure that elder prevailed over junior and male over female.

Weber's notion of "patriarchalism" has many limitations and needs to be significantly modified in order to be applicable to the Chinese context. Just to give one example, contrary to what Weber predicted, patriarchalism in the late imperial period was not significantly weakened by economic expansion and commercialization, or by the development of increasingly

STEVAN HARRELL AND GONÇALO SANTOS

powerful and far-reaching state institutions and legal structures (Hamilton 1990; A. Wolf 2005). But Weber's formulation is still valuable in another way, because he embedded it in his study of power and prestige generally, in which he distinguished between prestige categories and politico-economic ones. In the realm of social inequality, he distinguished between classes and status groups; in the realm of politics, he distinguished between power and authority. In both cases, there is a category defined in terms of hard social realities and a category defined largely in terms of cultural values of what is socially worthy and morally good. Weber's concerns were processual: he was interested in observing how these elements interacted with one another over time. However, with the waning of the historical comparative perspective in the social sciences, what today remains of Weber's processual account is a set of dualistically opposed categories (status and class, prestige and power), which in turn become lined up with other dualisms (soft and hard, idealism and materialism). In order to better understand the processes of change in the Chinese patriarchal system today, we need to return to a more integrated, processual analysis.

As mentioned above, however, some scholars have used the term *patriarchy* in a different way, which is hazardous to ignore. Beginning about 1970, the *Oxford English Dictionary*'s second definition of the term *patriarchy* began to take hold in anthropology, as second-wave feminist scholarship in many disciplines used it to refer more broadly to male dominance or masculine domination.[8] But in trying to understand how patriarchy as male domination actually worked, scholars such as Margery Wolf (1972) and Deniz Kandiyoti (1988) went beyond the simple truism that men had more power in almost all societies and looked at the ways women were both objects of male power and agents negotiating or maneuvering within a more general system of power and prestige that was biased against them. In other words, the attempt to explain patriarchy in this second sense—male dominance—turned out to work best when directly linked to a description or analysis of the particular social system through which that dominance is exercised. In the case of "traditional" China, that system is a variety of patriarchy in the classic sense laid out by Morgan, Engels, and Weber.

There are two major ways to think of the relationship between patriarchy in the narrow, classic sense and patriarchy in the broader sense of male dominance. One way is to think of male dominance or gender inequality *as a dimension* of a broader system of social inequalities, including those of class, race, ethnicity, nationality, education, and so on. This is the approach taken by third-wave feminist scholars under the rubric of intersectionality.[9] The other is to see male dominance *as both a motivator and an outcome* of the workings of a system of gender and generational dynamics in families that are, contra Thatcher, embedded in larger social-cultural and politico-economic structures. Here we combine these two approaches, observing Chinese patriarchy as a system of family and kinship that produces and is produced by gender and generational inequalities both within and beyond the domestic sphere, and we examine how the workings of this system change as they intersect with other variables such as class, education, sexuality, regional location, and, most importantly, China's rigid but loosening rural-urban divide.

Inequality in patriarchal systems encompasses both prestige and power, which are not always congruent but always interact over time. Many feminist anthropologists of the 1970s through the 1990s, operating under the broader definition of patriarchy as male dominance, recognized and analyzed the prestige-power distinction both generally and in specific societies.[10] These anthropologists started out with an account of gender that focused only on the level of prestige. For them, a gender system was a "prestige system"—a system of discourses and practices that constructed male and female not only in terms of differential roles and meanings but also in terms of differential prestige (see especially Ortner 1972; Ortner and Whitehead 1981). For these authors, the devaluation of women at the level of prestige categories was universal but did not necessarily equate to on-the-ground differentials of power.[11] In "Gender Hegemonies," Sherry Ortner (1990) systematized these findings. She pointed out that most societies are by definition "male dominant" or gender asymmetrical—men have culturally stated higher status everywhere, but there are many societies and contexts in which men have a lot of prestige but little power, and women have little prestige but a lot of power. Understanding these complexities, she argues, requires a more sophisticated approach to gender inequality, one that builds on Weber's processual account of the relationship between prestige and power. In this volume, we develop a similar processual approach, but we are concerned with "gender systems" primarily as *an element* of "family systems," rather than as independent structures of prestige and power. As we focus on "patriarchal configurations," our concern is with both gender and generational inequalities but primarily within the family.

CLASSIC PATRIARCHAL STRUCTURES BEFORE 1949

We define *Chinese classic patriarchy* in neo-Weberian terms as *a hierarchical system of domestic relations that includes multiple intersecting structures of inequality including gender and generational inequalities, among others*.[12]

It would be a mistake to think that this system of domination is strictly domestic. Late imperial patriarchal structures were both private and public. In addition to shaping lives lived inside the space of the *oikos*, they also connected both paradigmatically and syntagmatically to power relationships beyond the domestic sphere (Bray 1997). Paradigmatically, the ideal of the relationship between emperor and subjects was modeled on that between father and son or parents and children, and syntagmatically, domestic and extra-domestic structures reinforced each other: domestic relations enabled participation in the public sphere (Harrell 1997, 13), and powerful extra-domestic forces such as state institutions, legal structures, and processes of technological development and commercial expansion enforced and reinforced inequalities within the family. Taken together, these domestic and extra-domestic structures constituted a hegemonic system, but like all hegemonies, it gave birth to its own resistance, exemplified in the domestic sphere by the uterine family structure delineated by Margery Wolf (1972) and in the public sphere by critiques in such literary works as *Flowers in the Mirror* and chapter 16 of *Journey to the West*.

Our working model of Chinese classic patriarchal structures contains two major axes of both prestige and power in domestic relations: a generational axis and a gender axis. In terms of prestige, on the generational axis, elders had prestige over juniors, and on the gender axis, males had prestige over females; it is important to note, however, that the overall system was never totally consistent. For example, Confucian maxims held that a woman should always be subordinate to a man—to her father when young, to her husband when adult, and to her son when old—and at the same time that the primary obligations of a son were to *both* his parents. The two axes of domestic prestige and power also varied along other dimensions of prestige and power (such as social class) that had nothing to do directly with gender or generation. Because there was no clear norm, in ideology or in practice, about which axis prevailed over the other, actual power relationships assumed a more complex configuration. Young females were almost always subordinate; young husbands tended to have great power over wives. Similarly, fathers tended to have power over sons as long as the fathers were compos mentis. Women had opportunities to gain power as they grew older and became mothers and then mothers-in-law (M. Wolf 1972; Harrell 1981), sometimes resulting in what Stafford (2009) calls "matriarchy," or what we have heard informally referred to as "female patriarchs." Female power, however, seems to have been confined in almost all instances to the domestic sphere, while strict gender hierarchy prevailed in the public sphere of politics, and males were also heavily dominant in literature, arts, and business. And as in any social system, structure was only the starting point of relationships in particular families: personal abilities and specific circumstances allowed individual agents to maneuver within the system, something that continues to be the case, as illustrated by several examples in this volume.

This system of "traditional authority," which we call "classic patriarchy," derived its strength and its endurance from economic, institutional, and ideological foundations extending beyond the domestic sphere. Economically, as China was an agrarian society, probably 90 percent or more of families derived their livelihoods from family property, and by law and custom senior males controlled that property, passing their control down from generation to generation by patrilineal partible inheritance. Daughters were usually denied a share of that inheritance, or else were given a small share via dowries or small gifts inter vivos (Goody 1990; Harrell and Dickey 1985). Where patriarchs controlled property, they had power over both females and junior males (although, as mentioned above, senior females, particularly widows, could often assume control over patrimonial property and thus over the sons and daughters-in-law who derived their income from that property). While property relations were an important component of patriarchal power, this power was significantly reinforced by legal structures and ethical systems that placed a strong value on the sacredness of fatherly and parental authority. This is an important factor in explaining why the families of the wealthy were larger than those of the poor in the late imperial period (Harrell 1985): in addition to living longer and living better, wealthy patriarchs had more access to state resources and were better at mobilizing state authority to control the lives of the junior generations (Sommer 2000; A. Wolf 2005).

Outside the family itself, patriarchal authority was supported by two important customary institutions: patrilineal extended kinship and male monopolies on public positions of power. Patrilineal inheritance and virilocal residence gave males both control of property and the opportunity for kin solidarity. The epitome of kin solidarity came in places where the corporate patrilineage prevailed,[13] but even in the absence of strong lineage organization, residence and inheritance favored males and male solidarity. Public positions of power, particularly in civil and military government, were inaccessible to females and buttressed male domination in the domestic sphere. These institutional hierarchies were also built around generational inequalities. Patrilineal kinship institutions were based on ancestor worship and respect for the elder generations, and these ideological institutions legitimated and reinforced male monopolies on public positions of power.

Ideationally, Confucian social philosophy, which mandated filial obedience to parents as the foundational virtue of the whole ethical system and which strictly prescribed different hierarchical social roles for men and women, provided the elite, literate support for the two-axis system of power and prestige here described, while drama, festival, and folktale provided a more plebeian version at the level of folk culture. In addition, classic ideologies of gender difference postulated a specific gendered division of labor based on three dichotomies: inside/outside, heavy/light, and sometimes skilled/unskilled, with the first and more highly valued term in each binary usually associated with men. These binaries were not categories of fixed content but stereotypes that could take many different forms depending on the context (Jacka 1997; Hershatter 2007). These stereotypes were particularly powerful tools for the symbolic reproduction of gender inequality because they were deeply entangled in everyday life transactions. As Melissa Brown demonstrates in chapter 1, even the unconscious ideology of ordinary semantics defined any kind of work performed by women as mere "helping," while what men did was "real work." Similar ideological differentiations could be found in terms of generation. In South China, for example, there were clear-cut funerary distinctions according to seniority, and only parents over sixty were entitled to celebrate their birthdays. Even when a son had taken over the management of a household from an aged father, the old man's name was still on the door plaque, and the elder was the one who represented the household in rituals and ceremonies.

At the same time, women and the young were not without resources in classic patriarchal formations. Particularly at the social margins, where patrimonial property was weak and lineage organization nominal or nonexistent, kinship tended to be more bilateral, division of labor between the sexes more flexible, and norms of propriety honored in the breach in the face of practical necessities (Harrell 1982, 2013; Santos 2009). But even at the centers of power, where the orthodox system of economy, institutions, and ideology was at its strongest, there was still room for women and the young to maneuver within the system. As Margery Wolf (1972) demonstrated analytically, and classic literature had long illustrated, as women aged and became mothers of grown men and then mothers-in-law, they had the incentive to invest in classic patriarchal structures because they would benefit from being senior and receiving the filial obedience and respect that the ideology dictated alongside its mandate of subordination for females.

The two-axis system of inequality also had a strong affective component. If ideas ranging from Confucian philosophy to operatic moralism promoted a strict patrilineal, viricentric kinship system, everyday life gave rise to a rather different configuration of attachments and hostilities (Harrell 2013; Santos 2009). Fathers and sons were rendered distant or even antagonistic by the anticipation of the son and the dread of the father at the eventual generational transfer of property and primacy (M. Yang 1945; Ahern 1973), while mothers and sons were drawn close by the legacy of childhood attention and care, something that women could use to bolster their power as they got older (M. Wolf 1972). Marital distance and inequality were often mitigated by the emotional closeness of bed and the common interests of child rearing. So the strict patriarchal orthodoxy had its weak points, allowing women and juniors to strategize. When the economic, political, and ritual pillars of support were weakened at the social margins, a much less hierarchical, though still unequal, system of generational and gender relations emerged (Gates 1996). This flexibility in the face of everyday life provides us with a framework for understanding the configuration of changes that have happened in the sixty-five years since the Chinese Communist Party (CCP) proclaimed gender and generational equality as some of the goals of its program of revolutionary change, and particularly in the past three decades as China has seen much greater changes spurred by low fertility, the market economy, and relatively open access to new ideas about gender and generational relations.

PATRIARCHAL TRANSFORMATIONS UNDER SOCIALISM

As in any study of social change and historical transformation, periodization is important. We can divide the social history of Chinese patriarchy in the past hundred years into four periods:

- The Republican era, from the May Fourth Movement of 1919 to the Communist takeover of 1949. Proposals about gender equality and generational equality appeared in media and literature produced and consumed by intellectual and economic elites, and even influenced the legal codes of the Nationalist government (Glosser 2003; Tran 2015), but had little influence in the wider society. The most important transformations during this period, building on developments initiated in the last decades of the nineteenth century, were the abolition of footbinding and the beginning of the formal integration of women into an emergent industrial workforce (Ko 2005; Gates 2015).
- The Maoist era, from the establishment of the People's Republic in 1949 to the beginning of the Reform era at the end of the 1970s. Revolutionary reorganization of society included new norms of gender relations,

and patrimonial property was in effect abolished, leading to important changes in gender and generational relations, but new social institutions paradoxically allowed many earlier ideals, structures, and practices to survive or even flourish.

- The early Reform era, from the late 1970s to the mid-1990s, when market economy and new fertility regimes promoted significant reconfiguration of lingering classic patriarchal norms and practices.
- The late Reform era, starting from the mid-1990s, when massive labor migration, privatization of housing, the spread of mass education, large-scale urbanization, development of middle-class lifestyles, and an Internet wide open to discussion of gender and kinship issues (if still closed to more politically sensitive dialogues) accelerated the process of change.

Here we examine the changes of the Maoist era briefly and then look at the Reform era in more detail.

The Maoist Period: A Quarter of the Sky Collapsed

Revolutionary social and political change in the Maoist period affected the sphere of kinship and gender in a paradoxical manner. Even before the Communists assumed governance of the nation, they were committed to revolutionary changes in family and kinship, including nuclearization (Diamond 1975; Stacey 1983). As Barlow's classic article on the history of writing gender from the Qing to the early Reform era makes clear, the Communists were committed *in theory* to a paradigm that saw physiological sex as the ultimate ground of gender differences and thus created a new category of *funü* (or woman) that separated female people from their previous context of the patriarchal family organization, while at the same time conceiving their reproductive role as bearers and rearers of children as essential to the state, functions performed in the nuclear family of "mommy, daddy, and me" (1991, 277). At the same time, under the slogan of "Women hold up half the sky," the revolution would fulfill Engels's prophecy that abolishing patrimonial property and bringing women into the income-producing workforce as equal participants would end the power of men in marriage, abolish the power of elders over juniors in the family, and eliminate the tyranny of the patrilineage over ordinary rural families. Laws promoting free choice in marriage, freedom of divorce, and equality of inheritance were key elements of the revolutionary platform in the early years of the People's Republic (Diamant 2000; Hershatter 2007, 2011). These radical interventions led to significant changes in everyday practices, but the depth of change varied between the city and the countryside.

In urban areas, a more gender- and generation-egalitarian family model indeed emerged. Housing reform, which took many people out of traditional extended family courtyards and put them into small rooms in gray, concrete, walk-up apartment blocks inside the compounds of work units (*danwei*), promoted nuclearization of residence, if not necessarily of other family activities (Whyte and Parish 1984, chap. 6). Socialization of productive property took patrimonial control away from the elders of business families, mass propaganda and education about the new, modern social order allowed people to think in new ways about the proper roles of men and women, and universal primary and then secondary education for urban children of both sexes ensured that modernist ideas spread to the entire population. There was certainly a family revolution in urban China from the 1950s onward.

Still, many classic patriarchal norms endured. Even in the 1980s, the legacy of puritanical attitudes toward sex and marriage was evident, and what William Jankowiak and Xuan Li in chapter 7 call the "courtship model" of marriage selection prevailed: parents had the final say in selection of spouses, and even such demonstrations of affection as holding hands in public were effectively tabooed, especially for younger people. Marriage itself typically conformed to what Jankowiak and Li call the "dutiful spouse and harmonious relationship" model, in which personal attraction and romantic love still played minor parts. In short, in the cities of Mao's China, the generational axis was effectively transformed, while the gender axis experienced slower and more partial change.

Rural areas turned out to be more conservative. One might have expected that collectivization of all productive property, combined with intensive propaganda about gender and generational equality and opportunities for young people to assume leadership positions, would have severely weakened both the politico-economic and the ideational bases of patriarchy, but in fact several factors combined to protect lingering classic patriarchal relations.

The first way the Communist Party (inadvertently?) protected or even strengthened rural patriarchy was to take Engels seriously and assume that women's moving into so-called productive occupations—in the Chinese countryside, almost entirely agricultural—was the key to gender equality. This was very misleading because it was based on misrecognition of the productive contributions of women in the prerevolutionary period (Brown, chap. 1; Santos, chap. 4). Indeed the Party did encourage women to engage more fully in field work and compensated them for it. But the way they compensated women worked to the women's disadvantage in three ways. First, the work-point system, in giving points for agricultural work only, neglected both the subsistence contribution and the exchange value of women's handicrafts in the rural economy and thus did not compensate women for it. Second, the Party's efforts to pursue gender equality by socializing domestic labor were unsuccessful, so housework and child care continued to prevent women from taking full part in the "productive" labor force (Stockman, Bonney, and Xuewen 1995). Women and children continued to do almost all the cooking and housekeeping. Child care was never fully collectivized, and even in those rural areas where child care was subject to some form of collectivization, women and older siblings were the ones who did it, and it was compensated less than "productive" agricultural work (Santos, chap. 4). Finally, many collectives awarded work points according to the amount of physical strength required for particular tasks, so women received fewer points for the same hours of work than men did while working fewer "productive" hours. In short, women's labor, as Brown shows, was undervalued in the Chinese countryside before 1949, but the Maoist labor compensation policies exacerbated this undervaluation.

The undervaluation of the work performed by women was only one factor in the reproduction of lingering classic patriarchal structures in the countryside. Another was the continuing system of virilocal marriage and its formation of patrilineal households (Diamond 1975). As long as women continued to marry into their husbands' families, the families themselves continued to be organized around a patrilineal core, and women who married in were outsiders, giving them less power, at least until they became mothers-in-law. In this system, as Gonçalo Santos's informants recall (chap. 4), "the old still had the authority in the family," including the authority to arrange marriages, in spite of the provisions of the Marriage Law that mandated marriage by free choice. Youngsters did have more say in whom they married than did previous generations, and they were no longer betrothed at a very young age, but their marriages were still largely arranged by their parents and close relatives. And women's labor, even though undervalued in work-point terms, still contributed enough to family economies that people continued to pay brideprice; in fact, brideprice rose in many rural areas (Parrish and Whyte 1978; Siu 1993).

A third factor was the restrictions on migration up the administrative hierarchy, implemented as part of the *hukou* (household registration) system put in place after the failure of the Great Leap Forward in the late 1950s (Chan 2009). People could not leave the countryside except in special circumstances, so there was minimal opportunity for young people to escape the strictures of patriarchal family organization and make a living on their own. The fact that the property supporting them was now collective rather than patrimonial made little difference when authority still rested with patriarchs domestically and with male cadres at the village and higher levels of government.

Finally, there seems to have been a decision, sometime in the early 1950s, that family revolution was not a good idea in rural areas, as it was a threat to social stability and perhaps competed with class struggle for the attention of mass campaigns and their participants.[14] If the Marriage Law initially brought about a rash of real free-choice marriages, along with divorces from marriages previously arranged under the "old society," once the new society established nominal freedom of marriage, people entered into relationships voluntarily, by law if not in actuality, and so they were in effect stuck. And with their labor undervalued and living among strangers, young women in particular continued to be at a huge disadvantage.

In sum, in the sphere of family and kinship, the Communists' revolution was only fractionally revolutionary. People in the cities, with more access to education and almost all in salaried positions, were much more able to reduce the burdens of classic patriarchal structures, especially along the generational axis but also to an extent along the gender axis. But in the villages, the male-headed agricultural collective acted as a kind of institutional patriarch, controlling the property that fed and clothed people and reinforcing the longevity of key aspects of the classic patriarchal family.

Reform Era Transformations: The Lessons of This Volume

In the three and a half decades since the official beginning of China's Reform and Opening in 1979, and especially in the past two decades of global economic integration and accelerated social change, much more profound transformations have come to what was left of the classic patriarchal system. The factors that weakened urban patriarchal institutions in the Maoist period—increases in salaried occupations, universal education for both sexes, housing designed for nuclear families, exposure to modernist ideas about love and freedom—have all intensified since the start of the Reform era, and several new factors have been added: severe birth limitation, the collapse of the state welfare system, the ascent of middle-class values, and the valorization of romance and sexuality. The result is that urban China no longer fits in any way our description of classic patriarchal structures and marital relations. As mentioned, both Yan's model of individualization and Davis and Friedman's model of deinstitutionalization of marriage provide partial understanding of these changes. But a more processual approach to changes in the two axes of patriarchy affords a better understanding of just what has changed and how. The generational axis has changed much more than Davis and Friedman would allow—case studies in this volume show that this axis still exists in the form of emotions and felt obligations but has lost much of its power (read: politico-economic) dimension. The gender axis, while individualized and/or deinstitutionalized in some respects, remains male dominant, even though that dominance is no longer part of an integral system of patriarchy in the classic sense. Male dominance now rests more on gender roles defined and learned in the context of family interactions as well as in the extra-domestic sphere, and no longer on the classic pillars of virilocality, patrilineal inheritance, and the institutional power of patriarchs.

Elements of the classic patriarchal system still exist in the countryside, but in forms more attenuated and transformed than either of us would have suspected only a short time ago. The factors that held the transformation of rural patriarchy in check during Maoist times—devaluation of women's labor, virilocal marriage and patrilineal households, restrictions on mobility, and the de-emphasis on family reform compared to class struggle—have all weakened or disappeared, and modernist ideas, formerly restricted to urbanites with access to education and mass media, have flooded rural areas almost as much as they have flooded the cities. Still other effects have been more paradoxical. Birth restrictions exacerbated the importance of son preference and thus skewed the sex ratio in ways whose effects we still do not entirely understand. The lack of an effective social welfare system has kept the responsibilities of caring for the aged in the hands of their children, while opportunities to earn income through labor migration have put much more power in the hands of the junior generations, transforming but not eliminating the generational axis of inequality.

One way to sum up what has happened to what remained of the classic patriarchal system in the Reform period is to think of the hollowing out of the two main institutions of classic patriarchal kinship—the virilocal extended family and the corporate patrilineage. The focus of interaction, investment, emotion, and activity has shifted away from these institutions in two directions. An inward shift has brought an emphasis on the nuclear family—on conjugal relations of sexuality and affection and on intensive nurturing of one or at most two children. At the same time, an outward shift has spread many responsibilities to the public sphere. Some of these were already public in the collective period, particularly provision of housing and pensions in the cities and organization of agricultural production in the countryside. But now corporations and the mediasphere, even modern science and technology, are taking over. Insurance companies sell filial piety policies while state media outlets publicize the new twenty-four stories of filial piety (Zhang, chap. 12), and the way to deal with the inability to have a son has moved from adoption—there used to be lots of boys available—to artificial reproductive technologies (Klein, chap. 11). As the great middle-range institutions—the extended family and the patrilineage—have lost corporate power, the generational axis of patriarchy has weakened greatly and in some ways flipped altogether, and the gender axis, while not necessarily weakened, has been fundamentally transformed, held together more by gender than by kinship.

Weakening and flipping of the generational axis. The older generation has lost power in the Reform period, but it has not lost salience. Elders still monopolize public positions of power (e.g., the average age of the Politburo Standing Committee remains above sixty), but these monopolies go hand in hand with significant changes in intergenerational relations. The result is that the generational axis of classic patriarchal structures has been transformed from a strongly asymmetrical to a more balanced nexus of rights, obligations, and emotions. There are several facets to this transformation.

We can begin with demography and family size. Since the 1970s, China has changed from a high-fertility, medium-mortality society to a low-fertility, low-mortality society, severely altering the numerical balance between the generations. The Birth-Planning Policy, announced in 1979, has been a large factor in bringing down fertility, but the increased costs of bearing and rearing children in the context of new educational regimes and models of intensive parenting, the opportunity costs of child rearing for parents' careers, and the decline in mortality have all contributed to the decline in fertility to varying degrees in different places.[15] At the same time, life expectancy, even in older years, has increased, meaning there are fewer young and middle-aged adults available to care for an increased number of elders. In most urban areas, the so-called 4:2:1 family configuration has emerged, as the first generation born under the Birth-Planning Policy now bears its own singleton children.

Fertility, however, does not decline to zero. The great majority of Chinese still consider it not just a filial duty à la Mencius but an unquestioned part of life to have at least one child. For those who fail to conceive naturally, previous sources of children for adoption are drying up, as very few people have any children to spare. So, as Kerstin Klein illustrates in chapter 11, a discourse of rising infertility has emerged (no one really knows whether there has been an actual rise or not), and an industry of artificial reproductive technologies has developed, allowing people to obtain that precious little "only hope" (Fong 2004).

Fertility decline and the increased ratio of elders to younger adults, along with a decline in the pension system, have brought about what Hong Zhang (chap. 12) calls a "crisis of filial piety," in which young and middle-aged adults must bear increased burdens at the same time they deal with inflated career aspirations and expectations. In this crisis, a "filial piety industry" has arisen in which state organs actively promote the same traditional Confucian virtues that they attacked as feudalistic only a few decades ago. There are now state-sponsored contests for paragons of filial piety, along with a new set of twenty-four filial exemplars who provide very different models from those in the traditional stories. There is also a boom in old-age homes and home-care plans for those who can afford them, along with a lucrative market in elder-care insurance, advertised as the modern way to fulfill one's filial obligations.

People still take their filial obligations very seriously. In a telling case, Harriet Evans (chap. 9) shows how an alcoholic ne'er-do-well son and a licentious daughter in two Beijing slum families still pride themselves on being able to provide bedside care for his bedridden mother and her psychotic one. At the same time, however, the moral and emotional basis of generational relations seems to be changing. Yan characterized this as "the disintegration and ultimate collapse of the notion of filial piety, the backbone of old-age security in Chinese culture" (2003, 189), a great contrast to Davis and Friedman's assertion that there is "enduring respect for the value of intergenerational reciprocity" (2014, 26). Case studies in this volume point to a situation less apocalyptic than that described by Yan but less conservative than that described by Davis and Friedman. In the classic patriarchal system, and what survived of this system in the Maoist period, filial connection was an absolute moral imperative, to be fulfilled even in the absence of any affection, or even in the presence of concealed intergenerational hostility, particularly between fathers and sons and between mothers-in-law and daughters-in-law. This obligation was, of course, reinforced by elders' control of property and by obligatory gratitude for bearing and socializing the younger generation.

At the present time, however, elders have little institutional or economic control over the lives and careers of their adult offspring, and as grateful as the latter might be for their birth and upbringing, elders have lost the power to compel obedience or even force emotional connection. So filial piety has evolved into a relationship in which elders must earn, as it were, the support of their children by building emotional connections (Fong 2004; Ikels 2004a). Affection has become an important basis of the filial connection (Zhang Jun, forthcoming), and campaigns such as those described above stress affection more strongly than ethical obligations. This shift to affection does not imply that urban parents are no longer able to exert influence on the lives of their adult children. Analyses by Elisabeth Engebretsen (chap. 8), Roberta Zavoretti (chap. 6), and Evans (chap. 9) offer powerful illustrations of the extent to which urban parents are still able to do so, even when their children are married and live on their own.

In rural areas, the situation is slightly different. A strong sense of filial obligation remains in place, but in many cases the power relations on the generational axis are not just weakened but reversed. With the trend toward neolocal residence that accompanies the growth of the ideals of romantic marriage and the nuclear family, more and more old people are living alone, even in the villages. Cases of elder abandonment and elder abuse are increasingly reported in the press, as Zhang (chap. 12) points out. But even in less extreme circumstances, when members of the younger generation share a courtyard or live close to their parents, younger adults are increasingly absent for long periods as they migrate for labor or, in the ideal scenario, pursue higher education with a view toward obtaining an urban job in the bureaucratic or corporate world. As Santos demonstrates in chapter 4, this means that child-care obligations often fall on grandparents, obligations that Brown (chap. 1) reports are often resented by mothers-in-law of the "sandwich generation" who had to obey their mothers-in-law but now hold little or no power over their daughters-in-law. In the part of Guangdong researched by Santos, where fertility decline was slower than elsewhere, this has meant that grandparents are spending a huge amount of effort caring for their grandchildren (or their "little mosquitoes," to use the Cantonese term), effort for which they receive little credit either from the absent, anxious parents or from the public discourse that worries about "left-behind children" (see Wei 2016, chap. 2), whose grandparents are thought to be too ignorant and uneducated to bring up the little darlings properly.

Resource transfers between generations, which at one level have followed the pattern delineated by Caldwell (1982)—children have moved from being an economic asset to being a big liability for their parents—are still reciprocal because of the continuing sense of filial affection and duty. Helena Obendiek (chap. 3) describes a telling case in which upwardly mobile village youth still need to consider living arrangements for their parents, while Brown shows that even married women sometimes continue to remit some of their migrant labor wages to their parents and/or parents-in-law.

Aware of their own diminishing power and the growing asymmetry of generational relations in favor of the younger generations, old people can no longer assume that they have earned a place of leisure or semi-leisure in an extended family, cared for by sons and particularly daughters-in-law. Instead, they must now strategize to support themselves by saving and by continuing to work as long as possible into old age, as both Lihong Shi's (chap. 2) and Obendiek's (chap. 3) analyses point out. A discourse of "not becoming a burden" to their children has rapidly arisen, as Zhang (chap. 12) mentions. At the same time, old urbanites in particular increasingly turn to peer groups and recreational activities to pass the time and bring meaning to life, as exemplified by Zhang's description of a female retiree who has a schedule worthy of a middle-class American preteen, and poignantly illustrated in Angela Zito's film *Writing in Water*, about calligraphers in parks in Beijing.

Finally, new ideas, whether about romance and love or about the proper "scientific" ways of raising "only hope" children in today's hypercompetitive environment, have also contributed to flipping the generational axis. Suzanne Gottschang's analysis (chap. 10) of new ways of "sitting the month," or postpartum seclusion, illustrates this vividly. Young mothers in many cities still hew to the old belief that a new mother should take a month off to rest and recuperate, but they do not necessarily want to do the month the traditional way, eating fattening prescribed foods and observing taboos against brushing their teeth or washing their hair. So a scientific discourse of how to do the month in a modern way has arisen, along with sitting-the-month centers where young women can recuperate with their babies scientifically, away from the "superstitious" or "backward" beliefs of their mothers-in-law or their own mothers.

The generational axis of the classic patriarchal system is thus weakened in many ways, and what remains is no longer really asymmetrical in favor of the elder generation. The elder generation still enjoys high prestige in the family due to the continuing importance of norms of filial piety, but this high prestige does not necessarily translate into power in everyday life. One of Santos's informants sums this up beautifully: "We have already reached an advanced age, but we are not being looked after by the younger generation. Having worked hard to nurture one's own children is not enough; we still need to farm the fields to nurture the children of our children. Old people today are facing a lot of hardships."

Twisting the genderedness of the generational axis. At the same time that the generational axis has both weakened and flipped, it has also changed its angle somewhat: it is becoming less patrilineal and more bilateral. Part of this is due simply to fertility decline. Even in rural areas with a de facto two-child policy, one-fourth of couples will have only daughters, and in places where one child is really the rule (most of the cities and some of the more prosperous rural areas), the proportion rises to one half. In this kind of demographic situation, the relations between generations must become more flexible, as daughters increasingly take on a greater proportion of the changing roles in the filial relationship. Zhang (chap. 12) even mentions that sometimes couples with one son and one daughter claim that they prefer to rely on their daughters for help. At the same time, however, there is still a cultural expectation that the primary link in the intergenerational chain is a patrilineal one, creating contradiction and paradox.

At one level, patrilineal ideology remains strong in many ways. Andrew Kipnis (chap. 5) shows how recent migrants to the medium-sized city of Zouping in Shandong still organize their households around the patriline, and rights to land in home villages pass to sons. At the same time, however, he also makes clear that the degree of patrilineal bias in urban migrant households depends on where they have migrated from and on what kinds of property rights they hold. To simplify Kipnis's findings, former farmers whose villages have been swallowed up by a city, and who still hold local property rights, are the most viricentric; migrants from distant areas, who still hold property rights at home, are somewhat less so but still focus their lives on connections to husbands' villages; while migrants from nearby rural areas, who can most easily keep up connections with both husbands' and wives' kin, are the least viricentric. Even they, however, are by no means fully bilateral in their orientation; it is almost always sons, not daughters, who take rural parents into their heated urban apartments in the wintertime. Similarly, in rural Gansu, Obendiek (chap. 3) observes that "local understandings of the intergenerational contract remain skewed toward the patrilineal notion that it is above all the duty of the son (and daughter-in-law by association) to provide care for the elderly parents."

Looking down the generational axis toward the children's generation, in rural Northern Guangdong, mothers and paternal grandmothers formerly took care of children; the division of labor was both patrilineally biased and gender-specific. But now paternal grandparents of both sexes are the primary caretakers for children of out-migrating parents. In other words, the patrilineal bias remains, but the gender roles have merged.

There is also evidence of continuing patrilineal bias in unexpected and unprecedented places. An example comes from the rapidly growing artificial reproductive technologies industry, analyzed by Klein in chapter 11. Sperm donation, though encouraged by authorities as a solution to the perceived crisis of infertility, is thought of as more problematic than egg donation, because sperm donation means a couple will raise a child who is biologically unrelated to his or her father's patriline, while egg donation means merely replacing the less important maternal link. Never mind that sperm donation is a whole lot easier to accomplish.

At the same time, demographic change has forced people to rethink patriliny, in practice if not in theory. Couples in many places are still trying to have boys; there are many more boys than girls in recent birth cohorts (Cai 2013). There is considerable regional variation, however. Figures from the 2010 census show sex ratios at age 0–1 years ranging from 109 males per 100 females in Shanghai, just slightly over the human norm of 105 to 107, and around 112 in the three Northeastern provinces and Sichuan, while in Hubei the ratio was 124 to 100, in Hainan 127 to 100, and in Anhui, the evident capital of son preference, a whopping 130 to 100 (Feng 2011, 692).[16] In addition, there also appears to be class variation: both the very wealthy and the very poor have lower sex ratios (Guilmoto and Ren 2011).

People who do strongly prefer sons have resorted to undergoing illegal sex-selective abortions, abandoning girl babies, underreporting first births so that they can have a second or even a third child, and, in a few cases, even committing female infanticide, though the latter appears to be very rare. In areas where there are more boys, girls are, paradoxically, at a premium, and as Obendiek (chap. 3) reports, women are often able to call the shots when it comes to marriage payments, whether the marriage is one of the decreasing number arranged by parents or originates with the couple themselves.

In almost all cases, enduring patrilineal ideology, even in urban areas, dictates that the husband and his family pay a high brideprice to the wife's family—Obendiek presents a striking example of almost extortionate behavior on the part of a bride's family in rural Gansu. In addition to the brideprice, the husband's family customarily is required to either build a house (the most common practice in rural areas, as reported by Obendiek) or buy an apartment (more common in the cities, as reported by Zavoretti [chap. 6]) for the couple to inhabit in neolocal splendor. Expenses in excess of ¥100,000 (US$16,000) for brideprice, house, and wedding are not uncommon in many areas, and in cities like Shanghai, where housing is notoriously expensive, a monetary gift of ¥100,000 plus house means that the total brideprice amounts to more than ¥1 million.[17]

The increasing burden of this vestigial patriliny, however, has created a backlash in many areas. Shi (chap. 2) writes of a mother, upon the birth of her son, exclaiming, "Here comes my big debt!" and of a comment that whereas people used to "hope for a son" (*pan erzi*), they now fear a son (*pa erzi*) because of the ever-mounting expenses of rearing and paying for the marriage of a boy. There may be some evidence, just in the past few years, that sex ratios are beginning to decline again, although any large-scale trend is far from obvious. But at least in the rural Liaoning areas studied by Shi and the villages in Hubei studied by Zhang, people really seem to have little sex preference, or there may even be a bias toward daughters. Even in remote rural Gansu, Obendiek reports that preferences are beginning to shift.

One reason for the possible shift in sex preference is a perception that daughters are more likely to be emotionally attached to their parents. Part of this perception may stem from traditional virilocal family configurations, in which daughters generally had less fraught relationships with their parents, since their filial duties were severely attenuated after marriage. But part of it also has to do with the perception that daughters are more likely than sons to be filial when the basis of the filial bond shifts from duty to affection. Obendiek relates this to the observation that Gansu parents invest equally in education for their sons and for their daughters, if they are bright and capable, but that daughters perceive this investment as stemming from affection rather than obligation and are thus more likely to return both the affection and the material help.

So who takes care of aging parents—sons, daughters, or daughters-in-law? Shi reports from rural Liaoning and Zhang from both rural Hubei and urban Shanghai that sons (with their wives) and daughters contribute roughly equal amounts of money and care, but Evans, Obendiek, and Brown, writing about the urban poor, educated rural people, and migrant workers respectively, report various amounts of patrilineal bias in filial obligations. In almost all cases, however, the great burden of elder care continues to fall on women, although it appears to be shifting from daughters-in-law to daughters. In sum, even when intergenerational relations are much less exclusively *patrilineal* than they once were, they are still very *gendered*, the opposite of the changes in child-care responsibilities that Santos reports from rural Guangdong.

The gender axis itself. This brings us to what the reader probably thought the book was going to be about, namely male dominance, or, in Michael Herzfeld's usage at the Halle conference, andrarchy. We leave this aspect of the classic patriarchal system until last, not to denigrate its importance, but rather to emphasize the fact that it is so entangled with the generational axis that we cannot understand it thoroughly without taking into account the whole shifting patriarchal matrix in which it is embedded.

Simply put, with all the changes in the classic patriarchal nexus, China remains a heavily male-dominated, or andrarchical, society, even though women continue to have significant power both inside and outside the family. But with the huge changes in the generational axis, male domination has taken on a more basic, unmediated form. If sex and marriage are deinstitutionalized, in the sense that individuals have more freedom to script their lives, men still dominate in the newer, more flexible atmosphere. But men's domination is much less tied to their position in intergenerational patriarchal structures than before.

As with any system of gender relations, the current Chinese system has two primary aspects: division of labor and relative prestige and power. We know from comparative anthropological studies that there are, in fact, societies in which the gender division of labor is nearly absolute, but the prestige of one gender and the power it has over the other are minimal or even nonexistent.[18] This is not the case among the Han in China, but these examples remind us that the division of labor and the differential of prestige and power, although related, are not the same thing.

We have already noted that the Maoist attempt to promote gender equality represented only a partial challenge to the gender axis of the classic patriarchal system. In recent decades, the challenge has grown, but the asymmetry remains. Ideologically, everyone knows that "male and female are equal" and that "women hold up half the sky." Girls and boys not only have equal access to education, but in most areas, as Obendiek (chap. 3) and Kipnis (2011b) point out, parents are just as willing to educate girls as boys, even when they expect less material return on the investment. Professional and government jobs, with the possible exception of combat posts in the military, are open to both men and women, and women have occasionally risen to ministerial or higher levels of the bureaucracy. In education in particular, teaching and even high-level administrative posts seem to go without prejudice to either gender.

Still, strong male biases remain in job placement and mobility. At the highest level, no woman has ever served on the Politburo Standing Committee, and only a few have served as full members of the Politburo or at the next rank down as provincial party secretaries, provincial governors, or vice-premiers. There are well-known female entrepreneurs, but they are a minority. Office jobs, in both corporate and government sectors, are open to both genders, but women's advancement in such positions is curtailed by the expectation that both bureaucrats and businesspeople will spend a lot of time solidifying their important social relationships (*guanxi*) by playing—eating, drinking, flirting, and more with hostesses—in ways that are problematic if not impossible for women (Osburg 2013, esp. chap. 5).

Migrant labor has had a complex effect on gender subjectivity and gender relations. In the first great waves of labor migration in the 1990s, young women were dominant in several spheres, including assembly-line work (Pun 2005; Chang 2008) and domestic service.

As Hairong Yan (2008) in particular points out, learning to be "modern," raising one's personal "quality," or *suzhi*, was a big part of the migrant experience, and that experience changed young women's expectations for mate selection and the content of marital relations. Particularly if they were unable to stay in the cities long-term (as most of them were not), they found it impossible to readjust to rural life and particularly rural marriage, in which they were expected to return to both rougher material conditions and often the domination of a mother-in-law, "setting them up for heartbreak" (May 2010, 899).

From the start, men have dominated the higher-paying positions in migrant labor, whether in the construction industry, where they take the jobs requiring both technical skill and physical strength, or in the factories, where the composition of the workforce has changed as men have come to dominate the shop floor, where they have imposed a culture of "rough masculinity" (Deng 2012). And as Brown demonstrates in chapter 1, female migrant laborers may have their own bank accounts and make their own decisions about remittances to the senior generation at home, but in many cases boyfriends have access to those accounts, and even unmarried women often remit to their fiancés' families. We see these trends as evidence that although deinstitutionalization of marriage is definitely happening, marriages still end up being dominated by husbands.

In most cases, if one member of a married couple migrates for work, it is usually the husband. This often means that men may be bringing in more money, but it is primarily women who manage households, giving them everyday power where they lack prestige. It also leaves women at home with the duties of elder care. In some rural areas, as Santos (chap. 4) shows, young married women who engage in labor migration partially control the purse strings of the multigenerational household, and this has helped them impose themselves on their mothers-in-law as the newly dominant female figures in their households. Some of these women manage to become prominent beyond the realm of the family as some sort of powerful local public figures (see Chen Meixuan 2013, chap. 6), but these stories remain exceptional in the countryside. Moreover, because of the continuing idea that domestic labor is the province of women, and because such labor remains undervalued, as both Brown (chap. 1) and Zavoretti (chap. 6) point out, when there are career conflicts between a husband's and a wife's ambitions or job expectations, it is almost always the wife's that give way.

According to the 2010 census, 74 percent of working-age women were in the workforce. This figure stacks up well against other countries such as the United States and Australia, where about 75 percent of working-age women were employed in 2010 (Attané 2012). But China's figure is high because it includes rural women, most of whom are working either in the fields or away from home as labor migrants. If we focus only on urban women, we get a very different picture. In urban areas, a growing number of women are choosing to stay at home in order to take care of the children and the household. One reason for this is that they no longer benefit from the extensive network of public child-care facilities created during the Maoist period (Stockman, Bonney, and Xuewen 1995). This network was largely dismantled from the 1990s onward following dramatic cuts in public spending (Goh 2011). Today, most urban mothers have to rely on market services or else—as is most common—on grandparents and other relatives for childcare support, but this is not always possible and is not always considered desirable. Zavoretti's poignant example (chap. 6) illustrates this process of "housewifization," as a nurse in Nanjing gives up her dream of medical education in the United States in order to make her marriage work and provide a good environment for her only child. But perhaps the most telling example of male bias in marital negotiations about labor division comes from Engebretsen's study (chap. 8) of "fake marriages" between lesbians and gay men attempting to live a simulacrum of heteronormativity in order to get parents off their backs. Even in these purely performative marriages, Engebretsen shows us, the "husband" dominates the "wife" and sets the conditions for the administration of the false domicile.

In the ideological dimension, "half the sky" is balanced in many cases by what Evans (chap. 9), in describing what we might initially view as a self-abnegation of women's worth in a poor neighborhood of Beijing, calls "a gendered sense of self-worth" and "a sense of virtue as a wife," both of which compel at least nominal subordination to husbands and fathers as a part of female virtue. Many of Evans's acquaintances seem to believe that men are unreliable and childish but that it is still women's duty to follow them, because that is the way the world works. And as she also points out, conditions of poverty distance people from the effects of state ideologies of gender equality.

Finally we come to the large and complex topic of the social organization of the emotions: love, sexuality, intimacy, and affection. It is clear from the start that much has changed here from just a few decades ago. William

Jankowiak and Xuan Li (chap. 7) provide a telling quantitative demonstration: in Hohhot in the 1980s, only four out of thousands of couples walking together in the evening were holding hands, but by the early aughts of the present century, the majority were doing so. This is a public, physical demonstration of what appears to be a fundamental shift in ideas about dating, sexuality, and marriage.

As mentioned before, marriage is a social imperative that is still rarely violated, though there is much more stigma to being an "old maid" or "leftover woman" than there is to being a "bare stick" or bachelor (Zhang and Sun 2014). And childbearing and marriage are still very closely tied; whether or not there are a lot of pregnant brides in a community, almost all marry before the child is born, so that childbearing outside of marriage remains extremely rare (Davis and Friedman 2014, 26–27). But the way people get to marriage has profoundly changed. Harrell has observed in several rural areas in Sichuan that in the 1980s, almost all husbands and wives were actually introduced by parents, even though arranged marriages were technically illegal. But by the twenty-first century, almost all marriages in these areas were contracted by genuine free choice, and most couples actually lived together before marrying, to make sure they could get along in a common domicile. Liu Fuqin's research in a mountainous area in interior Zhejiang even found that the great majority of brides were pregnant at the time of the wedding (Liu, pers. comm.).

Urban areas in recent years have undergone what Jankowiak and Li (chap. 7) describe as a transition from the Maoist period courtship model, in which people cautiously got to know each other under close parental supervision, to a dating model, in which they go out together and get to know each other individually, often have premarital sex, and do not marry until their mid- or late twenties. In the 1980s, premarital sex was disapproved of and rather rare; by the early aughts, a majority of respondents in several surveys both approved of and engaged in premarital sex. With the emergence of this dating culture, sex, unlike childbearing, has become increasingly "delinked" from marriage (Farrer 2014, 64–65). And in dating relationships, Jankowiak and Li tell us, the woman often calls the shots, deciding on the pace and nature of increasing sexual and emotional intimacy. But this shot-calling is itself an indicator of contradictory ideas about gender equality: on the one hand, the woman controls the relationship and the man accepts the fact, if sometimes reluctantly; on the other hand, one reason the woman is in control is that she potentially would be more stigmatized than a man would be if she had experience with several sexual partners.

The ideal marriage, as exemplified in the studies by Jankowiak and Li (chap. 7) and by Zavoretti (chap. 6), is now one in which there is not only sexual but emotional intimacy. However, the unequal career obligations of the two genders, along with remaining patrilineal biases in many cases, mean that this ideal is not often realized, and that men, culturally expected to be less emotional and demonstrative, are still less likely than women to want to practice this model in reality. And both in choosing a partner and in continuing a marital relationship, practical considerations—house and job and even family background—never fall entirely by the wayside: it is still a rare woman who will marry for love when no house or apartment is forthcoming from her husband's family.

In chapter 7, Jankowiak and Li maintain that "whenever the love bond becomes a culture's dominant ideal and preferred practice, patriarchal values that highlighted the superiority of senior men and women over their offspring, and in a more localized context, a husband's preeminence over his wife, can no longer prosper, much less thrive." This is undoubtedly true, and we have seen some evidence that it is happening in China. However, weakening of classic patriarchal structures and values does not mean the end of gender inequality.

EMERGENT PATRIARCHAL CONFIGURATIONS

So how do we sum up what has happened to the classic patriarchal system after more than fifty years of large-scale industrialization and modernization? We know that the Maoist family revolution was not sufficient to bring about the collapse of the system, but what about the changes of the past three decades?

Clearly, China has moved away from the classic patriarchal configurations of the late imperial and Republican periods, a form of Weber's *Patriarchalismus*. At the same time, the current regime of generational and gender relations is very different from what standard modernization theories would predict. What is emerging is a new system of multiple intersecting structures of inequality, including gender and generational inequalities, among others. This new system of inequality continues to show significant class and regional variations, but it includes the following common features:

- Andrarchy, or male domination, is alive and well. Some aspects of gender inequality have gotten stronger; others have weakened in various ways. In particular, women's participation in every area of the public sphere has accompanied changes in their roles in familial and domestic life.

- Modernist ideologies of individualism and of gender and generational equality coexist uneasily with ideas inherited from the classic patriarchal configuration.
- The new configuration of generational and gender prestige and power is still built around the strong imperative to marry and have children and to create and maintain strong ties between the generations.
- The state has withdrawn from its previous commitments to providing social services of various kinds, from housing to pensions to medical care, meaning that the family has taken on many new obligations.
- The generational axis of the classic patriarchal configuration has not disappeared completely, but has weakened in some ways, flipped in others, and twisted its lineality in still others.
- Marriage is now defined as a voluntary contractual relationship based on individual emotional satisfaction, but it also involves monetary transactions that often include an apartment or house.
- Law favors deferral to individual preferences when regulating marital sexuality and conjugal property, but the state retains its prerogative to monitor reproductive practices while still maintaining that the only legitimate arena for reproduction is free monogamous (heterosexual) marriage.
- Sentiment and affection have partially replaced obligation as the basis of contractual ties between generations and between genders.

So can we still use the term *patriarchal* to describe current Chinese society and culture? Let us return to our modification of the classic definition derived from Morgan, Engels, and Weber, the first definition given in the *Oxford English Dictionary*: "a hierarchical system of domestic relations that includes multiple intersecting structures of inequality including gender and generational inequalities, among others." At a very general level, this definition still fits, but the "multiple intersecting structures" have changed greatly. Generational asymmetries are no longer based on coercive institutional forces, but they are still vital to the family and the social order. The gender axis has also been significantly restructured, but there is little doubt that it remains male dominant, or patriarchal in the more general sense of gender inequality. Whatever term one chooses to refer to the new system of multiple intersecting inequalities, that new term must make sense of the fact that we are dealing with an increasingly individualized system in which a single individual might be oppressed in some relationships and dominant in others.

In this volume, we analyze this shift toward a more individualized system as a move away from classic patriarchy in Weber's sense, but we continue to use the term *patriarchal* to refer to the newly emerged system of gender and generational inequalities in order to highlight the fact that contemporary family processes continue to be shaped by earlier deep-seated hierarchies. Herein lies the key paradox at the heart of this volume. On the one hand, present-day China resembles in many ways the industrial societies of North America and parts of Europe, in which patriarchy in Weber's classic sense no longer exists, while male dominance remains. On the other hand, family relations in today's China display many unique features, many of them linked to specific features of the Chinese patriarchal tradition. In this volume, we argue that making sense of these specificities requires adopting a model of patriarchy and social change that is sensitive to Chinese realities. Most theorizations—largely inspired by Western discourses and experiences—are based on a narrative of historical transformation that postulates the end of the patriarchy in Weber's classic sense and the rise of the nuclear family and affective individualism. This narrative of historical transformation has created a radical split between those who study historical forms of patriarchy (based on gender and generational asymmetries) and those who study modern forms of patriarchy (based only on gender asymmetries). In this volume, we argue that this intellectual division of labor does not fit societies like China, where modernity was not accompanied by as severe a decline in the significance of multigenerational family ties. In societies like China, the study of modern patriarchal transformations cannot just focus on gender inequality because gender asymmetries are closely related to generational asymmetries, whatever form the generational axis takes.

In this volume, we develop a model of patriarchy and social change that is more suitable to making sense of the complexities of the Chinese family system and its linkages to broader social-cultural and politico-economic structures. This model is historical in that we think that patriarchy is not a historical constant and that political action is crucial to maintaining or transforming specific patriarchal configurations. This approach has much in common with earlier feminist historical approaches to patriarchy in that—in contrast to standard theories of modernization—it envisions modernity not as the end of patriarchy but as its transformation. There is some disagreement in this volume as to whether the changes that occurred in the past five or six decades represent a form of progress, regress, or both, but there is broad agreement on the conclusion that there remain deep-seated gender and generational hierarchies. In this volume, we approach these deep-seated patriarchal structures from a perspective that has much in common with third-wave feminist intersectional approaches to gender inequality, in that we explore micro-level inequalities within families in the context of a broader system of multiple intersecting inequalities (e.g., class, race, ethnicity, nationality, education). This intersectional approach is critical of feminist accounts of patriarchy in Western societies based on a clear-cut opposition between private and public forms of patriarchy.[19] In this volume, we argue against such narratives of modernity postulating a clear-cut shift from a private to a public form of patriarchy. Patriarchy in its various forms (historical and contemporary) is never just private or public; it is always both private *and* public. This is especially true of patriarchal configurations in contemporary industrial societies, such as China, marked by increasingly entangled intersections between private negotiations and public dialogues at various levels in law, state policy, and media, among others. We hope the case studies in this volume present enough empirical data and analysis to allow for a better understanding of these complex private-public intersections as they are unfolding in the family lives and public lives of the world's largest country.

NOTES

1   We use the word *Chinese* here to refer to families among the Han and among those members of minority ethnic groups who have acculturated to mainstream norms. For comparable analyses of change in non-Han family systems, not all patriarchal to begin with, see Du and Chen 2011.

2   See, e.g., Croll 1981; Stacey 1983; Johnson 1983; M. Wolf 1985.

3   We use the term *Birth-Planning Policy* rather than the more fashionable *one-child policy* for two reasons. First, "birth-planning policy" is a literal translation of the Chinese term *jihua shengyu zhengce*, and, second, the actual number of children allowed has varied over time and space but the restriction to one child per couple has never applied to all citizens.

4   See, e.g., Giddens 1991, 1992, 1999; Beck, Giddens, and Lash 1994; Beck and Beck-Gernsheim 2002.

5   Hansen (2014) has recently analyzed education and student life in a rural middle school based on the observation that the individual is now the focus of both aspirations and socialization.

6   The term *deinstitutionalization* was coined by the American sociologist Andrew Cherlin (1978, 2004) writing about marriage in the US context.

7   "patriarchy, n." OED Online. September 2015. Oxford University Press. http://www.oed.com.ezproxy.kcls.org/viewdictionaryentry/Entry/138873 (accessed December 02, 2015).

8 See, e.g., Millet 1969; Firestone 1970; Mitchell 1971.

9 Walby 1990, 2011; Butler and Weed 2011; Cho, Crenshaw, and McCall. 2013; Patil 2013.

10 Ortner 1972; Rosaldo 1974; Ortner and Whitehead 1981; Ortner 1990.

11 Rosaldo 1974; Rogers 1975; Sanday 1981.

12 Chinese scholarship usually refers to "classic Chinese patriarchy" with the terms *fuquan zhi*, literally "system of paternal power," or *jiazhang zhi*, literally "system of household headship." Both terms were coined in the late nineteenth century, following Japanese usage, to translate the term *patriarchy* as used by Western social Darwinists and students of cultural evolution (Sechiyama 2013). Today, usage of these terms remains largely restricted to Chinese scholarly circles and the well-educated urban middle classes. In a survey undertaken in the city of Guangzhou in July 2014, only two out of thirty randomly selected well-educated middle-class respondents of different generations claimed that they had never heard the terms *fuquan zhi* or *jiazhang zhi*, and only one said that she was not clear about their meanings (Zhang Jun 2014). Most respondents defined *fuquan zhi* and *jiazhang zhi* as a hierarchical system of family relations shaped by both gender and generational inequalities.

13 Freedman 1958, 1966; Baker 1968; Potter 1968; J. Watson 1975b; R. Watson 1985; Santos 2006, 2008. In certain parts of China, especially in southern coastal provinces such as Guangdong and Fujian, patrilineal descent groups (*zongzu* or *jiazu*) were not just socially defined kinship groups; they were political organizations with corporate functions such as ancestral worship and mutual aid. Some of these corporate patrilineages were local in nature (e.g., village communities with only one or only a few patrilineal ancestors), but others were primarily translocal (e.g., lineage or clan associations bringing together people from different localities on the basis of common patrilineal ancestry) (Santos 2006).

14 Stacey 1983; Johnson 1983; M. Wolf 1985.

15 Greenhalgh 1988; Lavely and Freedman 1990; Harrell et al. 2011; Fong 2004; Kipnis 2011b; Cai 2013.

16 Sex ratios at birth in Tibet, Xinjiang, and Inner Mongolia are within the normal range of 105–107. Ratios in Tibet and Xinjiang are explained by the relative lack of son preference among Tibetans and Turkic Muslims, but there seems little explanation for Inner Mongolia, since Mongols, who in fact do not have strong son preference, are less than 20 percent of the population.

17 "Fit to Be Tied," *China.org*, July 30, 2013, http://www.china.org.cn/china/2013–07/30/content_29569666.htm.

18 Schlegel 1977; Ortner and Whitehead 1981; Ortner 1990; S. Du 2002.

19 Most classic feminist accounts of the history of gender inequality in Western societies postulate a clear-cut shift from "private patriarchy" (i.e., a system of gender inequality based on the exploitation of women in the private sphere) to

"public patriarchy" (i.e., a system of gender inequality based, not on excluding women from the public sphere, but on the segregation and subordination of women within the structures of paid employment and the state, as well as of culture, sexuality and violence) (Walby 1990, 1997, 2011).

STEVAN HARRELL AND GONÇALO SANTOS

PART ONE

RURAL RECONFIGURATIONS

CHAPTER ONE

DUTIFUL HELP

Masking Rural Women's Economic Contributions

MELISSA J. BROWN

THE Chinese patriarchal family system—which institutionalizes female subordination and exploitation in whatever kin and social relations obtain at any given point in history[1]—has been remarkably resilient from the late imperial period through the Maoist era to the global-capitalist present, although the institutional forms of that subordination that existed in practice have been very fluid.[2] The hegemonic idiom of "helping" has long elided rural women's economic contributions to household and society, an undervaluation that made even senior women vulnerable to kin demands for more labor. Moreover, Party-state policies exacerbated those vulnerabilities, completely eliding rural senior women's economic contributions, especially in clothing production, even as these policies created space for publicly crediting younger women's agricultural field labor.

Today, the organization of global capitalism in China has inadvertently created new potential for women—and particularly unmarried women— to gain control of their labor and earnings. Rural women migrate to cities for work and open bank accounts in their own names. However, "helping" has been brought forward into the global-capitalist present as central to the practical and emotional power of kinship and thus to the continued undervaluing of women's labor. Appeals for help are still used to encourage women's dutiful contributions. Unmarried women appear better able than married women to resist those appeals, although distancing themselves from their natal families may not be independence but an unacknowledged transition to upcoming marital families instead. In short, through the many transformations in the form of patriarchal relations across the twentieth century, there are remarkable continuities in the notion of dutiful help as an indicator of the undervaluation of the economic contributions of unmarried daughters, young married women, and senior (married) women.[3]

THE HISTORICAL HEGEMONY OF HELPING

The idea that rural girls and women are capable only of "help" (*bang* or *bangmang*)—not of work, in the sense of providing economic contributions comparable to that of their male age-mates—serves to rationalize patriarchy.[4] It portrays girls and women as (always) duty bound to provide whatever "help" is required by the patriline to which they are assigned and to gratefully accept whatever support is given them in return, implying that they do not contribute enough to cover the costs of supporting them.

Helping in Prerevolutionary Rural Families

The idiom of helping, used by both Chinese women and men, ideologically fueled the Chinese patriarchal system before 1949. It intersected with the ideology of "worthless daughters," who drain their natal patrilines of resources (food, clothing, houseroom) and take skills learned in girlhood to serve another patriline upon marriage (M. Wolf 1972; Ebrey and Watson 1991). These ideologies were entangled with the neo-Confucian principle that women should obey first their fathers, second their husbands, and third their sons but contradicted the older Confucian admonition to sons that they must obey their parents. Even maternal authority over sons did not and does not preclude the undervaluation of women's labor (the labor women actually perform). Since principles and cultural beliefs are not reliable predictors of customary practice, I view shared principles and beliefs as ideologies—some hegemonic, some resistant—whose relationship to practices must be explored.[5]

"Helping" is an *indicator*, linguistically marking the undervaluation of economic contributions by an individual or category of people. In the fluidity of social practice, use of the term *help* does not mean that girls or women never received any credit for their labor. Rather, "help" and "work" were credited distinctly, as if in separate cognitive accounting systems. In the early twentieth century, female labor was largely credited as "help"—provided to a man (e.g., father, husband) or a senior woman (e.g., mother, sister-in-law)—rather than "work." Boys' and men's labor, too, could be credited as "help," though women I have interviewed rarely spoke of male labor so. Ideologies associated with "helping" made it easy to undervalue or even dismiss labor contributions described with that language, particularly given many kinds of credit: time spent or earned (e.g., in agricultural labor exchanges) as well as meals, cash, or exchange-goods earned. Because the rural nonelite was cash poor, monetized value likely earned most credit. That textile labor was credited at the point of sale (Bray 1997) is further evidence that crucial labor—spinning—could be elided.

The belief that Chinese girls and women made little economic contribution was common, among Chinese women, their relatives, reformers, and scholars. Liang Qichao viewed footbound women as "parasites" (Ko 2005, 21). Mao Zedong himself in 1949 exhorted women to "unite and take part in production" (*tuanjie qilai, canjia shengchan . . . huodong*) as though rural women's labor had never before produced anything significant.[6] Scholarly analyses of the Chinese economy range from undervaluation of the contributions of daughters generally (e.g., Buck 1937, preface) to consideration of the economic value of the products of female labor (e.g., Bray 1997) while still undervaluing female labor inputs (e.g., Pomeranz 2000,101; 2003). Moreover, among those who consider female economic contributions important, only Hill Gates's (1996, 2001) research on the intersection between kinship and capitalism and, to a lesser extent, Philip Huang's (1990, 2002) research on mobilization of labor in the peasant family under involutionary conditions have previously considered kinship as integral to girls' and women's production. Gates (1996) argues that daughters who contributed economically to their families could expect to leave in "good" marriages, that is, marrying into marital families at or above the economic level of their natal families. This argument implies that female labor was accurately credited and, for an unmarried daughter in particular, created a social obligation on the family's part to secure marital comfort. By contrast, my analyses suggest that rural Chinese girls and women themselves, as well as their families, frequently undervalued their economic contributions. Using the idiom of help—integral to Chinese kinship—to describe female labor contributed to the view that Chinese women did little work.

The historical evidence presented here on female labor and earnings during the early twentieth century comes from collaborative research using orally administered structured interviews with 2,737 Chinese women, mostly born between 1915 and 1942, residing in twenty-two rural Han counties in eleven Chinese provinces (Brown et al. 2012; Brown and Satterthwaite-Phillips, 2016).[7] Methodological challenges revealed the idiom of help in masking female economic contributions. Mentioning "work" (*gongzuo, zuoshi, zuo laodong, ganhuo*) often elicited some statement that a woman interviewee herself, or women in general, did not work, even from women who had done agricultural labor in the Maoist period. For example, Ms. Li said, "[Before 1949] males did agricultural field work; females didn't go into the fields" (Dili de huo, nande zuo, nüde bu xia tian) (Hunan no. 2101146, b. 1935).[8] Handicraft labor was often elided as "helping" mothers (e.g., Shanxi no. 2902025, b. 1931) or mothers-in-law, who were credited with the product. For example, asked who spun in her marital household, one woman said: "My mother-in-law. My sister-in-law helped her spin" (Popo, saozi gei bangmang fang) (Anhui no. 1101032, b. 1916). To discover what labor women actually performed, we asked about specific tasks. Ms. Li planted, harvested, and dried sweet potatoes and soybeans for her natal family; she also picked cotton—labor that required going into agricultural fields. Footbinding, common in many rural areas before 1949, contributed to the perception that women did not work (Brown et. al 2012): "Footbound girls couldn't do any work; they could only spin and weave at home" (Baole jiao de nühai, zuobuliao shiqing, jiu zhineng zai jia fangsha, zhibu) (Jiangxi no. 2301118, b. 1932) (she was never footbound).[9]

The economic contributions of girls and women *were* significant to their households. Adele Fielde, a missionary in 1880s Fuzhou, calculated the value of assets held by her rural Christian converts and found the cloth, clothing, shoes, and bedding produced by female handwork equal in value to all the agricultural tools and draft animals used in farming combined, excluding land.[10] These handicrafts were necessary to survival, even in Fujian, one of China's warmer provinces. Contrary to expectations, footbinding could *boost* girls' handicraft production—for example, in spinning cotton—to levels higher than coerced from enslaved African Americans in the antebellum American South (Brown and Satterthwaite-Phillips 2016). Handicrafts produced—including thread, cloth, clothing, shoes, bedding, rope, fishnets, hats, grain bags, baskets, mats, white wax, hand-sorted tea, and opium—procured salt, oil, sugar, rice and other foodstuffs, clothing, and other goods (either by exchange of goods or via cash from wages or sale of handicrafts). Before 1949, girls and women who were skilled handicraft workers fed themselves and often other family members as well,[11] even if some of them did not believe it possible.

> CASE STUDY 1: Ms. Zhou's (ID no. 2302127, b. 1926) natal family
> in central Jiangxi owned 1 *mu* (about 0.067 hectare) of paddy land
> and 9 *mu* of dry land (the average local holding was 7.7 *mu*). They
> owned a draft ox and shared a house with extended patrilineal
> kin. Zhou was never footbound, as the custom had stopped
> locally by the time she was small. Around 1934, Zhou's family sold

their paddy and some dry land to release her older brother from the Nationalist army, which had seized him for conscription. Later, the family had to rent land but still ate rice regularly (only 40 percent of local families ate rice as a staple). Zhou "helped" her father and grandfather farming rice, wheat, soybeans, sesame, and cotton. Her field labor included weeding, working a water pump, harvesting, hauling crops from the field, and drying the grain. When her father plowed dry land, she would follow behind and break up dirt clumps with her feet.

Zhou's older brother ran a small workshop, pressing fried sesame for oil. The family's sesame crop was not sufficient, so Zhou twisted hemp into rope to exchange for sesame: 1 *jin* (about 650 grams) of rope exchanged for 1 *jin* of sesame. She made 1 "big" ounce (*liang*) of rope per day, requiring sixteen days to earn a *jin* of sesame to press. Zhou, along with her younger brother, "helped" in the workshop itself (*bangmang zha you*). They used their feet to stamp down the press and squeeze out the oil, repeating the process twice for each batch of sesame. Her older brother sold both the oil (for cooking) and the chaff (for fertilizer and feed for pigs).

Zhou's natal family owned a spinning wheel. Zhou initially said that her older brother's wife was the only spinner in the household. However, she acknowledged that, from about age nine, she would "occasionally help" her sister-in-law spin (*ou'er bang saozi de mang*). Zhou did not consider the thread her product because she spun only when her sister-in-law was busy cooking or taking care of the children, but these must have been frequent diversions. Zhou did no child care or cooking, and there were no other adult women in the house by that time. They jointly produced 2 big ounces per day, all of which Zhou credited to her sister-in-law. Her sister-in-law exchanged the thread for clothing and raw cotton (to spin). Zhou did not know how much the thread earned, another indicator that neither she nor her sister-in-law considered this product hers, for women interviewed who had sold their handicrafts themselves generally remembered how much the goods earned.

Zhou was essentially sold into marriage by her older brother, who was then family head. At about fifteen, she was married to a man seven years older (an only son) for a brideprice (*pinjin*) equivalent to 2,000 *jin* of unhusked rice and 10 *jin* of meat, fish and chicken.[12] As dowry, she took slightly more clothing and shoes than the local average and borrowed a chest and bed to accompany the bridal procession, but her husband viewed these as no dowry at all. No spinning wheel—a potential source of income, and a common but not ubiquitous dowry item for spinners—was included. Zhou's marital family was poorer than her natal family. They owned no land, renting all they worked. They owned a small house and shared a draft ox with another family, and their main staple was sweet potato, the staple of the poor. Zhou did not get along with her mother-in-law.

When first married, about 1942, Zhou worked with her mother-in-law to pickle beans for sale. Zhou also did almost every aspect of agricultural work necessary to grow rice, wheat, peanuts, soybeans, sweet potatoes, sesame, and some fruit (which they also sold): weeding, watering, fertilizing, harvesting, hauling the crop from the field, threshing, flailing, and drying.

After three years of marriage, Zhou bore her first child, a son. She had twelve children total and raised eight of them to adulthood (four died as newborns). With such a large family, handwork in her marital family consisted entirely of making shoes and clothing. Zhou also "helped" her husband with a sesame oil workshop but did not know how much the oil earned.

Zhou's life circumstances suggest that her economic contributions—both substantial and not dissimilar from other women—were given little credit. When asked if a woman could earn enough to support herself before 1949, Zhou herself said: "We didn't think so. Women gave all the money [they earned] to their parents, so they couldn't support themselves" (*yangbuliao*). By the time she was of marriageable age, her younger brother and sisters could replace her doing handwork, working in the fields, and pressing oil. Her marriage did *not* repay Ms. Zhou for her past contributions, since it thrust her into a household with less financial security (contra Gates 1996; cf. Brown et al. 2012), but brought *current* profit to her natal household via the brideprice.

Most rural Chinese women married at or above their economic standing: 46.5 percent of 7,314 women who married between 1907 and 1949 "matched doors" (*men dang hu dui*), and 31.1 percent married up, but like Ms. Zhou, 22.3 percent—one woman in every four or five—married down (Brown et al. 2012). The substantial number of these women involved in premarital labor activities—89 percent in agricultural labor, 89 percent in handwork

MELISSA J. BROWN

(67 percent produced textiles, with regional variation corresponding to the availability of raw cotton, and 77 percent produced other handicrafts)—suggests that, as with Ms. Zhou, families frequently overlooked daughters' past economic contributions when arranging marriages in favor of expectations of current and/or future earnings (via brideprice or affinal connections).

Helping during the Maoist Period

The view of women's labor as worth less than men's and often as dutiful help (rather than work) continued under Maoism (cf. Stacey 1983). Promoting rural production as strictly agricultural, the Party-state allowed rural handicraft production to continue as "backward" sidelines but did not give work points for it (Eyferth 2009, 2012). In other words, the Party-state transformed how people credited rural labor, institutionalizing work points as the highest form of value. These policies wrenched apart the interwoven crediting systems of "work" and "help," giving points only for "work" and erasing the value of labor described as "help." There was no ideologically correct way to credit "help" to the household, yet women still had to do handwork, since clothing, shoes, and bedding were necessary for survival in China's climate and most rural families could not procure or afford factory-made clothing or cloth (cf. Eyferth 2012). Rural young women, especially unmarried daughters, were publicly credited for agricultural labor—albeit earning work points at 70–80 percent of the men's rate—and these points were valuable to families (Davis-Friedmann 1983). Party-state policy, however, failed to credit rural women—especially married women whose duty it was to clothe children and husbands—for necessary, daily labor considered "help." It may have been this institutional masking of handwork contributions that prompted one Women's Federation official (interviewed in Yunnan in 2009) to remark that village women lost status in the transition to Maoism.

Older women received no work points for handwork, which was dismissed as "domestic" production (for home consumption) and rationalized in terms of ideologies about women as belonging to the "inner" (*nei*) quarters (Ebrey and Watson 1991). At times during the Mao period, however, other production for home consumption was collectivized and earned work points in rural areas: cooking in the dining halls, even child care in collective nurseries, and much agriculture. Earning no work points for handwork meant that some married rural women had to do their full-time day work—often field labor or caring for livestock—and then spin or weave at night, for their own use or for black-market exchange (e.g., Hubei no. 2001017, b.

1926 [cf. Eyferth 2012]). Domestic work became a Maoist "virtue" by which women were judged (Hershatter 2011), leaving women, especially older women not doing agricultural labor, vulnerable to expectations of ongoing uncredited contributions.

These demands cannot be understood only as a Maoist legacy disenfranchising elders, because grandmothers in Taiwan, who were never exposed to Maoist ideologies of generational equality, also face such demands for dutiful "help," as sons and daughters-in-law require child care (see Santos, chap. 4). In 1992, I complimented a Taiwanese (Han) woman, Ms. Lim, on the healthy two-year-old grandson playing in her living room, only to hear her grievances against her husband, son, and daughter-in-law for being forced to provide child care. She had just retired from years of factory work, and caring for her grandson required too much energy for comfort; she was exhausted; and her son and daughter-in-law did not even live with her! Ms. Lim explained, bitterly, that she had refused, despite her son's persistent pressure for her help. When her son finally appealed to her husband, she had expected her husband to support her refusal, but, instead, he told her to provide the child care so their daughter-in-law did not have to quit her factory job, which paid good wages. Despite her past significant wage-labor contributions, Ms. Lim found herself vulnerable to the patrilineal demands for current, dutiful help.

Thus, we see evidence that, across variation in its institutional forms, Chinese patriarchy has given more weight to girls' and women's current and future potential economic contributions than to their past contributions (contra Gates 1996). In addition to contemporary evidence of furious grandmothers forced to provide child care, there is also historical evidence of one in five downwardly mobile marriages (Brown et al. 2012) and the large number of children needed to reduce the risk of divorce (A. Wolf 1995)—evidence coming from prerevolutionary China as well as from Taiwan (which shared a patriarchal family system [e.g., Brown 2004]). Women are vulnerable at any age to demands for dutiful "help" from family members.

DUTIFUL HELP UNDER GLOBAL CAPITALISM

As Chinese patriarchy has returned to ideological respectability in the post-Mao Reform period, its institutional forms have shifted yet again. China has become "the world's factory," built largely on the labor of rural-to-urban migrants, yet questions still arise about whether families fully credit even female wage-labor contributions. The idiom of helping suggests why migrant girls and women may be viewed simultaneously as victims of structural violence from Chinese patriarchy *and* as independent agents seeking modernity and conjugal felicity (including the consumer pursuit of property or happiness [e.g., Gaetano and Jacka 2004]). Dutiful help is an affective hook that reels women into a patriline—whether natal, conjugal, or a husband's extended patriline—making it difficult to determine whether women are acting independently or as part of kinship units. Modern technology—direct-deposit, electronically accessed bank accounts—can potentially promote women's independence, or it can result in women's interdependence with kin and would-be kin (cf. Wallis 2011). Examining where migrant women's earnings go suggests that unmarried women's autonomy—their ability to act as individual agents—is subject to strong efforts to orient them toward marital kin units, sometimes even before marriage (cf. Hsiung 1996; Gaetano 2004); at the same time, it suggests that unmarried women's labor and earnings may still be undervalued.

The contemporary evidence presented here about migrant workers comes from orally administered surveys of 1,600 migrant workers in "Southern City," conducted in October 2010 (as part of a larger collaborative project [e.g., L. Liu et. al 2014]), and in-depth interviews with 27 women migrants in that same city in May 2011.[13] Survey participants were primarily factory workers. Most of the older women interviewed were employed as cleaners or cafeteria workers; most of the younger women worked on production lines or in factory showrooms. All had worked as migrants for at least three years before the 2011 interview.

> CASE STUDY 2: Ms. Zhang (SCity no. 1203026, b. 1990) finished
> middle school and did not test into high school. Her first job—in
> 2005—was working for her mother's brother, "helping" take
> production orders in a small Guangdong city. Her mother took
> her to her uncle's because she was afraid that Zhang would not be
> used to living "out"—away from home under the harsh, crowded
> conditions to which most migrants are subjected (cf. Gaetano
> and Jacka 2004; Chang 2008). She could live and eat in her uncle's
> home, rather than with the other workers, but Zhang stayed only
> a half year. Her cousin had told her that migrant work was hard,
> but she did not really believe it. By 2011, she knew migrant work
> was hard, but she could not go back (*hui qu*) because she'd been
> out too long.
>
> Several factors may explain why Ms. Zhang could not return
> to the house where she grew up. First, "just sitting around eating"
> was not an option (SCity no. 1203002). Zhang's father said that

if she wasn't in school, she must earn wages, but there was little opportunity in her rural hometown. Second, six years of independent decision making would have made returning to her parents' household difficult to tolerate. Third, after years of urban living, the daily inconveniences of rough country living might have been too difficult (see Obendiek, chap. 3). All these factors may have played some part, but I think personal autonomy was the most important. It would have been much harder to defy her parents over continuing the relationship with her boyfriend if she were living in their home.

In her first job, Ms. Zhang earned ¥600 per month (about US$72 at the time), for a total of ¥3,600 after six months; her aunt helped her save money. She gave ¥1,600 cash to her parents and clothing and red envelopes to her younger sister, younger brother, and grandparents (amounting to ¥650), remitting 63 percent of her total earnings in cash and gifts combined. Ms. Zhang used the remaining money to buy herself clothes and food, get her hair done, and go out with friends on the weekends. Her parents and grandparents wanted her to keep working at her uncle's—her grandmother told her it was safer—but Zhang could not stand having to spend all day on the phone and having no voice left at the end of the day. She may also have been chafing against personal restrictions: living at her uncle's would have given him responsibility for her behavior and her welfare in the family's view (cf. Gaetano 2004). Ms. Zhang's initial claims to adult status—at the age of fifteen, after six months of wage earning—were closely connected to dutiful remittances, symbolically emphasized because they were given at the lunar new year. She demonstrated commitment to her natal patriline and demanded autonomy in return for her contributions.

After the lunar new year, her mother's friend found Ms. Zhang a new job in a global-export city. Her first cell phone was stolen within the first month (cf. Wallis 2011). She thought the theft very sad because she could not get her old phone number back, so her friends could not find her. The thief also stole ¥700 (a month's salary) that she was on her way to give to an aunt to take home for her younger brother (he alone of the three siblings attended high school).

Ms. Zhang had a boyfriend. In 2006, he followed her to the first global-export city where she worked, later went to a different global-export city, and was in the fourth of China's major global-export cities in 2011. Although she had known him since middle school, they became boyfriend and girlfriend only in 2008, when they were home at the same time. Zhang reported that being so far apart was hard. He wanted her to move in with him, but she would not until marriage. Her parents and grandmother objected to their marriage plans because his parents' economic situation was not good. Her younger sister (also a migrant worker by 2011) agreed that Zhang could do "better," but Zhang said her boyfriend was good to her, so her younger brother (still a student and unmarried in 2011) accepted the relationship.

Ms. Zhang found the position she held in May 2011 with her cousin's help. She earned ¥1,775 per month, but as was common, her employer kept her first two and a half months of wages as a security deposit (to ensure sufficient notice before she left her position [cf. Chang 2008]). Zhang shared an apartment (with rooms for six people) with her cousin and his wife, paying rent and sharing food only after she was paid. She no longer sent money to her natal family, nor did she receive money from them. Rather, she was saving for her own apartment and marriage—for the wedding banquet and housing. When I commented that the groom's family normally pays these expenses, Zhang said she was "helping" (bangmang). Once married, Zhang planned to move to her boyfriend's city and "help" him open a business.[14]

Ms. Zhang opened a bank account in 2006 in order to carry less cash and to save money. She moved the account when she came to Southern City. Zhang never shared the account password with her natal family but did with her boyfriend. In 2011, he was using this account, putting money in it, so she could "help" him do some online trading. Zhang reported that her boyfriend put into the account about what he took out, but when I asked why he did not use his own account for online trading, she said he wanted her to "help" with some of his work. These remarks suggest that, despite her wage earning and apparent autonomy, Ms. Zhang's contributions are undervalued, for even if she did not lose money overall, her boyfriend's use of her account implies that he drew on her funds for his trading. There is no indication that he shared his online profits with her or that she expected him to do so.

Ms. Zhang's case illustrates the potential of the idiom of help as an affective hook, as well as the complexity of distinguishing independent versus kin-oriented actions. Ms. Zhang's independence from her natal kin grew as she shifted from remitting most of her earnings to sending nothing, though she also took nothing. But is this fading sense of duty autonomy, or is it a shift in allegiance to her boyfriend and his patriline? Ms. Zhang reported not sending money to her natal family in order to save for wedding expenses, in particular for costs usually covered by the groom's patriline. "Helping" with these expenses suggests a commitment to her boyfriend *and* his patriline. Ms. Zhang yielded control over her earnings to "help" her boyfriend and proffered her postmarital labor to "help" with his business. Despite the *possible* self-interest of increased conjugal income—her natal family thought she had better prospects—the idiom of help indicates an affective pull sufficient to elicit unconventional contributions and shows continuities with historic undervaluing of female economic contributions.

Ms. Zhang's contributions to her natal family from her first job were substantial, both in percentage and, for rural families, in absolute amount. In an initial comparison, she seems an exceptionally filial daughter: on average, unmarried women surveyed in 2010 gave 15 percent of their income to their parents (table 1.1). Moreover, estimation of Ms. Zhang's cash-only remittances had she worked a full year and contributed the same 44 percent of her wages (¥3,168, no correction for inflation) places her contribution well above the amount of cash unmarried women remitted on average and slightly above the average amount *married men* remitted (table 1.1). Not surprisingly, the mean cash amount of survey participants' self-reported remittances to parents—for men to their own patriline and for women to their natal patriline—was higher on average from men. However, because women's average annual income was only 56 percent of men's, women's remittances to parents constituted a larger *percentage* of their income than men's: 13 versus 10 percent. In fact, unmarried women—the lowest wage-earner category—sent the largest proportion of their income, on average, to their parents. Admittedly, since these are self-reports, these figures could indicate what people thought they *ought* to give rather than what they actually gave. Nevertheless, the data hint strongly that unmarried daughters are more susceptible than sons to patriarchal ideologies of filial duty (cf. Salaff 1995).

A closer comparison, to women interviewed in more depth in 2011, suggests that Ms. Zhang was not exceptionally filial, for pooling all unmarried women obfuscates an important distinction relating to women's independence. Unmarried women remitted more at the beginning of their migrant work period than later. Although 53 percent of women who were unmarried

TABLE 1.1 "Southern City" migrant workers' self-reported cash income and remittance to parents, October 2009–October 2010

	CATEGORY (N)						
	All women (567)	Unmarried women (265)	Married women (302)	All men (820)	Unmarried men, age ≤ 27 (304)	Unmarried men, age ≥ 28 (179)	Married men (333)
Mean annual cash income	¥19,453.2	¥18,732.0	¥20,040.0	¥34,706.4	¥29,197.2	¥30,884.4	¥40,435.2
Mean annual cash remittance	¥2,469.3	¥2,799.6	¥2,179.5	¥3,448.9	¥3,575.6	¥4,199.4	¥2,941.1
Percentage of income remitted	12.7	14.9	10.9	9.9	12.2	13.6	7.3

Note: Percentages are based on the number of individuals who answered that question (not every person answered every question). Percentages may not add up to 100, due to rounding.

at the time of their first migrant job reported sending home half or more of their salary in their first year,[15] *none* of the women who were unmarried in 2011, who had been working as migrants for three or more years, were still remitting more than half of their salaries (table 1.2 [cf. Gaetano 2004]). Such findings complicate our understandings of natal families' stated concerns about their daughters' safety living "out" and their efforts to find daughters jobs through relatives, as they did for 52 percent of the women interviewed.[16] Ms. Zhang's aunt helped her save the money remitted. A Hunanese woman (SCity no. 1203009), who gave all the earnings from her first job (in 2007) to her parents, said she could do so because her first job was "helping" at the business of a relative who covered her daily expenses (room, board) and even doctor visits.

Women's contributions to their natal families continued after marriage (cf. Judd 1989; Ikels 2004a), although once married, women's remittances to their parents declined (see tables 1.1, 1.2). In her first migrant job, Ms. Luo (SCity no. 1203015) sent her parents half of her salary and visited home every month. Six years later, married with children, she gave her mother only ¥500 for Mother's Day, though she did find time to buy clothes for her mother when she did not for her parents-in-law (cash and gifts for her mother totaled 3 percent of her annual salary). However, Ms. Luo sent her parents-in-law ¥700 each month (24 percent of her monthly salary). Most married women interviewed reported giving less than 10 percent of their

TABLE 1.2: "Southern City" migrant women's self-reported cash income and remittance to parents and parents-in-law for the first year at their first job and for May 2010–May 2011

	FIRST YEAR OF FIRST JOB		MAY 2010–MAY 2011	
	Unmarried (17)	Married (10)	Unmarried (5)	Married (22)
Mean annual cash salary	1983 = ¥356 (1) 1991–99 = ¥5,573 (7) 2000–2008 = ¥10,028 (9)	1994–98 = ¥12,871 (4) 2000–2006 = ¥11,462 (6)	¥21,700 (5)	¥17,455 (21)
			¥20,865 (26)	
REMITTANCES TO PARENTS (NATAL PATRILINE)				
Gave nothing	5.9% (1)	11.1% (1)	25.0% (1)	0
Gave 1–10% of annual cash salary	11.8% (2)	55.5% (5)	0	60.0% (12)
Gave 10–49% of annual cash salary	29.4% (5)	11.1% (1)	75.0% (3)	35.0% (7)
Gave ≥ 50% of annual cash salary	52.9% (9)	22.2% (2)	0	5.0% (1)
Mean annual cash remittance[a]	1983 = ¥356 1991–99 = ¥2,873 2000–2008 = ¥4,654	1994–98 = ¥1,238 2000–2006 = ¥1,480	¥5,086	¥2,463[b]
REMITTANCES TO PARENTS-IN-LAW (MARITAL PATRILINE)				
Gave nothing	–	37.5% (3)	–	15.8% (3)
Gave 1–10% of annual cash salary	–	12.5% (1)	–	31.6% (6)
Gave 10–19% of annual cash salary	–	37.5% (3)	–	21.1% (4)
Gave ≥ 20% of annual cash salary	–	12.5% (1)	–	31.6% (6)
Mean annual cash remittance[c]	–	1994–98 = 631 2000–2006 = 925	–	2,711
COMPARISON OF REMITTANCES TO PARENTS AND PARENTS-IN-LAW[d]				
Gave more to parents	–	60.0% (3)	–	23.1% (3)
Gave about the same to both[d]	–	0	–	15.4% (2)
Gave more to parents-in-law	–	40.0% (2)	–	61.5% (8)

Notes: Percentages are based on the number of individuals who answered that question (not every person answered every question). Percentages may not add up to 100, due to rounding.
[a] For a woman who worked at her first job for less than a year, annual remittance is estimated based on the percentage of salary she remitted.
[b] This mean would be ¥1,489 without the one woman who gave ¥20,000 for her younger brother's wedding. The median was ¥1,100.
[c] Women who gave less than 5 percent of their annual salary to both sets of seniors have been removed from the comparison, as these numbers inflate the "gave about the same" category. In their first job, three women gave nothing to both parents and parents-in-law, and in May 2011, five women gave less than 5 percent of their annual salary to both parents and parents-in-law.
[d] In this category, the amounts given to both sets of seniors are within 4 percent of the woman's annual salary.

income to their parents both in the first year of their first job out (67 percent) and in the year preceding May 2011 (60 percent [see table 1.2]).[17] Nevertheless, slightly more married women gave more from their first migrant job to their own parents than to their parents-in-law. Moreover, a substantial minority of married women—almost one in four—gave *more* to their parents than to their in-laws after three or more years out.

Further examination of married women's remittances challenges not only their sense of duty to their husband's patriline but even married *men's* sense of duty to their own patriline. Among women who were married when they came out for their first migrant job, half sent their parents-in-law less than 5 percent of their annual salary, and 88 percent—all but one woman—remitted less than 20 percent of their annual salary (see table 1.2). In May 2011, after at least three years out, 47 percent of married women remitted less than 10 percent of their annual salary to their parents-in-law, and 69 percent remitted less than 20 percent. Married men may have been remitting additional money without telling their wives. But it is very suggestive that, in the larger survey, married men's mean annual cash remittance to their parents (¥2,941)—which is such a low percentage of their own salary—represents 15 percent of *married women's* mean annual cash income (¥20,040 [see table 1.1]), and according to the interviews, married women's mean annual cash remittance to parents-in-law in the year preceding May 2011 (¥2,711) was 16 percent of their mean annual cash salary (¥17,455 [see table 1.2]).

Moreover, married women interviewed generally spoke as though they were responsible for remittances to parents-in-law, apparently from their own salaries. Ms. Luo, for example, spoke of giving her parents-in-law more money because she had no time to shop for gift items between work, running a household, and child care. Only one married woman, who reported giving her parents-in-law nothing at all, said that she did not know if her husband was sending them money, and only two women reported total remittances (to parents and parents-in-law combined) exceeding their annual salary. In one case, 123 percent of a woman's annual salary was reportedly given for her younger brother's wedding (SCity no. 1203011).[18] In the other case, in her first job out, a woman's reported remittances to parents and parents-in-law combined came to 110 percent of her annual salary (SCity no. 1203018). These women must have included contributions from their husbands (or money from savings) in their remittances.

If married women are indeed primarily responsible for remittances to both sets of parents, then gendered wage inequality bodes ill for rural seniors' old-age support (cf. Obendiek, chap. 3). In order to understand remittances to married men's patrilines, therefore, we need to know *not only* about their wives' sense of duty to kin *but also* about their wives' earnings. Most women *also* remitted money to their natal families (see table 1.2), so do their remittances to parents-in-law represent a lesser orientation to their husband's patriline? Or does the combined total of their duty-bound expenses—to parents, to parents-in-law, *and to children* (also part of the husband's patriline)—still take up the same proportion of their earnings that they once sent to parents?

Orientation to a marital patriline can begin before the wedding. Ms. Huang (SCity no. 1203016) gave nothing to her parents in her first three years working as a migrant because she was living with her boyfriend and giving money to him. However, she personally credited her contributions to the ¥30,000 brideprice—paid to her parents by her boyfriend's patriline so as to sanction the marriage—as including her remittance to her parents. Thus Ms. Huang justified remitting nothing in the previous three years. Although her money did go to her parents eventually, social credit for the brideprice goes to the groom's patriline, and it is not clear if they privately credited Ms. Huang's contributions. However, orientation toward her natal family did not completely disappear, because in May 2011, she gave approximately the same proportion of her income to her parents as to her parents-in-law (9 and 6 percent respectively).

In Ms. Zhang's case, it is hard to distinguish between contributions to her boyfriend's patriline and to her own anticipated nuclear household, especially in contributions toward housing.[19] The groom's banquet, too, would benefit her, as that ritualized celebration appears to be the moment when Ms. Zhang—and presumably her natal family—would consider herself married.[20] Despite her emphasis on the banquet, allocation of Ms. Zhang's earnings suggests that the couple's agreement to marry focused her orientation on her boyfriend and perhaps his patriline. Like Ms. Huang, Ms. Zhang stopped sending money to her natal family in order to contribute toward the groom's wedding costs, and she was contributing financially to her boyfriend's income by allowing him access to her earnings for online trading. It was not clear if Ms. Zhang's sense of duty to her natal kin would revive sufficiently to contribute to her brother's wedding costs, though this possibility complicates her brother's tacit approval of her boyfriend and hints at his orientation to her potential future economic contributions.

Modern technology does not, in and of itself, confer independence (see Wallis 2011, for a similar conclusion about mobile phones). Although having her own bank account may have facilitated Ms. Zhang's financial independence from her natal family, it also facilitated her boyfriend's simultaneous access to her earnings and undervaluation of her contributions. All women interviewed had bank accounts. Most (71 percent) got their first bank

MELISSA J. BROWN

accounts in their own names so their employers could pay them by electronic deposit—the dual global-capitalist expectation of employer convenience and individuals as the unit of labor. Although remittances to parents and parents-in-law were often routed through the bank accounts of younger family members living with or near the seniors, 91 percent of women interviewed had shared the password to *the bank account in which their pay was deposited*, including four out of five unmarried women! Thus women ceded their ability to control how much of their earnings others could access. Half the unmarried women shared their passwords with boyfriends, and the other half shared them with natal family members. As an unmarried woman, Ms. Huang shared her first bank account password with her boyfriend (whom she later married). Not surprisingly, 89 percent of married women shared the password to their own accounts or shared joint accounts with their husbands.[21] Only 55 percent had ready access to that joint account, thus ceding control of their earnings to their husbands, though two women did manage their joint accounts (cf. Cohen 1976). Most women, 88 percent, indicated that others who knew the passwords had taken money out of their accounts (ten husbands, one daughter, two boyfriends, and one natal family member). Bank accounts, then, may be used for financial independence or interdependence. Sharing of passwords, especially by unmarried women, reduces women's autonomy and increases their vulnerability. In this context, Ms. Zhang's usage of the idiom of help shows its affective potential for orienting a woman's sense of duty to a patriline while at the same time masking the significance of her economic contributions.

POLICIES AND PATRIARCHAL POTENTIAL

More rural Chinese women are gaining control of their labor and earnings as an unintended consequence of global capitalism, but the duration of their autonomy appears shockingly brief. Natal and marital families still appeal to women's sense of duty, with great success, based on the evidence of remittances. Even boyfriends appeal for help. Many Chinese women prove susceptible to these long-standing patriarchal ideologies. It may be too early, therefore, to posit a strong, individualized "girl power" (Yan 2009), for it seems—even in Yan's account of bridal agency—that what appear to be rips in the fabric of a duty-bound mentality to natal kin are instead merely a variation on women's traditional shift in orientation from the natal to the marital patriline.

There is great potential in the ability of rural migrant girls and women to decide the allocation of their earnings—whether they spend it on themselves or on remittances, and, if the latter, which patriline it supports. However, it is far from clear whether sufficient numbers of Chinese women will take this opportunity to wrest control of their labor and earnings, which would result in a significantly diminished Chinese patriarchy. Despite the many changes in women's labor-force participation and in the value of female labor that took place over the twentieth century, women's economic contributions are still subject to undervaluation—by individual women themselves and by their family members (both women and men). It is not women's contributions to family members per se that make for patriarchal (i.e., coercive gendered) relations but the failure to fully credit those contributions with status and voice and rights in the family.

Party-state policies will influence the trajectory of Chinese patriarchy—not only through policies about gender-based wage inequality but through other policies as well, policies about elder care, for example. Will institutionalized elder care be available and affordable? Will women's mandatory retirement age still be younger than men's? Will women who take care of elders—either by taking time off or after they retire—be credited for that work in their pensions? Such policy decisions will have a huge impact on women's vulnerabilities to emotional appeals from family for unpaid labor that is undervalued as "help." Given the difficulties in procuring child care in China today and the resultant increase in grandmothers' vulnerabilities, optimism is premature.

NOTES

I am grateful for the funding received from the US National Science Foundation (BCS-0613297, BCS-1238999, BCS-1063590), the Morrison Institute for Population and Resource Studies and Stanford University, the Radcliffe Institute for Advanced Study and the Fairbank Center for Chinese Studies at Harvard University, and the Minnesota Population Center. I thank my research collaborators for their many contributions to collecting and understanding the materials presented here: Laurel Bossen, Marc Feldman, Hill Gates, Chris Isett, Jin Xiaoyi, Li Shuzhuo, Liu Lige, Liu Yonghua, Damian Satterthwaite-Phillips, Matt Sommer, Wu Xu, Zeng Shaocong. I appreciate valuable comments on the manuscript from Steve Harrell and Gonçalo Santos, Laura Miller and Nicole Newendorp, Francesca Bray, and Janet Carsten and Rubie Watson, as well as Debbie Davis, Michael Herzfeld, Bill Jankowiak, Charles Stafford, and Woody Watson. I am most indebted to the Chinese women and men who shared information about their lives.

1   I focus on what Harrell and Santos (introduction) see as the "gender axis" of patriarchy. My empirical work suggests variation in age-related power dynam-

ics within households during the pre-Communist period, which I do not explore here (see Brown 2016).

2   I define the word *fluid* elsewhere (Brown 2004, 17) as "shifting of borders around individuals and groups who themselves do not necessarily change." That is the sense in which I use *fluid* here: shifting institutionalization around ongoing practices.

3   "Undervalued" does not mean "not valued at all." Undervalued contributions may well be—and often were/are—credited with some value; my point is that they are socially credited with *less* economic value than they actually produce. Carma Hinton's film *Small Happiness* captures this undervaluation when the young women picked more corn in the same workday than the men but were still awarded fewer work points for the same amount of labor time: the women's labor was valued (as work) in that it earned some work points, but it was *under*valued because the social credit ascribed was less than the value of the actual product when compared to the credit given to men for less product in the same amount of labor time.

4   Such ideologies may have existed in urban areas, but my evidence comes from rural sources.

5   Brown 2007; Brown and Feldman 2009; Brown et al. 2012.

6   Inscription for the magazine *Women of New China* (Xin Zhongguo funü), printed in its first issue, July 20, 1949; see Mao 1966, 554–55.]

7   Interviews were conducted in a form of Chinese that the women understood; in some research sites, that meant using local or southwest versions of standard Chinese (Mandarin); in other sites (Gan, Xiang, etc.), migrant women were usually interviewed in standard Chinese. Where the interviewer did not speak the necessary local language, local people were hired to translate between standard Chinese and, for example, Gan. (For further discussion of methods, see Brown et al. 2012; and Brown and Satterthwaite-Phillips 2016.)

8   All names of research subjects are pseudonyms.

9   The view that spinning and weaving did not count as work was shared by foot-bound women (e.g., Hunan no. 2102057, b. 1930). It could reflect the low value of women's handwork before 1949 or subsequent devaluation of handwork in the Maoist period.

10 Fielde 1884; cf. Gates 2001 and Brown et al. 2012.

11 Cf. Gates 2001; Bossen 2002; Brown et al. 2012; contra Huang 2002.

12 I translate *pinjin* as "brideprice" because money and gifts from the groom's to the bride's family has been widely understood among Han as buying the woman herself—her body and her labor, as well as her progeny (in contrast to the African case, see Tambiah 1989, 415–16, for a summary). In testimony in Qing legal cases, for example, non-elite people referred to "bride price" (*caili* 財禮) interchangeably with "body price" (*shenjia* 身價) (Sommer 2009, 2015). Ethnographic and sociological accounts also report money and gifts to the bride's family as buying a woman—especially in southern China, in Taiwan,

and among diaspora Chinese (e.g., Gates 1987, 265–66; 1996, ch. 7; Siu 1993; Jaschok and Miers 1994)—but purchasing brides is an ongoing issue throughout China (e.g., Zhao 2003; Minter 2014). Ms. Zhou's point is that she was sold.

13 My Chinese research collaborators requested that I not name in which of the four major southern global-export cities our joint project occurred. Shenzhen and Guangzhou in Guangdong, Xiamen in Fujian, and Shanghai all have high numbers of migrant workers, though migrants are a majority only in Shenzhen and Xiamen.

14 See Hsiung 1996 for discussion of the myriad, undervalued ways that bosses' wives contribute to family businesses.

15 These were not necessarily unrequited remittances. One woman (SCity no. 1203020) who remitted 92 percent of her first year's salary later received ¥10,000 from her parents when she and her husband opened their own business.

16 There *are* safety issues facing young migrant women (Gaetano and Jacka 2004; Chang 2008).

17 Married women surveyed reported giving 11 percent of their income, on average, as cash remittances to their parents (see table 1.1). Bear in mind that the mean gives an inflated impression of most married women's remittances. Among married women interviewed, the mean cash remittance was 9.6 percent of the mean cash salary for first jobs in the 1990s, 12.9 percent for first jobs in 2000–6, and 14.1 percent for jobs in 2011, although the majority of married women remitted less than 10 percent (see table 1.2).

18 She sent ¥20,000. Often, such large payments are long-term, low-interest loans between relatives, necessary to cover brideprice and housing costs.

19 Such contributions seem rather different than women's pre-1949 "private money" *(sifang qian),* because women I interviewed had full control over their private money. Husbands and mothers-in-law often did not know such funds existed.

20 Women interviewed disagreed about the dates their marriages began: at the bride's family banquet, at the groom's family banquet, when the couple moved in together, when they moved the bride's household registration *(hukou)* from her natal household to her husband's place of registration in his natal village, or when a child was born. The couple often moved in together first and moved the household registration last, sometimes years later.

21 One married woman (SCity no. 1203025) had her adult daughter manage her account, to which her husband did not have access.

MELISSA J. BROWN

CHAPTER TWO

FROM CARE PROVIDERS TO FINANCIAL BURDENS

The Changing Role of Sons and Reproductive Choice in Rural Northeast China

LIHONG SHI

T HE patrilineal and patriarchal tradition among the Chinese has rendered sons economically responsible for supporting parents in old age and culturally crucial to continuing the ancestral line. More specifically, adult sons are expected to serve as care providers for their parents in old age, whereas the filial obligation of daughters is transferred to their parents-in-law upon marriage.[1] With sons playing such a crucial role in fulfilling the filial obligation and continuing the patriline, there has been a strong preference for sons among Chinese parents. Although Chinese families have also desired daughters, sons have been considered indispensable (Skinner 2002).

This desire for sons in reproductive choice has come into direct conflict with China's Birth-Planning Policy. Implemented in 1979, the policy limits the majority of Chinese couples to only one child. While the Chinese state has strictly enforced the birth limit through various measures, a large number of rural couples in particular have strongly resisted the policy in order to achieve their reproductive goals, in most cases to have at least one son.[2] Some of the most violent forms of resistance include female infant abandonment and sex-selective abortion, which has caused a male-biased sex ratio at birth in China.[3]

Recently, however, the reproductive choice of having at least one son has undergone drastic transformations, and a new reproductive pattern is emerging in Northeast China, where an increasing number of couples have chosen to stop with a singleton daughter. Although the Birth-Planning Policy has been relaxed since the mid-1980s to allow rural couples whose first child is a girl to have a second child, the couples I studied have decided not to take advantage of the modified policy and to forgo a second child. What is the scope of this reproductive pattern, and what are the socioeconomic factors contributing to the weakening of a preference for sons?

RESEARCH COMMUNITY AND METHODOLOGY

Data collected for this chapter come from seventeen months of ethnographic research between 2002 and 2012 in Lijia Village, a rural community in Liaoning with a population of eight hundred in 2007.[4] Lijia residents grow corn and take temporary nonagricultural jobs outside the village.[5] Young Lijia men and women typically start to work after they finish junior high school or in their late teens. Once married, men continue to do nonagricultural work, while a large number of women also find temporary employment when they can secure child-care assistance from their parents-in-law or, in some cases, their natal parents. The postmarital residence pattern is primarily patrilocal. Within a few years following a wedding ceremony, a young couple typically establish their nuclear household in a separate house or in a separate room in the husband's parents' house and keep separate finances. About one-fourth of married Lijia daughters either are married to a Lijia man and live in the village or have moved back to the village with their husbands, to take advantage of employment opportunities in the nearby factories. The majority of those who marry out of the village live in the same township or in the county area. Frequent bus service and the availability of motorcycles provide convenient means for married daughters to return to Lijia Village to visit their natal parents.

The Birth-Planning Policy has been strictly enforced in Lijia Village since its initiation in the 1970s. As in villages elsewhere in China, a Women's Federation leader has been responsible for enforcing the policy by delivering contraceptive services and monitoring women during their peak childbearing years to make sure that there are no unauthorized births. Beyond the village level, a township office for family planning is responsible for delivering birth-planning guidelines and providing contraceptive services and ultrasound tests, as well as other services related to the Birth-Planning Policy, such as assisting qualified couples applying to the county office of family planning for a one-child certificate.

Research methods for this project combine participant observation, a household survey, and interviews. During my multiple field trips, I lived with two host families; one family was a couple in their late seventies in 2007, and the other family was a couple in their mid-thirties who had a singleton daughter in 2007. I also conducted semi-structured interviews with couples who had singleton daughters and elderly parents with married sons and daughters. Lijia villagers speak the northeastern dialect of Mandarin, and I conducted my field research in that dialect.

EMBRACING A SINGLETON DAUGHTER: EMERGING REPRODUCTIVE CHOICE UNDER THE BIRTH-PLANNING POLICY

Since the initiation of the Birth-Planning Policy in Lijia Village in 1980, the government has made a few modifications that allow some couples to have a second child. One major relaxation of the policy, implemented in 1986, allows a couple whose first child is a girl to have a second child. During the early years of enforcement of the policy, the majority of Lijia couples who were qualified took advantage of the modified policy and had a second child. In fact, all except one couple who had a singleton daughter by 1986 chose to have a second child. Since the 1990s, however, an increasing number of couples have decided not to take advantage of the modified policy and have chosen to have singleton daughters. This emerging reproductive transition has been demonstrated by a large percentage of couples with singleton daughters who have obtained a one-child certificate.[6] In 2010, 165 Lijia couples in which wives were below the age of fifty had at least one child. Fifty of these couples had singleton daughters. Thirty-four (68 percent) of them had obtained one-child certificates. My interviews with these thirty-four couples and the village women's association leader reveal that only one couple made the choice due to health issues. Although a couple who has obtained a one-child certificate is allowed to have a second child as long as they return their one-child certificate and the money they have received, this practice was very rare in the village, according to my interviews with birth-planning officials. This emerging reproductive transition is not an exception in the township area. In the other seventeen villages in the township, the reproductive choice of having a singleton daughter is also emerging, demonstrated by an increasing number of couples with singleton daughters who have applied for a one-child certificate.

Unlike couples in rural Guangdong who have preferred to have small families with two children and at least one son (Santos, chap. 4), this emerging reproductive choice suggests that couples in rural Liaoning not only have chosen to have small families but no longer consider sons to be indispensable. A combination of various sociocultural and economic factors contributes to this reproductive choice. For example, one major factor is the rising cost of child rearing and the preference for focusing limited family resources on one child in order to secure the best possible upbringing for that child. Like urban parents who have experienced a "consumer revolution" (Davis 2000) and have lavished family resources on their children (Croll 2006a; Fong 2004), Lijia parents have faced the rising costs of child rearing in the daily consumption of products and the heavy burden of financing their children's education. Like rural parents in Gansu who supported their children's education in the hope that their children could convert their college degrees into income-earning capacity and would be able to support them in old age (Obendiek, chap. 3), Lijia parents consider education a significant factor in achieving upward social mobility and therefore have strongly supported their children's education. Parental support for a child's education is not gender specific, and parents have supported their daughters' education in an unprecedented manner. Due to the rising cost of child rearing and strong parental support for children's education, young and middle-aged Lijia parents prefer to concentrate resources on one child, to give that child the best possible opportunities. This child-rearing preference has contributed to the reproductive choice of having a singleton daughter.

The reproductive choice of having a singleton daughter is also a result of the declining belief in the significance of having a son to continue the family line. While ancestral rituals, such as visiting ancestral graves and burning paper money for ancestors, are still widely practiced in Lijia Village, a large number of villagers admitted that they visited ancestors' graves to put on a show for other villagers so that they would not be criticized as unfilial to their deceased family members. In the past, a family without a son was referred to as "finished" (*juehou*), considered the worst curse for a Chinese family. This stigma no longer exists in the village. Instead, young and middle-aged couples consider having strong financial capability more important than having sons. Villagers look down on families with few financial resources with which to support their children, even when those families have male heirs.

These two factors are among those contributing to the reproductive choice of having a singleton daughter. Perhaps even more important is the drastic transition of the role of sons from care providers to financial burdens. Parents no longer consider sons to be reliable providers for their old age, due to a decline in the practice of filial support. Furthermore, sons have become financial burdens for their parents as a result of the skyrocketing cost of financing their weddings. Such a drastic transition in the role of sons has had a significant impact on the reproductive choices of young and middle-aged couples. Instead of holding "a desire for sons" (*pan erzi*), the current generation of rural couples in Northeast China have developed "a fear of sons" (*pa erzi*).

"IF SONS AREN'T FILIAL, IT'S NO USE HAVING A SON": SONS AS UNRELIABLE PROVIDERS FOR OLD-AGE SUPPORT

Elderly Lijia residents typically support themselves by farming well into their late sixties or early seventies. In addition to farming, some elderly men also find temporary employment or herd cattle for extra income. They usually do not require financial and physical support until they stop farming or their health significantly declines. Elderly parents typically exchange land for financial support from adult children. Usually the son who farms his parents' land provides food for his parents. For some families with more than one son, sons divide their parents' land and share the responsibility for financial support. When elderly parents have significant medical expenses, all children are usually expected to help with the cost.

Elderly parents try to postpone dependence on their children for nursing care as long as they can. When one spouse requires nursing care, the other spouse usually becomes the primary care provider, assuming responsibility for cooking and other household chores. When both parents become physically fragile and have difficulty performing daily chores, they usually live with the family of one son or in a house separate from their son's family but have meals with the family. Lijia villagers call this practice *guigei erzi*, which means "becoming the responsibility of a son's family." The son who supports his parents until their deaths inherits his parents' house.

The arrangement between one elderly Lijia couple and their sons exemplifies the practice of elder support in Lijia Village. In 2007, this couple was in their late seventies and had four sons and one daughter. The elderly mother had long-term conflicts with the oldest daughter-in-law, and as a result, the oldest daughter-in-law refused to offer any support to them. The second son was physically disabled after suffering a stroke and lived by himself while his wife migrated to the city for employment. Their third son and their daughter lived outside the village. The youngest son lived in the village, and the couple got along better with him and his wife. The elderly couple supported themselves financially by renting their land to their youngest son. All except the oldest son bought them food occasionally when visiting and offered them money on holidays and their birthdays. When I visited the couple in 2011, the elderly father was in his early eighties and was showing signs of dementia. When I returned to the village in 2012, the couple had moved in with their youngest son's family for support.

However, the above arrangements are seldom made without disagreements among multiple sons or frustration and disappointment for elderly parents. A plethora of literature has revealed intergenerational conflicts (Davis-Friedmann 1991; Zhang 2004) and a renegotiation of intergenerational exchange in contemporary China.[7] In Lijia Village, intergenerational exchange and filial support are also undergoing significant transformations. In families with more than one son, adult sons sometimes disagree about their shared responsibilities. In particular, when a son and his wife feel that the husband's parents have not given them as much support as they have to other siblings, such as providing child care for one grandchild but not for others or offering more money to finance one son's wedding, they are usually reluctant to fulfill their filial duty. As demonstrated by the above-mentioned case, when elderly parents have severe conflicts with the family of one son, usually with a daughter-in-law, that son's family often refuses to provide any support.

When all adult children abandon their filial responsibilities, elderly parents have no choice but to turn to the village head, who can serve as a mediator or file a lawsuit against adult children. Since the laws in China stipulate that adult children are responsible for providing support for parents in need, the court usually favors elderly parents in such lawsuits. In recent years, a few elderly Lijia parents sued their adult children for sufficient financial support, and all won their lawsuits. However, this is seen as a last resort, because it is considered extremely disgraceful to bring a family dispute to court, thus making it public, and doing so can severely harm relationships with adult children.

Even among the elderly who receive financial and physical support from their children, many complain that the quality of care has significantly declined compared with their own practice of filial support to their parents. Some elderly parents lament that their adult children are inconsiderate and disrespectful. For example, a few elderly parents who were living with their sons' families complained to me that their sons and daughters-in-law were not considerate enough to prepare food that was easy for elderly people to chew and digest. Some elderly parents resented the lack of respect shown by adult children who had verbal confrontations with them and, in a few cases, abused them physically.

As women still take the major responsibility for household chores, such as cooking and doing laundry, elderly parents usually rely on daughters-in-law for daily support. When elderly parents do not get along with a daughter-in-law, it can significantly affect the quality of care they receive. Even when elderly parents make an effort to establish a good relationship with a daughter-in-law, the delicate nature of the relationship can create emotional stress for elderly parents, as exemplified by the story of Wang Li. Wang Li's husband died of cancer in his forties. Her husband had worked as a village electrician, so her family was better off than most Lijia families. She managed to finance a wedding for her only son a few years later and lived in the same house with the young couple. According to the villagers I interviewed, Wang Li did not intend to remarry and had planned to live with her son's family for the rest of her life. However, her daughter-in-law preferred to have a private conjugal life and frequently expressed discontent when her husband demonstrated his close bond with his mother, such as offering an ice cream bar to his mother before giving one to her. Eventually, Wang Li decided to remarry so that her son would not be put in a difficult situation and accepted a marriage proposal from a widower in another village. One villager, who lived in Wang Li's old neighborhood, told me, "On the day she left for her new husband's village, she left everything with her son and daughter-in-law [out of love for her son] and took only one wrapped package with her. It was sad to watch."

While the role of a son's family as care provider for elderly parents has significantly declined, young and middle-aged couples have explored alternative means of old-age support. Couples with singleton daughters have tried to cultivate close bonds with their daughters in the hope that they can rely on the daughters for support in old age. While filial support from a daughter-in-law can never be taken for granted, a large number of daughters have proved to be reliable and filial to their birth parents. According to my interviews with thirty-four elderly parents with married sons and daughters, elderly Lijia parents defined filiality as expressing intimate care, showing respect, and providing financial and physical support (Shi 2009). The majority of these elderly parents considered daughters to be more filial than sons. Like daughters who have maintained intimate bonds with their parents and who have even shouldered filial responsibilities for their natal parents in other areas in China,[8] an increasing number of Lijia daughters have become valuable sources of emotional support and nursing care for elderly parents. When elderly parents have conflicts with their sons and daughters-in-law, some married daughters have shown their emotional support by visiting their parents and comforting them. When elderly parents become physically fragile, some married daughters have provided support by bringing meals and doing laundry for them. In addition, when a married daughter's financial situation allows, she usually supports her parents in need, such as by buying food and clothes and pay-ing for medical expenses.

An increasing number of Lijia couples have also prepared for self-sup-port in old age by maximizing the family income in order to build up their savings. Some couples told me that they would work hard to make as much money as possible while they still could. If their child became unreliable when they reached old age, as long as they had savings, they could find a way to take care of themselves, such as by paying someone for help. A husband and wife who both held positions at the township government hired someone to take care of the husband's elderly mother. Some villag-ers mentioned this arrangement as a possible option when explaining their plans for the future.

The decline of filial support and the preparation for alternative means of support in old age suggest that sons are no longer considered reliable pro-viders for old-age support. This transformation has a significant impact on reproductive choice among Lijia parents. During my interviews with cou-ples who had singleton daughters, the majority admitted that their decisions had been greatly influenced by the declining practice of old-age support provided by sons. They frequently told me, "If sons aren't filial, it's no use having a son" (Erzi buxiao, you erzi ye meiyong).

Lijia couples faced with the decision of whether or not to have a sec-ond child are usually care providers for their aged parents. Not only have these couples witnessed the tension and conflicts between elderly parents and their sons and daughters-in-law, they even engendered the decline of filial support. Some of these couples used their own stories to explain their choice not to have a second child. During my interview with a Lijia man who had a singleton daughter, he told me, "It's no use having a son. Take the example of my family. My mother has four sons and needs support now. If each of us gave her ¥500 (approximately US$80) a year, it would be enough. But none of us is willing to give her any money!"

"HERE COMES MY BIG DEBT": SONS AS FINANCIAL BURDENS

While the role of sons as care providers for aging parents has undergone a drastic transformation, the escalating financial obligation of paying for a wedding has turned sons into financial burdens for their parents. In Lijia Village, both dowry and bridewealth have been offered during marriage transactions. While the amount of dowry provided for a daughter is only a fraction of the amount of bridewealth due from the groom's parents and is easily affordable, the rising cost of bridewealth and other expenses for a wedding becomes a heavy burden for the groom's parents.

Bridewealth is demanded by a bride from her groom's family before an engagement ceremony. As the majority of young couples are introduced by their relatives and friends, the amount of bridewealth is usually requested after the couple has met a few times and has expressed willingness to continue the relationship. If the man's parents refuse to pay the requested amount, the woman often discontinues the relationship. Instead of giving her bridewealth to her parents, nowadays a bride can claim ownership of her bridewealth and make decisions on how to spend the money. The cost of bridewealth has increased from an average amount of around ¥300 between the mid-1970s and the mid-1980s, to ¥4,000 in the 1990s, and to more than ¥22,000 in the aughts (Shi 2011). In addition to bridewealth, a new or well-renovated house is also critical for a marriage proposal. In 2006, the cost of building or renovating a house ranged from ¥30,000 to ¥70,000. Other expenses included three pieces of jewelry, a motorcycle, and household items such as furniture, a television set, and a washing machine, as well as an engagement dinner and a wedding banquet.[9] In 2007, the amount required to finance a son's wedding could add up to ¥100,000, and it could take at least several years of hard work to make such a large amount of money (Shi 2011).

Due to the unbalanced sex ratio in men and women of marriageable age, as well as the obligation of the groom's family to finance the wedding, young women have been empowered to demand a large amount of bridewealth (Shi 2011). Recent studies reveal an emerging notion of self-worth by which love and marriage have been measured by material possessions among middle-class urban residents in China (Li Zhang 2010). Such a materialistic notion of self-worth is also salient among young brides in Lijia Village. The amount of bridewealth that a woman is given indexes the degree of appreciation from the groom's family. Therefore, young women often compare their offers of bridewealth to the amounts requested for the most recent marriage transactions, and when the amount of bridewealth requested by others is higher, prospective brides will try to match it.

In February 2007, Xiaohua, the granddaughter of one of my host families, was trying to decide whether she should ask for ¥30,000 or ¥40,000 in bridewealth from her boyfriend's family. At that time, ¥30,000 was the amount that a few recently married Lijia daughters had requested. When I visited Xiaohua one day, she asked me about the amount of bridewealth requested by the girlfriend of Haitao, who was the nephew of my other host family and whose family was negotiating the amount of bridewealth with his girlfriend. I told her the amount was ¥40,000.[10] She promptly replied, "She asked for ¥40,000. I will ask for the same amount." The next day, Xiaohua and a few family members went to meet the matchmaker, whom they called "Uncle Liu," to discuss the amount of bridewealth. Xiaohua told Uncle Liu that she requested ¥40,000 and three pieces of jewelry. On behalf of her boyfriend's family, Uncle Liu suggested that she request ¥40,000 but no jewelry. Xiaohua refused to compromise. The negotiations were in a stalemate for two hours. Xiaohua's uncle, the husband of an aunt with whom she was very close, reminded her that she should be flexible so as to avoid putting Uncle Liu into a difficult position. Her aunt then suggested that her boyfriend's family offer her ¥40,000 plus one piece of jewelry. Eventually, everyone seemed satisfied with this arrangement.

The next day, however, when I visited Xiaohua, she had obviously changed her mind. She blamed her uncle for making the compromise and Uncle Liu for negotiating on behalf of her boyfriend's family. She said, "I am going to talk to his [her boyfriend's] parents. I will just say Uncle Liu was drunk yesterday and told them the wrong amount." When I mentioned that her boyfriend's parents had bought her two pieces of clothing during her first visit, she said, "The girls in my restaurant all got money—¥200, ¥300, or even ¥500—when they first visited their boyfriends' families.[11] His parents think that they are very generous. But every family offers money now." Although her boyfriend's family eventually accepted her initial request, she later broke up with him anyway and soon began dating a coworker.

As the amount of bridewealth has skyrocketed, this financial burden has become an unavoidable responsibility for parents with a son. The majority of Lijia parents take their responsibility very seriously as a demonstration of their genuine love for their sons and their status as responsible parents. Such a strong sense of parental love and responsibility is demonstrated by my conversation with a Lijia mother in 2005. When I offered my congratulations on her son's recent graduation from college, his new job in the city, and her fulfillment of the duty to support her son through college, she said, "My duty is not done (Haimei wancheng renwu). I need to prepare the money to buy my son an apartment for marriage."

In Lijia Village, in a few cases, the parents did not have the resources to finance a son's wedding, nor were they willing to borrow money and then pay off the debt through years of hard work. These parents were severely criticized by other villagers for being "irresponsible" (bu fu zeren). Not only did villagers criticize these parents; their sons also blamed them. Bachelors who have passed the most suitable ages for marriage sometimes express resentment and even anger toward their parents. In one family, a twenty-five-year-old son was frustrated with his parents for being unable to provide engagement money to a young woman to whom he was introduced. One day, after a verbal confrontation with his parents, he broke a window in their house and left home. Thus, financing a son's wedding not only fulfills a crucial parental obligation but also avoids criticism from other villagers and blame from sons.

Due to the heavy burden of financing a son's wedding, couples with a son usually start to make preparations when the son reaches his mid-teens. Because housing is a major financial burden, the first step is to rebuild or renovate a house. If a house is still in good condition, a couple will renovate the house, making improvements such as replacing the doors and windows, paving the floors, and covering the kitchen and exterior walls of the house with ceramic tiles. If a house is considered too small or requires major renovations, a couple will usually rebuild it. Couples usually leave some parts of a house unfinished, such as decoration of the ceiling or division of a large room into two smaller ones. When the son is ready to marry, they will finish the renovation in the latest style. In 2006, four Lijia families either rebuilt or made major renovations to a house. Two of these families each had a teenage son, and the parents of a son in his early twenties were asking their relatives and friends to introduce a girlfriend to him.

A Lijia mother whose son was eighteen years old in 2007 had the following plan for financing her son's future wedding, which is representative of the plans of a majority of Lijia parents. On a winter day in 2007, I met this woman on her way back from inspecting an old house for sale in the village. She told me that because her house was in bad condition and the yard did not have enough space for another house, she and her husband were looking for an old house that they could either rebuild or renovate. She and her husband were each working in a factory to make money for a house. She told me that they should be able to afford a house by using their savings and taking out loans. Once the house was finished, they would spend a couple of years paying off their debts. By then, their son would have reached the age to start looking for a marriage partner. When their son was ready for marriage, they would use the money that they would be earning and would borrow some from their relatives and friends to pay for bridewealth and other wedding expenses. According to this plan, she and her husband would have to keep working even after their son's wedding to pay off all their debts.

Such a heavy financial burden for a son's wedding has had a negative impact on the reproductive choice to have a son. Because young couples, women in particular, are the driving force behind the increasing burden of paying for a wedding, they are well aware of the power dynamics in the negotiation of marriage transactions and understand that this ever-increasing financial burden is unavoidable. Some young couples expressed their unwillingness to have a son because of the financial burden, as demonstrated by the story of Liu Hong. Liu Hong was pregnant in the winter of 2006. I interviewed her two days before she gave birth. Because doctors are not allowed to disclose the sex of a fetus during an ultrasound examination, she did not know whether her baby was a boy or a girl. She told me, "It is better to have only a girl. If the child is a boy, we will have to work for him for the rest of our lives." She continued, "In the past, everyone desired sons (*pan erzi*). Nowadays, people have developed a fear of sons (*pa erzi*)." Two days later, Liu Hong gave birth to a healthy baby boy. When I visited her in the hospital, she looked at her son and said to me, "Here comes my big debt!" (Da jihuang laile!).[12]

Some parents who chose to have a second child and ended up with two sons complained about the rising cost of weddings and expressed bitterness or even regret over their decision. A mother who had a teenage son told me in 2007, "When I gave birth to my son, ¥10,000 was absolutely enough for a son's wedding. Now it is so much more, and who knows how much more it will be when my son is ready to marry? . . . Back then, if I could have envisioned that it would cost so much for a son's wedding nowadays, there was no way that I would have had a second child." She continued, "I said this to my son: 'In the past, the Japanese [soldiers] forced people to work for them, pointing guns at their backs. You are exactly like the Japanese!'"[13]

◆　◆　◆

The dramatic shift in the role of sons from care providers for their parents in old age to financial burdens has contributed to a weaker preference for sons as a reproductive choice. This transformation has significant implications for family dynamics and gender relations in China. First, the crucial role of sons in a Chinese family has been shaken, while the status of daughters has been reevaluated. Sons are no longer considered as reliable and the only source for old-age support, nor are they regarded as indispensable for a family. Meanwhile, a large number of married daughters have proved to be even more filial than sons and have been valued for their potential role in supporting their parents in old age.

Second, while filial obligation to aging parents and the parental duty of financing a son's wedding are both highly expected, middle-aged couples have chosen to take their parental duty more seriously. Lijia parents often expressed a deep sense of guilt when they mentioned their failure to provide better living conditions for their children during the years of financial hardship in the family. However, such a sense of guilt was rarely expressed when these parents were confronted with their failure to fulfill their filial obligation to their own aging parents. For the current generation of middle-aged couples, the focus of family obligation has shifted from the older generation to the younger generation.

Despite these drastic family transformations, it may be too simplistic to conclude that the patriarchal system in rural Northeast China has come to an end. In his discussion of the rise of "girl power" in Xiajia Village, Heilongjiang, Yunxiang Yan (2006) documents young women's agency in challenging patriarchal power in the arenas of courtship, marriage negotiation, and family division. However, Yan argues that the empowerment of young women in marriage is the result of shifting power relations between the senior generation and the junior generation, and therefore girl power challenges the generational axis of patriarchy more than the gender axis. In contemporary Lijia Village, during power negotiations between young daughters-in-law and their mothers-in-law, young women have gained the upper hand in providing filial support and demanding a high amount of bridewealth. However, as Yan's analysis suggests, the power that young women enjoy now probably will not be carried on as "mother power" when these young women become mothers-in-law.

Furthermore, by gaining the upper hand in bridewealth negotiations and in providing filial support to their natal parents, young Lijia women have transformed certain aspects of patrilineal and patriarchal practices among the Chinese. However, their agency does not necessarily challenge the long-standing patrilineal and patriarchal ideologies that are deeply rooted in Chinese society. For example, when a young bride asks for bridewealth from the groom's parents, she justifies her request by claiming that the groom's family should pay bridewealth for the benefits of her future labor contributions and children, a rationale behind marriage transactions in the patrilineal Chinese tradition. With the same rationale, when a Lijia woman disputed her husband's disapproval of her gift of ¥100 for her father's birthday, she claimed that since she was married to him and bore children for his family, and her natal parents had raised her without receiving anything in return, they well deserved the money for their birthdays. On the one hand, one could argue that these young women utilize commonly accepted patrilineal and patriarchal ideologies in order to achieve their goals, such as providing support to their natal parents and receiving a large amount of bridewealth. On the other hand, their claims reinforce both the patrilineal ideal of a married woman shifting her membership from her natal family to her husband's family and the commodification of a woman during marriage transactions.

NOTES

I would like to thank Stevan Harrell, Gonçalo Santos, Michael Herzfeld, Priscilla Song, and participants at the conference at the Max Planck Institute for Social Anthropology for their insightful comments and suggestions. Funding for fieldwork for this research is provided by a grant from the Wenner-Gren Foundation for Anthropological Research, three summer research grants from the Department of Anthropology at Tulane University, and a Women's Studies Research Grant from the Newcomb College Center for Research on Women at Tulane University.

1   Baker 1979; Hsu 1948; R. Watson 2004a; M. Wolf 1972; Wolf and Huang 1980.

2   Greenhalgh 1994; Greenhalgh and Winckler 2005; Shi 2014; Wasserstrom 1984; White 2006.

3   Chu 2001; Johnson 1996; Murphy 2003; White 2006; W. Zhang 2006b.

4   To protect the privacy of informants, I use pseudonyms for the name of the village and the names of informants.

5   Lijia residents take wage-labor work at construction sites, in a few factories in the vicinity of the village, and in ceramic factories in a nearby economic development zone. An increasing number of young villagers have also migrated to urban areas for temporary employment opportunities.

6   A one-child certificate is a pledge to the government not to have a second child. In 2006, as an incentive, a couple received ¥10 a month until the child reached the age of fourteen. Since 2005, the Chinese government has granted ¥720 each year to rural couples in Liaoning who have one child or two daughters when they reach the age of sixty as a reward for abiding by the birth limit and as financial assistance in their old age. According to my interviews with Lijia parents, the money was not a large incentive to have only one child. However, because a one-child certificate was required for receiving the monetary incentive, once a couple has decided not to have a second child, they usually apply for a certificate. Therefore, I use the application for a one-child certificate as an indicator of the reproductive choice to have a singleton daughter

7   Croll 2006b; Guo 2001; Ikels 1993; Yan 2003.

8   Fong 2004; Evans 2008; Judd 1989; H. Zhang 2007a.

9   In 2012, a desktop computer became a new item requested by a bride for her wedding.

10 I was told that in Haitao's girlfriend's village, ¥40,000 was the newly requested (and accepted) amount of bridewealth at that time.

11 Xiaohua was working as a waitress in a restaurant in the city before she went home for the matchmaking. Her coworkers were from rural areas in neighboring counties.

12 In Lijia Village, the local term for debt is *jihuang*, and borrowing money is called *la jihuang*. The word *jihuang* meaning "debt" is widely used in some regions in China, and this definition has been listed in Chinese dictionaries.

13   Although Lijia villagers of her generation did not have the experience of liv-
      ing under Japanese colonization in Northeast China during the first half of
      the twentieth century, mainstream media reports and movie and television
      dramas portraying Japanese colonization in China overwhelmingly pres-
      ent images of the brutality of Japanese soldiers and the suffering of Chinese
      civilians.

CHAPTER THREE

HIGHER EDUCATION, GENDER, AND ELDER SUPPORT IN RURAL NORTHWEST CHINA

HELENA OBENDIEK

I T has been argued that in China the Communists' attack on patriarchal power as the core of the Confucian social order, along with a number of developments in the Reform era, such as state-induced fertility decline, rapid industrialization, the young generation's greater mobility and exposure to new values, have profoundly altered the power relations between the genders and the generations.[1] In rural China, the decline in the dominance of the senior generation brought about a severe crisis in the family-based elderly support system, all the more so since the demise of high socialism left the elderly with few resources to be deployed as bargaining chips in claiming old-age support from their offspring (Ikels 2004, 2006). Without alternative sources of elder care, many rural parents have been adapting to the new circumstances by preparing themselves to live independently as long as possible (Thøgerson and Ni 2008; H. Zhang 2004). At the same time, the young generation, and in particular young women, in the countryside have been empowered in various ways (Yan 2003, 2006). Married daughters, whose filial obligation used to be transferred to their in-laws in the traditional patrilineal and patrilocal Chinese family system (Baker 1979; Hsu 1948), came to take on new roles in elder care for their natal parents.[2] Even though in some rural regions new reproductive patterns give evidence of a weakening of son preference (see Shi, chap. 2), my research in rural Gansu points to continuous preferential parental investment in sons, showing that local understandings of the intergenerational contract remain skewed toward the patrilineal notion that it is above all the duty of the son (and daughter-in-law by association) to provide care for elderly parents. Such gendered obligations of old-age support also affect the younger generation's life planning and, not least, their intragenerational gender relations.

Interplay between higher education, gender, and obligations of elder care is evident in Huining, an economically deprived county in Gansu. In this region, rural parents usually have no source of income when they get too frail to work in the fields or migrate to the cities to sell their labor. With no elder-care provision by the state, they become fully dependent on their offspring's support in practical as well as financial matters.[3] At the same time, many parents in the region push their children to pursue higher education, even though the expenses clearly exceed their financial resources, forcing them to deplete all family savings and often even to incur heavy debt. Yet, the "return" on educational spending in terms of career options for the graduate has recently become highly insecure. Rapid expansion of national university enrollment quotas in the late 1990s and early aughts, as well as the concurrent abolition of the state job-allocation system for graduates, have led to fierce competition in the newly established academic employment markets in which graduates from poor rural family backgrounds have little to offer other than their academic degrees.

Gendered roles in elder-care provision intertwine with local parents' motivation to support their offspring's higher education, while a high level of education has different effects on young men's and women's lives, including their obligations and capacity for providing family support. Parents' educational support for sons and daughters causes a shift in the way filial obligations are gendered while at the same time putting the implicit contract between the generations on a new basis. Moreover, continuous notions of patrilineality shape intragenerational gender relations of recent graduates from the region.

BACKGROUND

Given its arid climate, hilly topography, and lack of infrastructure, Huining County, located on the eastern rim of China's Loess Plateau about 150 kilometers southeast of the provincial capital of Lanzhou, offers few opportunities for earning cash income. With an average annual income of about ¥1,300 (about US$210) among the rural population, the county belongs to one of China's most impoverished regions.[4] When I lived in a village in Huining for more than six months in 2007, local people grew wheat, corn, potatoes, lentils, linseed, peas, and alfalfa in crop rotation with one harvest per year.[5] Due to continuous scarcity of rainfall in recent years, yields had been just enough to secure pure subsistence. In order to earn the cash needed, mainly for health-care and educational expenses, many middle-aged men (up to their mid-fifties) left the region to look for wage labor somewhere else, with some returning during agricultural season to help their wives and elderly parents with farming. The younger generation obviously felt that life in the countryside did not have much to offer, and almost everybody who finished middle school (or dropped out of school even earlier) opted to leave the village, either by joining the tide of migrant laborers or by pursuing high school and tertiary education that, it was hoped, would lead to regular white-collar employment in the cities and thus permanent rural-to-urban mobility.

During the first two decades of Reform socialism, when graduates from secondary vocational and tertiary educational institutions were still allocated steady employment by the state, educational achievement was a rare but secure ticket enabling rural residents to cross the strict administrative divide between urban and rural society installed by China's unique socialist system of household registration (*hukou*). Every graduate was granted not only a regular salaried position but also permanent urban residency rights and eligibility for the comprehensive social welfare protection that went along with it. In the late 1990s, a new wave of market reforms, including rapid expansion of university enrollment quotas, rising tuition fees, and the abolition of the state job-allocation system for graduates, turned the pursuit of higher education into a financially risky endeavor, especially for poor rural families (Bai 2006). Nevertheless, almost all rural Huining parents pushed their offspring to pursue higher education. With the local fertility rate in constant decline since the late 1970s, reaching about two children per woman in the 1990s,[6] it seemed that every child who had at least a minimal hope of succeeding in the educational race was supported, if not pressured, to continue schooling. Accordingly, there was fierce competition for enrollment at one of the five local high schools that offered places for slightly more than one-quarter of the respective age cohort.[7] After all, compared with the insecure working and living conditions migrant laborers had to face, educational achievement was still believed to be the better option. Despite all investment insecurities, higher education at least allowed the hope that graduates in the end would achieve regular employment with reliable salaries and social benefits, however small such a chance had in fact recently become.

From the point of view of rural Huining parents, the educational mobility of their offspring did, however, entail particular consequences for their own old-age security. First, given the fact that the average per capita annual income in rural Huining corresponded to just about one-sixth of the

HELENA OBENDIEK

expenses for one year of university education,[8] supporting a child through years of secondary and tertiary education meant that local parents could hardly accumulate any financial reserves as security for their old age. Their situation thus differed considerably from parents in other regions of China who were eligible for pension payments and/or had already accumulated savings in order to live independently as long as possible (see Zhang, chap. 12). At the same time, the educational mobility of their offspring resulted in different outcomes in intergenerational resource flows, depending on the child's gender.

CREATING INDEBTEDNESS

Living arrangements in rural Huining demonstrate that the conventional patrilineal and patrilocal ideal of at least one son co-residing with and taking care of elderly parents in exchange for inheriting the patrimony was becoming difficult to realize. Quite obviously, rural Huining parents had few assets to offer their children in exchange for providing support during old age. In the case of sons, parents could at least use inheritance of the house as a bargaining chip to strengthen their position. Even though most young men hoped that labor migration would allow them to settle elsewhere in the long run, the option of returning to the parental courtyard was still important backup security for them, should efforts to set up a life somewhere else fail. Moreover, some couples with small children decided to have wives live in the village together with parents-in-law in order to take care of the toddlers there. Others left their children in the custody of grandparents in the countryside while both parents continued to work elsewhere. If a son and/or his wife returned to the village and co-resided with his parents, relationships between the generations often turned out to be strained. The power shift to the advantage of the younger generation became most obvious to the public when elderly parents moved out of their houses to live independently somewhere in the neighborhood, usually under much worse conditions.

Given local notions of patrilineality according to which daughters have no right to inherit the parental estate, parents had even less to offer their daughters in the intergenerational contract. In a long conversation about his two older sisters, Wang Yadong, a first-year university student from a rural Huining family background, commented about the fragile bond between local parents and those daughters who migrated in search of temporary work: "In the places they go to, migrant laborers like my sisters find someone they like and who is good-looking, and then they marry him. The parents are not involved in that process; they just have no control over the situation. If they object, they just risk having their daughter leave anyway and breaking off all contact with them." Obviously, when rural Huining youth left the village in search of temporary employment in other places all over China, their parents lost control over their lives, particularly in the case of daughters.

The situation was different for those rural youth who took the educational pathway and later graduated from institutions of higher education. As graduates, they were expected not to return to the countryside but to set up permanent lives in the city. If they returned to their home county, they at least should have secure employment as teachers or as cadres in the local administration. In any case, as persons "with culture/education" (*you wenhua de ren*), graduates were believed to have left the peasant lot behind. They thus enjoyed a much higher social standing than their "peasant" family and kin, a fact that also mattered when it came to marriage. On the marriage market, which was stratified according to the candidates' level of education, among other factors, an academic degree could thus well outweigh the disadvantage of originating from an economically deprived region like rural Huining. Advancing their offspring's marriage options thus was also an important motivation for local parents to support their children's education (cf. Obendiek 2016b).

The recent academic employment crisis meant that higher education no longer enabled male graduates to fulfill the intergenerational contract in the way their predecessors, who had benefited from state job-allocation, had been able to do. The latter's privileged position often had allowed them to bring their parents to the city to live with them there. It had at least supplied them with sufficient resources to provide viricentric support of various kinds to their parents and other kin back in the village (cf. Obendiek 2016a). Recent graduates who entered the labor markets after the late 1990s found the opposite situation. In their case, insecure employment prospects as well as the heavy financial burden of buying an urban home and, in the long term, of high expenditures for their children's educations, made it rather unlikely that many resources would flow back to parents in the village. Moreover, rural parents hardly could afford to provide housing in the city for the newlyweds, an obligation that still fell to the male's family. The patrilineal logic of preferential investment in sons as a means of securing fulfillment of the intergenerational contract thus had become highly questionable. While supporting a son's higher education exhausted all family resources, new insecurities concerning the graduate's future career, as well as the skyrocketing costs of settling in the city that burdened mainly the groom's side, made education-based rural-urban mobility an endeavor that put male graduates' ability to fulfill their role in the intergenerational contract at particular risk. In the future, the heavy financial burden of assisting a graduate son in purchasing urban housing as a precondition of marriage may even make local parents reconsider son preference in their reproductive choices (see Shi, chap. 2).

Compared to the exorbitant costs of a son's education-based pathway out of the village, pushing a daughter to attend higher education implied much less financial risk. Above all, in her case, parents did not have to worry about financing a neolocal urban home when she married.

Irrespective of the offspring's gender, parents' willingness to shoulder the heavy financial burden of supporting their children's higher education was certainly rooted in the hope that, despite all difficulties and insecurities, educational achievement would still improve their offspring's career and marriage options, in addition to the "intrinsic" values associated with becoming persons "with culture." At the same time, educational support also produced the side effect of altering the basis of the intergenerational contract: as a kind of pre-mortem inheritance (J. Goody 1973) it indebted the children to their parents, thus keeping them attached emotionally. After all, educational support went along with clear expectations of the students' whole-hearted gratitude toward their supporters. Such gratitude, it was assumed, would induce not only the obligation but also the wish to reciprocate the help received.

Chinese parents have been described as quite explicit in expressing the reciprocal claims entailed in their upbringing of and care for their offspring (e.g., Croll 2000, 2006b; Fong 2004). However, such explicitness was much less common in relationships between parents and their educationally successful children in rural Huining. Here parental intentionality and anticipation of a "return" on educational spending was rather played down, if not denied. Only during longer conversations would parents admit holding any expectations at all. "I do not need much. It is enough if they remit some money later and sometimes come home to see me" was an often-heard statement. Sometimes a concrete (e.g., a car) or more general ("filial piety") wish that they hoped would be fulfilled by their children would shine through a parental joke, or a student might overhear how his father, when drinking with his friends, bragged about his "educated" son who would later bring him to live in the city. Many students from rural Huining family backgrounds recalled how during their childhoods their parents had frequently retold stories of children from the village who had made education-based careers outside the locality and later had supported their families in all possible ways. Moreover, when graduates failed to send money home to their families in the village, their parents' disappointment was widely known and discussed in the neighborhood. In a quite indirect fashion, rural Huining children thus learned early on that their parents' educational support for them was connected to rather definite expectations of a return.

Certainly, local parents were not purely rational actors who only calculated the potential return from their educational "investments." Yet these parents surely did worry about how to raise their children's capacity—and willingness—to support them at a later stage in life. After all, without any alternative sources of old-age care, they simply were not in a position to ignore the question of how their relationship with their children would develop in the future.

In his study of village life in Northeast China, Yunxiang Yan (2003) argues that in view of the waning power of the senior generation, rural parents felt they had to invest in sustaining the emotional bonds with their children, for example, by approving early family division, in order to secure their offspring's support during old age. In rural Huining, parents' "gift" of educational support is aimed both at strengthening the emotional bond with their children and at incurring the latter's obligation to reciprocate the support received. After all, according to Chinese *renqing* ethics, the popularized version of the Confucian social theory of proper social relationships and reciprocal gift giving (L. Yang 1957), the material exchange of giving a gift or doing a favor is congruent with the feelings it evokes between the people involved (Yan 1996; Kipnis 1996). In close resonance with the classical anthropological discussion about the Maussian concept of the "gift" (e.g., Mauss [1924] 1990; Sahlins 1978), the concept of *renqing* denotes not only the medium transferred in social exchange, such as a favor or a gift, but also the social norms and moral obligations that should guide the social interaction of reciprocal exchange. Moreover, *renqing* also connotes "human feelings," in particular a distinctively human empathy toward the other's emotional responses in social interaction (Yan 1996, 122–46). Material exchange thus is not only expressive of good human relations but can also be used to create, maintain, acknowledge, or intensify good feelings, since gifts "embody the desired closeness of a relationship which they help to construct" (Kipnis 1997, 67). With such close interrelation between emotional attachment and instrumentality, it is no contradiction that parents' educational support may be motivated by a complex mixture of emotional closeness, parental obligation, and calculation of a future return.

Huining students and graduates were well aware of the double nature of the "gift" of educational support. They often stated that although their parents surely did not primarily count on a return on their educational spending, it was just natural that such was their "second thought." Huining parents, on the contrary, seemed eager to present themselves as having minimal or no expectations at all. "Everything for the children" was the frequent description of parents' position regarding their children. Parental sacrifice is conveyed by the following narrative: Since historical circumstances had deprived their generation of the opportunity to change life for the better, all they could do was to exert all their energy toward supporting their children's efforts to achieve lives that were different from the hard lot of a poor peasant. Parental sacrifice was recurrently displayed in front of students when parents' thriftiness (e.g., through saving on food, postponing house repairs, and even shunning urgent medical treatment) was justified by the wish to save all possible resources to pay for their children's education. The picture of hardworking parents who, when tilling the fields, "bent down, facing the dry loess earth while the sun burns on their back" (*mian chao huangtu, bei chao tian*), all for the sake of their children's education and future, was also inculcated in pupils at local schools.

Such deployment of the notion of sacrifice connects to a long-standing Chinese tradition of parental sacrifice as an act of giving that entails the obligation of reciprocity (Kipnis 2009; Feuchtwang 2002). At the same time, local Huining parents' constant reference to the hardships they underwent in order to meet their children's desires was their investment in the emotional bond between the generations. After all, in view of the lack of other kinds of resources to bequeath to the next generation, and "tradition" having lost its binding force in the intergenerational contract, strengthening emotional attachment based on gratitude for parental sacrifice seemed the only means of bridging the increasing gulf between the generations (cf. also Kipnis 2009). The "dividend" parents might gain from such a strengthened parent-child bond thus would be less the direct repayment of the material debt the younger generation incurred and more the relationship created (cf. also Schweitzer 2000; Brandtstädter 2003). Moreover, with more and more local parents preparing to live independently as long as possible, the emotional support that was likely to result from an emotional bond between the generations became an increasingly important resource for them.

Aspects of emotional support were particularly relevant in local parents' relationships with their daughters. In contrast to sons, whose obligation to care for their parents according to patrilineal logic was represented locally as "natural," a matter of "heavenly rule and earthly justice" (*tianjing diyi*), daughters' contributions to their natal parents' elder support was seen as based on "feelings" (*ganqing*), not obligation (*zeren*), and thus not reliable.

While female students generally professed the same deep feelings of indebtedness toward supportive parents as did their male counterparts, some claimed that, being aware of persistent gender bias in the intergenerational contract, they understood their parents' spending for their education to be even less instrumentally motivated than in the case of their brothers. First-year university student Zhao Mei, whose family hosted me during my research in the village, explained this to me:

> I have discussed this issue with my parents. . . . Parents lose a lot of money when raising a daughter, especially when they have to support her, as in my case, from elementary school until university. In that case, it is better to have a son. I think adult daughters used to contribute less to support their parents because of the circumstances they lived in. After marriage, women usually relied on their husbands for their living. They themselves had neither money nor social standing; . . . they just had no resources to support their natal parents. . . . But when women in my generation graduate from university, they will have their own income and will be able to live on their own. We will not depend on our husbands. After graduation, I plan to live together with my parents, but I am aware that such an arrangement will mean much social pressure for us. In our region, almost no parents live with a daughter. Parents may visit their daughter for a certain period of time, but they will return to their own place sooner or later. . . . People just do not trust that a daughter will be able to care for her parents when they become frail. Therefore, if I really want to live with my parents, we will face quite some social pressure.

Reduced fertility spurred by the Birth-Planning Policy certainly favored the redefinition of a daughter's role in elder care (see also Zhang, chap. 12). Supporting a daughter's higher education thus was reasonable for local parents in many respects: Higher education would not only enhance the daughter's access to location-independent financial means and, due to greater mobility, also put her in a better position to realize practical support for her parents. It also was likely to advance her chances on the marriage market and strengthen her bargaining position in her marriage should she wish to support her natal family from the conjugal budget. Moreover, since the customary notion of the gendered intergenerational contract made daughters believe that their parents' spending on their education was even less instrumentally motivated than if they had been sons, daughters could be expected to feel at least as indebted as their brothers, if not more so, to their parents for the educational support they received. Not least, strengthening their emotional bond with a daughter might make up for diminished filial piety from an empowered daughter-in-law. After all, the latter may have benefited from her own parents' educational support and could be expected to feel much obligation toward them.

GRADUATES' PRESSURES

Students, of course, bore the main burden of passing through an educational system that demanded extraordinary discipline (cf. Kipnis 2001, 2011b). Fierce educational competition started when pupils prepared for the decisive senior high school entrance examination that divided rural youth into those with an option for higher education and those whose fate as "peasants" and, most likely, migrant laborers was sealed. Pupils who were accepted at senior high school spent most of their three years there constantly learning by rote from early morning till late at night, six and a half days a week. For both girls and boys, the motivation for such an investment of mental and bodily discipline was clear-cut: all they strove for was the opportunity to live a life different from that of their parents. Such a "change of fate" did, however, also imply changing the situation of the whole family. After all, against all odds, local students as well as their parents still hoped that educational achievement would give graduates access to all kinds of support resources from which the whole family would benefit.

While educational achievement rewarded rural Huining pupils with high social standing and feelings of pride during high school, life at university became a rather bitter experience for them, given the wide range of socioeconomic discrepancies in the family backgrounds of university students. Students from rural Huining usually believed that they could overcome any weakness in comparison with their urban and richer classmates' intellectual achievements by taking a highly disciplined approach to their studies.

What really bothered students was their shortage of economic resources. Lacking the financial ability to reciprocate often led them to make up flimsy excuses for declining an invitation to participate in social events. More importantly for young men from the region, lack of financial means made them feel inescapably disadvantaged in terms of attracting girlfriends. After all, everybody was convinced that all costs incurred on a date were to be assumed by the man. Liu Jingzhu, an unemployed Lanzhou university graduate, complained:

You can't imagine how much money I spent during the years we were dating at the university. After I met her, my monthly expenses almost tripled. Before, I had spent ¥400 per month, and then expenses suddenly rose to more than ¥1,000 per month. Each time you date, even if you do not go out to a restaurant, you still cannot avoid having a drink or a snack somewhere on the way. As a man, you always have to pay the bill. A bubble tea here, a little snack there—it is always you who has to pay. And then, there are these days like her birthday, or Valentine's Day, and so on; you have to give her a present on these occasions. Moreover, university dormitories are gender-segregated, and if you want to have some privacy, you have to rent a small room outside the university. That is very expensive. And now, after I spent all that money, she left me because I am poor and do not have a job.

Not all male students from rural Huining were willing to spend that much money on maintaining a love affair while at the university. Some argued that they just could not enjoy a love relationship if it meant having to spend their parents' scarce money.

After graduation, when these young men of rural Huining family backgrounds were about to "enter society," the financial burden in their partnerships became even more severe. Having to find urban employment but lacking connections (*guanxi*) as well as the financial means of influencing decisions in job assignments to their advantage made some graduates from rural family backgrounds feel desperate. Others lowered their expectations and hoped that their experience in diverse temporary jobs would eventually help them qualify for better kinds of employment later in their careers. What really gave male graduates from rural Huining headaches was the challenge of finding a fiancée and getting married. Duan Weilan, who had been lucky to find steady employment in the provincial capital quite soon after graduation from Lanzhou University, explained: "Living in Lanzhou puts a lot of pressure on me. I have to find a wife. For that, I need to buy an apartment. Life is already too difficult to manage for me alone, so how should I ever be able to find a wife under these conditions? It just does not feel realistic. The biggest problem we face is buying an apartment. You need to have your own house or home; that is how we see it." The notion that it is the man who has to fill the role of financial provider in the partnership, especially the obligation to provide a house as a precondition of marriage, made the humiliation of being poor even more severe for male than for female students and graduates. For many male graduates with rural Huining family backgrounds, the task of finding a bride thus turned into a real challenge. While female graduates were assigned less responsibility for the financial matters involved in setting up lives in the city, they still had to struggle with feelings of indebtedness to their supporters when it came to making central decisions in life. With career expectations generally lower for daughters than for sons, some parents put pressure on their daughters to return to Huining, preferably as teachers, a profession that was believed to perfectly suit women because it offered security and was less characterized by competition than life "in society." When parents expressed clear expectations that their daughters should stay in the vicinity, they also hoped to be able to draw on their support (cf. also Judd 2009).

That the conditions of planning their future differed for male and female graduates because patrilineal notions continued to assign divergent roles in elder care to each gender became most obvious to me in the case of Zhao Mei. As described above, when Zhao Mei was still an undergraduate student, she clearly professed her wish—particularly since she was a daughter—to reciprocate the educational support she received from her parents. When I met her again six years later, she was just about to finish her master's studies at Lanzhou University and faced a dilemma that was quite typical for many female graduates with rural Huining family backgrounds: in planning her future, she was torn between her own career plans, her mixed feelings toward her boyfriend and prospective marriage partner, and her family's objections to him because of his low career prospects. Her fiancé's rural Huining family was not only economically worse off than hers but, more importantly, lacked an influential person in the wider network whose support he could rely on when looking for a job. After trying in vain to find employment in Lanzhou city for more than a year, he had accepted an offer in township government in Huining. To return to her home county was, however, not the future Zhao Mei's family had anticipated for her, given the investment they had made in her education. Central to her family's plans was an influential paternal uncle of Zhao Mei's who was a government official in Xining, the capital of neighboring Qinghai. This uncle had little contact with his two daughters from two former marriages and was childless in his present marriage. The family's plan was thus that this uncle would use his influential position to help Zhao Mei and her younger brother find employment in Qinghai. The siblings would then bring the parents to Qinghai and take care of all of them, parents as well as the uncle and his wife, during old age. Under these circumstances, it was understandable that Zhao Mei started to doubt her relationship with her boyfriend, as it became clear that it jeopardized her family's plans (cf. also Obendiek 2016b). After all,

Zhao Mei's uncle was not willing to help further by arranging a job for her fiancé, whom he believed lacked the abilities as well as the ambition necessary for a career outside his home county.

In this standoff, it became obvious that Zhao Mei and her younger brother, both recipients and prospective providers of family support, still faced quite different future prospects. While Zhao Mei had been accepted at the national key university on account of her merits, her educationally less successful brother had depended on his uncle's help to get admitted to a less prestigious teacher's college in Xining city. When her brother introduced his prospective bride to the family, quite to the astonishment of both Zhao Mei and her brother, the woman's economically very deprived family background did not cause any discussion in the family, and everybody agreed to the engagement. Moreover, the uncle helped Zhao Mei's brother get a regular job in Xining city right after graduation. The job he had planned to arrange for Zhao Mei, it turned out, was at a state grain station in an upland Tibetan region in Qinghai that would earn good money as compensation for the harsh local conditions, but such a prospect was clearly much less appealing than the future in the provincial capital the uncle had arranged for her brother.

When Zhao Mei's father, an uneducated worker in the local electricity company, was killed in a work accident, it became particularly obvious that such differential treatment of the two siblings was related to a gendered understanding of their family support roles. The father's death left the mother alone in the house in the village. Both Zhao Mei and her brother professed a desire to invite her to live with them as soon as they had gotten married and settled down. Yet the division of the compensation payment of ¥690,000 paid by the electricity company to the bereaved made it clear that the familial support roles of the two siblings were clearly gendered: while the mother received ¥200,000 to pay for her living expenses, Zhao Mei's brother was allotted the remaining ¥490,000, a sum that was supposed to enable him to buy an apartment as a precondition for marrying his girlfriend.

In this situation, Zhao Mei, who had always proclaimed her intention to care for her parents and who, after her father's death, had immediately obtained her fiancé's approval for offering co-residence to her mother, defended such a practice by referring to the patrilineal argument that "he is the one who is responsible for taking care of my mother during old age." As it was, Zhao Mei had no other option but to depend on her fiancé to raise the money for an apartment as a precondition for marrying him. "If I had the money, I would help him buy the apartment. But as it is, he's the one who has to raise the money," she maintained. She estimated the sum to be ¥420,000 for an apartment of suitable size in the prefecture-level city where both of them were presently working, with 30 percent of the price paid in cash upon purchase. Additional costs were expected to be about ¥100,000 for internal construction and furnishings. Moreover, costs for the wedding would add up to ¥30,000, and his side would have to pay another ¥60,000 as a brideprice, of which ¥20,000 would be retained by Zhao Mei's mother, while the rest, as a kind of diverging devolution (J. Goody 1973), was transferred back via her to become part of the marital budget. Altogether, her fiancé thus had to raise about ¥300,000 as a precondition for marriage. To make things worse, he still had to pay back ¥20,000 of student loans to the university. Even though Zhao Mei was willing to help him shoulder the burden, she would be able to save just about ¥30,000 until the planned date of marriage. Despite the seeming hopelessness of the situation, her fiancé, who earned slightly more than ¥3,000 per month in his present job, professed his optimism about being able to borrow the sum from a number of sources.

At first sight, local understanding of the male side's obligation to buy an apartment as a precondition for marriage seemed to benefit young women, who could claim corresponding requests from their fiancés. Yet Zhao Mei's example also shows that gendered roles in elder care continued to influence differential investment in offspring. In the end, preferential investment in sons keeps women dependent on the male side as the main provider, thus underpinning the latter's dominant position in the marriage. In this context, it is remarkable that new Chinese marriage regulations introduced in 2011 restrict the scope of marital property by stipulating that in case of divorce all pre-marriage investments return to the original owner (Davis 2014). Thus a woman still depends on the success of her marriage to secure her living, should the apartment she lives in have been financed by her husband's side. In terms of her role as a daughter in the intergenerational contract, a female graduate's ability to reciprocate the educational support received depends on her ability to convert her degree into income-earning activities in a job market that itself is quite gender-biased (e.g., Cohen and Feng 2009; Guang and Kong 2010).[9] Only a regular salary will give her the standing in her marriage to bargain in favor of caring for her parents in practical, financial, and emotional terms, so that the support her parents have provided for her will not turn into "water spilled on other people's gardens."

• • •

The pursuit of higher education thus affects power relations between the genders and the generations in a poor rural region of China in several ways. On the one hand, educational achievement empowers the younger generation in relation to their often more or less illiterate parents, who thus lose parental—and particularly paternal—authority. On the other hand, local parents' only means of keeping their offspring indebted and—so it is hoped—emotionally attached to them is to exhaust scarce family resources and even go into heavy debt on their children's behalf. Most local parents believed that the best way to do so was to support their children's secondary and university educations.

Parents' educational support was aimed primarily at fulfilling their parental wish and duty to advance their offspring's career and marriage chances. At the same time, reduced fertility and the need to secure support for their old age turned educational spending into a viable strategy for changing the character of the intergenerational contract: with tradition alone having lost its binding force and inheritance of the house being of little value for the younger generation, the "gift" of educational support, backed by the deployment of parental sacrifice for the sake of the children's well-being, could be expected to sustain "modernized filial piety" (see Zhang, chap. 12), that is, an emotional bond between the supported children and their parents based on feelings of gratitude and indebtedness. While such emotional bonding was likely to translate into emotional support for the elderly, a resource much valued by those parents who tried to live independently as long as possible, parents' educational support surely also came with some expectation of a more material return. Being based on a mixture of motivations that were at the same time emotional and instrumental, educational support thus was an investment in a reciprocal parent-child relationship that, it was hoped, would "pay off" in the future. As a kind of pre-mortem inheritance, it went to daughters as well as sons, despite the gendered effects their mobility had on their parents' elder-care situation.

Continuing notions of patrilineality, along with the necessity of providing newlyweds with neolocal housing in the city that accompanied education-based rural-urban mobility, led to skyrocketing expenses for male graduates and their rural parents. While the obligation to act as financial provider presented many male graduates from the region with severe problems finding marriage partners, it also meant that a son's education-based rural-to-urban mobility put the intergenerational contract at particular risk.

In contrast to their male fellows, female graduates, as well as their parents, found the effects of higher education to be less disruptive. Women clearly benefited from parental spending on their education—it facilitated

HELENA OBENDIEK

their financial independence and urban residence—while the pressure to "repay" their parents was much less severe for them than for their brothers. Nevertheless, female graduates felt as indebted, if not even more indebted, to their parents for the educational support they received. At the same time, due to their contribution to the marital budget, they could be expected to be in a position to support their natal parents. However, their bargaining position in their marriages depended very much on their ability to convert their academic degrees into corresponding income-earning activities.

Female graduates thus seemingly benefited from the local understanding that assigned the male side the obligation of providing urban housing as a precondition of marriage. However, such gender expectations also kept female graduates dependent on their husbands as economic providers. Even though educational support empowered daughters to bargain in favor of taking care of their natal families, their parents' investment, in the end, still favored their brothers. Female graduates thus still suffer from local notions of patrilineality that limit their independence from and equity with their husbands and boyfriends.

NOTES

1   For example, Yan 2003, 2006; Ikels 2004a, 2006; Davis and Harrell 1993.

2   For example, D. Wang 2004; H. Zhang 2005, 2007a; Shi 2009.

3   During field research in rural Gansu in 2006–7, the New Rural Co-operative Medical System, which offers reimbursement for a certain percentage of medical costs, was just being introduced. The New Rural Old-Age Insurance that guarantees a monthly pension of at least ¥55 for all rural residents age sixty and above was introduced to the region in 2009.

4   According to statistical data provided on the official website of the Huining County government, per capita cash income among the county's rural residents has been ¥1,310.19 (about US$210) in the period between January and October 2007; http://www.huining.gov.cn/zfxx/ShowArticle.asp?ArticleID=1737 (accessed January 8, 2013).

5   Research was carried out in a village and in the county seat of Huining County, at Lanzhou University, and among graduates from the region living in Huining and Beijing between August 2006 and September 2007 with funding from the Max Planck Institute for Social Anthropology in Halle (Saale), Germany. Short visits to the field site followed in 2012 and 2014. All verbatim quotes in this text are translations from tape-recorded interviews and conversations, done by the author in standard Chinese (Mandarin). Villagers in Huining County often speak only Huining dialect, a local version of the northwestern dialect of Mandarin. In conversations with parents and other villagers, a local student

or graduate usually helped with translations to standard Chinese. Names of informants have been changed.

6 Data collected in the village and among students and graduates originating from rural Huining indicate that the national average fertility rate of about six children per women during the 1960s and early 1970s was also valid locally. In the mid-1980s, more than half of the families still had three or more children, while in 2007, the majority of the families in the village with children under eighteen years of age had two children, usually one of each gender.

7 About 40 percent of the pupils at local secondary high schools were girls. National expansion of university enrollment was reflected in the fact that within just three years, between 1999 and 2002, the admission quota among participants at the national college entrance exam in Huining County quintupled, from 15 percent to 85 percent (including admission to university short courses) (Yun 2007, 225). This phenomenon certainly further increased local parents' determination to have their children strive for academic careers.

8 Tuition fees vary according to the kind of university and the subject studied. In 2007, annual costs for tertiary education usually amounted to about ¥10,000 (including tuition, accommodations, and expenses for a frugal lifestyle).

9 At several job fairs I visited during field research in Lanzhou in 2007, specification of the prospective candidate's gender, usually to the disadvantage of female applicants, was a common practice.

CHAPTER FOUR

MULTIPLE MOTHERING AND LABOR MIGRATION IN RURAL SOUTH CHINA

GONÇALO SANTOS

I can't go anywhere now. My daughters [who have married into neighboring lineage communities] tell me I never visit them, but I don't have time. My third daughter-in-law is away from the village running a small vegetable farm in Nanhai [near Guangzhou], and she asked me to take care of her "little mosquitoes" [a local term for small children] (*sai-man-jai*),[1] so I can't leave the kids by themselves. I only have four now. In previous years, I also had to take care of my second daughter-in-law's four "little mosquitoes," but their father returned to the village last year. My wife is looking after the eight "little mosquitoes" of our fourth and fifth daughters-in-law including a few young babies. We live in separate houses: I stay at our third son's and she stays at our fourth's. . . . Taking care of children is hard work. . . . I feel more at ease when the mother of the kids is around [about three or four times a year].

THUS explained a sixty-five-year-old grandfather, whom I will call Bright Moral, in January 2000,[2] a few weeks before the lunar new year celebrations, a major festive occasion when many migrant villagers return home for the big family reunion of the year. At the time, a significant proportion of the population of Harmony Cave, a Cantonese village in western Yingde, Northern Guangdong, was already engaged in temporary labor migration to the highly industrialized and urbanized areas in the Pearl River Delta. This trend has intensified, and in mountain townships like Yellow Flower, where the village of Harmony Cave is located, temporary labor migration has become a way of life.[3]

A few days ago one of my grandsons' classmates injured himself quite severely. It's the winter break now, so the kids spend a lot of time playing and running around. On the day of the incident, the boy's grandmother [a fifty-eight-year-old illiterate lady who lives alone with six grandchildren] left home early in the morning . . . to go up the mountain to get firewood for the cooking stove. That morning, the six-year-old boy fell out of a big tree and broke his leg quite badly. The boy would eventually recover, but the hospital bill—about ¥30,000 [approximately US$4,600 using today's currency exchange rates]—bankrupted the family. The boy's parents returned to the village as soon as they received the bad news via pager. Upon their arrival, the boy's mother [a very outspoken thirty-one-year-old woman, also illiterate] scolded her mother-in-law in public for not taking proper care of the children. She said that they are working very hard away from the village to earn money and that it is not easy to be away from the children, so they expect her to take responsibility and avoid leaving the kids alone. The boy's mother was not happy that her mother-in-law had gone up the mountain to fetch firewood when nowadays one can purchase dry firewood in the village. She said that going up the mountain to fetch firewood is a "backward" practice, and she repeatedly referred to her mother-in-law as a "stupid old woman."

But the boy's grandmother cannot really be blamed because she is not given enough money to take proper care of the children and because she is doing it all by herself [her husband having died a few years before, and all her sons and daughters-in-law being away]. Moreover, the incident could have happened even if she was at home. Watching "little mosquitoes" is not an easy task; no one can prevent them from running around all day. . . . But this is not what people are saying. Most people who hear the story blame the old woman, and no one reproaches the daughter-in-law for not showing respect for her mother-in-law.

. . . [So] I stay at home as much as possible. If something happens to my grandchildren in my absence, I will also be in trouble with my daughter-in-law. She is the boss, you know, and I prefer to be careful. Ancient people have a saying: One wrong step can cause a thousand regrets (Yat chi sat juk chin gu han).

Back in 2000, there were already many children like the boy above who were "left behind" by their migrant parents under the care of grandparents, but this phenomenon was not yet widely discussed in the national public sphere as a major social problem that needs to be addressed (see e.g. Nie, Li, and Li 2008). This way of framing the issue has since become common among the growing urban middle classes and is actively promoted by various kinds of social policies, nongovernmental organizations (NGOs), and media discourses. This shift goes hand in hand with important changes in urban family life due to the Birth-Planning Policy launched in 1979 and the increasing popularity of global middle-class ideologies of intensive child rearing built around the conjugal family. In this new climate of intensive parenting, parents (especially mothers) are subject to unprecedented levels of public scrutiny and expert analysis, and they are expected to be closely involved in the upbringing of their children.[4] Leaving children "behind" under the care of grandparents or other close relatives is considered a form of neglect that is dangerous to the children in question and to society as a whole. In the past five years especially, incidents involving so-called left-behind children (SC, *liushou ertong*) often make headlines in the national media, and the situation of these children has become a matter of significant public concern and online discussion. This phenomenon is thought to be particularly worrying because, according to a well-known survey undertaken by the All China Women's Federation, there are at least 61 million "left-behind children" in the countryside (ACWF 2013). That is nearly a quarter of the nation's children and almost a third of its rural children. About 15 percent of these children are thought to be unable to see their parents even once a year.[5]

This chapter parts ways with these normative discourses to approach rural practices of "surrogate parenting" not as a social pathology but as a window onto something of more general significance in Chinese family life: the importance of grandparents as child-care providers. Although child care by grandparents is widespread in both rural and urban areas (Silverstein, Cong, and Li 2007), research remains limited. Most recent urban research tends to focus on parent-child relations, even though grandparents play an important role in child-care provision (Goh 2011). This strong reliance on grandparents in urban areas is not just linked to Reform era processes such as the dismantling of the public child-care system and the rising costs of child care; it also shows important continuities with earlier gendered practices of multiple parenting and caregiving built around the joint family. This chapter explores these historical continuities in emerging rural practices of surrogate parenting involving grandparents. The analysis proposed here owes much to classic anthropological conceptualizations of child rearing as a collective effort of caregiving that can take many different shapes depending on context (Mead and Wolfenstein 1955; E. Goody 1982). But instead of assuming that such collective child-rearing structures—what science and technology studies scholars would call a "socio-technical system" involving multiple caregivers (Cowan 1983; Bijker 2010)—are the product of unchanging cultural traditions, the emphasis here is on how human action transforms these structures, and how this process of "transformation" involves complex power struggles and negotiations (Bourdieu 1977; Ortner 1996, 2006).

This chapter draws on materials collected in an impoverished rural township in Northern Guangdong, but the changes described reflect broader transformations in the Chinese countryside. In most rural areas in China, the Maoist attempt to put into practice the "Engels strategy" of pursuing gender equality by including women in the formal labor force had very limited effects in the sphere of child rearing, so the development of a public network of nurseries, crèches, and kindergartens did not really take off (Stockman, Bonney, and Sheng 1995, 144–45). By the end of the Maoist period, the joint family remained the most important safety net for the provision of child care, and the work of child rearing remained strongly associated with women despite several campaigns aimed at challenging this normative assumption.[6] More specifically, the work of child rearing remained in the hands of a female-centered intergenerational parenting body supervised by the child's mother under the authoritative guidance of her mother-in-law (the child's paternal grandmother) (see Santos 2004, 215–62).[7] This multiple mothering formation could include more or fewer members depending on the size and circumstances of the family, but its function was everywhere similar. The main function of this "multiple mother" (ibid., 224) was to help new mothers get on with their child-rearing duties without completely neglecting their productive responsibilities.[8] The use of the term *help* here may be somewhat misleading, as Melissa Brown (chap. 1) reminds us. This multiple mother was not just an informal structure of collaboration and mutual aid; it was also a site of patriarchal exploitation. Although its very existence can be conceptualized as a celebration of female power, many of its structural features—including its normative emphasis on the authority of the senior generation and its conventional definition of the "inner" realm of the household as the proper place for women—play an important role in the reproduction of the broader system of intersecting generational and gender inequalities we call "patriarchy." This patriarchal multiple mothering formation was reconfigured from the 1980s onward so as to allow ordinary rural families and women to engage with a radically new mode of livelihood based on labor migration. This process of reconfiguration was possible only because of a broader intergenerational power shift within rural families that both challenged and reproduced existing patriarchal arrangements.

The incident that opens this chapter illustrates this transformation starkly. Local marriage customs are shaped by strict rules of virilocal or at least "viricentric" (Kipnis, chap. 5) residence. Brides are expected to move into their husbands' villages upon marriage and to transfer their filial devotion to their parents-in-law, especially their mothers-in-law. Both before 1949 and under Mao, there were many instances of everyday life conflicts between daughters-in-law and mothers-in-law, but for old grandparents like Bright Moral, there was something special about the incident described above. For Bright Moral, this was not an ordinary incident of unfilial behavior but part of an emerging pattern of incidents pointing in the direction of an important change in local family life: a new balance of power between the generations had emerged as the young set off to work in the city. As in other parts of rural China, this restructuring of the "classic" patriarchal order was initiated by radical reforms and campaigns implemented during the 1950s, 1960s, and 1970s, but it was only in the 1980s that this reconfiguration was accelerated. Labor migration played an important role in this process because it allowed the younger generations to "break free" from local conventions and assert their economic superiority and position of power in relation to the senior generations. New multiple-mothering formations developed, based on a clear-cut generational division of labor: the senior generation took over the work of the mother-in-law-centered "feminine" network of everyday care and vigilance, while the younger generation focused on the "masculine" work of earning income away from home. These new multiple-mothering formations are more balanced in terms of intergenerational power structure than their predecessors as young mothers (and fathers) as breadwinners have taken over from grandmothers (and grandfathers) as the dominant figures. The emergence of these formations does not represent a breakdown as much as a reorganization of earlier patriarchal interdependencies in the context of increasing local engagement with nationwide reforms and global capitalist processes.

SOJOURNERS FROM THE HILLS OF GUANGDONG

The township of Yellow Flower is located in a mountainous area of western Yingde, away from major waterways, and about three hours' drive from Guangzhou. In 2012, Yellow Flower had a population of more than fifty thousand. The township is often praised by visiting urbanites for the beauty of its agrarian landscape of paddy fields and figure-shaped limestone mountains, but this agrarian impression is largely an illusion. With the reforms, villagers increasingly participated in money-oriented activities away from the fields, which led to the growth and diversification of the local economy. In the mid-1980s, the younger generations (initially only men) started to engage in temporary labor migration to the Pearl River Delta region.

The first wave of migrants targeted specific areas close to Guangzhou and Foshan where they leased land from former agricultural collectives and started cultivating vegetables for sale in local markets. By the late 1990s, when I first arrived in Yellow Flower, a clear-cut migration pattern had already emerged: while unmarried youngsters (both boys and girls) favored working as unskilled wage laborers in factories, married couples favored becoming self-employed vegetable gardeners. This pattern is still in place today at a time when more than 70 percent of the households registered in the township have at least one member working away from home.

Yellow Flower migrants are critical of official restrictions on rural-to-urban migration that place significant constraints on their prospects of integrating more fully into city life, but most see themselves as sojourners and remain strongly tied to their native township and village. Foremost among their investments at home are new forms of private housing that people call "mansions." But migrants are not just investing their savings in expensive "mansions" and the related work of keeping up with ever-changing notions of family modernization and what Veblen (1899, chap. 3) called "pecuniary decency." Their economic success is also evaluated in terms of their capacity to contribute to community building efforts, and their contribution to the "revival" of "old" lineage structures of political and ritual organization has been particularly important.[9]

THE WORK OF BEGETTING CHILDREN

Emerging in the context of the new political economy of the Reform period, present-day structures of lineage organization are very different from their prerevolutionary counterparts, but they also display remarkable continuities, for example, in their emphasis on ritual ideologies of patrilineal descent and ancestor worship. Historically, these ideologies have nurtured the development of a reproductive culture that emphasized the importance of having many children, especially male heirs (M. Wolf 1972, 1985; R. Watson 1985). In Yellow Flower, the overall pronatalist orientation of this "traditional" reproductive culture was not significantly challenged by the reforms of the Maoist period (Harrell et al. 2011; Santos, forthcoming). In the late 1970s, when decollectivization was initiated, local reproductive practices remained strongly pronatalist in large part because the Communist emphasis on the primacy of the agricultural sector only reinforced the local emphasis on reproductive achievements.

This started to change only in the Reform period, mostly because of the implementation of birth-control policies (Harrell et al. 2011; Santos, forthcoming). In Yellow Flower, the Birth-Planning Policy—launched nationwide in 1979—was not vigorously enforced on the ground until 1988, and even then, it was initially treated as a relatively flexible "two- to three-children policy." This policy generated significant popular discontent, and the vegetable gardens in Foshan and Guangzhou played an important role in local strategies of resistance. These vegetable gardens offered married women a safe refuge from annual birth-planning inspections or a place to give birth to "unplanned" children. The gardens also allowed many village families to earn enough money to pay the fines for "unplanned births," thus delaying sterilization and having more than the usual two or three children. By the late 1990s, however, the success of the policy started to become apparent as overall fertility levels dropped below those of a fertility regime with universal third births. By then, giving birth to "unplanned children" had become extremely expensive, so it is not surprising to see a young migrant mother—as in the opening story—showing signs of utter distress upon hearing the news that her son had broken his leg. That boy (her third son) had cost her a lot of money in birth-planning fines, not to mention the price of sterilization.

Today, village folks in this part of Northern Guangdong are still concerned with the importance of having children, especially male heirs, but most young couples tend to have no more than two children. One reason for this is that the local birth-planning policy has become less permissive. The other is that reproductive ideals have changed. Most young couples say that they would like to have at least one son, but they often say that the ideal would be to have one son and one daughter. Some would be happy to have only one daughter, but they complain about peer pressure and parental pressure to do otherwise, a state of affairs that is somewhat different from what is going on in rural Liaoning, where sons have become too expensive and the decision to stop after a singleton daughter is increasingly accepted (Shi, chap. 2).

Despite the shift toward fewer children per couple, *the work of begetting children* remains central. A common pattern—in place since the late 1990s—is to drop out of school either toward the end of primary school or toward the end of middle school and work in factories for a few years before marriage. Most people get married in their early twenties (usually to someone from the same township or a neighboring township) and have their children within the first ten years of marriage while continuing to engage in temporary labor migration. Some manage to integrate their employment situation in the city with the duties of family life and the care of multiple children by working on vegetable farms, but not all migrant couples are vegetable farmers, and running a vegetable farm demands a lot of labor, so who takes care of the children while the parents are working?

MULTIPLE MOTHERING AND SURROGATE PARENTING

Back in the year 2000, Bright Moral was telling me how busy he and his wife Palm Sister were taking care of sixteen grandchildren between them. Their situation was already quite common. More than 50 percent of the village population was working away from home, including many migrant parents who left their children "behind" under the care of grandparents. This phenomenon has intensified in the past decade to the point that many lineage communities in the township have only grandparents and children around.

Palm Sister explained a few years later in the summer of 2005:

> When I married into this village [around 1960], I brought with me one son and one daughter [Palm Sister's two previous husbands passed away very early]. After marriage, I gave birth to four sons and two daughters. I am now over seventy years old and have five daughters-in-law and twenty-one [patrilateral] grandchildren, eleven grandsons and ten granddaughters. That's a lot of grandchildren, so we need to help our daughters-in-law. Without support, our sons and daughters-in-law would never be able to go out of the village to earn money, and without this money, they would never be able to have as many children or build as many new "mansions" as they did. Getting married and having children these days is very costly, and building a new house costs more money than ever before. . . . The only way to do it is to seek work away from the village, but we are too old to do anything. Our sons and daughters-in-law go out to make money; we can only help them take care of the children. I bathed all my grandchildren when my daughters-in-law were "doing the month" [the period of convalescence following childbirth], and I carried them all on my back [with the support of a sling] before they started to walk by themselves [usually around two to three years old]. . . . Mothers want to stay close to their children, but this is not always possible because they need to work hard on the vegetable farms [or in factories], and the environment down there is not good for

children. Once the children start to walk, or even before that, mothers prefer to leave the children in the village. We watch them and feed them and make sure they go to school.

Such "surrogate parenting" arrangements do not represent a radical departure from earlier strategies and procedures of child rearing. Palm Sister continued:

> When I had my children [back in the 1960s and 1970s], I had to take care of them largely by myself because there was no mother-in-law [Bright Moral lost his parents at a very young age]. Everything was harder without a mother-in-law, but I had more freedom. In those days, the old still had a lot of authority in the family, and mothers-in-law were quite often in charge of household matters. . . . Children were taken care of by the "mother" (a-me) under the guidance of the "old mother" (lou-ma) [grandmother]. Young girls usually started taking care of younger siblings at around five or six. My eldest daughter helped me take care of her younger siblings, and when I was a small child, I helped my mother and grandmother take care of my younger siblings. In those days, it was important to have a lot of people around to help take care of children because this made it easier to manage labor and coordinate the work in the fields. If a daughter-in-law needed someone to watch her young children while she was working in the fields, she could always ask the support of her mother-in-law or other close relatives in her production team. In those days, this support was not as important as it is today because mothers did not need to go out of the village to earn income, and the work in the fields was not as intensive as the work in factories or on vegetable farms.

Almost everyone in Yellow Flower was brought up by a small army of caregivers under the control of two main characters: the "mother" and the "old mother." This "multiple mother" figure can take many different forms, and have many different functions and effects, but its overall purpose is to help young mothers cope with child-rearing duties so that their productive activities both inside and outside the household are not completely disrupted. Grandmothers, sometimes also grandfathers, were always important actors in this process. In the 1960s and 1970s (when Palm Sister's children were born), just as in the 1930s and 1940s (when Palm Sister was a child), grandmothers commonly provided child-care guidance as mothers were actively engaged in productive activities in the fields, but their assistance was less critical than it is today. In the era of labor migration, having both paternal grandparents alive and available to offer full-time child-care support has become a critical resource (see Silverstein, Cong, and Li 2006, 2007; Cong and Silverstein 2012). Parents lacking this resource have their labor migration prospects significantly constrained. Some couples obtain the support of maternal grandparents, but this is still uncommon and is usually a supplementary arrangement.

This increasing reliance on the child-rearing contributions of the senior generation also reflects a lack of alternatives. Migrant parents have limited access to social welfare and educational facilities in the city, and they cannot afford paid child care. For them, the broader family remains the most important source of social support, and grandparents are the most economical and trustworthy option when it comes to child care. In urban settings too, limited day care for preschool children, expensive private babysitters, and mistrust of domestic helpers all made grandparents a comparatively trustworthy source of child care after dramatic cuts in publicly subsidized child-care programs (Du and Dong 2010). In this new political conjuncture, there emerged a 4–2–1 child-care pattern, that is, four grandparents and two parents jointly raise one child (Goh 2011). In reality, there may not always be four grandparents caring for one grandchild—sometimes there are only two or even just one—but the term refers to an overall trend, a new model of child care in which both paternal and maternal grandparents collaborate with parents on raising a single child.

In Northern Guangdong, this 4–2–1 model makes little sense. Local families have many "little mosquitoes," not just one "little emperor," but there is also the fact that there are only two not four grandparents, and these two (paternal) grandparents are expected to attend simultaneously to the child-rearing needs of many middle-generation couples. This means that grandparents like Palm Sister and Bright Moral have to rotate from one middle-generation couple to the other, and this involves a lot of negotiations over who is going to help take care of whose children, when, and where. Most migrant parents (especially mothers) I interviewed say that they would be happy to take care of their children by themselves, but they also note that this is a full-time job that is best done by someone with experience and expertise. Accepting support from the senior generation allows them to focus on something that they consider far more important and far more valuable in the age of "getting rich first": the work of earning income that keeps the whole family running.

This commitment to income-earning activities is perhaps nowhere more clear—in the case of mothers—than in weaning practices. As late as the 1960s and 1970s, mothers did not wean their children until around two or three years of age (with gender variations), and some women vividly recalled the sight of children as old as five being breastfed while their mothers were working in the fields. Migrant laborer mothers almost invariably wean their infants at around three to six months, and from then onward, babies are fed solely with rice porridge and (since the late 1990s) powdered milk. Back in the 1960s and 1970s, prolonged breastfeeding was considered a good option because it was affordable and did not disrupt the mother's capacity to work in the fields. Prolonged breastfeeding today is no longer a good option because it affects the income-earning capacities of mothers working in factories or on vegetable farms.

Most migrant mothers, as Palm Sister notes, would prefer to stay close to their children and spend more time with them, but this is not always possible because the mothers must return to work as soon as possible after childbirth. It is difficult for grandparents to go to the city to offer child-care support, because they have to consider the needs of other daughters-in-law and find it difficult to live away from their villages for long periods of time (some can barely endure a bus journey to the city because of motion sickness). So the only option for migrant mothers (and fathers) is to part ways with their children from a younger age and leave them in the care of grandparents back in the village. This option is also favored because the environment in the city (i.e., the suburban areas where vegetable farms are located) is considered not very suitable for children. In 1999, for example, two children, four and five years old, were found drowned in waterways bordering the vegetable farms of Yellow Flower migrants, somewhere on the edges of Guangzhou. These tragedies were very powerful in making the point across the migrant community that it is better to leave one's young children safely back in the village than expose them to the dangers of the urban environment.

Leaving children with grandparents is not a form of abandonment, as assumed by expert commentators and state media news sources (see, for example, Li Yifei et al. 2015). Most migrant mothers (and fathers) are convinced that they are doing what is best for their children, and they certainly do not see themselves as having renounced their parental duties and responsibilities. They may not be providing everyday care for their children, but they are working hard to earn the money that pays for food, clothes, education, and so on. In their view, the work of mothering, and more generally the work of parenting, can be partitioned into different roles and shared by many actors, so when they say that they are committed primarily to their income-earning duties rather than to the actual work of raising children, they are saying that they prefer to work on their maternal/parental identity as "breadwinners" rather than as "everyday caregivers." This is not to say that they have completely dismissed the importance of acts of everyday caregiving (for example, when mothers return home from the vegetable farms, they are very keen on sleeping with their children and showing motherly love through various kinds of material practices), but they prefer to present themselves as "nurturant breadwinners" as opposed to "nurturant caregivers." Both conceptions of maternal/parental identity contribute to the "nurturing" of the child but stand in a hierarchical relation to each other. Those focusing on the work of earning money are the ones people refer to as "the boss" (*lou-baan* or *lou-sai*).

THE DECLINE OF THE AUTHORITY
OF THE SENIOR GENERATION

When I spoke to old Bright Moral back in 2000, I had not yet met "the boss," his third daughter-in-law. When I finally got to meet her face-to-face a few weeks later, I realized that she and Bright Moral actually maintained a very good relationship, and that this was the reason he had chosen his third son's place as his "official" residence a few years earlier. This was the kind of daughter-in-law who would buy a new pair of trousers during the Spring Festival period upon realizing that Grandpa has only three old, patched pairs. What was so scary about this daughter-in-law? I asked him a few months later.

> When I was a "little mosquito" [back in the 1940s and 1950s], old people were in charge of family matters. It was the duty of parents to organize the marriages of their children, and family division was delayed until all sons were married. When young women married into the village, one could see that they were afraid of their mothers-in-law. . . . By the time I got married and started to have my own children [in the 1960s and 1970s], old people were still in charge [*a-gung leung-gung-po wa-si*], and daughters-in-law were instructed to take proper care of their children. There were many incidents of unfilial behavior, but there was community pressure to show respect toward the senior generation. Nowadays the situation has changed. The villages are empty. Everyone is away making money. There is no community pressure anymore, and the old rules of family division no longer apply. Sons establish

their own independent "stoves" immediately after marriage as they set off to the city to earn money. Old people are no longer in charge. Daughters-in-law are in charge, and they instruct the old to take care of their children.

Youngsters are not just telling old people what to do; they are instructing old people to do the job with little money:

Daughters-in-law like to say that they work very hard in the city in order to send money to the village and pay for all expenses back home, but this is not what is happening. The old are complaining that they are not receiving enough money. I do not mean pocket money; I mean money to survive. Most have to farm the land to feed themselves and their grandchildren. . . . We have already reached an advanced age, but we are not being looked after by the younger generation. Having worked hard to nurture our children is not enough; we still need to farm the fields to nurture the children of our children. Old people today are facing a lot of hardships.

More than ten years later, in March 2012, I met Bright Moral at the house of one of his close village brothers, old Splendid Omen, and his wife, Third Sister, a seventy-two-year-old illiterate grandmother who, like most village grandmothers, is very proud of having bathed all her grandchildren in the first months of life:

We have six [paternal] grandchildren. Our three sons are all working away from the village. . . . Our second son is still a bachelor; he lives with his younger brother and his wife. . . . Our sons are all cultivating vegetables in the city to earn money; we stay in the village to take care of the children. We already took care of the four children of our eldest son [back in the 1990s and the aughts of the present century]. . . . We are now taking care of the two children of our youngest son, a boy and a girl. The boy is eleven years old and attends primary school [grade 5] in the market town. The girl is still very young. She's three years old and needs a lot of care. We get about ¥600–700 per month to get by with these two children. It is not a lot of money, but many old people receive even less. The only way to get by with this money is to save money on rice, vegetables, peanuts, corn, and ginger, so we are still farming the land to have food to eat. Next year we'll

stop cultivating rice. I'm half blind already [due to cataracts],
so I cannot help my husband in the fields anymore. We want to
help our children, but we are getting too old to do anything. . . .
I know that my sons would give us more money every month if
they could afford it. But what we are getting at the moment is not
enough to fill the stomach. Yesterday I took the young girl to the
doctor to get an injection because she was sick. Just that cost ¥50!

Although old people themselves realize that this is an exploitative relationship, they nevertheless uphold the idea that they have to help and support their children until they can give no more. Of course, their efforts to
render help and support create all kinds of frictions and contradictions on
the ground. Old people are not simply being told to do things like take care
of grandchildren on a very tight budget, Third Sister says, they are also being
scolded for not doing it the right way:

Daughters-in-law nowadays do not have to listen to what we say,
and no one criticizes them when they mistreat us. They often
say that we are good for nothing, and they like to scold us for all
kinds of reasons. . . . They say that we are old and "backward"
and that we don't even know how to take care of children. If they
actually had some sense, they would think something along these
lines: "They are so old already, nurtured so many children, how
can they not know how to take care of children?" But this is not
what they say. What they say is that we are "useless."

Third Sister gives a concrete example:

Sweet potatoes . . . I know you find them tasty. . . . We ate a lot of
sweet potatoes over the years. . . . We could even say that without
sweet potatoes, we would probably not be here. . . . We also gave
a lot of sweet potatoes to our children [growing up in the 1960s
and 1970s] . . . . There is nothing wrong with sweet potatoes. They
nurture people. But when our daughters-in-law return to the
village, they criticize us for cooking sweet potatoes. They say that
sweet potatoes are not tasty and are not nourishing enough. And
when we give them a bowl of rice instead of sweet potatoes, they
criticize us for not adding enough salt and oil. . . . Sometimes they
also say that the food lacks sugar or that it lacks soy sauce. . . .
I don't really understand what they want. . . . People of our age

never add sugar or soy sauce, and we are not used to adding a lot of salt and oil. All we need is a bit of salt to add taste. . . . Today a bit of salt is not enough. They also want monosodium glutamate, sugar, ginger, and whatnot. It may well be that cooking in this manner makes food tastier. . . . But our economy does not allow for it. . . . You need money to cook food with all those things. . . . Who pays for it? They certainly don't!

It is not just that the middle generation is failing to show respect toward the senior generation, Third Sister says, but the junior generation (grandchildren) is also not responding to the senior generation's instructions. Local authorities commonly refer to the senior generation's lack of authority as an important factor behind recent policies and market developments, from 2008 onward, leading to the creation of full-day kindergartens and boarding primary schools for the children of migrant parents. The other major factor is the perceived lack of "quality" of the senior generation. Echoing the overall orientation of the Reform era movement known as "education for quality" (SC, *suzhi jiaoyu*), the current schooling regime is built around the assumption that children are better off in the hands of professional experts (i.e., local teachers) than in the hands of "backward," illiterate grandparents. Those migrant parents who can afford it have embraced this development not just because they want to jump on the bandwagon of modernity and provide the best possible education for their children but also because— and this is an important point—fathers want to act like "good sons" and mothers want to act like "good daughters-in-law" and reduce the babysitting workload for their parents/parents-in-law. This trend toward "grandparenting outsourcing" (Zhang, chap. 12) is already having a visible impact on the local landscape in that a growing number of children are attending full-day kindergartens, some of which are privately run. There is also the fact that a growing number of children are no longer attending primary schools close to their villages but are studying in a very large boarding school located in the market town. These children go home to stay with their grandparents only during weekends and public holiday periods.

GRANDPARENT BABYSITTING AND
THE NEW PATRIARCHAL ORDER

These examples converge in many ways with recent accounts of the so-called breakdown of patriarchal extended family structures in other parts of rural China (see especially Yan 1997, 2003, 2009), but they point not so much to a breaking down as to a restructuring of existing patriarchal hier-archies. As in other parts of rural China, this process of restructuring was initiated during the Maoist period, but greater changes came about with China's late twentieth-century and early twenty-first-century reforms. The situation in Yellow Flower draws particular attention to the role played by labor migration in triggering a major shift away from an agrarian mode of sociality built around tight-knit community structures, but this transfor-mation did not take place as predicted by standard Euro-American mod-els of globalization and modernization that postulate the conjugal family and the parent-parenting dyad as the end product of a so-called collapse of patriarchal family structures.[10] These models are very popular in China as prescriptive ideologies of development, widely regarded as the path that the country needs to take in order to achieve global modernity (Green-halgh 2010), but they are not very useful for making sense of contemporary Chinese family relations, because they ignore both grandparents and the continuing relations of interdependence between the senior and middle generations.

The growing power of the younger generations in rural Northern Guang-dong should be conceptualized not as a "triumph of conjugality" (Yan 1997) but as a reconfiguration of the relations of gendered generational interde-pendence typical of patriarchal family structures. These interdependencies are increasingly common globally under conditions of late capitalism and a worldwide erosion of public child-care support (Attias-Donfut and Segalen 2002; Swartz 2009), but they cannot be overlooked in the contemporary Chinese context, especially in rural areas where public welfare structures remain limited. In rural Northern Guangdong, as in other parts of rural China, the work of child rearing continues to be built around gendered generational interdependencies, which were reconfigured from the 1980s onward so as to cope with labor migration. This process of reconfigura-tion gave rise to new multiple mothering formations in which grandparents have become largely responsible for the "feminine" work of everyday care and vigilance, while mothers and fathers started to redefine their parenting duties primarily in terms of the "masculine" work of earning income outside the village. This transformation has empowered the middle generation, but it has *not* led to the collapse of the intergenerational contract. If anything, it has resulted in the emergence of a new patriarchal configuration in which middle-generation mothers and fathers have more bargaining power in the negotiation of gendered generational interdependencies. As Deniz Kandi-yoti (1988, 275) notes, "patriarchal bargains are not timeless or immutable entities, but are susceptible to historical transformations that open up new areas of struggle and renegotiation of the relations between genders"—as well as between generations.

In the "classic" patriarchal order, local girls were betrothed or adopted as daughters-in-law at a very young age and had no say whatsoever in whom they married. After marriage, they were expected to move to their husbands' villages and work very hard under the authority of their parents-in-law, especially their mothers-in-law, and their position was not really secure until they managed to give birth to at least a few male heirs. Many things have changed with the implementation of the Marriage Law of 1950 and subsequent reforms aimed at protecting the rights of women and youth. In the 1950s and 1960s, the lives of local peasants started to unfold in the context of tight-knit agricultural collectives built around a newly emerged ethical system of collective responsibility and self-sacrifice, but this Maoist shift to socialism did not bring about the collapse of the "classic" patriarchal order. Despite significant gains in personal autonomy for women and youth, the process of marriage (read: *patrilocal* marriage) continued to be controlled by the senior generations and to involve payment of material compensation to the bride's natal family, a form of bridewealth locally known as "corporeal body money" (*yuk-san-chin*). After marriage, young brides continued to be subject to the demands of their husbands' patrilineal corporations. They also continued to face strong social pressure to defer to the authority of their parents-in-law, especially their mothers-in-law. As in earlier periods, young brides were positioned at the bottom of the local patriarchal pecking order, but they were not completely powerless in their efforts to cope with the hardships of patriarchal demands. One of the reasons women continued to choose marriage and bear harsh lives as young wives was the prospect of holding power over juniors, first as mothers and then as mothers-in-law (M. Wolf 1972, 1985).

This remains true to some extent in the new patriarchal order that has emerged in the reform period, but the strategy no longer pays clear-cut dividends. This is the main reason behind the resentment expressed by the babysitting grandmothers and grandparents described in this chapter (see Brown, chap. 1). The grandmothers suffered under the "classic" patriarchal order, both before and after the Communist revolution, and endured it in the hope that one day they would get to boss around their own daughters-in-law, but this did not happen, and they feel cheated. These grandmothers, unlike women of the younger generations, do not find reproductive duties degrading or unfashionable, so they do not resent having to do the work of babysitting. What they really resent is being told what to do by their daughters-in-law and being mistreated and put-upon by their juniors. This resentment is made all the worse because the elderly today routinely live longer than in times past, and their increased longevity leads to an accumulation of pressures that often results in conflicts. Some grandmothers resort to suicide as a way of expressing their grievance (Zhang, chap. 12), but most end up coping with the new order of things because they love their sons and grandchildren and because they come to understand, if not accept, that times have changed. Young girls today are no longer as docile, unschooled, and village-bound as in earlier times. Most are allowed to go to school, and once they become adults, they start seeking work outside the village so that they can earn their own money. These girls have a strong say in whom they marry, and they no longer think that a "good" daughter-in-law has to behave *as if* she owes unconditional support and obedience to her parents-in-law. Marriage for them is not about living under the shadow of their parents- and mothers-in-law but requires the establishment of separate family stoves and, if economic circumstances allow, construction of separate houses.

This dynamic of "individualization" (Yan 2003, 2009, 2010) is an important part of what is going on in much of today's rural China in the age of global capital, but this development goes hand in hand with a parallel process of reconfiguration of earlier patriarchal interdependencies. Massive labor migration in rural Northern Guangdong from the 1980s onward would have not been possible without the emergence of reconfigured patriarchal structures. This process of reconfiguration has created patriarchal interdependencies that are more balanced in terms of generational power relations, but the local patrilineal ideology is still strong enough to skew the whole system in a patrilineal direction, suggesting that gender relations are changing more slowly than are generational relations. This is particularly visible in places like Yellow Flower, where marriage continues to entail the payment of bridewealth to brides' natal families to signal the transfer of the brides' filial obligations to their parents-in-law. In the past few decades, bridewealth has undergone a dramatic process of monetization and inflation that has "normalized" the practice of paying a high monetary price for a bride (see Obendiek, chap. 3). Many families return part of this payment to their daughters in the form of dowry gifts, but the money spent on these gifts is usually only a small fraction of bridewealth. This system of marriage transactions is based on the idea that brides have to be purchased by patrilineal family corporations, and there are reasons to believe that this "purchase" makes brides more vulnerable to the demands of these corporations. This vulnerability is made all the worse because most local married women—despite significant improvements in earning power—continue to have limited economic autonomy. This lack of economic autonomy is not just linked to the continuing hold of customary patrilineal inheritance structures; it is also linked to the enduring power of familist values of self-realization. For most local young women, life outside (virilocal/viricentric) marriage remains a non-option, and the pursuit of economic independence within marriage continues to be depicted as amoral. In interviews and informal conversations, most young women I know tend to depict marriage as an inalienable relationship built around a common property regime, and many do not see the point of keeping an independent bank account, not even as a way of protecting themselves against the increasing uncertainties of marital relationships.

NOTES

1   All Chinese terms and expressions quoted in this chapter are in the Cantonese language as spoken in the region of Northern Guangdong. Cantonese is transcribed with the Yale romanization system, without tone marks in order to facilitate reading. Terms and expressions in standard Chinese (Mandarin), the official language of the People's Republic of China, are labeled SC and are transcribed with the standard pinyin system of romanization. For Chinese characters, please consult the glossary at the end of this volume.

2   All names of places and persons referring to my fieldwork area are pseudonyms. I chose English-language pseudonyms instead of romanized Cantonese pseudonyms in order to facilitate reading and give a sense of the semantic richness of local naming practices.

3   My research in this Cantonese-speaking township (also called Brightpath in other publications) stretches over a period of fifteen years. My first fieldwork in the region was a long-term stay of fourteen months between 1999 and 2001. During this period, I lived in three different households in Harmony Cave and accompanied villagers to their migrant abodes in the city. In addition to undertaking participant observation and writing a systematic body of field notes, I used methodologies such as household surveys and semi-structured interviews. Between 2005 and 2015, I returned to Harmony Cave on six occasions for follow-up research.

4   Jing 2000; Fong 2004; Gottschang 2007; Kipnis 2011b. On the rise of a global culture of "intensive parenting" and "intensive mothering," see Hays 1996; Furedi 2002; and Faircloth, Hoffman, and Layne 2013.

5   See "Baipishu cheng Zhongguo jin qianwan liushou ertong 'yiniandaotou jianbudao ba ma'" [White Paper says China's close to 10 million left-behind children go a full year without seeing their parents], *Chinanews.com*, June 18, 2015, http://www.chinanews.com/gn/2015/06–18/7353603.shtml (accessed July 22, 2015).

6   Stacey 1983; M. Wolf 1985; Judd 1994.

7   The theme of multiple motherhood and/or parenthood has a long history in China. See, for example, Bray 2009 on late imperial medical discourses and notions of "multiple motherhood."

8   See the works of Francesca Bray (1997, 2013), Gail Hershatter (2011), and Hill Gates (2015) for a critique of the neglect of women's productive activities in standard accounts of late imperial China; for South China, see Siu and Chan 2010. Bray (1997, 270) suggests that this historiographical bias was probably shaped by "the Western cultural predilection for construing female identity in terms of biological reproduction and its control."

9   Santos 2008, 2011, 2013, forthcoming; Santos and Donzelli 2009. For similar processes in other parts of Guangdong, see also Potter and Potter 1990; Aijmer and Ho 2000; Ku 2003; Oxfeld 2010.

10 Goode 1963; Cowgill and Holmes 1972; Giddens 1991, 1992, 1999; Beck and Beck-Gernsheim 2002.

PART TWO

CLASS, GENDER, AND PATRIARCHY IN URBAN SOCIETY

CHAPTER FIVE

URBANIZATION AND THE TRANSFORMATION OF KINSHIP PRACTICE IN SHANDONG

ANDREW B. KIPNIS

N December 2012, I attended the wedding of a relative of a Chinese friend, after bumping into him on the street and being invited to tag along. The wedding took place in Zouping, a midsize Shandong city of about 350,000 people. Both bride and groom worked in urban white-collar jobs, and the couple lived in a city apartment purchased from the groom's work unit. The wedding was run by a private company, which arranged for the hotel banquet room and supplied an emcee to run the ritual as well as photographers to document every moment of it. Though it took place in the large hall of an urban hotel restaurant, the emcee, following directions from the family, structured the wedding in a standardized manner known as a "rural wedding in the city" (*nongcun hunli chengli ban*). As was traditional in the patrilineal, virilocal rural weddings of this area, only the groom's friends and family attended; no one from the bride's family was present (Kipnis 1997). At the start of the ceremony, the emcee directed the bride to formulaically address her father-in-law as "Dad," her mother-in-law as "Mum," and her husband's paternal grandparents as (paternal) "Grandma" (Nainai) and (paternal) "Grandpa" (Yeye). As she addressed her new relatives, each of them in turn handed her a red envelope (*hongbao*), supposedly filled with cash. The ritual thus announced the bride's incorporation into the husband's family rather than a mutual blending of families. After the kin-addressing part of the ceremony, the Party secretary of the single-surname village (located roughly ten kilometers north of Zouping) where the groom had grown up and where his paternal grandparents still lived was invited to give a speech. He concluded by urging the new couple to have children soon (*zao sheng guizi*) for the glory of their lineage and their village. I was not able to interview the participants in detail, but my curiosity was piqued, and a series of questions quickly formed in my mind: How often did this wedding ceremony company (*hunqing gongsi*) put on this type of wedding? What other forms of wedding did they perform? Why did the couple select this form of wedding? What did the bride's family think? How did the patrilineal spirit of the ceremony relate to the practical living circumstances of the couple? Who paid for their apartment? Would relationships between the couple and the bride's parents be parallel to or distinctly different from the couple's relationships with the husband's parents?

The city of Zouping has grown rapidly over the past fifteen years, with both its population and geographic area increasing more than sixfold. As I did research on the household situations of the newly arrived families in this rapidly growing urban area from 2008 to 2011, I came across many households that seemed both linked to and distinct from the type of kinship arrangements I had observed in villages in the same county during research carried out on two occasions roughly five (Kipnis 2009, 2011b) and twenty years earlier (Kipnis 1997). Like the wedding I attended, these arrangements could be depicted as being simultaneously "in the city" and marked by their rural origins. Also like the wedding, these arrangements raise as many questions as they might answer.

The arrangements varied according to the particular geographic origins of these newly urbanized Zouping residents, with at least three distinct groups clearly apparent: "villagers-in-the-city" (*chengzhongcun ren*), those who lost their agricultural land as the city expanded and thus were incorporated by the city rather than moving to it; migrants from villages inside the same county or from villages in the bordering regions of neighboring counties that were within a forty-minute motorbike ride of the county seat; and migrants from farther afield (some of whom came from as far away as Yunnan or Gansu).

Analyzing the transformations of kinship practices that mark each of these groups, or even the differences among them, requires positing a baseline for change and thus structural definitions. For heuristic purposes, one could distinguish among three anthropological concepts that often but not always interrelate in Chinese contexts: patrilineal reasoning (thinking kinship primarily in terms of agnatically related men, and tracing kin relations over time through agnatically related descendants), virilocal patterns of residence and care (married couples residing with the husband's family rather than the wife's and, consequently, enacting closer and denser material, labor, and emotional exchanges with members of the husband's family

ANDREW B. KIPNIS

than with those of the wife's), and patriarchal power (a pattern of familial power relations in which men dominate women and the elderly dominate youth).[1] But however one defines or pulls apart these concepts, daily practice seems to move in directions that simultaneously invoke and move beyond particularly defined modes of patriliny, virilocality and patriarchy. A straightforward version of modernization theory, in which neolocality, bilaterally imagined kinship, and more balanced gender relations automatically replace patriliny, virilocality, and patriarchy, cannot explain the types of transformations that occur in Zouping.

The problem is perhaps exacerbated by my methodology. I rely primarily on household interviews. Though I interviewed more than one hundred households, I did not do ethnography with any of them, making questions of power relations especially difficult to grapple with. Judging who in a particular household dominates whom, if possible at all, generally requires living in that household. But the fluid nature of human relations also makes such judgments difficult. New living circumstances create new practical problems as well as provide new opportunities for social advancement. Family members always reshape their kin relations in reaction to changing circumstances but also always are shaped by cultural memories both physically embodied and engraved in the wider social environment, that is to say, kinship is a practice in the Bourdieuian sense (Bourdieu 1977, 1990). In addition, perhaps moving beyond typical Bourdieuian approaches, cultural memories are also moved by conscious, imaginative attempts to manipulate them, as is suggested by the structure of the wedding ceremony described above. This chapter addresses questions of transformation in kinship by simultaneously engaging practical adaptations to changing circumstances and the modes of cultural memory that are apparent in enacting the adaptations.

URBAN ENVIRONMENTS

As it has in many new cities in China, the spectacular growth of Zouping has been structured in a tripartite division of urban space (Hsing 2010). The old town, especially its shopping district, has been rebuilt and continues to expand gradually; a new city district (*xincheng*), consisting primarily of government buildings, parks, and housing estates, has sprung up from scratch; and a large development zone (*kaifa qu*), filled with both factories and the housing and amenities needed to service the factory workers, has urbanized large sections of previously agricultural land. This chapter focuses on the newer residents of the development zone, where most of the population growth has taken place.

The Weiqiao Group is the economic cornerstone of the development zone. Over the past five years, it has employed between 100,000 and 160,000 workers at a time, depending on demand for the cloth, clothing, aluminum, and other products that it produces. Its workers are divided between relatively permanent "contract" (*hetong*) workers and "temporary" (*linshi*) workers who are laid off when demand slackens. Its expanding production spaces and housing facilities take up more than half the area of the development zone. It maintains free dormitory beds for up to 100,000 workers and has more than 25,000 apartments for sale to married contract workers at heavily subsidized prices (many factory workers marry other factory workers, so most of these apartments house at least two people who work for Weiqiao). The Weiqiao Group physically relocated much of its production and its staff to the development zone from the nearby town of Weiqiao in the early aughts, as part of a deal struck by the county government when it decided to establish the development zone.

In many senses, urbanization in Zouping involves most of the changes that classic forms of modernization theory would predict. It has been accompanied by and spurred on by industrialization, and the majority of new urban residents are factory workers. Urbanization and industrialization have been accompanied by a rapid increase in the number of years children spend in school; a rapid increase in the ability of citizens to speak the national language in addition to (and sometimes even instead of) local dialect; a demographic transition (enforced by the Birth-Planning Policy); a rapid increase in incomes and corresponding expansion of practices of consumption; and "time/space compression" (Harvey 1989), brought about by road building, the availability of motorcycles and cars, cell phones, and the Internet.[2] But whether and how these changes relate to transformation in practices of kinship is a rather more complicated matter than straightforward modernization theory can explain. Rather than the simple demise of patriliny, virilocality, and patriarchal power, what seems to be taking place is a complex transformation of their formats. Moreover, this transformation does not proceed at the same pace or in the same manner for everyone. Consider, then, the particular situations of the three groups identified above: villagers-in-the-city, migrants from nearby, and migrants from farther afield.

MIGRANTS FROM NEARBY VILLAGES

Migrants to Zouping city from villages in the same county or nearby regions often maintain close relationships with their families in their home villages, living lives that are split between village homes and apartments, rented

ANDREW B. KIPNIS

rooms, or dormitory beds in the development zone. The construction of paved roads means that almost all villages in the county are less than forty-five minutes away by car or motorcycle from the county seat, and as factory workers have gotten richer (with most salaries exceeding ¥2,000 [US$330] per month in 2011), almost all of them can afford at least a motorbike. For those who do not like to drive their own vehicles, there are regular buses from the county seat to all of the townships, with stops within a kilometer or two of all but the most isolated of villages. Many possibilities for concrete living arrangements are possible. Workers, married or single, can live in village homes and commute daily to jobs in the county seat. Young single people regularly shuttle back and forth between dormitory beds (which are free) and their parents' homes in villages. Those wishing to have some privacy, perhaps because they have boyfriends or girlfriends, can rent a room for ¥100 a month in one of the villages bordering on the development zone and shuttle between their rented rooms and village homes. Many married workers purchase one of the company apartments but also return regularly to their village homes on days off and/or host family visitors from their village homes.

Here let me focus on married worker couples who purchased apartments from the Weiqiao Group. I was able to interview these couples by establishing research projects in the primary schools that their children attended. I divided my time between a second-grade class and a fifth-grade class, with the result that the couples I interviewed were of two, overlapping age cohorts. The parents of the second-graders were born during the late 1970s and early 1980s and, because of the onset of the Birth-Planning Policy in 1980, averaged many fewer siblings than the parents of the fifth-graders, who were, on average, a few years older. In all, I interviewed thirty such couples for this project.

Though they lived in apartments in the city, most of these couples still had land rights in the villages where the husbands had been born. As is commonly the case throughout rural China, upon marriage, women in rural Zouping lose land rights with their families and in the villages where they were born and gain them in the families and villages of their husbands. This virilocal pattern of land allocation influenced the kinship practices of these couples. In the majority of these households (twenty-four out of thirty), the couple's land was farmed by the husband's parents, with help from the husband during busy periods (such as the wheat harvest) and on weekends. Eighteen of the husbands said that they went back to their home villages every Saturday or Sunday to visit their parents and help with farming. Of the six households in which the husband did not help with farming, in four cases, the husband had a brother who lived in the village and had taken charge of farming the family's land; in one case, the husband's parents had died and the couple chose to rent out their land to neighbors; and in the final case, the couple's family had lost their land rights when the husband's parents agreed to take factory jobs in a township-run enterprise in exchange for those land rights. In none of these thirty households did either the husband or the wife help out with the farming chores of the wife's parents.

Partially as a result of their farming work, the husbands in these households tended to work fewer hours in Weiqiao's factories and, consequently, to receive lower salaries. The shift and salary structure in Weiqiao was very complex, as the group produced a variety of products and paid more for work that was tiring, required night shifts, or demanded relatively rare technical skills. But one basic difference in compensation was between that paid for a standard day-shift workweek (*changbaiban*), of five eight-hour daytime shifts, and a rotating-shift workweek (*lunban*), of six eight-hour shifts including day, evening, and night shifts. Rotating shifts paid about 25 percent more than standard day shifts because they involved 20 percent more hours and because of bonuses paid for the night shifts. In the eighteen households where the husband regularly did farmwork, the husband always worked the standard day shift, but in ten of these households, the wife took a rotating shift. This situation corroborates the findings of Alan de Brauw et al. (2008), who debunk the myth that farming is becoming feminized in China. It also runs against the stereotype that in most households, husbands work longer hours outside the home and earn more than wives.

Clearly couples who own apartments in the city and live there with their children but not their parents can be labeled as exhibiting neolocal residence patterns in standard anthropological kinship terminology. But such a label masks not only the ongoing labor exchanges these households enact with their parents but also the fact that relationships with the husbands' parents and those with the wives' parents are not equivalent. Perhaps because of the standard way land is allocated in Zouping, these exchanges exhibit a virilocal character and are labeled here as "viricentric households."

The viricentricity of these households was also apparent in patterns of child care. In the families of the second-graders especially, the parents desired after-school care for the children. In twelve of the fifteen Weiqiao apartment households with second-graders, one or both of the paternal grandparents regularly came to the household to care for their grandchildren. As Gonçalo Santos (chap. 4) demonstrates, child care by grandparents is common in China. In most of these Zouping households, the child-care provider was the paternal grandmother. Often, the paternal grandmother lived with the couple during the week and sometimes returned to the village on weekends with the father when he went back to farm. In such households, the paternal grandfather would spend most of his time in his village home. In some households, both paternal grandparents would move back and forth between their village homes and their sons' apartments, usually traveling by bus. Only in one of the fifteen households did the couple rely on the wife's parents for child care. In this household, the parents had a daughter in the second grade and a one-year-old son who lived with his maternal grandparents in their village home. But the husband in this household had several brothers, one of whom lived with his parents in their village home, so the paternal grandparents had less need and less time for a close relationship with this household.

Sometimes these viricentric arrangements were justified with a patrilineal mentality; that is to say, when I asked why the paternal rather than the maternal grandparents provided child care, the response would be that the children and paternal grandparents were of the same lineage/clan (*jiazu*). The logic of viricentric child care was also apparent during summer vacations, when many children spent weeks or sometimes the entire vacation in their paternal grandparents' village homes but only occasionally visited the homes of their maternal grandparents.

The Birth-Planning Policy has made multi-son families illegal in Zouping, exacerbating the logic of viricentricity among the Weiqiao apartment dwellers. While first-born daughters usually have a younger sibling, couples whose first child is a son are not allowed to have another child. As in the case of maternal grandparents providing child care, the apartment dwellers were much more likely to have relatively limited relationships with the husbands' parents when the husbands had brothers. Sometimes limitations on relationships with the husbands' parents led to increased interaction with the wives' parents. In other cases, there seemed to be less interaction with both sets of parents. As the Birth-Planning Policy has been strictly implemented in Zouping, the younger male contract employees overwhelmingly come from households in which they are the only sons. In addition to the Birth-Planning Policy, financial pressures of the sort described by Lihong Shi (chap. 2) also limit the desire to have more than one son. As a result of the diminishing number of men with brothers, the households with second-graders exhibited slightly more viricentricity than the households with fifth-graders, a trend that will likely become stronger over time.

A third aspect of viricentricity among Weiqiao apartment dwellers was apparent in their patterns of elder care. Of the thirty couples, ten said that the husband's parents lived with them during the winter months. The Weiqiao apartments had free heat during the winter, but village homes, for the most part, were without heat. In addition, there was little farmwork to be done during the winter. Couples told me that by letting the paternal grandparents live in their apartments during the winter, they could protect their parents' health. None of the couples, however, reported hosting the wife's parents during the winter. The couples' parents were generally too young (mostly in their fifties) to require significant care, but the pattern of inviting the husbands' parents to live in the apartments during winter months seems a harbinger of larger quantities of viricentric elder care in the future.

While the Weiqiao apartment dwellers are almost entirely of rural origins, I interviewed two households of people of local origins who lived in the development zone but did not live and work at Weiqiao and were not of rural origins. One was a family of workers from a nearby township. The household of six was made up of two schoolchildren, their parents, and the paternal grandparents. They had come to the development area after the parents lost their factory jobs in a nearby township. The parents and paternal grandfather had picked up factory work in the development zone, and they were able to purchase a three-bedroom apartment on the open market by pooling their income. The paternal grandmother cooked and provided child care. The second household consisted of two schoolchildren and their paternal grandparents. The apartment had been purchased by the children's parents, both of whom lived and worked for the government of a neighboring township. The parents purchased the apartment as an investment and because they felt that the schools in the development zone were better than those in the township. The grandparents took care of the children during the week; on weekends, the children went back to their parents' home. In both of these cases, viricentricity is apparent in the fact that the significant intergenerational exchanges take place between the couples and the husbands' parents rather than with the wives' parents. I discovered no three-generation households involving the wife's parents.

Two final points might be made in terms of a comparison between development zone viricentricity and practices observed in (fully virilocal) Chinese rural settings. First, a point of contrast: Ellen Judd, who also did research in rural villages in this part of Shandong, has pointed out the importance of agnatic kinship in the subordination of women in village settings (Judd 1994). After virilocal marriages, village men are surrounded by close relatives with whom they grew up, while women can be isolated. Such settings can place women at a profound disadvantage in cases of spousal conflict or divorce (Sargeson 2012; Sargeson and Song 2010). In the development zone, women living in viricentric apartments do not suffer this particular disadvantage. Yet a parallel exists between the pattern of development zone wives working longer hours than their husbands and the traditional uterine families of rural Taiwan discussed by Margery Wolf (1968, 1972). In both cases, it seems that women respond to their lack of position in an extended (patrilineal) kinship grouping by focusing their labor on more narrowly defined kin groups. For the women from rural Taiwan, this required investing extra affective care in their relationships with their sons. For those in Weiqiao apartments, it means earning money that can be streamed into the budget of narrowly defined households rather than expending labor on farming, which would benefit the more broadly defined patrilineal extended family.

MIGRANTS FROM FARTHER AFIELD

A large number of development zone workers, including many Weiqiao temporary employees and some contract employees, came from rural areas far away from Zouping. Eighteen of the twenty-eight such households I interviewed came from distant parts of Shandong, usually from the western, poorer parts of the province, about an eight- to ten-hour bus ride away. The rest came from other provinces, including Sichuan, Yunnan, Gansu, Henan, and Hebei.

Their living conditions were typically much worse than those of people who had purchased their own apartments. They usually rented rooms in villages at the fringes of the development zone, where the monthly rent at the time of my research was about ¥100 per room. They saved money by skimping on rent, sometimes living with their children in a single room with no bathroom or running water (there might be a collective toilet or tap in the larger compound, but in some cases only a poorly maintained public toilet someplace in the neighborhood). Some saved their money in order to purchase a private apartment in Zouping someday, while others planned to return home after a number of years with enough money to retire on. Because most were not contract workers, they typically were not eligible to purchase Weiqiao's subsidized apartments, but even those who were eligible to do so did not, as Weiqiao does not give the deed (*fangchan zheng*) for these apartments to the purchasers, and people from outside Zouping did not trust Weiqiao enough to make such a purchase.[3]

Perhaps in part because they tended to live in crowded conditions, these twenty-eight households consisted uniformly of nuclear families. Because the development zone has good schools and liberal education policies that allow the children of migrant workers to attend for free, most migrant workers brought their school-age children with them. Some even said that the only reason they stayed in Zouping was because of the quality of the schools available to their children. But none of the households I interviewed brought either the husband's or the wife's parents with them; none even planned on bringing them in the future. These families visited their distant village homes at most twice a year (for some of the Shandong households) or as little as once every three years (in the case of the household from Yunnan), with most making the traditional once-a-year migration home over the Chinese New Year holidays.

These households often lacked child care, and even the second-graders had to find their own way home after school. Despite the lack of child care, some couples were so desperate to save money that both parents worked rotating shifts, with the result that the children were forced to supervise their own homework and sometimes even prepare their own meals using hot plates and water fetched from elsewhere, as rented rooms had no proper kitchen. While some of these children did well in school, others did not, and teachers often felt that the biggest troublemakers came from such households. Perhaps not surprisingly, teachers typically blamed such problems on the parents' "low quality" (di suzhi), rather than on their difficult circumstances.

In short, despite coming from rural settings that were probably not that different from those of nearby villages, the kinship arrangements of migrants from far away were much more nuclear than those of workers from nearby. Though some such households spoke of learning of the opportunities available in Zouping through networks of people linked to their places of origin, few had the time to regularly socialize with people from the same place. They were focused on earning money and getting their children through school and acted as individuated household units. Their situations resembled the type of kinship practice that many modernization theorists would predict—a simplification of kinship ties resulting in nuclear families. While local migrants' householding and economic strategies seemed to lead to greater reliance on viricentric kinship bonds, economic pressures on more distant migrants seemed to lead to rather individuated forms of alienation. Children received less care, adults constantly complained of tiredness, there was little trust in the company that employed them, and socializing with neighbors was rare. Efforts were focused on accumulating capital for the future. If these migrants are successful, however, perhaps broader forms of kin ties will reemerge later in their lives.

Stevan Harrell (2013) has presented Chinese patriliny as dependent on a material property base that necessitates patrilineal thinking for survival. He shows quite clearly how flexible Chinese kinship practice has been and how patriliny and virilocality disappear when the material conditions for their reproduction are negated. But his analysis cannot predict what would happen if the material conditions for patriliny and virilocality reappear after a period of disappearance or, perhaps more importantly, if material conditions are such that households or men or women actually have a choice about the types of families they would like to create. While the prevalence of neolocality among the migrants from afar supports Harrell's thesis, whether patrilineal thinking or viricentricity might reemerge when they return home or even after they establish themselves in Zouping is an open question. When I asked these families about their visits home, they reported visiting the husband's family rather than the wife's. While women in such households often took advantage of return visits to see their own parents, they would do so only after spending a few days at the homes of their parents-in-law. Husbands sometimes would not visit their in-laws at all.

VILLAGERS-IN-THE-CITY

Village farmers whose land was absorbed by the expanding city were usually among the wealthiest urbanites of the three groups explored here. The terms of land appropriation in Zouping have generally been quite good. Households that had lost their land receive annual payments equivalent to the value of the harvest at that year's market rates for thirty years. In addition, the village as a whole often receives a section of land on which it can develop its own real estate projects, passing the profits down to the individual households. In villages where the houses are razed, those losing houses are given heavily subsidized apartments in new urban developments. Households that keep their houses and are located near factories can develop lucrative rental businesses by building as many as twenty ¥100-a-month rental rooms on top of and inside their courtyard homes.[4]

The exact routes to prosperity can be quite various for villager-in-the-city households, but the generality of their prosperity can be seen in the fact that there were only two factory workers of this type among the twenty-five households I interviewed. Though they had on average no more education or skills than the migrants working in factories, most felt factory work to be too "bitter" (*ku*) and preferred to start their own businesses or take easier (even if lower-paying) jobs. One man explained his wife's choice of a low-paying department store job as follows: "Our household has many sources of income, the 'money replacing agricultural income' (*dunliang qian*) and rental income as well. Factory work is too tiring; retail work pays less, but it is more pleasant."

These households exhibited many viricentric tendencies. Thirteen of the twenty-five households included paternal grandparents, and none included maternal grandparents. Pressure to live with grandparents increased in those villages with lucrative rental markets, as living in separate households wasted potential rental space. But though they economized on space, none of the rentier households I visited economized on the quality of their homes. While the rental rooms attached to the main sections of the house were generally quite basic, the space they occupied—which always included separate bedrooms for grandparents, parents, and children, as well as a living room, a kitchen, and a private bathroom—was usually beautifully decorated and full of high-quality fittings.

In these households, the grandparents never took formal jobs. Having lost their land, they had no farming to do, and none felt the need to find employment. They took care of their grandchildren and socialized with neighbors. Generally speaking, the villagers-in-the-city had the most active social lives of all the groups. They still lived in relatively organic communities and had more leisure time than the factory workers, who, if from nearby villages, were juggling full-time factory work with farming or, if from farther away, were dealing with extensive factory work, a lack of child care, and living circumstances that made cooking and washing more difficult. While the households were viricentric, their socializing involved both agnatically related fellow villagers and visits to affines, who were usually within easy commuting distance if not from the same village. Unfortunately, my research was not detailed enough to provide data on the relative importance of socializing with different groups of friends and relatives.

A final aspect of viricentricity and patriliny was visible in the patterns of inheritance in these villages. One of the villages-in-the-city that I visited was quite wealthy. The village had done extremely well with its collective real estate holdings and earned enough money to provide subsidized apartments for all village households, private health insurance for all villagers, four-year-tuition scholarships for all village high school graduates who were accepted to tertiary institutions, and monthly stipends that in 2009 were set at ¥380 for those under the age of fifty-five, ¥450 for those between fifty-five and sixty, and ¥760 for those over sixty. To prevent the dispersal of these rights over time, the village had decided that rights to these benefits could be passed on to only one household in each generation. While this household could be the household of a daughter, and had to be for households with no sons (somewhat more common as result of the Birth-Planning Policy), rights still went to sons more often than daughters. The village Party secretary told me that of the nine households in this village in which there was both a son and a daughter and the rights had been formally transferred, in seven cases the rights had gone to the son. In the other two cases, the daughters had received the rights because the sons had settled in elsewhere and did not want to return to Zouping. Households, he explained, chose sons for this privilege because stable material resources greatly enhanced a son's marriage prospects but did less for those of a daughter. As Helena Obendiek (chap. 3) shows, such inheritance patterns reinforce viricentric patterns of intergenerational obligation. The fact that uxorilocal marriage was relatively common in this village (households with daughters but no sons had to marry their daughters uxorilocally or lose their benefits) may have intensified competition for good uxorilocal male partners. If so, this competition would have exacerbated the pressure for virilocal marriages for households with a son and a daughter.

Just as villages in farming regions must determine rules for the allocation of land, all of Zouping's villages-in-the-city with collective real estate income must set up rules for issuing various forms of benefits and dividends. Although these rules are usually framed in a gender-neutral way, in practice they often involve logics and patterns that resemble those allocating land rights in villages where patrilineal, virilocal kinship predominates. While I did not research cases of divorce in Zouping's villages-in-the-city, it seems likely, given the findings of Sargeson and Song (2010) in other parts of rural China, that the person who marries into the village will lose out on benefit rights after a divorce, and that such people are more likely to be women than men. If these property arrangements mean that women have more to lose from divorce than men, then such arrangements also could form the material underpinnings of continued private patriarchy, either because the husband is more able to dominate his wife or because the husband's parents manipulate the husband into using the threat of divorce to make their own demands on the wife.

◆ ◆ ◆

The problem of defining terms in anthropology is always difficult. Clear terms usually emerge from particular social situations. The term *virilocality* makes sense in farming communities, where people control the land they farm and live nearby in extended families. If one accepts the argument that "modernity" or "capitalism" has resulted in an increasing conceptual and physical separation of home from work, of familial reproduction from laboring for an employer to earn a wage, then one would have to say that virilocality makes the most sense in "premodern" farming communities (Graeber

2001). In such societies, the location of one's home correlates closely to the setting where one labors and therefore the family that benefits from one's labor. In the context of rural Shandong in the 1970s and early 1980s, the flavor of virilocality was shaped by several factors: that most people were farmers who approached the labor of farming and familial reproduction as joined tasks, that most people lived in villages of 250–1,000 people, that transportation between villages could be difficult and time-consuming, and that many villages were dominated by agnatically related men or by men who grew up together and created imagined agnatic kin links enabling the use of kin terms when addressing one another. When terms like *virilocal* are used to capture such a lived reality, there is always an excess of local factors that shape specific uses of the term—that is, what *virilocality* meant to anthropologists working in Shandong during the 1970s and 1980s was not entirely contained in the broader anthropological definitions of the term itself. Comparison, whether across cultural borders or over different time periods, always has the potential to stretch the definition of the terms. I use the term *viricentricity* not because it is easy to define but merely to point at aspects of continuity in the kinship practices of those who move from Chinese agricultural village settings, where work and home blend together, to industrial urban ones, where work and home become more separate.

Virilocality in 1980s rural Shandong was clarified by the practice of "dividing the household" (*fenjia*), which delineated exactly who belonged to which household (Cohen 1976). But the practice of dividing the household never clarified everything about the material and emotional exchanges that were to take place between households and individuals. In the case of migrants to Zouping city from nearby villages, there is much ambiguity about whether they had formally divided the household. Legally, most families attempt to do whatever is necessary in the home village to maximize their land allocation. But whether a given household had been formally divided did not determine the extent of visiting, labor exchange for farming, child care, and the like, that took place between the couple's household and the household of the father's parents. Given the existence of two separate dwelling spaces (the apartment in the city and the village home), the households felt separate even if they shared a budget and maintained close ties.

The three groups examined in this chapter all move from predominantly rural, agricultural (presumably patrilineal and virilocal) village settings to residential settings in a new urban area, but there are observable differences in their kinship practices. These differences relate to their ongoing ties to their former homes. The villagers-in-the-city live in their former communities, even if some of these communities have been relocated or rebuilt.

Favorable land appropriation policies have given these new urbanites a more advantageous class position in the new city compared to the positions of the other two groups. Critically, there are strong continuities in the way in which the ownership of property is divided among individual households and the village as a collective. When the village was rural, its primary asset was agricultural land. Though its assets are now either real estate investments or rights to "money to replace agricultural income," the processes of divvying up the benefits entail relationships similar to those associated with virilocality, patrilineal thinking, and patriarchal power relations. The migrants from nearby areas maintain regular contact with their relatives in farming villages and the practice of farming itself, though these are less significant than they would have been in the past. Perhaps because virilocality intersects with the allocation of land rights, this contact seems to entail viricentric patterns of intergenerational relationships as well. Migrants from distant villages are forced by circumstances to severely attenuate the extent of their lived ties to their home villages. This attenuation reduces the extent to which they are able to enact viricentric exchanges of labor and care. Nevertheless, perhaps I could have picked up on other aspects of viricentricity had I been able to follow these migrants on their visits back to their home villages or to follow up on those households that plan to retire in their home communities or even on those who settle in Zouping and build long-term futures there.

While there are clear differences among the groups, there are also linkages to wider patterns of social expectations that are shared by all of the groups. This is likely to be the case in the argument about marriage markets by the Party secretary from the village-in-the-city described above. Patrilineal thinking, in which the production of children from a marriage is imagined as more important to a husband and his extended family than to his wife and her family, and patriarchal ideology, which sees marriage as more "natural" when the husband and his family have greater control than the wife over the joint property of a household, conjoin in expectations that the husband and his family, rather than the wife, should bring more material resources to a marriage. Such expectations, while not necessarily universal throughout China, are apparent in patterns of marital ads in even the largest, most cosmopolitan cities in China (Dong et al. 2011).

The modes of cultural memory evident in the continuities of kinship practices in urbanizing Zouping are doubtless multiple. But material processes of labor and property division are also practices of memory. In very concrete ways, consciousness about gender and generational relations, about the paths of creating relatedness, is reproduced in processes of exchanging labor and sharing property. The three groups discussed here enact very different forms of familial property relations. For many villagers-in-the-city, heritable property constitutes an important aspect of family income. For migrants from nearby villages, farming income is a supplement to factory wages. Migrants from afar are totally dependent on wage labor. In the context of a marriage market in which property makes men desirable, the existence of heritable property might be thought of as both an incitement to and a mode of patrilineal thinking.

In depicting property as a form of memory, I do not wish to enter general arguments about whether "consciousness" determines "social being" or "social being" determines "consciousness" (Marx, in Tucker 1978, 4) but rather intend just to indicate that the two are endlessly entwined. In marital markets, "consciousness" of what constitutes desirable male and female partners, if widespread or hegemonic, is experienced as a material, social force. Perhaps it would be best to deconstruct the entire material/ideological dualism and accept that symbols and ideas are material as well.

NOTES

1   In the context of this chapter, I refer primarily to what Silvia Walby (1990) called "private patriarchy." Of course power relations within the family and the types of desires they generate both affect and are affected by gendered power relations outside the family, or what Walby calls "public patriarchy."

2   Elsewhere I have written extensively on various aspects of Zouping's modernization. See especially Kipnis 2016.

3   At the time of my research, these apartments were being sold at roughly one-third of their market value. Purchasers could keep the units until they either quit Weiqiao or passed away, at which point the purchase price was supposed to be returned to them or their heirs. Non-locals did not trust this arrangement on many levels but most of all feared that if a conflict with their employer caused them to leave Weiqiao, they would be forced to give up their apartments without receiving the refunds.

4   The extent to which land appropriation is beneficial to former villagers across China is quite variable. There are undoubtedly cases in which villagers' rights are trampled (e.g., X. Zhu 2014), but there are also many others, especially in the Pearl River Delta, where the villagers are transformed into a privileged rentier class. For depictions of the latter sort of place, see Chan, Madsen, and Unger 2009; Chung and Unger 2013; and Tomba 2012.

CHAPTER SIX

BEING THE RIGHT WOMAN FOR "MR. RIGHT"

Marriage and Household Politics in Present-Day Nanjing

ROBERTA ZAVORETTI

IN the People's Republic of China, the idea that older people, and in particular old men, hold power over younger people and women has been an important discursive weapon in the hands of different political actors, including different state leaderships, at least since the end of the nineteenth century. At different times, political movements as well as newly established political leaderships have proposed themselves as the agents of young people's and women's emancipation from patriarchal power, often in the name of the need to "modernize the country" (Barlow 1991, 1994; Duara 2000). Nowadays, however, the term *patriarchy* does not seem to be so prominent in state efforts to conceptualize China as a "Socialist Harmonious Society,"[1] perhaps because it conveys the idea that society is not only about cohesion but also about contradictions.

Patriarchy has been used as an analytical category in the social sciences, and in particular among scholars belonging to the "second wave" of Euro-American feminism. The debates within and around the feminist movement, however, quickly led to a radical questioning of the existence of a universal "female" subject and of "women" as a homogeneous group (Butler and Scott 1992; Kandiyoti 1998). Accordingly, the concept of patriarchy underwent repeated scrutiny in activist and academic circles. In the context of these debates, Deniz Kandiyoti (1988, 1998) drew on the concept of patriarchy in order to grasp the multifaceted dimensions of household politics.

Kandiyoti looks at patriarchy as a system of domination of the young by the old and of women by men. In the countries of the so-called patriarchal belt that includes the People's Republic, women are excluded from the lineage and from the inheritance of property, which is called "patrimony." In this (oversimplified) scenario, young men have a clear stake in the perpetuation of patriarchal norms due to their prospect of inheriting the status of family head and family property; young women's compliance, however, cannot be easily explained through models based on rational choice. Following anthropologist Margery Wolf (1985), Kandiyoti (1988) questions how and why women participate in the perpetuation of a system of power that so plainly discriminates against them.

Other studies discuss the different extents to which women in the patriarchal belt were excluded from the control of property at different times in history (J. Goody 1990; R. Watson 1991). While acknowledging the noticeable historical variations and the role that dowry (either provided or earned through work) played in women's autonomy and in the reproduction of class and status, these works highlight the fact that daughters relinquished further claims on the family estate by receiving their dowries (J. Goody 1990, 89–91, R. Watson 1991). Margery Wolf's (1985) influential account of patriarchal relations in China anticipates Kandiyoti's (1988) conclusions: under the unfavorable condition that patriarchal families impose on young brides, the strategy women pursue most in order to gain autonomy and prestige is to bear sons.

Notwithstanding its limits, this model was effective in showing that the patriarchal household was not a place of stark black-and-white oppositions but one of bargaining and negotiations. Young women enjoyed limited economic autonomy, little recognition for their work, and a low social status both within and outside the family. However, they were not helpless and voiceless victims; on the contrary, they strategized in order to improve their own lot, albeit within the limits of patriarchal power. The prospect of holding power over the younger women as mothers and mothers-in-law was one reason most women were inclined to bear a harsh life as young brides.

In reconsidering her earlier work in the context of post-structuralist debates on sex/gender, Kandiyoti (1998) noticed that her previous model did not address subject formation, which was central to third-wave feminist debates, and that for this reason it could not always adequately grasp the complexities of household relations. Kandiyoti's and Wolf's work can serve as a point of departure to show how patriarchal norms are reproduced in affluent urban China through everyday bargaining. These bargaining processes and the reproduction of gender-specific hegemonic roles are in turn intimately linked with the role that state-sponsored class models play in people's visions of a desirable family life.

These processes are evident in the life of Wang Rui, a young woman from Nanjing who went through the process of courtship, marriage, and child-bearing between 2007 and 2012 together with her fiancé and then husband, Li Han. Both came from financially comfortable, urban-based families and enjoyed similar levels of education at marriage. By background and educa-tion, Wang Rui saw herself as a "modern," educated woman and was, to some extent, committed to "gender equality" (*nannü pingdeng*) and professional development; at the same time, she was close to her parents and ostensibly keen on building a harmonious, "high-quality" family. Living and working in Nanjing allowed Wang Rui to foster a relationship of reciprocal care with her parents. Besides, she enjoyed the amenities offered by this prosperous provincial capital and preferred it to stressful and expensive global cities like nearby Shanghai.

During the five years when we were in contact, Wang Rui and Li Han were grappling with issues that commonly worried unmarried young people in China: finding a suitable spouse, advancing in their professions, finding affordable housing, having a child, and maintaining good relations with their in-laws, spouses, and parents. All these issues were interconnected. It would have been difficult for Wang Rui to make a decision about her career with-out thinking about marriage or childbearing age; it would have been hard for her to decide on courtship and marriage without giving any thought to home ownership and living arrangements.

The issues that generally affect the lives of young people like Wang Rui and Li Han highlight how power relations within the household reinforce, and at the same time are reinforced by, power relations that emerge in extra-household settings like the housing and labor markets. At the same time, as the household constitutes a fundamental site for the provision of emo-tional, social, and economic security, power relations within the home tend to be pragmatically "dealt with" rather than openly challenged. Finally, the young couple's keenness on maintaining an appearance of "harmony" and on "keeping everybody happy" at the expense of their own personal (and sometimes different) wishes sheds a light on the symbolic importance of having a "harmonious family" in present-day urban China (Engebretsen, chap. 8).

Wang Rui and Li Han's desire for a strong conjugal bond did not over-ride their filiality (Jankowiak and Li, chap. 7): intergenerational and conjugal relations were closely intertwined. As they both shared ideals of conjugality and intergenerational harmony, each eventually took different trajectories in order to embody those ideals. On the one hand, Wang Rui continued to work at her nursing job, pooling her income with that of her husband's family; however, she eventually renounced pursuit of further professional development and invested her energies in sustaining her role of working mother. On the other hand, Li Han gradually became more focused on his career, assuming the role of the main breadwinner; in addition, he would eventually inherit the house his parents had bought for the family.

As Wang Rui became part of a happy and prosperous three-generation household, she did not only gain long-term economic security. Firstly, she proved herself a successful competitor in a tough marriage market; secondly, she gradually reconciled her modern persona with a dutiful "respect" toward Chinese "family values." After bearing her son, Wang Rui could aim to embody the state-sponsored model of "high-quality" mother and wife: good educator, keen support to her husband, devoted daughter and daughter-in-law.

WANG RUI AT TWENTY-FIVE: LIVING IN THE FAST LANE

I first met Wang Rui in late 2007. At that time, she was working as a qualified nurse in one of Nanjing's main hospitals. She had earned her degree in nursing from an important university in the north of China and was in her mid-twenties. Wang Rui's family background was not wealthy but comfortably stable: her mother and father, both Nanjing residents, had managed to ensure that both she and her younger brother would get a university education. Wang Rui's parents were happy that she had managed to get a good job in her native city of Nanjing after getting her degree. In the meanwhile, her brother had moved to another provincial capital to pursue his own university studies.

Wang Rui and I met during a dinner party organized by common friends; she arrived later than the rest of the party, just after getting off her shift at the hospital. She mentioned that she was toying with the idea of migrating to the United States to pursue a degree in medicine. We started meeting regularly. Other friends defined her as an "open" (*kailang*) personality: trusting, honest, and broad-minded. As a young, unmarried professional, Wang Rui believed that she was at a critical point in her life. Should she pursue her professional ambitions further and try to become a doctor? Yet, as she told me, the fact that she was approaching the age of twenty-six made her worry about her chances of getting a good fiancé. After twenty-six, she said, women had a harder time finding a good prospective groom. Despite my skepticism, she was adamant that she would be much less eligible as a prospective bride in a couple of years and felt she had to act fast.

What about her plan to go to the United States to study then? Would she put that aside? "Well," she answered pragmatically, "if that went through, the whole situation would change. As far as I understand, foreigners do not mind marrying a bit later. If I migrate to the United States, I can probably wait until I am thirty to marry and get my degree in the meantime." I was intrigued by how Wang Rui pursued *both* marriage and career through such careful planning. She was investing much time trying to get her English-language certifications so that she would be in a position to apply for graduate programs in the United States. In the meanwhile, however, she was working hard at her job (which she enjoyed very much) and was also participating in social events and keeping her eyes well open in case "Mr. Right" might show up.[2]

Wang Rui and I continued to see each other regularly and go out with mutual friends; although she was always busy, she often managed to save some time and energy for social events. She was curious and sociable: there was no topic she would shy away from discussing, no place or company she would not try to see for herself. Significantly, she happily followed me when I suggested going to a club. Although this might sound like a banal outing, many "respectable girls" would have considered a club way too shady of a place for them. In addition, many women felt strong pressure in terms of appearance: girls who hung out in clubs invested considerable time, effort, and money making themselves attractive and fashionable, and the most successful ones were hired as promoters. Wang Rui had had a fairly sheltered upbringing; however, she agreed to go to the club out of curiosity. Many of her social activities took place away from her parents' gaze, although they lived together. In fact, Wang Rui shared an apartment in the city center with two colleagues, where she slept after her late shifts.

The fact that I was from Europe influenced my friendship with Wang Rui and other informants in important ways. As a European woman, I was not only a stranger—and hence not in a position to gossip with colleagues or family members. Most importantly, I was easily identified with an ideal, imaginary "Western" society in which young people, and in particular young women, enjoyed boundless freedom of thought, experience, and expression. For this reason, it was possible to talk with me about sensitive topics without the fear of being censored. Wang Rui was sure that a "foreigner" would not judge her for "unruly" behavior.

During our conversations, Wang Rui was rather disappointed to hear that "the West" was not as free from social pressure as she had imagined. She also vented her concerns on courtship and marriage as she experienced them. One such concern was the issue of virginity. Wang Rui believed that, had she lost her virginity before marriage, she would not have bled on her wedding night; as a consequence, her husband would have eventually rejected her. I tried to minimize the issue, suggesting that most women did not even bleed on their first intercourse, yet I could understand her concerns. Many young men I had spoken with did hope to marry someone who had not had previous sexual partners and thought sexual intercourse was acceptable only after engagement. Accordingly, most parents expected their daughters to refrain from full sexual intercourse until marriage. Wang Rui was open-hearted on her desire to have sex, but she was also adamant that this was a risky business.

Wang Rui was not the first young woman who had voiced her doubts about virginity with me; this was a recurrent topic among young people from "respectable" and comfortable backgrounds and invariably led to animated discussions among boys and girls (Farrer 2014). The widely shared expectations of female chastity did not mean that unmarried women necessarily *did* refrain from full intercourse. Many young women in Nanjing, for example, were working and living away from their parents and enjoyed economic independence and personal space. In addition, cities in the Reform period feature a plethora of public and commercial spaces where women and men can freely associate and experience "romantic" encounters. One should be careful, however, to equate these interactions with a generalized "sexual liberation"; young women are keenly aware of the imperative to marry (Engebretsen, chap. 8) and the prime value that a competitive marriage market confers on female sexual propriety (Fang 2013). Women who are not pursuing higher education are largely expected to marry just after reaching legal marriageable age and thus access socially approved intimacy. Professional women like Wang Rui, however, need to keep a respectable persona *while* freely socializing with men at an age in which most are sexually active. For this reason, for example, many of them avoid clubs, which are often considered disorderly (*luan*) places where promiscuous people look for one-night stands (*yiye qing*).

Situations vary greatly from one case to another, yet most young, unmarried women go to great lengths to conceal their intimate lives from their families and, eventually, their boyfriends. Many parents just assume that their daughters are behaving "respectably," occasionally turning a blind eye to what daughters actually do. Other parents are aware that a long engagement is likely to imply sexual relations but tolerate them as long as they happen discreetly; at the same time, a lengthy public engagement allows parents to trust that the young man will eventually take their daughter in marriage (*qu*). The general understanding is that sexual intercourse should be part of a committed relationship (Farrer 2014) and not an encounter aimed solely at short-term pleasure. Unsurprisingly, some young women do craft a more provocative persona for themselves and avoid concealing their sexual relations, yet this is perceived largely as a challenge to custom, an excess that might be acceptable only in other, more "open" (*kaifang*) societies.[3] Wang Rui was not ready to spoil one of her few assets—respectability—just to satisfy her curiosity. For her, the idea of sex evoked the anxiety of building an exclusive relationship with the right person. The absence of information on sexual health did not lessen these anxieties and reminded Wang Rui that marriage was still the only legitimate arena for sexual activity as far as the state was concerned. While Reform era publications targeting young people promote "sexual gratification as one of the great bonuses of the reform programme" (Evans 1997, 82), they remind the same young readers that they should practice restraint. Media productions regularly describe female sexuality as passive and in need of being awakened by male active desire, notably within the state-approved and socially accepted arena of marriage. As wifehood and motherhood are regularly depicted as women's natural destiny, premarital sex is produced as an irresponsible behavior, potentially dangerous for young women's psychophysical health (Evans 1997, 82–83, 104–11; see also Farrer 2014).

Wang Rui talked a lot about the men she met in her search for Mr. Right. One evening, at a social event for people interested in migrating to the United States, she made friends with one of the organizers, a man in his late twenties. After giving a presentation at the event, the man had approached her and complimented her for being attractive. Wang Rui was pleased by the compliment and found the man attractive as well; however, she said, he had seemed controlling from the beginning, telling her that she should pursue the profession of social worker (instead of doctor) as a way of going to the United States. Wang Rui felt the man had been arrogant in his effort to push this idea on her. He had also told her that he expected his wife to focus on the home rather than on her profession, and, notwithstanding her keen desire to have children, Wang Rui recognized this statement as a clear sign of "machismo" (*dananzi zhuyi*). After this first encounter, Wang Rui was pretty sure that, although attractive, this man was not going to be an ideal husband for her. As a consequence, she declared that she would not meet him anymore.

WANG RUI AT TWENTY-SIX: THE ARRIVAL OF MR. RIGHT

Wang Rui never left China. In the summer of 2008, she announced that she had met someone she really liked—"on the Internet," as she put it. They quickly got engaged, and one evening she introduced me to her Mr. Right in a teahouse near her workplace. Her boyfriend, Li Han, struck me as a good-natured, sociable man of her age; he had a good job in the field of law and, like her, was looking forward to marrying and having a family. After we spent the evening together, they insisted on driving me home, since he had just bought a car; it did not matter that my flat was only five hundred meters away from the teahouse. As they were calling it "our" car, it obviously represented the first step toward the gradual institutionalization of their union.

Wang Rui and her Mr. Right got along well, yet their path toward marriage was not smooth. Their families engaged in fierce negotiations around the purchase of a house. Wang Rui's father and mother expected the groom to buy an apartment for the new family. This expectation was common in Nanjing as well as in comparable urban milieus, where estate prices had boomed after the privatization of the housing market. Helen Siu (1993) highlights how the spread of this custom after the Reforms cannot be read as the simple reemergence of pre-Liberation brideprice payments but rather is a way in which families participate in the realignment of class in Reform era China. The reinforced association of property with the male child does not only imply an increased burden on the family of the groom but also highlights the gendered dimension of home ownership and class formation in the contemporary period (L. Zhang 2010).

Despite the expectations of his prospective parents-in-law, Li Han was not able to buy a house at that moment. The flat in which he was living, which had been provided by his employer, was occupied by his parents, who hailed from a different city and wanted to be close to their son. Wang Rui felt she was between a rock and a hard place: she very much liked her fiancé, but she understood her parents' concerns. Her boyfriend's parents thought only about their own wish to live in the big city, and not about their son's need to provide a house for his new family. Wang Rui went on to tell me that any young man in Nanjing would be expected to do so. For her parents, accepting Li Han without a house would imply a loss of face. They had raised her properly and paid for her university studies; they were keen on her making the best possible marriage. I asked about how her fiancé was handling the situation. She replied that he was in a predicament similar to hers: he wanted to marry as soon as possible, but in no case could he have asked his parents to leave his house, as this would have been plainly unfilial behavior. Wang Rui felt all the more helpless as she empathized with Li Han: she was herself an affectionate daughter and understood his desire to maintain a good relationship with his parents.

The young couple decided to stick together in the hope that time would bring about a solution; they thought that their parents would eventually cool down and find a compromise. In the meantime, Wang Rui kept renting a room in the city center. This allowed the young couple to meet on their own, at least occasionally. Wang Rui was now in a committed relationship that, she was sure, would lead to marriage. This implied that she did not need to worry too much about chastity because, in the end, the person she was spending the night with was her husband-to-be. Did her parents know? "Certainly not," she said, "they would never agree." Instead of worrying about sexual propriety, Wang Rui was bothered by the need to hide her intimacy with Li Han and postpone their marriage. At the same time, their delayed yet impending marriage also prompted her to put aside the opportunity to work abroad. This was a dilemma, since she deeply wanted to have a family but was also driven to pursue new professional avenues and travel abroad.

MARRIED AT LAST

Wang Rui and Li Han married in early 2010. At that time, unfortunately, I was not in Nanjing. I met her the following summer. She was happy, although the couple had not yet found a way to live under the same roof; they were saving to buy an apartment, and meanwhile she was still living with her parents and spending the occasional night with Li Han in town. Property prices were too high, she complained, and they needed to buy a flat in an expensive location, because they both worked in the city center. Even for a couple with good jobs, it was impossible to save enough money to qualify for a mortgage without parental support.

In October 2011, Wang Rui gave birth to her son; she moved into a new apartment on the outskirts, together with her husband and his parents (her mother-in law's house, "*pojia*," as she called it). After forty days of ritual rest, also called "sitting the month" (*zuo yuezi*), Wang Rui told me that she still felt it was too cold to be out much with the baby and that she would ask me to come to her when "conditions would be better." After Spring Festival she got in touch, and I visited her. It took roughly one hour to travel to her new neighborhood by underground. When I arrived at the underground station, she saw me and came to greet me. I recognized her only after a few seconds: everything about her had changed except her cheerfulness and wit. She had put on much weight, had cut her hair short, and had adopted a much more casual dressing style. We walked a few hundred meters to reach her place.

Wang Rui explained that we were going to have tea with her mother, who had rented an apartment in the area after Wang Rui had given birth. She described her arrangement: she, her husband, and the baby spent the night at her mother-in-law's; in the morning, her husband would leave for work and she would go to her mother's flat. She and the baby would spend the rest of the day there, until her husband returned from work. This arrangement highlighted the fact that Wang Rui had ended up doing what she had refused to do all along, namely, live with her in-laws. Her mother's presence could provide her not only with child-care help but also with a homey space (removed from her in-laws) where she could spend the day until her husband came back from work between eight and nine o'clock at night.

"So late?" I asked. "He works overtime every day!"

"Yes," she replied. "Nowadays this is common in China. On top of that, he now has a new job."

She proudly added that her husband was now employed in a key sector of the provincial administration, a huge improvement over his previous position. In the meanwhile, we had arrived at her mother's place. As we were walking up the five flights of stairs to get to the apartment, I realized that the climb was challenging for Wang Rui, who was used to staying at home most of the day. As we entered, her mother came to welcome us and led us into the living room. The apartment was pleasant and had a southern exposure; in the living room stood a gigantic wedding picture portraying a smiling Wang Rui in a shimmering white gown and her husband in a tuxedo. Just as I had not been able to identify Wang Rui at the train station, I had a hard time recognizing my friend as the fairy-tale princess smiling from the picture. Wang Rui brought around her baby son, who was half asleep. We played with the baby and looked at uncountable pictures of the young family.

After a couple of hours, Wang Rui and I went to a nearby restaurant for dinner, while her mother stayed at home with the baby. Wang Rui told me how both she and her husband were happy about the arrangement, which, however, looked rather complicated to me. "My relationship with my mother-in-law is not bad (*hai keyi*). And it's good to have my mother around," she said. "Everything else is going well. Because of my husband's new job, we already have a place in one of the best kindergartens in the city. Imagine, almost all the children going to that kindergarten are boys!" As a nurse, Wang Rui was more than aware of the lengths to which people went in order to give birth to a male child. As far as she was concerned, she could read the ultrasound results herself.

Wang Rui's four-month-long maternity leave was coming to an end. She did not at all like the prospect of going back to work in a couple of weeks. I objected that she used to like her job very much; Wang Rui replied that she still did, but she feared that she would not be able to cope with the double burden of working at the hospital and caring for the baby after her shift. Wang Rui was not short of child-care help. On the contrary, it was likely that two sets of grandparents would eventually compete to care for her baby. But her job was taxing, and it was difficult to get a good night's sleep with a baby in the house. In addition, her new home was far from the hospital where she worked. "What happened to the flat you and your husband bought in the city center after marrying?" I asked. She mentioned that they were in the process of selling it, because it was too small for the whole family. She would have had to commute to work and back every day by underground. As we were chatting, her husband called to tell her that he was heading home in his car. They quickly arranged to meet at her mother's place and go together to Wang Rui's mother-in-law's. After dinner, Wang Rui walked me to the underground station and then went back to her mother's to pick up her baby and meet her husband.

NEGOTIATING A SUCCESSFUL MATCH

The problems that Wang Rui and her husband Li Han had to face during the few years preceding and following their marriage are common to large numbers of young people and their families in urban China today. Wang Rui's marriage can be considered a "successful" match: one that combined personal preference and affection with substantial pooling of material resources across families and generations. Despite several moments of crisis, the tensions never led to a breakup between the two young people or the two families or among family members. This was facilitated by a generalized forbearance, in particular on the part of the young couple, but also by more material factors: for example, the fact that both families had similar economic positions and were affluent enough to invest in real estate. Last but not least, Wang Rui had been lucky enough to produce a son relatively quickly after marrying.

Wang Rui and Li Han expended much effort on keeping their parents happy. They postponed their marriage for more than a year, without the absolute certainty that their parents would eventually reach an agreement and give their approval (*and* material support) to the match. In the meanwhile, they engaged in sexual intercourse but concealed it so that their relationship would be seen as respectable in the eyes of their parents. This situation was particularly uncomfortable for Wang Rui: as a woman, she was aware that she was losing ground in the marriage market with the passage of time. While she liked her fiancé enough to hold onto him, she was doing so at her own risk and was aware that she could have looked for someone who would be able to marry her straightaway. In addition, her decision to have sex with her fiancé implied total commitment in her eyes (and in his). If she was wary of losing her virginity to any man, she thought that Li Han was the man whom, sooner or later, she was going to marry. She concealed this situation from her parents, however, because she knew that "they would not approve." If the marriage had not taken place after all, Wang Rui would not have lived up to her own ideas regarding female sexual conduct, let alone those of her parents.

Wang Rui and Li Han put up with this uncomfortable situation for a while, since marrying against their parents' wishes was not an option for either of them. The couple did not have enough money to pay for the ceremony, nor had they saved enough money to qualify for a mortgage. They could have married without celebrating, but in a context in which wedding banquets were the rule, the absence of a proper public celebration would have come across as the most obvious signifier of parental opposition. Wang Rui and Li Han could also have done without buying a flat and rented an apartment for themselves instead so that they could live together after marrying. However, they did not consider this to be a sensible option. Rents in Nanjing were too high to plan a life in rented accommodations. Financially speaking, they both thought that the wisest choice would be to buy a flat. This was what their parents hoped for them and what their friends wanted for themselves as well. The idea of buying a flat in order to have a safe haven for one's new family was part of the "common sense" of middle-class life in Nanjing.[4]

Wang Rui and Li Han agreed on the importance of having a proper celebration and of buying an apartment. In fact, these important expenses were integral parts of "marrying" for both parents and children. For the parents, approving and facilitating their children's marriage perhaps constituted the most important milestone in their practice of care and nurturing (*yang*) (Stafford 2000). By pursuing their parents' approval and support, the children accepted this relationship of *yang*, which was mutual and underlined their implicit obligation to care for their parents in old age. Only through this mutual relationship could parents and children regard themselves as "good parents" and "good children." Notably, after the marriage, Wang Rui's mother moved close to her and helped her with child care. This suggests that Wang Rui, like many other daughters in urban China, will eventually assume the duty of care not only for her parents-in-law but also for her own parents.[5]

A WOMAN WITH A PLAN

Between 2007 and 2011, Wang Rui strategized in order to get what she wanted: a reliable partner and a stable and prosperous family. She made no mystery of the fact that she recognized in Li Han the features that she had very rationally established as the markers of Mr. Right. In turn, before marrying, she constantly adjusted her own deportment in view of the all-important event of marriage. For example, when she was single, Wang Rui was keen on having a full social life in order to multiply her chances of meeting eligible men. As a nurse, she worked day and night shifts, and at times she would join a dinner party, even if this meant cutting down on precious rest and personal time. She did this mainly in the hope of meeting new potential matches. When Wang Rui did meet a man who was of interest to her, she would try to figure out the man's life and outlook as quickly as possible, in order to decide whether or not to pursue the acquaintance. If there was something about the man that did not sound reassuring in terms of marriage prospects, he was rapidly sidelined.

Wang Rui also made clear that marriage was her priority through her sexual conduct. Although she longed for sexual contact well before marriage, she preferred to wait; men might or might not have been able to tell whether or not she was a virgin, but she thought that it was better to play it safe. When she finally met her Mr. Right, she waited to establish a relationship of trust before allowing herself to have full intercourse with him. Even when the couple had a formal arrangement (delayed yet impending marriage), she did not openly admit to her parents that she had lost her virginity to her fiancé. Her parents knew that they had no control over her sexuality, but they preferred not to investigate their daughter's life too carefully. If making a "good" marriage was not always compatible with sexual fulfillment, Wang Rui had her clearly set priorities. Although she thought that her parents' views on premarital sex were limiting, she was not keen on challenging them openly. Large numbers of Chinese women marry at a younger age than Wang Rui did. It is highly educated, affluent women who have to find strategies for maintaining a socially acceptable persona while being unmarried well into their twenties and thirties. While it is generally accepted that young men should experiment and talk about their sexual exploits, young unmarried women have more discreet sex lives, precisely because they "should wait for Mr. Right."

PATRILINY AND PATRIARCHY

Wang Rui's story reveals forms of relatedness that cannot be reduced to a rigid patrilineal system (Stafford 2000). It shows how age, sex, and marital status remain important factors when establishing what kind of person each family member is and what his or her rights and needs are (Moore 1994). While informants often describe relationships of mutual nurturance and support (*yang*) in benevolent terms, these linkages are likely to include conflict and negotiation.[6] During the years in which I was friends with Wang Rui and Li Han, both had to bargain and strategize carefully in order to marry despite their parents' early, unsympathetic stands. Wang Rui held on to her fiancé even though her waiting implied sex-specific risks. As she built her relationships with her parents, parents-in-law, and husband, she invested much emotional and material work, watching her own conduct, pooling her income with her husband and in-laws, changing her professional plans, and adapting to unfavorable living arrangements. Wang Rui's efforts were not acknowledged in any particular way because this was the kind of behavior she was supposed to maintain as a good daughter, wife, and daughter-in-law.

Although Wang Rui's marriage was successful and happy in most respects, she still felt that she had missed out. Before she married, the pressure to find a partner before the age of twenty-six dominated her life. This led her to spend a substantial amount of energy in finding a fiancé and to constantly monitor her conduct. After marriage, she focused on caring for her baby with the help of her mother, who also offered her a space removed from her in-laws' house. Li Han's life, meanwhile, was changing in different directions: focused on a fast-advancing career, he was now spending most of his time out of the house and delegated responsibility for domestic affairs to his wife and his mother. Wang Rui was aware of the fact that her wish to marry and have children clashed with her desire to travel abroad and pursue further training to become a medical doctor. Keeping her job as a nurse was a compromise between her desire to embody the role of caring mother, wife, and daughter-in-law and her wish to pursue further professional and personal development.

By improving his professional position and prospects, Li Han had acquired a higher status in his household: he performed as a filial son toward his parents, who were living with him in a bigger house, as they had wished, and as a good provider to his wife and his son, who was already enjoying the privileges that his father's newly acquired position could offer him. Wang Rui, too, enjoyed a good status in her mother-in-law's house, but this was due mainly to her forbearance facing the ever-changing living arrangements, as well as because she had given birth to a son. While she had invested her own money in the first apartment she had bought with Li Han and pooled her income with the rest of the family members, it was her husband who had clearly become the main breadwinner of the family.

In the past thirty years, Chinese young people and their parents have started to worry about finding jobs, buying houses, and embodying the new middle-class dream of distinction. For many people like Wang Rui and Li Han, in fact, there was an almost complete overlap between the prospect of marrying (and having a child) and that of buying a house. It is thus not surprising that talk about marriage, relationships, and self-worth was repeatedly framed in material and even financial terms (L. Zhang 2010).]

When I first met her, Wang Rui struck me as a confident young woman who loved her job, had an active social life, and enjoyed a good relationship with her family. However, her feelings of self-worth were bound to her perceived likelihood of striking a "good bargain" on the marriage market. The asset she had to offer in this deal—her youth—was rapidly deteriorating. At this stage of her life cycle, Wang Rui was keen on marketing herself as the ideal bride: pretty and smart, but also respectable and committed to building a family. After five years, Wang Rui was a wife and a mother and did not seem to be putting effort into making herself attractive or fashionable. As a prospective bride, Wang Rui felt she had to make herself attractive to men, in particular to those who could be her Mr. Right; as a mother, she had to be a dutiful wife, daughter-in-law, and caregiver for her son. Throughout the years, her own subjectivity and feelings of self-worth appeared to be tightly bound to her reproductive role of wife and mother.

At the beginning of their relationship, Wang Rui's and Li Han's educational and professional status was similar: both were university-educated young people at the beginning of their professional journeys. After their marriage and the birth of their son, however, the division of labor within their household acquired a clearly gendered dimension. Like many other urban, well-off women, Wang Rui had to juggle multiple demands on her time: working outside the household in order to contribute to the family budget (and retain some source of autonomy), caring for her baby, and supporting her husband in his own career. This is the model of the ideal wife sponsored by the current Chinese leadership through official propaganda and continuously re-proposed by market-sponsored family models (Evans 1997). This home-focused middle-class model of wifehood has been compared to the Maoist working wife and mother (Rofel 1999) but should not be read as its simple opposite; different generations of women *continue* to fulfil their roles as daughters and mothers, wives and workers, albeit in ways that are "inscribed with different meanings and possibilities of self-identification and practice" (Evans 2008, 116).

While the young couple had been lucky enough to secure a place for their son in one of the best kindergartens in the city, they still needed someone to support them with babysitting, cooking, and cleaning because of their long working hours. As they had been dependent on their parents in order to marry and buy a house, they were now dependent on them (in particular their mothers) for help with housework and child care. While this situation of interdependence is considered the norm in urban China (Davis-Friedmann 1983; Evans 2008), it was a good reason to keep relations in the larger family as "harmonious" as possible; in turn, the family's ability to negotiate and maintain a "harmonious" appearance certainly benefited the status of all family members within their wider social circles.

The ethnography reported in this chapter indicates clear continuities with Kandiyoti's idea of "patriarchal bargains" (1988, 1998). Wang Rui and Li Han needed the support of the older generation not only in economic terms but also in order to endow their new family with essential moral propriety. Their household, although prosperous and apparently "harmonious," was in reality a site of continuous negotiation. In this context, Wang Rui was not a helpless victim: she had wanted this marriage and she retained some autonomy thanks to her job and the support of her parents. However, it was the birth of her son that endowed her with an increased sense of self-worth and an unprecedented status within the family. The building of this "harmonious family" implied the need for Wang Rui and Li Han to take gradually divergent paths after their marriage; it also prompted Wang Rui to rely on her own mother, which suggests that she will have to care for her, as well as for her in-laws, in the future. Wang Rui and Li Han's "modern" and successful marriage highlights how normative binaries, like the gender dichotomy grounding specific patriarchal bargains, are often reproduced through what can be otherwise perceived as changing social practice.

NOTES

The author thanks Janet Carsten and Deborah Davis for their extended comments on an earlier version of this chapter, as well as Stevan Harrell and Gonçalo Santos for their helpful editorial contribution. Conversations with Elisabeth Engebretsen, Harriet Evans, and Sara Friedman have also contributed to the final version of this chapter.

1   Li Peilin, scholar and theorist of the notion of Harmonious Society, maintains that patriarchy in China came to an end with Liberation, of which women's liberation was part and parcel. According to him, "The early stage of the feminist movement (*nüxingzhuyi yundong*) coincided with the movement

for women's liberation (*funü jiefang*). In the framework of class analysis and of struggle against class oppression, (its) basic proposition was to stress the reform of old institutions, opposing patriarchy (*fuquanzhi*) and the (preferential) right of the husband (*fuquanzhi*). . . . The current feminist movement hopes to go beyond the topic of women's liberation in general and pay more attention to the reform of women's (*nüxing*) social ideal, social mentality, and social consciousness'" (2006, 275). The words *funü* and *nüquanzhuyi* ("woman" and "feminism" in Maoist political discourse) have been replaced by *nüxing* and *nüxingzhuyi*, which are based on the idea of the essential difference of sex/gender.

2   Wang Rui herself jokingly referred to her ideal husband as "Mr. Right" in English. This expression was not uncommon in her milieu.

3   While *kailang* is a positive and politically correct term, *kaifang* simply indicates openness; therefore it can eventually be used to define an excess of openness, for example, in the context of sexual mores.

4   The term "common sense" is used in the Gramscian sense of "the uncritical and largely unconscious way of perceiving and understanding the world that has become 'common' at any given epoch" (Gramsci 1971, 322).

5   Evans 2008; Stafford 2000; Whyte 2003.

6   Croll 2000; Ikels 1990, 1993; Whyte 1997, 2003.

CHAPTER SEVEN

EMERGENT CONJUGAL LOVE, MUTUAL AFFECTION, AND FEMALE MARITAL POWER

WILLIAM JANKOWIAK AND XUAN LI

URBAN China's shift from a world of restrictive social insularity to a more open, fluid, and mobile society is readily apparent in the rampant growth in home ownership, the reemergence of distinctive social classes, and a greater tolerance for privacy and personal idiosyncrasy. Contemporary China is a society teeming with myriad social worlds and alternative, albeit quasi-secret, lifestyles. Research has just begun to explore some of these social worlds, which range from homosexual communities (Kam 2012; Engebretsen 2009, 2014; and chap. 8 in this volume) to migrant families (Shen 2011, 2013), to new rich social classes (Goodman 2008; Osburg 2013), to youth cultures (Kloet 2008). The newly formed micro-universes often include domain-specific values that enhance individuals' self-awareness and heighten their sense of subjectivity.

China's drastic social change has transformed the normative consensus that shapes public discourse, and a new consensus has yet to emerge. There are contradictory and often competing voices, especially pertaining to gender issues that involve romantic relations such as dating and marriage. Whenever the love bond becomes a culture's dominant ideal and preferred practice, patriarchal values that highlighted the superiority of senior men and women over their offspring, and in a more localized context, a husband's preeminence over his wife, can no longer prosper, much less thrive. Current changes show that urban Chinese society is heading in this direction.

In China's Reform era, which started in 1978 in parallel with the beginning of the implementation of the Birth-Planning Policy, members of the single-child generation are encouraged to expand and develop their selves (Fong

146

2007). This value, extended to development of self-respect, protection of dignity, privacy, and individual space, is readily apparent in the domains of courtship/dating and marriage. Among China's youth, the emergent value given to individual expression contributes to undercutting an individual's commitment to the patriarchal expectation that offspring are obligated and subordinated to the larger family's interest.[1]

Urban China's single-child generation, especially its college-educated members, has more or less embraced an "emotionally egalitarian" model of marriage based more on shared empathy and mutual affection than on duty. But an emotionally egalitarian marriage does not mean that men and women perform similar familial roles or have the same emotional life orientations or behavior. In the domain of marriage, however, the presence of a gendered division of labor as well as personality differences does not mean that marital relationships are unequal. Likewise, the presence of mixed, converged, or even reversed sex roles does not imply that a marital relationship is fully egalitarian. In this chapter, the central criterion for equality is the degree of appreciation, admiration, indebtedness, respect, and trust each spouse has for the other. By the definition presented here, an authentic love marriage is based substantially in feelings of fairness, shared esteem, and, ideally, immense mutual appreciation. An emotionally egalitarian marriage is more likely to be built around the "language of love" as opposed to the "language of duty" (Santos, pers. comm., 2014).

This shift to the language of love is apparent in the emergent institution of dating and in the new value placed on formation of a conjugal love union. The new importance placed on creating conjugal love has also altered the ways ordinary men and women think about intimacy and romance and, more fundamentally, how contemporary men perceive women as respected, if not admired, individuals. The desire to create and sustain a love union modifies men's and women's behavior away from detached performance of roles, toward a willingness to create bonds of emotional interdependence and empathic mutuality. Other chapters in this volume explore in more detail the underlying structural inequalities informing the urban shift toward marital relationships based on emotional interdependence and empathic mutuality.[2] Here we are more interested in understanding this emergent cultural schema of marriage than in exposing its contradictions (see Quinn 1996).

First, a word on research methods is in order. William Jankowiak's initial research was conducted in Hohhot, the capital of the Inner Mongolia Autonomous Region, in 1981–83 and again in 1987. In this research, he focused on various aspects of the lives of 75 key families (45 Han, 30

Mongol). This included observing public and semiprivate arenas in which husband and wife interacted, addressed each other, joked with each other (rarely), quarreled, discussed ordinary events, and so forth. He also visited, observed, and interviewed other residents of the city. His 2000–2012 data were obtained through extensive observation of male-female dating interaction, in-depth interviews with 37 married or formerly married men and women, and a 2006 survey that included 34 individuals and a larger 2008 survey that explored thoughts and opinions about love, courtship, and marriage given to 132 individuals between the ages of nineteen and twenty-five. His 2008 survey was supplemented with several group and focus-group discussions concerning what the single-child generation thought made for a positive girlfriend-boyfriend relationship and then what made for a quality marriage. Xuan Li (2014) conducted an extensive 2011–12 Nanjing study of parent-child interaction that included more than 100 families (see also Li and Lamb 2013). Her research focused primarily on parent-child interactions and practices. However, while interviewing parents about their children, she was also able to observe couples' interactions and witnessed their touching, smiling, criticizing, and seeking to positively validate each other in their parental roles. Taken together, we employed a variety of mixed methods that relied on the use of surveys, open-ended semi-structured interviews, and intense active listening in order to document and support our analysis of the historic changes that have taken place in the institutions of Chinese marriage and family.

FROM A COURTSHIP TO A DATING CULTURE: THE PURSUIT OF INTIMACY

The relationship between sex, romance, and companionate love is not always stable or straightforward. These relationships need to be continuously renegotiated within and between the specific partners involved. For example, romantic love and a higher degree of sexual interaction are more typical of the beginning than of the middle phase of a relationship. Further, the love bond always has a social component and thus wears an ethical face. Whatever an individual's personal dilemmas, the negotiations never take place in a vacuum. The intertwinement of love, sex, and ethical issues ensures that a couple's negotiations follow a pattern and are not the simple by-product of an idiosyncratic impulse. In this way, love and sex are as much about ethical considerations as they are about an emotional experience.

The discourse of love and sexual expression has moved out of China's urban shadows and into its commercial arteries. While intimacy and affection were once forbidden in public, they are now the currency by which individuals seek to demonstrate their continuing commitment and mutual involvement. In this new cultural setting, singleton children no longer think marital life should be organized around two individuals meeting the social expectations of desired family life, as manifested by the husband's assertion of authority and the wife's willing obedience, but rather should be based on mutual consideration, spontaneous cooperation, empathy, and shared respect. In pursuit of the "good" marriage under these new standards, urban Chinese have become more concerned with the development of an equal, intimate conjugal unit. The shift in emotional and ethical weight given to conjugal intimacy has contributed to the redefinition of dating as a meaning system and social practice.

Chinese youth today, much like their parents, continue to date and marry for a variety of reasons that range from the desire to gain material and social resources, to the fulfillment of social expectations, to proving self-worth. The conception of love articulated by singleton youth is also similar to that expressed by their parents' generation, which married in the 1980s. For example, a 2008 focus group found that, much like the 1987 Hohhotian focus group, the romantic love experience is characterized by feelings of excitement (e.g., "maddening," "a hot feeling," "crazy feeling," "amazing feeling," "it makes us excited"), empathy ("it makes us happy, it makes us worried"), and exclusivity ("you do not want to share"). Significantly, there is little gender difference in the values men and women associate with being in love. For example, to the question "How do you know you are in love?" posed to a Hohhotian focus group in 1987, young Chinese males responded, "I cannot sleep without her," "I miss her; I think about her constantly," while their female counterparts similarly answered, "You feel a hurt in your heart when he is not around," "He is my only one; without him I cannot live," "Love is determined. I will obey this arrangement till I die."

When Hohhotian youth were asked again in 2000 and 2008 to describe how their experiences and mental processes of love translate into everyday practices in today's China, the interviews found the following comments representative: "You show you care," "You do everything for the person," "You help one another," and "You want your lover to be happy." A twenty-two-year-old female added, "When I feel in love, I want a lot of affection and want to give a lot of affection. It involves simple things like holding hands, sitting close together, snuggling up on the sofa to watch a late night movie. It also means speaking and acting kindly and with respect for each other."

Among the single-child generation, status symbols and material accomplishments do attract attention and garner women's potential interest, but they cannot in and of themselves compel anyone to cherish, reflect upon, or value another. In short, a man's material wealth can command female interest, but not love (Osburg 2013). A 2014 survey of 151 college participants (114 females and 37 males) at Fudan University found around 70 percent of males and females agreeing that romantic love can last forever. Thus marriage, for the single-child generation, is not viewed as the tomb of love but rather as a lifetime arena in which previously established romance would be sustained or even flourish (Jankowiak et al. 2015). However, the new cultural understanding and expectation that the ideal marital relationship is based on mutual love require both parties to make a strong commitment that often goes beyond (even significant) material manifestations. Power, tradition, and force hold a minor place in the domain of love. Instead, the desire to form a love bond softens men's attitude and behavior toward the women they want. Women, who would have had their voices silenced and agency denied in a conservative patriarchal society, can now more easily control the pace, frequency, and degree of relationship intimacy, especially in a dating relationship's early phase.

Such transformations give dating and marriage in today's China a strikingly different configuration from that of the courtship culture that dominated China as recently as the 1980s. China's courtship culture at that time was based on established semi-ritualistic transactions linked to individuals getting to know each other en route to marriage (Bogel 2001). Unlike rural Spain in the 1960s, where courtship practices were chaperoned and organized around double-standard ethics that allowed males greater freedom of behavior within the courtship ritual (Collier 1997), courtship culture in urban China was less asymmetrical. Chinese women did not have to grant sexual access if they did not want to. Instead, throughout the 1980s, neither gender had greater freedom. Men were also constrained by courtship norms and wider conceptions of decency (Jankowiak 1993, chap. 7). For example, if a man got a reputation as a philanderer or was simply known to have had a few previous "girlfriends," his reputation as a virtuous and steadfast fellow would be damaged and his prospects for marrying a woman of good repute were ruined. Consequently, men and women strove equally to be reserved or at least discreet about their personal involvements. The strong ethos of emotional/sexual chastity was a powerful incentive, and it resulted in restraining personal behavior and lowering expectations of sexual experimentation and intimacy.

Dating in today's culture, in contrast, is less about finding a life partner and more about finding personal enjoyment and satisfaction. Practical concerns remain central when it comes to marital choices (see Zavoretti, chap. 6, and Obendiek, chap. 3), but dating, which is often organized around issues of practicality, is now talked about primarily in terms of feelings and emotions. There remain some reservations about talking openly about sexual matters (see Zavoretti, chap. 6), but these reservations are no longer as strong as in earlier times. Unlike the informal or secret meetings common to the socialist work unit era, contemporary dating is conducted explicitly and publicly. It is flaunted more than denied. For example, when a high school student was asked in 2008 if her male companion was a classmate (*tongxue*), she burst out, "No! We are lovers." In this way, dating, with its embrace of love and its creation of interpersonal intimacy, constitutes a profound transformation in the dominant structure of intergenerational authority away from the senior generation's desire to control the sexuality of its youth and in favor of the junior generation's determination, albeit not always successful, to overcome their parents' suggestions.

The social transformation in the meaning and value placed on being a couple has resulted in a cognitive shift away from the preference for homosocial circles to an increased focus on closer heterosexual intimacy. China's new value orientation is readily apparent and visible on Chinese city streets. For example, of well over a thousand couples observed walking together in public in 1987, only four couples around the Inner Mongolia University neighborhood were holding hands during an evening stroll. By contrast, in 2000 and then again in 2008, more than half of all couples observed held hands while walking down a street.

What is particularly significant is the change in the use of public behavior as a means of signaling intimacy. It has changed from a "wall between us," whereby male and female tended to demonstrate, especially in public, disinterest in the opposite sex, to a "wall around us," whereby couples use the indifferent gaze of the public as a way of signaling their exclusive union to each other. Young couples in urban China, much like young American couples, use the public arena to exclude others and make "an open declaration of unity," thereby expressing mutual concern to each other (Weitman 1973). In Reform era China, most couples prefer to form autonomous islands of egalitarian informed privacy. Here, intense intimacy and emotional egalitarianism fuel each other and jointly characterize the dating culture in today's China.

CONJUGAL LOVE: INTIMACY VERSUS DUTY

Reform era Chinese youth's increasing awareness of the importance of marital intimacy is due, in part, to the greater acceptance of individualism. Robert

Bellah et al. (1985) believe the arrival of an individualistic ethos in the United States resulted in the release of people from repressive institutions. No longer having to organize married life around the demands, expectations, and responsibilities derived from living in an extended family, Chinese husbands and wives today become more focused on the development of their own conjugal units (Dong and Xie 2013). Although intergenerational exchange retains a significant role in the life of the nuclear family, such transactions are no longer prioritized as they were in previous eras, especially given the changing living arrangements that release young couples from the constraints of living in larger families (Santos, pers. comm., 2014).

Longitudinal interviews and observations of couples interacting in the 1980s in Hohhot and in the aughts of the present century in Hohhot, Shanghai, Chengdu, Nanjing, and Beijing found that a cultural shift had taken place in Chinese society whereby one model of marital relations had bifurcated into two prevalent forms: the "dutiful spouse" model (prevalent among people born between the 1960s and 1977) and the "emotionally involved" model (prevalent among younger people born after 1978). Each model is organized around different assumptions about the meaning, value, and behavior expected in the making of a "good" marriage. The "dutiful spouse" model, grounded in the ordinary life of family practicalities and explicit duties, stresses the diligent and responsible fulfillment of family duties by both spouses and, when necessary, an accepted sexual division of labor. While a "dutiful spouse" marriage can begin as "pure love," it must be transformed by other, more pressing pragmatic concerns such as career demands, housework requirements, care duties, and the schooling of offspring. Post-marital interaction quickly becomes perfunctory, with value given to harmonious, albeit task-oriented interaction. Chinese spouses, like those in 1950s British working-class marriages (Bott 1957), go on to live parallel lives and associate mostly with same-sex friends.

Family responsibilities are still recognized for their loving and caring connotation, of course, even in the Reform era. In the aughts, men of the single-child generation continue to believe, as they did in the 1980s, that it is their responsibility and not their wives' to achieve promotions, increase household income, and expand personal connections. It is an obligation and expectation that men find demanding and take seriously. Failure to perform satisfactorily often results in a wife's complaint that her husband "let the family down," a complaint that a man does not want to hear for its power in denying his success as a family man. Males acknowledge that fulfilling that role in the setting of the newly competitive economy, in which work is essential and often exhausting, places more pressure on them. It was repeatedly stressed to us that men are obligated to find good jobs, buy apartments, and support their families financially, if not emotionally as well. Out of 122 male and female Hohhotians surveyed in 2008, 115 readily concurred with the statement that while young married women in their thirties struggle to stay on top of everyday events at work and in the family, "men have more pressure (*yali*) than women."

In accordance with their husbands' conscious striving to fulfill their responsibilities as the man in the family, women are acutely aware that a happy family requires, in the words of one young woman, "two people who want to cooperate and have a life together." Chinese women in the "dutiful spouse" model willingly take on their share by covering the "backstage" work at home to support their spouses. "I want to be a good wife who is a good mother too. I am loyal, devoted to making the family a greater good." A thirty-four-year-old divorced woman described how she tried to help her former husband: "I tried to help my husband and make him secure. . . . I knew he worried about money and tried to suggest ways of getting money or saving some of it." Several women readily admitted what one woman noted, that "behind every successful man is a woman who worries about and supports him."

The dutiful marital model does not necessarily seem to have produced much marital satisfaction, even for those who grew up with the "dutiful spouse" model. A fifty-year-old female who had embraced the dutiful wife role readily admitted, "In my generation, few couples are happy or satisfied. Younger people can select a spouse, and more of them appear happy. Our marriages were arranged, and we did not have a helpful understanding of each other. In time, we grew into indifference." Yet this model is not necessarily hostile or fragile. A thirty-two-year-old male stressed the value placed on familial-role responsibility when he noted: "A wife is linked with family, and there is mutuality, and it is hard to let that go. A lover, on the other hand, has no reason to be with you other than that she loves you. The wife is more complicated. . . . You have responsibilities for family concerns." After a lengthy pause, he added: "My wife should love me, but I should return the love too." Such "concerns" are what tie the family together even when feelings fade, as a fifty-three-year-old woman worded it: "Chinese women seldom divorce for love. They will stick with their family responsibilities."

By contrast, the "emotionally involved" model is more often a result of free, spontaneous, and mutual attraction independent of much external intervention. In this model, the husband and wife prefer to define themselves as socially interconnected and, ideally, intensely emotionally intertwined. Partners use marital strategies similar to those Sandy To (2015), in her typology of women's mate selection, calls "satisficers," women look-ing for egalitarian men despite their compromised socioeconomic status, and "innovators," women looking for nontraditional, emotionally fulfilling relationship forms outside marriage. Family responsibility and role perfor-mance are both valued, as in the "dutiful spouse" model, but there is also an explicitly articulated idea that husband and wife should have conversational intimacy and that both should enjoy and contribute to the warm feelings of being together and the closeness in the marital relationship. The closer, more intimate marital bond is valued in present-day China, at least as an abstract ideal, and love or connection in coupledom has now become a posi-tive criterion for forming and remaining in a relationship. A 2010–13 survey of 110 Shanghai college students found that 93, or 86 percent, considered love an essential quality for a good marriage. This is in stark contrast to a 1983 survey that found love absent from most people's list of criteria for mate selection (Jankowiak 1993). For today's younger generation, marital life is no longer organized around a husband's willingness to provide and a wife's willingness to be obedient to her husband and senior in-laws; instead it is based on shared empathy and mutual respect, alongside other recipro-cal processes such as consideration, cooperation, and compromise. In the words of a twenty-seven-year-old female, the small, conjugal family should be "the best place to relax" and "a warm place to be."

Many respondents vividly depicted their ideal of an emotionally defined "good marriage." A twenty-six-year-old woman admitted that a "good mar-riage is based in harmony. When we are together, I hope we have many good times, such as cuddling up to go to sleep, holding hands while watching the sunrise and sunset, chasing each other on the beach, walking beside riv-ers, watching TV and movies together. Love needs tolerance, understand-ing, and trust. We need not promise each other too much—our behavior will prove that what we feel is true love." Her loving sentiment is echoed in a twenty-two-year-old Tianjin woman's elaboration on the qualities of a good marriage. She acknowledged that a good marriage involved "being polite, respectful, and considerate. These values are essential for sustaining every marriage." She further noted that couples often refer to this as "being respectful to each other because both are guests." For the most part, men shared a similar expectation of the ideal marriage. For example, a forty-two-year-old college-educated man told me that, "after marriage, you should eat together, go to the movies together, and always strive to be an ideal couple."[3]

Under the halo of intimacy, however, equality and independence must be ensured. Couples understand that they will need a certain amount of privacy and their own space in order to accomplish different things. This will produce a boundary between husband and wife as each person lives in separate, albeit overlapping, spheres. A twenty-three-year-old female acknowledged that "we will have nice moments together, but I will not be controlled by the person I love, . . . and yet I know I am also a submissive woman. I will sacrifice everything for him. I will make a full commitment to him. I will believe in and trust him." When asked if she was a genuine (*zhen*) submissive, she smiled and stressed that "there are limits to what I will tolerate." Her qualification is significant. The word *sacrifice* is a metaphor for the value she places on the importance not only of family harmony but also of emotional unity. Unstated is the expectation that her husband has similar values and will also reciprocate emotionally. Another female seconded this and acknowledged what may have been wrong with her first marriage: "I spoiled my husband and made him very comfortable being with me, and he stopped reciprocating. This was a mistake. A husband must appreciate his wife's actions and be willing to reciprocate. He too must be willing to dedicate his life to the family and be a responsible husband and father." Cooperation and mutuality are not only expected in the everyday life of a couple but also deemed essential.

As in many Western marriages, the features of the two types of marriage are not mutually exclusive, and one type often transforms into the other over time. Sometimes, an aloof, albeit dutiful, marriage blossoms into an emotionally interdependent marriage. Other times, a solid intimate marriage can gradually slip into a dutiful, albeit aloof, marriage (see Zavoretti, chap. 6). For example, in 2006, a fifty-two-year-old woman reminded Jankowiak, "If you remember, at the beginning of our [1980s] marriage, my husband and I did not get along. We were indifferent to each other. Now we are closer. *He has adjusted*" (emphasis added). She notes, however, that this transformation is unusual, though not impossible. In reverse, those who cherish the initial phase of their "love" marriage need to make tremendous efforts to maintain and revive their marital intimacy. One example comes from a twenty-eight-year-old woman who had been married almost three years. When asked if her marriage was closer now than it had been, she immediately answered in the affirmative, although she admitted that this is not always the case among her married friends. When asked why her marriage was different, she stressed that she and her husband made plans to do things together over the weekend, while her friends did not. She thought that planning how to rejuvenate their marriage bond contributed to making their marriage stronger. Her intuitive sense of how to forge closer emotional bonds is consistent with Jankowiak's 2000–2008 observations of marriages in the singleton generation and those in their parents' generation: Couples who plan things together and maintain habits formed during courtship seem to have the more satisfying marriages. Those who expect that the marital bond "will [naturally] grow and grow" and focus solely on their careers or friends, thereby "letting the marriage take care of itself," often drift apart. In these instances, Jankowiak's urban investigations in the aughts found that some men and women sought emotional satisfaction with lovers instead of with their aloof spouses (for a similar pattern among Shanghai middle-aged couples, see Farrer and Sun 2003).

MARITAL COMMUNICATION: THE TRANSFORMATION OF FEMALE MARITAL POWER

Though the Chinese family, much like the Mexican family, is considered by some to be among the most conservative of social institutions and the last refuge of male authority, we found, like Matthew Guttman (1996), that "it is not easy to dismiss what takes place between wives and husbands . . . as the simple exercise of male prestige and power" (256). In China, the benchmark of "good" relationships has drifted away from fulfilling the demands, expectations, and responsibilities involved in living in an extended family to a dyadic relationship in which males and females, as individual agents, jointly construct mutually cooperative bonds based on respect and admiration, if not also in profound love. In this setting, men are much less successful at controlling their spouses, while women, by effectively using closeness and intimacy as bargaining power, are obtaining increasing power in the marital bond. For example, in 2008, a group of middle-aged married men spontaneously discussed how their wives "make a fuss over nothing" (*mei shi zhao shi*) and why women "got angry so quickly" but could not quite figure out what caused the, from their perspective, unexpected outburst.

A possible explanation may arise from most Chinese women's demonstrative involvement and thus willingness to undertake emotional labor that is oriented toward the management of their marriage (Duncombe and Marsden 1993). This particular mind-set requires, at least from a woman's perspective, constant effort, attention, and verbal presence. In highly satisfying marriages, women strive to keep their husbands involved in the marriage. They are the de facto managers of family emotional life. At the same time, women often strategically withdraw their attention and focused concern in order to draw their male partners' involvement. This behavioral style is especially evident during the dating period (yet less so in the marital arena when the husband's commitment is more or less ensured). For example, when couples quarrel, a common strategy is for wives to withdraw emotionally and not respond to their husbands' words or gestures. A Hohhotian husband acknowledged that whenever his wife misses him and does not want him to leave, she looks at him with pleading eyes. Although he insisted this did not happen often, whenever it does, "I must cancel my outing and spend time with her." In another instance, a young Hohhotian wife, upon learning of her husband's affair with a masseuse, immediately moved out of the apartment and did not return until her husband (almost in tears) begged her to return. Another effective response is to threaten divorce whenever there is a quarrel, which, depending on whether her husband loves her or not, may be effective in changing his negative behavior. Still another is to accuse the husband in a fit of anger of "not truly loving" her, which, in one instance, caused the husband to plead that he, "unlike other husbands, gives her his yearly bonus" (thus demonstrating his commitment to her and the family).

While Chinese youth continue to place weight on material factors as important mate selection criteria, they also put a high value on joint activities, shared feelings, empathy, and mutual trust; this is especially true among those in the urban, college-educated stratum. According to Marshall (2008), true intimacy thrives only when spouses have developed either quiet or explicit empathy for each other's feelings. Because the close romantic bond builds on patient, attentive listening to the other's concerns and unconstrained, effective expression of feelings to the other, the development of reciprocal couple intimacy is difficult, if not impossible, in the context of the asymmetrical relational model associated with classic patriarchal family organizations. In effect, true love implies emotional equity and does not accept total control by one over the other or dominance by one party.

The gradual transformation of marriage into a zone of vibrant conjugal union has given more weight and importance to the expression of interpersonal subjectivity. Our observations of dating couples' interactions found, in accordance, that while those who got married during the socialist era still cherish affection that is quietly transmitted under mutual consensus, members of the single-child generation are more comfortable and willing to openly communicate their feelings within a relationship context. A forty-three-year-old divorced woman told Jankowiak the following story about a friend who married twice. Her friend was twenty-four years old when she first married. Her husband, a hotel manager, was romantic: he always expressed his love in words, took her out to dinner, or sent her flowers. But when he was home, he refused to do housework. He always made a mess and never cleaned it up. She divorced him, as she could not stand living with him anymore. Three years later, she remarried and is happy. Her husband is so sweet; he seldom takes her out for dinner, but he cooks for her. The informant then asked rhetorically which husband loved her more. For this forty-three-old-woman, her friend's second marriage was better because of her husband's dedication, consideration, and commitment, which is not verbally transmitted but demonstrated by alternative means. In contrast, a thirty-three-year-old woman, while acknowledging that in a "Chinese marriage, responsibilities and duty are important," articulated her hope that "[her] future husband knows how to express his love to [her] either with words or actions." Similarly, a thirty-five-year-old woman expressed her idea of a perfect marriage by acknowledging the importance of her expression of devotion to her husband: "I will show my husband warmth and joy so we can live a common life together as one." Confirming this, most Hohhotian female participants in the 2006 survey (N=37 out of 44) responded positively to the question "Is it important for a husband to express love (i.e., communicate) to his wife?" It is college-educated women's heightened expectations of good marriages that make them the primary agents in the push to transform the meaning and performance of conjugal intimacy.

The change in the meaning of marriage and family life is seen in the way Chinese women embrace what Francesca Cancian (1985) refers to as a "feminization" of love ethos that yearns for more intense and frequent expression of emotional intimacy. When marriage was defined as performance of familial and marital roles, a male's emotionally reserved posture was tolerated. In Reform era China, where men no longer have institutionalized authority to advance their interests (Palmer 2007), they must, often out of self-interest, strive to please their wives by altering their conduct to meet their wives' expectations. Like contemporary Japanese women, single women in Reform era China who are no longer satisfied with the dutiful spouse role expect men to change (Mathews 2014). Many college-educated women, having taken the step themselves, insist that their husbands engage or try to engage in more frequent verbal intimacy. For example, a forty-six-year-old woman aptly summarized the opinion of the majority of mature women interviewed in acknowledging that "all humans have love in their hearts. The difference is that some would like to use words to express their love, while others use another way to express love. I think nowadays most Chinese prefer to express their feelings and talk about their love. As for me, I prefer to speak to my husband and show my feelings. Love comes from both of us, and we need to show our feelings." When men refuse to change, women are increasingly using divorce as a means of sanctioning male behavior. In this way, women are not only redefining the standards for good marriages but also actively shaping men's notions of how to be a man through their mate selection decisions and justifications for changes in relationship status.

The changes are not as fast as expected, however. Many urban Chinese young men continue to find comfort in the replication of their fathers' more reserved, albeit responsible, action-oriented, verbally nonexpressive role in the family. For example, female college students admitted that "we tell our boyfriends we love them, but they are reluctant to tell us." A fifty-three-year-old man seconded her opinion and pointed out, "In China, people express their feelings differently. Maybe the woman will say she loves her husband, but men prefer to express themselves through actions and not words." Throughout the aughts, the frequency with which married working-class (twenty out of thirty-six) and college-educated men (twenty-three out of thirty-one) voiced their marital angst and, more explicitly, their disappointments suggests that they feel more ambivalent and less secure about their position within the family and society than in former times. Significantly, many men admitted they often quarreled with their spouses despite the unpleasantness this caused. Based on interviews, we suspect that most people in China's middle generation (forty to sixty years of age) are uncomfortable discussing emotional issues, and that for many, quarreling is a final effort to establish some sort of emotional exchange in an at best bearable living arrangement so as to avoid complete detachment and divorce.

Nevertheless, the cultural shifts currently taking place have had a corresponding impact on urban Chinese men's conceptions of themselves as husbands and fathers. Some men detected these changes in the urban Chinese social landscape. A thirty-four-year-old professional commenting on his marriage, which everyone considered to be a good one, noted, "I want an interesting wife and not a boring dutiful wife. Thus my wife has a strong personality and is interesting to talk to. I want this. However, we often quarrel about the amount of time I have to spend with her. So we discussed my work schedule. I agreed to be home for dinner twice a week and do things with her over the weekend. However, there is reality, and thus my professional job requires that I work till midnight, and I cannot come home earlier." Here, while admitting that his job usually stands in the way of realizing these plans, this interviewee's intention reflects transitions in the marriage culture among men, which involve greater respect for their female partners and an increased yearning for their lovers' attention.

Still, there are class differences among men (but not so stark among women). Working-class men interviewed in both the 1980s and the aughts appeared to be more defensive than college-educated men: they were more adamant in appealing to conventional sex role norms and were reluctant to alter their style of conjugal interaction. Jankowiak found during his 1980s and aughts interviews that seven out of twenty-eight working-class men in the 1980s, and twelve out of thirty-six working-class men in the aughts were overtly responsive to their wives' requests. In contrast, both Li and Jankowiak found that urban college-educated men are more comfortable with open discussions with wives about everyday arrangements and (when professional schedules allow) are more likely to spend more time with their families. Our observations and findings are consistent with research that found that college-educated men are quicker than working-class men to give women equal authority and play the "partner" role (McLanahan et al. 2002). In contrast, working-class men continue to favor the dutiful spouse role. For them, compromise implies the inability to achieve mastery of their social role. In the face of their wives' obvious disappointment, it was not uncommon for some men to insist that "they did other things for their wives" and that it was inconvenient of their wives to demand that they cease "having fun."

Unlike men from the socialist *danwei* (work unit) era, who felt largely secure about their positions in dealing with their female partners, Reform era men are often confused about their exact behavioral norms as good boyfriends and husbands and are equally puzzled by females' visible frustration when they fail to conform to these expectations. It is perhaps because of the variance in the extent and pace of Chinese men's change in emotional expression in marital life that Chinese women have emerged as the "emotional managers" in the family. For example, whereas a woman prefers to speak softly on a date, once married she is likely to shout commands at both her child and her husband. In the 1980s, a male worker of mild temperament, accustomed to listening to his wife issue pronouncements, matter-of-factly said, "Women shout a lot. It's their way. We just have to accept it." His perception of being marginalized within the family is representative of the period and has not changed. Several rounds of interviews in different Chinese cities in the aughts suggest that men continue to feel at times that their spouses are hypercritical, while many realize that their wives are devoted to them and, if the marriage continues to be based on affection, appreciate the role women assume in emotionally managing the family as well as promoting their self-confidence. A fifty-four-year-old male admitted, "I appreciate my wife's participation in my affairs. It can be a pain at times, but not having her would be worse." He added, "Life is more interesting with her involvement."

In the sociocultural milieu of Reform era China, in which neolocal marriages dominate, the direction of dependence in marital relationships is no longer clear: while men still enjoy advantages in financial and social resources in marriage, couples who are united by love bonds are usually emotionally dependent on each other. Thus, Chinese males, compared to their fathers and grandfathers, are more willing to strive to meet their wives' needs and expectations (Cancian 1985, 96). The increased weight given to the romantic love bond has contributed to wives' ability to better influence, manage, and, at times, control their marriages.

• ◆ •

Throughout the 1980s, most middle-aged Hohhotian couples endured more than loved each other and maintained rather than enjoyed their marriages. By contrast, the singleton generation is strongly inclined to form emotionally based, affectionate marital relationships. In present-day China, young men and women are more intertwined with each other's lives than they are often willing to acknowledge, and readier than previous generations to voice their need for emotional intimacy. Chinese males and females of the singleton generation now typically use their adolescence and early adulthood— if not also later life stages—as a dating period during which they seek to understand themselves and explore their own rules for closeness, intimacy, and companionship.

The shift in the meaning of Chinese marriage away from a role-performance institution and toward an affectionate union has also undercut many, but not all, of China's lingering patriarchal values and ideologically charged sentiments. Most singleton men no longer believe that men, as a social category, are the "intellectually superior gender," nor do most men prefer or expect to marry obedient wives (Jankowiak and Li 2014; Ding and Xu 2015,71). In this new cultural milieu, the reciprocal nature of intimacy has granted both sexes, but particularly women, control over the quality and progress of romantic relationships. More than before, men need to make an effort, and sometimes must plead. The increased value given to the formation of a love marriage has also contributed to the alteration of the power dynamics in China's intergenerational relations that resulted in the breakdown of wider family arrangements, including but not restricted to the relationship between the mother-in-law and daughter-in-law. The wife's new source of power—her husband's desire to form a love bond— has enabled her to renegotiate the marital obligations customarily owed to her mother in-law.

Today's college-educated urbanites in China view adulthood less as a series of social accomplishments (e.g., marriage and parenthood) and more as a process of becoming emotionally responsible to one's self. This changed view brings new challenges, however, not least the difficulty of creating the conditions necessary to sustain marital intimacy while engaged in intense work schedules and other "default" family duties such as parenthood and elder care. Women and men can become impatient, anxious, and, at times, angry, at the shift in cultural norms, making it difficult to interpret the other's intentions. This new ethical and emotional environment leads some women and men to delay marriage, as their needs can easily be satisfied in alternative social arenas. This poses something of a paradox: On the one hand, both genders have benefited from the opportunity to explore their inner lives and perhaps achieve a deeper sense of fulfillment. On the other hand, they may also remain anxious about their inability to find suitable mates who can fulfill their ideas of "what makes life worth living." Their search for life partners who are also ideal soul mates is based on a strong cultural fantasy that is constantly articulated in women's and some men's public and private conversations but is less often realized. For China's single-child generation, the marital ideals and relationship values common to their parents' generation can no longer thrive, and what remains instead is a tangled web of alternative paths that are often at odds. In this setting, individuals are more or less on their own in their effort to find life satisfaction in a culture that is no longer sure of itself.

NOTES

We acknowledge the following people for support, assistance, and inspiration: Gonçalo Santos, Stevan Harrell, Gordon Mathews, Robert Moore, Tom Paladino, Peter Gray, Alice Schlegel, Shen Yifei, and Yuezhu Sun.

1   This does not mean that the needs and expectations of parents are not taken into consideration. They often are. In order to understand the strength of parents' authority over their offspring's mate selection, Jankowiak (2000) queried youth as to whether they had a previous boyfriend or girlfriend. If they answered in the affirmative, he asked them to provide an explanation for the breakup. Through these explanations, he discovered that, in contrast to the 1980s, when no one abandoned a boyfriend or girlfriend because of a parental objection, more females (n=27) than males (n=5) admitted to breaking off an intimate relationship due to their mothers' relentless negativity.

2   See Zavoretti, chapter 6; Engebretsen, chapter 8; Evans, chapter 9; and Gottschang, chapter 11.

3   Zavoretti (chap. 6) discusses how a couple also embraced the intimate marriage ideal before gradually shifting into something like a dutiful marriage.

CHAPTER EIGHT

UNDER PRESSURE

Lesbian-Gay Contract Marriages and Their Patriarchal Bargains

ELISABETH L. ENGEBRETSEN

> Contract marriage is a way for lesbians [*lala*] and gays to resist the
> marriage pressure from society and family. It is premised on a non-
> sexual relationship and intends to maintain both partners' economic,
> physical, and personal independence in the guise of a husband-and-
> wife relationship.
>
> —EDITORIAL, *LES+*

IN a society in which marriage remains a universal imperative, finding viable coping strategies for the pressure to marry is one of the most
important challenges that Chinese lesbians and gays face.[1] Providing
information and support is therefore a priority task of lesbian/gay activist
groups and a hot topic in lesbian/gay online chat rooms as well as in offline
communities. In this context, *xingshi hunyin* (henceforth *xinghun*), or contract marriage between a lesbian and a gay man, has become a popular strategy—at least in principle if not always in practice—because it appears to
conform to hetero-marital norms but in reality aims to allow for "both partners' economic, physical, and personal independence."[2] In principle, *xinghun* seeks to *resolve* intense marriage pressure by faking marriage. Indeed, it
is often termed *jiahun* (fake marriage) because, ideally, these marriages are
pro forma agreements with little or no marital implication beyond public
recognition of what appears to be a hetero-marriage. In short, a *xinghun*
arrangement seeks to perform compliance with the social and familial order

by faking marriage and therefore requires strict, ongoing compartmental-ization between a secret (or tacitly open) lesbian/gay personal life and the heteronormative social facade. This balancing act is difficult to maintain successfully over time.

In China, as elsewhere, marriage is certain to raise conflicting emotions and views in the context of sexual and gender minorities. The ideal of same-sex marriage equality has become enormously influential globally, marking the advancement of progressive modernity and liberal democracy (Sanders 2012). Chinese lesbians and gays—especially activist networks—also par-take in this globally traveling rhetoric of marriage equality (Hildebrandt 2011; Kong 2011). But most lesbians and gays consider *xinghun* a better and more appropriate strategy, because it is seen as an ideal compromise between personal desire and social and family duty. The most common practice, however, remains heterosexual marriage, whether it be in terms of giving up one's lesbian/gay life altogether or attempting to balance nor-mative married life with a secret lesbian/gay life on the side. Recent media and activist attention to the plight of the "wives of gay men," or *tongqi*, has clarified that the universal marriage pressure leads to casualties regardless of sexual orientation and gender (Yiu 2012).

This chapter discusses urban, college-educated lesbians' and gays' negotia-tions of marriage pressure by offering selected *xinghun* narratives and media discourse.[3] Why do so many women and men with same-sex desires find *xing-hun* to be an ideal arrangement at a time when emerging individualism and modern social values, inspired by global flows of culture and politics, may seem to have allowed for greater autonomy and choice in personal lifestyle (see Jankowiak and Li, chap. 7)? It details how some Beijing-based lesbians and gays negotiate and experience *xinghun*, demonstrating that structural pres-sures remain omnipresent, and teasing apart the complex factors that shape individual practices in this regard. Thereby, "the event of *xinghun*" is shown to straddle multiple, often paradoxical, conflicting desires—the felt desire to be normal, to conform to (hetero)normative social duties, at least on the sur-face—and crosses regulatory axes of sexuality, gender, generation, and class. In general, married status carries social and familial recognition that is other-wise unattainable; remaining single carries deep social stigma (see Zavoretti, chap. 6). Despite the intention to solve an existential dilemma and balance competing relational desires and expectations, the *xinghun* strategy, rather than resolving marriage pressure, generates post-wedding complications that reaffirm the dominance of the heteronormative family as society's basic moral and social unit. As with South Korean contract marriages, conformist pres-sures to marry dominate lesbian and gay lives to the extent that *xinghun* often becomes a social reality due to the coercive power of hegemonic cultural ideologies and practices, often defined as patriarchy (Cho 2009, 413). This chapter complements this research as well as many of the careful analyses included in this volume (see Evans, chap. 9, and Zavoretti, chap. 6). It is also a skeptical response to the oft-made argument that the emergent egalitarianism of romantic intentions and personal agency now offset and even sideline "traditional" socio-familial and state-sponsored policy-driven imperatives in ways that are good for women (see Yan 2009 for a fuller analysis of China's complex path toward individualization).

Although *xinghun* puts women at particular disadvantage—risking their hard-earned personal autonomy upon entering marriage—due to the privilege afforded men and husbands within this social system, it is important to keep in mind that patriarchy is not simply an ideology of male dominance over women and structural devaluation of all things feminine. In order to adequately account for why and how lesbians and gays experience pressure to conform and their desire to comply strategically, it is necessary to focus on intersecting systems of oppression in which gender, sexuality, generational cohort (age), and socioeconomic class are central factors. This broader definition, keenly inspired by feminist insights (e.g., Patil 2013; Valentine 2007), troubles simplistic assumptions regarding gender and sexual oppression or liberation and attends instead to the specifics of contemporary regimes of normalization and social control. This perspective, moreover, highlights the connections between multiple systems of oppression—including traditional patriarchal values and how they transform and converge with late capitalist and globally circulating systems of inequality and difference—while also identifying alternative political interventions that challenge systemic forms of hegemonic power (Valentine 2007).

Chinese social norms still emphasize family duty and respectability above all else; individuals are defined according to the social recognition of their status roles and their assumption of appropriate responsibilities therein; the corresponding imperative toward marriage and childbirth is unavoidable for anyone regardless of gender or sexuality. The broader context of patriarchal regimes of normalization and differentiation deters openly lived homosexuality and women's equality, devalues the integrity of any public or social claim to lesbian/gay existence and equality, and stresses the superior integrity of the public realm and social imperatives that value stability, conformity, and harmony in order to build the Chinese dream of progressive modernity and global power.

Finally, an engaged ethnographic exploration of *xinghun* contributes to our understanding of the rapid changes to China's family and kinship practices by demonstrating that marriage involves the concerns of not just the two spouses but also the different generations in both sets of families. In this sense, marriage becomes an affair of not just two but (at least) six people, straddling at least two generations, or oftentimes three, all of whom define propriety and values quite differently. Recognizing the variegated, intersecting levels of this problematic is key to understanding, for example, the psychological power of the older generations to pressure reluctant, well-educated women to go along with conjugal pressures, or why postmillennial cosmopolitan gay men highlight a desire for very traditional gender ideals when advertising for lesbian "spouses" online. Adding to existing literature that has examined these emerging family dynamics (Brandtstädter and Santos 2009; Evans 2008), a focus on *xinghun* tactics problematizes underlying heteronormativity and compulsory heterosexuality—not only in Chinese society but also in much anthropological scholarship on contemporary Chinese society.

CONTRACTING MARRIAGE: PEIJING'S STORY

We begin with an account of one woman's deliberations over available marriage options, her reluctant choice to engage in *xinghun*, and the ways in which complex social and family duties influenced this choice. This account brings out the diverse ways in which normative pressures and conventional desires shape the subjective experiences of choice and compliance, and why *xinghun* emerges as the best strategy. It further complicates simplistic notions of choice, agency, normativity and patriarchal oppression, because factors related to gender, sexuality, class, and age are complex and shifting in intricate ways.

Peijing was twenty-nine years old, university-educated, and employed by a large company in downtown Beijing.[4] Her family, including a younger, married sister, was from a provincial town outside Beijing where they still lived. Peijing was by now an expert at putting off introductions and arranged dates with men. She would change the subject when family and colleagues brought up marriage in conversations and play "stupid" on dates to discourage a man's interest. Her sister had married young, but Peijing was approaching thirty and did not even have a boyfriend. Now parents and relatives were asking increasingly direct questions about why she was still single. For years, Peijing had struggled to create an independent life for herself, making use of the educational and career-related opportunities available to women to advance their status outside the family realm. However, she felt intensely guilty about disappointing her parents and not meeting social expectations, and exceedingly frustrated about both. In our conversations, she expressed a strong dissatisfaction with the life expected of her and struggled with the pressures closing in on her from all sides. Sometimes she thought about marrying conventionally, just to give herself a comfortable life and to "reduce pressure." This resembled what many other lesbians would say; they were "tired to death" (*leisi le*) of hiding, pretending, resisting the pressure— "I can't take it anymore!" (Wo shoubuliao!). At the same time, Peijing acknowledged that this pressure was not just externally imposed (social), but also, she wrote in a chat conversation, "sometimes from my own heart. . . . It is natural that I hope to have a family and children." She often spoke of her deep desire for a child and worried that the only way to raise a child was within a conventional marriage. Being twenty-nine, she continued, was the most difficult time to deal with these conflicting demands, as the "current choice will lead [to a] different future path, and I am facing my life crossroads." On a family visit during the Spring Festival holidays, Peijing discussed marriage with her mother. In a later e-mail, she wrote:

> My parents are so eager for me to get married, but they are too afraid to ask me face-to-face anymore. Instead they get other relatives to inquire and try to persuade me. My other relatives are alright; they just don't want to see my parents disappointed. So now I have contacted this gay guy [she had replied to his online ad about contract marriage] again, and we decided to have a good talk when I return to Beijing. . . . I tried to tell my mum this time that I don't want to get married. She told me that she would be very upset if I didn't. I said to her that I know she wants me to be happy, but happiness for me is not about being married. And you know I really don't want to hurt my parents—I am Chinese, after all. . . . It's impossible for her to change her mind. She was born in the 1950s in the countryside, and she hardly has any education [due to the Cultural Revolution in the 1960s and its chaotic aftermath]. It's near impossible to communicate with her about this; she doesn't understand anything else. She would be devastated if I were to remain unmarried. You know, she is also pressured by her environment—neighbors, other older family members, and so on. I should understand her.

Peijing's narrative exhibits a strong emotional attachment and sense of responsibility toward her parents: she told her mother that she did not want to get married; she explained that for her, happiness and marriage were not compatible, but her mother clearly could not fathom the possibility of her eldest daughter remaining unmarried and childless. Perhaps this was due in part to the social pressure the family experienced in the town where they lived, where a family's reputation relies on individual family members conforming to social duties defined by patriarchal notions of gender and kinship. As Peijing put it, "[My mother] is also pressured by her environment—neighbors, other older family members, and so on."

Undoubtedly influenced by these difficult discussions, she decided to pursue *xinghun* talks with a gay man she had met in an online *xinghun* discussion group. Later that spring, Peijing announced to her parents that she now had a boyfriend, Zhongqian. Overjoyed by this long-anticipated news, her parents accepted him readily as good husband material and made it clear they were looking forward to the wedding. Zhongqian was an only child, and his family, who lived in westernmost China, were keenly anticipating the wedding, urging Zhongqian and Peijing to decide on a date very soon. But it quickly became apparent that the marriage plans—intended as a solution to the constant conformist pressure—were becoming a very real problem due to many other, related, expectations. This was mainly because of Peijing's and Zhongqian's different views on the practicalities of everyday married life and the implications of gendered autonomy. While it was family pressure that had initially concerned Peijing, she realized that Zhongqian, supported by his domineering parents, harbored old-fashioned ideas about married life and a wife's role. One issue was the post-wedding residential arrangement. Zhongqian, sponsored by his parents, had already purchased an apartment in Beijing, with the expectation that she would come live with him. Like many gays, he believed that living together made the marriage more "real." Peijing, however, worried about the implications if she moved to his apartment. First, the travel distance to work would increase considerably, which she dreaded. Second, living with him would make it harder to lead an independent life—socially, romantically, and financially. For example, her mother had already announced that she would live with them for a while, to help the new couple settle in. This would make it even harder for them to keep up appearances and live their own independent lives. Third, Peijing worried about having to share her husband's financial obligations, including mortgage payments and apartment furnishings. When initially considering *xinghun*, she had hoped that having a boyfriend would be enough to put a stop to marriage talk, or at least would buy her time. In addition, she was now imagining the possibility that she could remain unmarried after all. This idea was encouraged in part by professional fulfillment. She had recently begun working for an international organization, which inspired her greatly in matters unrelated to work as such and also enabled her greater financial independence. The emergence of multiple *xinghun* issues as she was negotiating with Zhongqian and her growing exposure to online and international alternatives for defining a "good life," including criticism of *xinghun* in the lesbian/gay community and its growing support for same-sex marriage, meant that she had become more confident that another life was possible, beyond marriage.

Still, the practical and emotional entanglements of intergenerational family bonds and the corresponding albeit diffuse structures of social duty did not ease but rather intensified the marriage pressure. When Peijing and I talked online about one year later (in 2007), she updated me on the events since. Because Zhongqian's parents had ordered him to get married no later than the end of the year, Zhongqian gave her an ultimatum: she had to decide by June or he would find someone else. Peijing told me she was now even more hesitant about going through with it. Whereas Zhongqian's parents were obsessed with his marriage, although they lived far away and the marriage thus would have little practical impact on family relations, Peijing's parents now rarely mentioned it, and her sister was supportive of Peijing's resistance to marrying. It was likely that Peijing's sister's being married and having given birth to a daughter had pacified their parents and family sufficiently. Moreover, Peijing's educational and career accomplishments probably appeased social opinion. In contrast, Zhongqian's experience speaks to the pressures on only sons to fulfill filial duties, even as contemporary ideals of romantic love and individualism are taking hold of the public imagination. Long-standing collective family ideals, with their rigidly defined gender, class, and intergenerational implications, are hard to change.

I returned to Beijing one year later and reunited with Peijing, who in the meantime had married Zhongqian. However, they lived apart and led separate lives, except when family visited. She had also become active online, finding community support for her *xinghun* and meeting lesbian friends. Better still, she had met a girlfriend online, a Chinese businesswoman who lived in Europe. Peijing was contemplating getting a divorce and moving to Europe to live and work with her girlfriend, and indeed, she did exactly that in the following year.

FINDING A "CONVENIENT" PARTNER

Peijing's experiences illustrate the difficult pressures that young women and men endure, most of which come directly from their own immediate families but also via complex social and family structures that reward conformity and compliance and punish transgression. Her story showcases the continued willingness of younger generations to submit to the older generations' emotional pressure in these matters, despite their exposure to individualism and greater personal autonomy. In short, married offspring reflect favorably on the social status of all family members and also alleviate the felt personal pressure to conform. Resisting is emotionally exhausting, while conforming enables one to relax. Remaining single (as Zavoretti also highlights in chap. 6) is regarded as a personal failure that also reflects badly on one's family and therefore comes at an emotional and material cost that is simply too high for most people. As research on Shanghai lesbians has shown, unmarried women older than the most suitable age for marriage (between twenty-five and twenty-nine years of age) are considered a social problem because they are avoiding their gendered social responsibilities toward family and society (Kam 2012). Overage unmarried women (*lao guniang*) are defined as physically unattractive, with bad social skills, poor health, and personality defects. Married status is therefore associated with a gendered internal essence. The normalizing discourse of *sheng nü* (leftover women) has emerged in mainstream and political discourse as a category that describes unmarried women over the age of twenty-seven. It is part of a deeply stigmatizing discourse on single women and complements the immense normative pressure for young women to marry and thereby contribute to strengthening the overall quality of the population, and, by extension, the nation (Fincher 2014; Zhang and Sun 2014). Note that singledom is also deeply stigmatizing for men. Alongside the denigrating *sheng nü* and *lao guniang* discourse, the notion of *guanggun* (bare branches/sticks) describes the rising number of men unable to find wives, due to poverty, rural *hukou*, and skewed demographic consequences of the Birth-Planning Policy (Greenhalgh 2013; Jiang and Sánchez-Barricarte 2012).

These intersecting factors are important reasons why the *xinghun* strategy has become a desirable option and perceived solution for many lesbians and gays. Following this, the most immediate issue is to find a suitable partner for a convenient marriage arrangement. But what is meant by "suitable" and "convenient"? Let us consider the practicalities of actual married life. Whereas the *xinghun* discourse in lesbian/gay community circles stresses *xinghun*'s ability to balance personal desire and socio-familial conformity, the structural milieu in which these marriages exist presents two major challenges. First is the basic requirement for strict compartmentalization between lesbian/gay life and married life. These challenges can only increase with time because the onus is entirely on lesbians and gays themselves to manage them correctly. Second, and equally important, the prevailing patriarchal underpinning of gender relations and social norms means that the lesbian woman is far more likely to face constraining social pressures and an effective decrease in personal autonomy in her post-wedding life.[5] As Cho (2009) and Kam (2012) argue, social expectations for maintaining good contact with in-laws and one's own family rest on the wife, as do the entertaining of visitors and caregiver responsibilities. A wife's ability to successfully attend to these tasks entails status implications for herself as well as her husband and their wider families. Boys and men, too, have filial responsibilities, of course (Miège 2009), but girls and women customarily shoulder the bulk of this burden. This has considerable consequences for personal autonomy in practical and emotional ways and contributes to the current reversal of gender equality policies (Tatlow 2012).

Finding a "good" gay man and defining the values and personality likely to ensure a successful *xinghun* is a central discussion topic in lesbian/gay communities. In order to illustrate the most common concerns, consider the following two personal advertisements written by gay men seeking wives on the popular web portal Baidu's Contract Marriage Forum (Xingshi Hunyin Ba):

> I am a forty-year-old "gay man [*tongzhi*]," Beijing resident, restaurant owner, who is now looking to find a LL [lesbian] for *xinghun*. Requirements: no interference in each other's lives. The baby issue [*haizi wenti*] can be considered later. However, I do not really intend to have children, to avoid making the woman suffer [*tongku*].

> I am an army officer in training in Beijing. . . . My measurements are 170-70-76-1;[6] my physique is robust, I'm in great shape, "MAN" [masculine], and it's impossible to tell I am "GAY." . . . My monthly income is more than ¥4,000 [approximately US$650]. After I am married, I am entitled to military housing. . . . I am college-educated, my personality is graceful, MAN, responsible, considerate, understanding. I am filial toward my parents and on good terms with them. I am looking for a LL for contract marriage who fits the following requirements:
> 1. First of all, you must be filial toward your parents. My wish is that we will be equally filial toward our parents-in-law as to our own parents.
> 2. You should not look too MAN but be a bit feminine and not have a too small or stocky figure.
> 3. You should want to have a child. Even though many oppose

this, I think we have come to this world only this once, and we should leave a mark, don't you agree?

4. You should have Beijing *hukou* and be financially self-sufficient; your personality should be average, nothing extraordinary, and you should have a healthy outlook on life. . . .

5. You must behave cordially toward my army comrades, friends, and contacts. . . .[7]

The emphasis on economic independence and status tied to educational attainment, employment, and residential matters (living alone, having Beijing *hukou*) is striking but not surprising. These factors indicate an aspiration for cosmopolitan middle-class status, which, in turn, is perceived as granting access to sufficient resources to maintain the necessary split between the socially recognized normative married life and private gay/lesbian life. Moreover, the ads demonstrate the importance placed on a gendered version of conformity and the symbolic ideals and material realities of personal autonomy in the successful strategizing of *xinghun*. The second advertisement in particular demonstrates particularly well the oft-mentioned obsession with conventionally gendered appearance and behavior. Indeed, a common belief was that a particularly effeminate gay man or masculine lesbian would be more likely to cause suspicion and problems with family and colleagues. Gender-conforming lesbians and gays were considered less risky (more likely to pass), more trustworthy, and capable of acting their prescribed *xinghun* role. Exceptions existed, especially with regard to sexual behavior. Many lesbians worried that gender-conforming gay men might inflict sexual violence, even rape, and force them to become pregnant. This appears to reflect a larger issue related to common understandings of heteronormative sexuality that I repeatedly encountered in conversations with both lesbians and straight women, whereby sexual intercourse is a husband's "right" and a woman's desire and consent are deemed less important. In addition, a common belief was that a gender-conforming gay man would likely have many casual sex partners, and some lesbians discussed this as a health risk that could mean a wife would be responsible for paying the costs of treating sexually transmitted infections and even HIV. As noted more recently by Yingyi Wang (2015), many lesbians would define *xinghun* ideally as chosen kinship, brother-sister relations, or friendship. Consider this lesbian couple's personal ad:

> We live in Shanghai but may relocate to Beijing. We are looking for a G [gay] couple. My GF [girlfriend] and I are an emotionally

stable couple, graduates, with stable employment. Now we hope to find a pair of honest G, of the 1979–85 generation, college educated (just for the parents' satisfaction), and with stable jobs.

Our appearance is not masculine [*bu nan*], and we hope that you are not effeminate [*bu nü*]. We do not have any other requirements. We just want good people [Zhi yao ren hao].

Note again the prominence of the ideal of gendered conformity in appearance and personality. It speaks to the broader aspiration to "fit in" and live "normal" lives so as to generate and maintain respectable social status, with all this implies for resource acquisition, although the desire to please parents and families is significant, however much it ultimately reproduces hegemonic regimes of normalcy.

ENDURING MARRIAGE: YINGYU'S EXPERIENCE

The combination of complex familial desire and personal desire is illustrated in the following narrative. Yingyu was a confident media professional and self-defined T (tomboy; masculine lesbian) in her early thirties, whom I befriended early into my fieldwork period (2004–6). She decided on a *xinghun* after discussing it for many months with friends, lesbian activists, and her girlfriend. Yingyu and Qibing, her gay husband, met via online *xinghun* advertisements. They were both accomplished in their respective careers and aspired to a cosmopolitan lifestyle. They soon became friends, aided by their shared views on marital practicalities around finances (to be kept separate), living arrangements (to live apart, remaining with same-sex lover), and mutual support vis-à-vis family and work. After a year of courtship and negotiations, they married in January 2005. For them, this meant registering for the official legal marriage certificate and then hosting a wedding banquet for family and close friends.[8] Qibing's relatives lived far away and were unable to travel to Beijing to attend the party. His long-term partner in Beijing, as well as their gay and lesbian friends, including Yingyu's girlfriend, took part in the wedding banquet. Yingyu's family, including a frail elderly grandmother, however, was oblivious to the considerable gay and lesbian presence.

Interestingly, Yingyu came out to her father years earlier, in a conversation about why she did not want to marry. At the time, she was in her first serious relationship with a woman and believed it was filial to be honest about who she was. So she told her father, "I prefer women" (Wo xihuan nüren). Her father simply replied that she still should marry, because two women together was "not good" (*bu hao*) and would cause problems in life.

Yingyu felt that her coming out and marriage refusal were not taken seriously, which was probably the case. Pressure to marry from her parents and coworkers intensified as she approached thirty, and that was why she had decided that a contract marriage would be the best solution.

After registering their marriage, Yingyu and Qibing hosted their wedding reception for family and relatives just before the Spring Festival holidays. They had their wedding photos taken at a professional photo studio and ordered photo albums to distribute to family members as gifts at the reception. To reduce expenses, maintain T integrity, and resist the customary over-feminization of the bride, they wore their own clothes. Yingyu shouldered most of the costs, including for the photos, food, and drinks. Her father had given her some money, but my understanding was that Yingyu paid for most of the wedding out of her own savings. The rationale was that the reception was a ritual intended for her family, not the groom's, so it was only fair that she pay for it. Indeed, the only guests who knew Qibing were his boyfriend and one gay friend.

The family reception was a deliberately low-key affair, both to save money and to minimize the wedding's significance, but impressive enough to satisfy Yingyu's family. Yingyu's pre-wedding preparations were concerned mainly with coordinating with Qibing and his boyfriend (who lived together elsewhere in central Beijing) to make it appear as if Qibing and Yingyu actually lived together. This included removing every possible trace of Yingyu's girlfriend, including strands of her long hair in the bathroom and on the couch, and hiding her possessions, while moving in some of Qibing's for the day. They also prepared detailed stories about their everyday life together, including how they had met and "fallen in love." The reception ended in the late afternoon, and the parents and other relatives returned to their hotels. By the next day, they were back in their hometown outside Beijing.

The day after the wedding, Yingyu and Qibing invited a large group of gay and lesbian friends for brunch and drinks. Unlike the wedding, the brunch was a relaxed and joyful celebration, held in a downtown restaurant. In this way, they balanced the public wedding reception with a more intimate celebration with lesbian and gay friends and their respective partners. Although the party was held in a public place, their privacy was maintained; restaurants often allow for a kind of privacy-in-public by offering separate rooms for guests. This is popular with groups of gay and lesbian friends, as it allows for open displays of affection and conversations on any topic imaginable.

Yingyu and Qibing sought to lessen the significance of the *xinghun* wedding and downplay the "fake" performance of marital love, thereby also attempting to minimize the guilt they felt for deceiving their blood families.

Expenses were an important factor here; Yingyu sought to reduce the wedding expenses as much as possible without triggering her parents' suspicion. Their wedding banquet performed several central rituals uniting the two families and demonstrating customary respect and filial relations. During the lunch, there were many festive toasts and speeches, including Yingyu and Qibing toasting and bowing before their elder family members and each other. Yingyu showed me one particularly striking photo in which she and Qibing, each holding a glass of beer, bow to each other in formal ceremonial style. In the background, family and friends are gathered around them, looking pleased. Yingyu's mother is in the foreground, next to the couple, perhaps directing the ritual. She is smiling broadly and gazing at the bride and groom, her delight evident from her elated facial expression.

In another photograph, Yingyu and Qibing are in Yingyu's apartment, surrounded by their friends, two lesbian couples and Qibing's boyfriend, who stands behind Qibing with his hands resting on his lover's shoulders. Both smile brightly and look very happy. In stark contrast, Yingyu, normally a very confident T, looks very unlike herself in all the photos, having borrowed feminine clothes from her P (femme) girlfriend: a knee-length skirt in a flowery pattern, a black blouse, a colorful silk scarf around her neck, and high-heeled black boots.

After the wedding, Yingyu had mixed feelings about the marriage's success in solving her problems. Although her parents had stopped nagging her, she believed they would soon start asking about children. Still, she thought this kind of pressure was less onerous than marriage pressure, and it did not seem to be as all-consuming. Furthermore, being married meant that her home was now the conjugal home, not that of her parents, which in practical terms meant she was not expected to visit and stay at theirs at every opportunity. This change brought a sense of emancipation, and she proceeded to spend the Spring Festival holidays in Beijing with her girlfriend and lesbian friends under the pretense that she was spending it with her new husband. Echoing the custom that women are seen to marry out and the oft-made point that daughters are more mobile than are sons, Yingyu argued, "I'm gone now" (Wo yijing zoule) and "They don't mind me anymore" (Tamen buguan wole). Talking about this on one social occasion, she smiled about her life-changing events: One year earlier, she had been single and unmarried, worrying about her future life and the exasperating relationship with her parents. Now, she had both a *laopo* (wife) and a *laogong* (husband)!

Despite this, and related to the official onset of married life, Yingyu was now experiencing other sorts of pressure in her everyday life. Neighbors were curious about the continuous absence of her husband and the presence of a young woman who was living with her. That she had married was public knowledge, given that the wedding celebrations took place in her apartment and festive double happiness (*shuangxi*) symbols were plastered outside her door. Yingyu always had to be on the alert, ready to produce stories and remember those she had already told. There were similar problems at work, where colleagues asked seemingly innocent questions, such as "What are your plans for the weekend?" or "What did you and your husband do last weekend?" Stories had to be invented, remembered, and modified according to the circumstances. Once, while having dinner with her girlfriend and some other friends in her apartment and talking about this, Yingyu suddenly broke down in tears. For an otherwise strong-willed, confident T, this naked display of emotional distress was extraordinary. As her girlfriend comforted her and her friends stressed their support (*zhichi*) and admiration (*peifu*), she quietly said that she hoped her experiences could prove helpful for others.

Yingyu's *xinghun* experience shows that the social and public reality of marital imperatives dominated lesbian-gay *xinghun* strategies for providing personal relief and ending conformist pressures. These concerns are of course not limited to lesbians and gays; they are shared by men and women, straight and gay/lesbian alike. However, a significant part of the *xinghun* problem is living with the guilt of lying to parents: pretending to be straight and thereby knowing that one is acting not just against one's personal desires but also against one's parents' expectations and the omnipresent heteronormative moral order. Yingyu's narrative illustrates the nuances of these tensions, especially when she broke down in tears, thus evidencing the enormous psychological strain the arrangement brought.

The *xinghun* practices and discourses discussed here demonstrate that a number of factors intersect in shaping lesbian and gay strategic responses to heteronormative, normalizing pressures. First, *xinghun* complicates simplistic understandings of patriarchy and necessitates a nuanced, intersectional approach that reaches beyond customary notions of traditional filial hierarchy and men's systemic oppression of women. Normalizing pressures rely on preexisting "traditional" filial ideologies as well as recently arrived, globally traveling normative understandings of social order and gender systems, with gender inequality as perhaps the most central factor. This situation continues to have serious implications for the ability of girls and women to attain full personal autonomy in symbolic and economic matters. In turn, this is why lesbians have the most to lose in *xinghun* arrangements, and usually do, compared with gay men, for whom personal independence and access to resources are much less curtailed by entering *xinghun*. Therefore, contemporary regimes of normalization and gendered social convention appropriate preexisting patriarchal ideology; some are locally Chinese, and some partake in globally circulating discourses of modern identity and propriety. An essential ingredient in this discursive regime is a dualist (naturalized masculine/feminine) and intensely politicized gender system, which is predicated on performing compulsory heterosexuality and heteronormative gender expression. This system, in turn, is formalized through the marriage predicament. This is why openly lived same-sex relationships and coming out as lesbian/gay are impossible for most. The female body, its conduct and social status, remains crucially "wedded," then, to a heteronormative reading of personal status. The contemporary global neoliberal system that China partakes in defines the good-"quality" (*suzhi*) citizen as middle-class, cosmopolitan, and a keen participant in a consumer economy that utilizes heteronormative discourses and imaginaries (romance, sex, marriage) to sell proper modern selfhood. Central to this globally circulating imaginary is a gendered model of (hetero)sexual complementarity, including the objectification of women's bodies and gendered "innate" qualities.

The *xinghun* narratives also accentuate a temporal differentiation between the ideas and values of the current historical moment, when the women in my study came of age and learned vocabularies for negotiating the marriage predicament, and the ideas and values of the pre-Reform era when their parents grew up. The women's difficulties with communicating meaningfully with their parents regarding their same-sex desires (Yingyu coming out to her father) and personal views on happiness (Peijing resisting marriage in discussions with her mother), for example, demonstrate a significant intergenerational gap in this respect. This may be a reason why their parents—mothers in particular, as seen in Peijing's narrative—cannot fathom the different life trajectories of their daughters today. Due to improved access to education and employment, fewer births, and political campaigns highlighting the value of girls and women, there has been considerable improvement in women's social status and personal autonomy (Evans 2008; and see Jankowiak and Li, chap. 7 in this volume). Still, newly intensified socioeconomic inequalities and economic transitions have stalled movement toward gender equality and restated the dominance of hetero-patriarchal social structures (Fincher 2014; Tatlow 2012).

XINGHUN'S PATRIARCHAL LIMITS AND LESBIAN-GAY FUTURES

The detailed examples of *xinghun* strategies that tacitly subvert—or attempt to subvert—family and gender norms show us that their success can only be relative and temporary, rather than absolute and permanent. A *xinghun's* potential to provide relief from heteronormative pressure relies almost entirely on lesbians and gays themselves: their capacity to assume and maintain a sense, not just of imagined or actual control, but also of social responsibility and personal risk for the duration of the fake marriage, and to negotiate a range of compensatory life strategies for alleviating normative pressures. The common markers of "good" strategies are, first, reticence or tacit expression of difference (coming out is impossible) and, second, not to overstep boundaries that preserve (the appearance of) equilibrium and social harmony.

Xinghun's long-term success, then, rests on the complicit deployment of the idea that homosexuality must remain invisible, or at least (appear to be) without social consequences. Even if known, such as when Yingyu came out to her father, homosexuality must fold back into the socio-familial system and be effectively overridden, erased, by a social order that denies that homosexuality can be a viable and visible life choice. According to the logic of filial duty, lesbian subjectivity and desire cannot have consequence or make the kind of difference that would somewhat alter hegemonic gendered and familial norms, which rejecting marriage would do.[9]

The *xinghun* narratives presented here point to the human cost of maintaining complicit reticence in compartmentalizing the articulation of lesbian love. Women invariably described themselves as "exhausted," having "no other options," and struggling with guilt and contradictory desires to comply but also reaching out for alternatives, imagining different futures. The human cost of seeking and trying out coping strategies is gendered in ways that make lesbians particularly vulnerable to the repressive regime that renders homosexuality silent and invisible. Lasting strategies are those that can be translated into known hetero-familial roles that do not upset hierarchical structures, including the "chosen kinship" practices of "second daughter," caregiver, or the neutral-sounding "friend." Again, same-sex love remains socially invisible for what it really is. The general obligation of childbearing within marriage further genders this complex terrain. Peijing's narrative illustrates that for many lesbians and gays, childbearing is invested with strong personal desire, socio-familial duty, and certain moral conundrums that are specific to gays and lesbians; I spoke to many lesbians who felt that it was morally wrong to bring up a child in a non-heteromarriage setup, for example, out of fear of homophobia. Childbearing, then, becomes a strongly felt concern when facing marriage pressure and adds significantly to the stress lesbians and gays endure, although this stress is gendered in ways that oftentimes make the experience of stress different for gays and for lesbians.

The question remains, can there be a subversive potential to *xinghun*? At the outset, complicit lesbian-gay marital strategies illustrate how the hegemonic hetero-patriarchal system denies same-sex desire and relationships a place in social and public life, forcing dissenting individuals to retreat into a socially invisible, private space. Although it is possible for some couples to strategize symbolic and material capacities toward achieving a sense of tolerance, any direct, unambiguous recognition of homosexuality is almost impossible. There is, however, potential to challenge the status quo through these strategic appropriations of hegemonic norms; as we have seen, however, the human cost is often too great, the emotional pressures too complex to resolve fully. Many if not most pre-*xinghun* negotiations therefore never reach agreement or formalization, and many *xinghun* end in intra-*xinghun* conflict and divorce. Still, it may work out for some, such as Peijing, who over time came to realize there was a way out, that a life of happiness was possible, that marriage was not the only solution: she divorced and migrated abroad to begin a new life with her girlfriend. Through this lengthy process, her parents came to tolerate her unconventionality and, finally, the divorce; this was undoubtedly facilitated by their having another daughter who had married and given them a grandchild.

Xinghun demonstrates that patriarchal ideologies remain a core normalizing structure that positions gender inequality as central to contemporary kinship practices but, at the same time, operates through the intersecting factors of sexuality (homo/hetero and reproductive) and generation. The success of a *xinghun* depends on a complex set of specifics regarding family composition (having a conforming sibling, for example), parental rigidity (often classified as either "modern" or "backward"), and overall personal autonomy, such as having the imaginative resources to hope for a better and different future life. Perhaps the growing awareness of the limitations of *xinghun* arrangements within lesbian and gay communities is the reason that now, in the new millennium's second decade, many lesbian/gay networks support same-sex marriage equality and dedicate their resources to anti-homophobia activism.

Spatiality and migration are important in shaping these strategies. While the narratives here have focused on university-educated lesbians and gays in urban settings, who already live away from their parents, it is important to keep in mind that fighting the normative pressures is much harder for those who enjoy less personal autonomy, for example, those who live with or near parents in provincial small towns, have less educational attainment, and depend on family networks for support. Women stuck in small-town or lower-class settings, near their and their husbands' families, endure considerable pressures to fulfill gendered caregiver roles.[10] In sum, an array of intersecting emotional and practical factors beyond a simplistic "women are oppressed" rhetoric shapes the realities and imaginative possibilities of *xinghun* to alleviate normative pressures to comply in any meaningful, lasting way.

Still, the event of *xinghun* offers at least *some* bargaining power and scope for imagining a future lived otherwise. An intersectional approach to *xinghun* negotiations and hetero-patriarchal imperatives brings out the everyday workings of normative constraints over time (pre- and post-wedding) and shows how performances of strategic complicity become social semifacts when private life goes unrecognized, socially and legally. Despite this, *xinghun* discourses and practices go some way toward articulating same-sex lifeways as valid alternatives, by increasingly building up—via new media and globally traveling imaginaries of freedom and openness—lesbian/gay community visibility and solidarity. This reality challenges the hegemonic ideology of the paramount need for an absolute split between the normative public imperative of (what appears to be a) hetero-marriage and invisible same-sex love. Finally, in temporal terms, it allows time to think and to bargain with manifold expectations. It is at this drawn-out event of *xinghun*, then, that lesbians and gays rethink and sometimes rewrite customary norms for the good life, even as such strategies remain a complicated affair of hearts of many different persuasions.

NOTES

Thanks to Stevan Harrell and Gonçalo Santos for inviting me to the "Chinese Patriarchy" workshop at the Max Planck Institute for Social Anthropology in 2013 and for their helpful comments on the original paper; paper discussants Janet Carsten and Deborah Davis for their incisive remarks and support; and the anonymous reviewers. I am grateful to Henrike Donner, Harriet Evans, Sara Friedman, Suzanne Gottschang, and Roberta Zavoretti for inspiring conversations and support.

Epigraph: *Les+* 2009, 33. *Les+* was a Beijing-based activist lesbian 'zine published between 2005 and 2012.

1   I use the English terms *lesbian* and *gay* loosely, as a way of pointing to a diverse collectivity of women and men with same-sex subjectivities and intimacies.

2   Contract marriages are sometimes called "fake" (*jiahun*), "cooperative marriage" (*hezuo hunyin*), or "marriage of convenience" (Chiu 2013; Davison 2011; Kam 2012; Wang Yingyi 2015). I prefer to use the term *contract marriage*, as it alludes to the intended purpose of the practice in part as a ritual performance.

3   This chapter draws on ethnographic material researched for my first mono-
     graph (Engebretsen 2014). The original fieldwork took place in central Beijing
     from 2004 to 2006, as part of my doctoral work at the London School of
     Economics and Political Science, and was funded by the Economic and Social
     Research Council. Follow-up fieldwork took place in 2009 and 2012, funded in
     part by a Professional Development Grant from Duke University (2009) and a
     research grant from the Helsinki Collegium for Advanced Studies (2012).
4   All names are pseudonyms to protect confidentiality.
5   See Wang Yingyi 2015 for a compelling analysis of *xinghun* arrangements,
     including what Wang considers a new ethics of lesbian-gay solidarity as a
     result of such conjugal cooperation.
6   These numbers refer to height (cm), year of birth (1970), weight (kg), and
     sexual role (the numeral 1, meaning active, also implicitly refers to being
     masculine).
7   The ads were retrieved from the Baidu website's Contract Marriage Forum
     (Xingshi Hunyin Ba), posted in 2009; http://tieba.baidu.com/f?kz=199837558
     (accessed May 20, 2012). Identifying details have been removed or altered.
8   It was inappropriate for me to attend because the wedding was a family affair.
9   Elsewhere I detail two alternative strategies: live-in caregiver for elderly
     parents and kin instead of marriage (out); and *er nü* (two daughters), a form of
     chosen kinship whereby a daughter's girlfriend appropriates the role of second
     daughter in her girlfriend's family. These women are usually in their thirties,
     and therefore the most intense marriage pressure has receded (Engebretsen
     2014; regarding gay men, see Fu and Zhang 2013.
10   Engebretsen 2014; Miège 2009; and see Evans, chap. 9 in this volume.

CHAPTER NINE

PATRIARCHAL INVESTMENTS

*Expectations of Male Authority and Support
in a Poor Beijing Neighborhood*

HARRIET EVANS

P OOR women in the Dashalanr neighborhood of Beijing have experienced profound changes in their lives over the past half century, presenting successive generations with unremitting difficulties as well as new opportunities. At the heart of these changes are the patriarchal configurations of gender and generational power. Women's shifting modes of engagement with these configurations are influenced by a series of linked factors, including their poverty; their relative lack of engagement with state narratives and institutions; their strategic perceptions of where power lies and how they can manipulate it; the changing strategies of the patriarchal figures in their lives, including husbands, fathers, and mothers-in-law; and their own moral sense of the gendered responsibilities of wives and mothers. These women are making a "patriarchal bargain" (Kandiyoti 1988) as they negotiate the changing configurations of power in their households, families, and neighborhood.

Extending this argument, the notion of investments in a reconfigured patriarchy refers to the personal and familial returns—calculated or not, material, affective, and moral—that women anticipate through accommodating male authority in the household. Their investment in "the men's family" (M. Wolf 1985, 189) is not based on pragmatic considerations alone. Their awareness of their disadvantage and their desires for emotional companionship are folded into an understanding of ethical responsibilities and sensibilities—of being a moral person—that is inseparable from a gendered sense of self-worth. Despite their negotiations and exchanges for personal material benefit, their

crucial role in maintaining their families' welfare, and assertion of independence, their sense of self as a moral person—as a "good" person—is grounded
in an understanding of family obligations ordered by an inextricable mix of
gendered and generational obligations. Their actions are thus caught in an
apparent paradox between implicit challenges to male authority in household
affairs and continuing attachments to patriarchal ideas about and practices
related to marriage, reproduction, family, and kinship.

DASHALANR

Dashalanr is a small neighborhood just southwest of Qianmen at the southern end of Tian'anmen Square. During the late Qing and early Republican
eras, its warren of alleys and lanes (*hutong*) was home to popular theaters
and opera houses, brothels, and provincial association lodges, and its main
street was a bustling thoroughfare of itinerant vendors, small eateries, and
artisan shops. By 1949, it had long since passed its heyday, and despite
numerous projects launched between the 1950s and 1970s for reconstruct-
ing its "old and dilapidated houses," it remained one of Beijing's poorest and
most overcrowded neighborhoods (Beijing Shi Bianzuan Weiyuanhui 2000,
208).[1] New policies and strategies to regenerate the neighborhood were for-
mulated in the 1980s, but it was only in 2005 that demolition began, involving the relocation of large numbers of local residents. In West Street—its
poorer area, where I have been working—demolition and reconstruction
(*chaiqian*) began only in the winter of 2008, with migrant laborers working
alongside bulldozers late into the night to lay new pipes and wiring, leaving
a tangle of open wires and piles of rubble in the tiny pedestrian margins
left at the sides of the street.[2] By then, many residents had already moved
out. Others remained, renting out their small rooms in order to maximize
their returns, or too poor and too resigned to find affordable accommodations elsewhere. These residents live mostly in single rooms in crowded *da
zayuan*, compound courtyards, some of which still house up to twenty or so
households. Dilapidated and damp, with no sanitation and minimal cooking facilities, these courtyards are the material and spatial evidence of the
poverty of the capital's "underclass" (Strand 1989).

Dashalanr, then, is a neighborhood in which everyday life for its residents has been shaped by the effects of long-term neglect. To this, in recent
years, have been added the relentless noise, dust, and detritus of demolition and reconstruction. All *da zayuan* residents generally know one another's names and occupations, where their children attend school, and their
household comings and goings. Far from the place depicted in the nostalgic

tones of journalistic reports about the loss of the *hutong*, the spatial arrangement of the *da zayuan* breeds a hotbed of gossip about local relationships and family quarrels, and social and personal relations are fraught with tensions and potential conflict (Wu 1999, 114).

The lives of the people discussed here have long focused on the material exigencies of getting by from one day to the next. Many—and among those I know, particularly men—are unemployed and, with minimal welfare support from the state, lead a hand-to-mouth existence, picking up odd jobs wherever they crop up, helping local shopkeepers repair shop signs, rolling up "traditional Chinese paintings" to sell as tourist souvenirs, and trying to steer clear of the ever-watchful local patrol officers. At best, among the residents I know in the neighborhood, individuals might find employment for a few months at a time washing up in a local Kentucky Fried Chicken, waitressing in a local café, or working as "hygiene officials" (*weisheng guanyuan*)—rubbish collectors, road sweepers, and cleaners of the public toilets. Everyday energies go to developing strategies of survival in informal and often extralegal activities—driving a pedicab without a license, making trinkets for unauthorized vendors to sell on the street—that signify a constant interruption of official plans for local transformation. Each of the three following case studies reveals a different aspect of local understandings of changing patriarchal interdependencies.

THE GAO FAMILY

Old Mrs. Gao lived for seven decades on a lane that she first moved to in 1937 when, at age seventeen, she married a local man who worked as a security guard for the Nationalist police. She rarely left her *da zayuan* home, a big room divided by a partition, until her relocation in 2011 to a second-floor apartment in a popular area farther south, where she died in the autumn of 2013.

Old Mrs. Gao became bedridden in 2009. Painfully thin, and very frail, she spent her days on the big bed, lying back against a pillow, knees raised, watching the television on the dresser in front of her, dozing, or just looking around. Her youngest son, Young Gao, had a chronic lung condition that he claimed made him unfit for regular employment, so he spent most of his time with his widowed mother, sitting at the small table by her bed. Since his wife was often out at work, he was left to care for his mother, helping her with the bedpan and rearranging her position to make her comfortable. But his wife undertook these tasks as soon as she returned from work; she also did the daily shopping for food, the cooking, tidying up, and cleaning, despite her husband's complaints about her negligence. Occasional comments his wife and sisters made about his drinking habits implicitly criticized him for not pulling his weight, but neither his wife nor his mother openly reproached him, at least in my presence.

Old Mrs. Gao was the youngest of four. Her father died soon after she was born, and her widowed mother tried to make ends meet by picking up whatever work she could, cleaning, gathering fuel left on the streets, and making shoes. At age five, Old Mrs. Gao was sold as a child bride (*tongyangxi*) into a household where she was treated as a skivvy. She repeatedly ran back to her mother, and her mother repeatedly returned her to her in-laws. She managed to leave, finally, at the age of ten and went to live with one of her married elder sisters, earning a bit of money doing odd jobs for neighbors. When she was thirteen, she found a job in the house of a local shopkeeper, collecting coal and cleaning, but her elder sister insisted that she return to her mother. Her elder brother found a position as an apprentice to a shoemaker who lived near Dashalanr's Guanyin Temple, and it was through his connections there that Old Mrs. Gao was introduced to the man who became her husband.

Old Mrs. Gao's life centered on her home after her marriage. Her husband was a good-looking and mild-mannered man, but as time passed, he seemed to her to be weak and inept. He worked for the local vegetable depot, selling vegetables on a mobile cart, but he always undersold his produce and brought little money back home. Life was tough, and Old Mrs. Gao had to struggle to keep the family going, especially during the first decades of her marriage, the 1950s and 1960s, when she had to take various menial jobs—folding paper to make book pages and making matchboxes—allocated to her by the neighborhood committee and which she could do in her *da zayuan* home. During the famine years in the early 1960s, she had to scavenge on the lanes and sent her older children out to the suburbs at night to forage for wild plants. Tellingly, her eldest daughter once commented that her illiterate mother might have done better had she stayed with the man to whom she was "married" as a child bride.

Old Mrs. Gao's husband died some years before I met her, but her children's references to her suggested that they had long regarded her as the emotional mainstay of her household. Her infirmity did not diminish this role. People used to come and go; they would sit at the table to eat and watch television and would chat, drink, and smoke cigarettes, keeping her company as she dozed. Her long life, her determination to keep her family going, and her reputation for generosity to neighbors who were down on their luck made her the linchpin in her family's unity and survival.

When I first met Young Gao, his right arm, which he had broken in a collision with a local rickshaw cyclist, was in a cast. His mother had just come out of the hospital. Before I met him, he had had a job at a local vegetable depot but was laid off when he was admitted to hospital for an operation. By June 2007, he had been sacked from a job as a night watchman after he was discovered drinking while at work. He received ¥300 yuan (approximately US$40) a month from the government as basic welfare payment (*dibao*), but this lasted for only one year, so he largely depended on the income of his wife, Xiao Xi. In 2007, she worked as a pedicab driver until pedicabs and itinerant street vendors were officially ordered off the streets as part of the neighborhood's "prettification" before the 2008 Olympics. She then found a job in a factory, working six night shifts every week.

Xiao Xi was an extremely capable and hardworking woman and a dutiful daughter-in-law and wife. She also had an independent spirit that made her a marked contrast to her husband. Yet despite the contrast between her abilities and her husband's evident weakness, she was deferential to him. She would wait on him and serve him his food, and even if she told him from time to time not to drink too much, she never directly criticized him. Occasional comments she made indicated that she was aware of the potential affront to her husband's authority that her employment and income might imply. Nevertheless, the reasons for her deference were far from clear, and it was only when Young Gao died in late 2010, and when negotiations about Old Mrs. Gao's relocation began, that I came to understand a bit more about the apparent contradictions in Xiao Xi's behavior.

One morning in the summer of June 2009, Young Gao seemed unusually depressed. He had lost a lot of weight and spent more time in the hospital for fluid on the lungs. Though it was only ten in the morning, he had already started drinking strong sorghum spirits. His mother's condition had deteriorated, and financial difficulties were on his mind. But as he talked, it became apparent that there was another reason for his distress. He had been quarrelling with his eldest sister, had not slept well, and woke up thinking about his father's death a few years before. Young Gao had developed pneumonia, but he tried to ignore his condition so that he could look after his father, who was then seriously ill in the hospital. Eventually, Young Gao had to be hospitalized and was not released until after his father died. "So I couldn't make it in time before my father passed away. What regret. I cried, I really cried. Aiya!"

Old Mrs. Gao and her daughters sometimes praised Young Gao for the care he gave her, attending to her needs as described above. Yet neither their attempts to assuage his distress nor his claim that the "Communist Party doesn't let me work" could hide his sense of inadequacy as a husband and son unable to fulfill his familial and filial duties. He once remarked that it would have been better had his mother not given birth to him. His distress was compounded by the precarious future his family faced. Some, like Xiao Xi, were quite pragmatic in their response to the prospect of moving: "If we have to move out, then that's what we'll have to do." Young Gao could not, or chose not to, confront the idea; for him, it was unimaginable. "We can't think about the future," he said, "since all we can do is get through today. All we can do is wait."

Before Young Gao died in late 2010, news was already circulating in Dashalanr that the alley where the Gao family lived was going to be partially demolished. By June the following year, Xiao Xi and her mother-in-law were preparing to relocate to subsidized accommodation provided by the local government. For them, this seemed a better option than the alternatives, of accepting compensation and finding their own accommodation or being rehoused in another *da zayuan* in the neighborhood. Given that compensation would be based on the floor area of their Dashalanr home, it would be too little to afford commercial rent elsewhere, and remaining in Dashalanr could be only a temporary measure at best, since it would all be demolished sooner or later. Old Mrs. Gao was more than ninety years old, and no more than a few years were left to her. Through long negotiations with her in-laws, and despite the discomfort and distress to the old lady, Xiao Xi insisted on relocating and accepting the government's arrangements.

It was at this point that Xiao Xi's interests as a widow, and an "outsider" in her husband's family, as she put it, came to light. She hoped that the contract for the new apartment would pass to her after her mother-in-law's death. When Old Mrs. Gao eventually died in 2013, Xiao Xi's in-law siblings wanted her to leave the apartment in return for monetary compensation. Xiao Xi insisted that as she had no alternative residence, and in return for the long years of fulfilling her filial obligations to her mother-in-law, they should respect her moral right to the apartment. Underlying her deference to her husband, despite his inadequacies, and her filial care of her mother-in-law lay an aim to secure her own residential and material security after her mother-in-law's death. Folded into her material self-interest, however, was also an ethical sense of self, as wife and daughter-in-law of the "men's family." Her investment in the trappings of patrilineal and patriarchal authority was rooted both in her pragmatic interests in material returns and in her gendered notion of integrity and "self-worth."[3]

Through the long decades of her life in Dashalanr, and with little apparent support from either her husband or the state, Old Mrs. Gao performed the key role of safeguarding her household against fragmentation (Stafford 2000). Like many elderly people, she liked to dwell on her childhood and youth. Her recollections of her mother's destitution and her own childhood suffering were particularly acute, sometimes bringing tears to her eyes. Reaffirming the bitterness of her childhood highlighted her determination to care for her uterine family during the 1950s and 1960s, even though it also explained her lowly status as a "dependent housewife" (*jiashu*) outside the formal state system of employment. The bitterness of her past life, therefore, became the reference for a self-legitimation articulated through her roles as daughter, mother, and wife. Her claim—backed up by her children's acknowledgment—to having fulfilled her family duties was a virtuous vindication of her attachment to ethical and gendered values associated with the "traditional" roles of daughter, wife, and mother in the face of a state that denied her recognition.

Her son's narrative, in contrast, fluctuated between resentment of a state that, in his terms, subjected him to its power without offering any benefits, and his sense of inadequacy as a husband and son. His self-validation—or lack of it—was rooted in his sense that he had failed to assume the gendered responsibilities expected of him as husband and son. For his mother, the place and space of her home and neighborhood acquired a sense of interiority as the center of her performance of her obligations and responsibilities as a woman, but for him, they had a different meaning. His sedentary occupation of his home alongside his bedridden mother confirmed his weakness as an uneducated, unemployable man whose everyday care of his mother should, in the proper gendered order of things, have been the responsibility of his wife. For Xiao Xi, facing relocation and without evident support from her natal family, respect for her mother-in-law's and husband's positions offered a path to material security, as well as to a sense of integrity as a woman who had fulfilled her obligations to her husband's family. Like Hua Meiling in the story that follows, Xiao Xi's continuing investment in the authority of the "men's family" was not just linked to material uncertainties; it was also linked to a strong attachment to gendered values of filiality and family obligation.

HUA MEILING AND HER DAUGHTER

Hua Meiling lives with her twenty-three-year old daughter in a small single room, registered under her mother-in-law's name, at the back of a *da zayuan* on the same alley where the Gao family lives. The room has a double bed that Meiling shares with her daughter, a small sofa, a computer that her daughter uses, a television, and a small table. It is always tidy and feels like a decidedly feminine space, with pink cushions and a pink coverlet on the bed, a couple of pictures of cute puppies on the wall, and a lace mat on the small table.

Born in the late 1950s to cadre parents, both of whom worked in a state ministry, Meiling grew up in what she described as a cold and austere family environment. Her parents were demanding and, in her eyes, were more interested in their public status than in caring for their children. Her father used to beat her and her siblings, and when she finished high school, Meiling ran away from home and fell in with a bad lot who used to offload stolen goods on her for safekeeping. But she wanted to have fun, as she put it, and used to go out to eat with her friends and hang out with boys, and eventually she became pregnant. A painful abortion did not interrupt her activities, however, until the early 1980s, when she was arrested for prostitution and sent away for "reeducation through labor" for three years. Upon her release, she found a job in a local pastry factory, where she met the man who became her husband and the father of her daughter. She moved into his mother's *da zayuan* in Dashalanr, but after they married, he lost his job and could not find work, beat her, and eventually started an affair with another woman. He was then imprisoned for twelve years for violent robbery. Instead of divorcing him as she said she wanted to, she "ran around after him. . . . I didn't do anything to him that I'm sorry about," she commented. With a child to bring up on her own, with parents who had disowned her, and with little prospect of stable employment, Meiling's main hopes for her own and her child's welfare lay in sustaining her marital links and the material security—in the form of a place to live—that these gave her.

Meiling's husband died not long after he was released from prison. She then got to know another man through a neighbor who often facilitated introductions between his friends and "girlfriends." Meiling's new acquaintance ran a small clothing factory and gave her a job there as a cook, and she liked him. As a former prostitute with a husband in jail, she had long had to put up with neighbors' gossip, and following her husband's death, she had had to endure repeated criticisms from her mother-in-law and sister-in-law about her lack of filial respect as daughter-in-law and her failure to give her own daughter, Xiao Hong, a proper upbringing. Meiling could give as well as she got, and in conversations with me, she often derided her mother-in-law for her gambling habit and her sister-in-law for her loose behavior. Meiling often said that she would give anything to leave Dashalanr but was prevented from doing so, she claimed, by her mother-in-law's refusal to consider moving. On many nights, she also had to share her bed with her mother-in-law when the latter's room in the *da zayuan* was occupied by her daughter and grandson. So, constrained by her residential dependence on her mother-in-law and surrounded by gossip, Meiling welcomed the companionship and care she felt her lover offered her, as well as his protection against the advances of other men. He was also good to her daughter, who called him "uncle," even though she rarely saw him, as he usually visited when Meiling was alone. Meiling cooked for him on the single-burner cooker in her small room and always made sure that she looked good. Over fourteen years, they had developed a close and companionable relationship, which she did her best to hide from her *da zayuan* neighbors. She did not want to fuel their gossip about her. "He's got a strong sense of justice, he plays things straight, so after I got to know him, I felt that I would be able to lead a happier life." Despite occasional fights, Meiling felt that her arrangement with her lover constituted a sound exchange: he gave her a monthly contribution toward her and her daughter's expenses, companionship, and a sense of self-worth, so she willingly provided the food, warmth, and intimacy that they both seemed to enjoy.

Meiling repeatedly referred to her sense that men were unreliable, but this did not interfere with her insistence that her daughter, Xiao Hong, should find a husband with a stable job. "All I want is that she finds a man with a good job, and as long as she treats him well, and he finds a clean house when he comes home and hot food on the table, he'll be happy." Her daughter suffers from a hyperthyroid condition that affects her facial nerves, and her mouth is permanently lopsided. "Who wants someone like that?" Meiling asked, meaning not that she would have preferred a son—Meiling never said anything to that effect—but that finding a husband would be difficult. "An operation would be several thousand *kuai*, but I don't have enough money for food let alone something like that." Meiling's daughter did not have the education or the skills to find a decent job; she lacked social skills and had little motivation to find work. She liked clothes and makeup, however, and dreamed of taking a cosmetics course. She spent a lot of time online, looking at fashions and films, and although her mother objected, she also spent time on dating websites. When I first got to know Meiling, her daughter had gone off to Fujian with a man she had met online. "She doesn't understand that in love you have to be responsible. Today, she'll get together with this guy she likes, and tomorrow another. I always tell her off about this." Xiao Hong eventually returned to Beijing after several months when her boyfriend's parents would not agree to their marriage. By 2011, she had found another boyfriend who not only had a job but access to an apartment. Meiling reserved judgment about whether she approved or not. What she was convinced of, however, was that her daughter's security lay in finding a man with prospects on whom she could depend.

Since I first got to know her in 2007, Meiling has had a succession of short-term jobs, preferring this to relying on the meager welfare payments from the local government. She worked in the kitchen of her elder sister's restaurant until she decided to quit because she felt that her sister was treating her badly. She then worked in another restaurant, washing up and cleaning the floors, and in 2010, she found a job as a cleaner in a cosmetics shop near Wangfujing. In all these places, she had to work long hours, arriving on her bike early in the morning and returning home in time to make the evening meal for herself and her daughter. She was constantly worried about her daughter's activities while she was out at work, but as the only breadwinner, she had little choice but to leave her alone. Moreover, Meiling was proud of being independent, active, and self-reliant; she never talked with her daughter about her past and felt that Xiao Hong respected her for her hard work and care.

Meiling's story reveals an attenuated attachment to patriarchal practices and values through her gendered and generational commitments. Her status as a single mother living with her daughter removed her from the need to accommodate the presence of a senior male, but pragmatic considerations about her residential security tied her to her husband's family. The same pragmatic considerations explained her tolerance of her husband, including the long years he spent in jail and the violent ways he sometimes treated her. She was proud of her performance as a hardworking single mother, able to keep going and stand up to a social world that disdained her. At the same time, and despite her history of violent abuse by her father and husband, she continued to rely on men's capacity to offer protection and material security, evident in her advice to her daughter about the benefits of subservience to the "men's family."

In all this, the contradictions in Meiling's behavior echo both Deniz Kandiyoti's general suggestions about women's "bargains" with patriarchy as well as others' arguments about the pragmatic and ideological reasons sustaining women's adjustments to patriarchy in China (Judd 1994; Stafford 2009). But there is something to add to this. Just as Old Mrs. Gao's and Xiao Xi's self-legitimation centered on their fulfillment of gendered values of filiality and family obligation, so Meiling repeatedly referred to her sense of virtue as a wife who had stood by her recalcitrant husband, a committed mother, and a constant if reluctant daughter-in-law. She was a "good person," she constantly reiterated, who had never let anyone down and had never harmed anyone. Her claims to virtue were rooted in her observance of her familial duties. With a history that earned her social disrepute, this virtue could become a source of self-validation that she could hurl in the faces of those who disdained her.[4]

THE ZHAO FAMILY

Zhao lives with his mother, wife, and stepdaughter in a partitioned room of a *da zayuan* housing eight families on an alley off Dashalanr's West Street. His wife, Xiao Yan, has another small apartment not far from Dashalanr, where she and her daughter generally stay at night. Old Mrs. Zhao came from a small landlord family well known for its martial arts expertise, on the outskirts of Beijing. Her husband was the son of an optician known to her father who ran a business in the Zhushikou neighborhood south of Dashalanr. As members of politically problematic families whose businesses were disbanded and nationalized during the early 1950s, Old Mrs. Zhao and her husband had limited access to stable employment, and their conditions of existence were precarious. They had a fractious relationship, which did not improve when they were housed in cramped *da zayuan* accommodation in Dashalanr during the late 1950s. With four children, they had to make do with one bed, and Zhao and his siblings had to sleep on wooden boards laid out on the floor. Poor as they were, the Red Guards ransacked their room as the Cultural Revolution got under way, and Old Mr. Zhao was repeatedly beaten up in front of his wife and children.

Old Mrs. Zhao's neighbors all called her mad. She suffered from terrifying paranoid delusions, which ranged from a conviction that her neighbors wanted to burn her room down and claims that the police wanted to arrest her, break her knees, and decapitate her, to an insistence that even the Party's general secretary, Hu Jintao, had issued orders to that effect. She had a temperament that veered unpredictably between meek submissiveness and angry indignation. Zhao's local reputation was not much better than his mother's, and neighbors considered him slow-witted and irascible. His younger and only brother had died many years ago, and he had little contact with his two sisters, who offered no support for their mother.

Zhao and Xiao Yan married in 2000, three years after Xiao Yan's first husband died and a year after Zhao divorced his first wife because, as he put it, she was unfilial to his mother. Xiao Yan also had a daughter. Her deceased husband had left her nothing upon his death, and even though Zhao's cousin warned her that both Zhao and his mother were "a bit mad," she felt that he was a good man who was able to weather hardship and who would take care of her and her child. For his part, Zhao thought that Xiao

Yan showed appropriate filial respect toward his mother. He did not want to have another child, even though, as a childless partner in a second marriage, he was legally entitled to do so: he felt that his circumstances were too limited to be able to offer another child a good upbringing. In return for Zhao's taking on Xiao Yan's daughter as his own, Xiao Yan agreed not to have any more children. An explicit exchange grounded in mutual requirements for support—on the one hand, care of the mother, and on the other, of the child—underpinned the couple's decision to marry.

Zhao had a succession of jobs after he was laid off from a private vehicle parts factory in 1998. He had been an itinerant fruit seller and a construction worker, and when I first got to know him, both he and his wife worked as pedicab drivers. They also had a small mobile street stall from which they sold Buddhist trinkets. But without a license for either their pedicab or their mobile stall, they were circumspect about the hours they worked, and when the local government launched its campaign to clean up Dashalanr's main streets in preparation for the Olympics, they stopped this work altogether. But Zhao was a resourceful man, and he was often out and about, trying to make a bit of money on the side. His wife found work washing up in a Kentucky Fried Chicken in a nearby neighborhood, but with a daughter to look after, she could not work the long hours required of her, so she found another post looking after an elderly man who lived alone not far from her mother-in-law.

Zhao's mother's condition made it dangerous for her to be left on her own, so between them, Zhao and his wife took turns looking after her while the other went out to work. One night in the early summer of 2010, when I was leaving Dashalanr, I heard Zhao's mother calling to me for help from the other side of the street. She seemed frantic, and her disheveled appearance drew the attention of passers-by. She was convinced that her neighbors had locked her out, and since her son was at his wife's apartment, she had no means of getting in. I took her back home, where the door was open, and phoned her son to come over. He sounded unsurprised when I described to him how I had found her and told me to lock her door; he would be over in the morning.

Zhao and his mother often quarreled, sometimes quite loudly. One issue was her medication, which she resisted taking on the grounds that it made her want to go to sleep. Her son often invented small chores to keep her occupied, only to become impatient at her ineptness. With neither material resources nor personal connections to draw on, Zhao had no access to the professional help that he knew his mother needed. He was under no illusions about the severity of her condition but had little alternative but to share the task of looking after her with his wife, and the relentless demands of attending to her during her frequent bouts of terror and anger left him exhausted. However, he did not complain about his responsibilities and took his filial duties extremely seriously. He considered taking care of his mother to be a moral obligation that, as the son and only "senior man" of his household, he could not relinquish, whatever the physical and emotional cost to himself. He often expounded, at some length, on his opinions about "big matters," as he called them—the relationship between family, society, and the universal values of Buddhism, Christianity, human rights, and Confucianism. The core of his personal philosophy rested on the view that personal integrity and inner strength offered the way to weather material disadvantage and that personal integrity began with fulfillment of family and filial obligations.

Xiao Yan's deference to her husband masked tensions that she only rarely allowed others to glimpse. On one occasion, she complained that her husband went out too much and was never up front about his activities. She also hinted at an affair he had had, although she quickly brushed it aside, claiming that she didn't care. However, she was appreciative of the support he offered her daughter, as well as his attention to her schoolwork and ideas about future employment. And even if Zhao's long lessons in philosophy and family values did not exactly excite his stepdaughter, both he and his wife hoped that they would inculcate in her the importance of being a good person. As noted above, Xiao Yan's marriage to Zhao was built on mutual benefit; accommodating her husband's shortcomings was preferable to a life on her own. Their marriage therefore was the pivot of arrangements for social support that sustained patriarchal attachments, values, and practices: on the one hand, of Zhao's authority as the "senior man," filial son, and supportive husband and father, and on the other, of his wife's obligations as daughter-in-law.

PATRIARCHAL INVESTMENTS

None of the lives described in this chapter correspond with the arrangements associated with the orthodox model of Chinese patriarchy, summarized by Rubie Watson (2013) as the "authorized exercise of power by senior men over women and younger men," and largely overlapping with the notion of "classic patriarchy" defined by Kandiyoti (1988, 278) as the patrilineal-patrilocal complex subordinating women to the power of men and senior women (see also the discussion in the introduction). Had Zhao's and Young Gao's fathers been alive, their household arrangements and relationships might well have produced other developments. Nevertheless, while the households described here are singular in their experience, practice, and articulation of Reform era historical conditions, they converge in sustaining the authority of the male head of the household, directly and obliquely, and in his presence and absence. Wives, mothers, daughters, and daughters-in-law share recognition of his authority, whether in the form of the desired husband for Meiling's daughter, the indispensability of Zhao's role as filial son, or Young Gao's place alongside his widowed mother and as guarantor of his wife's material security. The women are "strong" characters, conscious of their abilities and protective of their independent activities yet at the same time accommodating of patriarchal practices and values for pragmatic, ideological, and ethical reasons.[5] Their stories illustrate expectations of family order that center on gendered and generational notions of patriarchal authority, reconfigured by the specificities of household, family, and marital arrangements in conditions of social and economic disadvantage. Patriarchy is not sustained simply by economic disadvantage; considerable evidence suggests that women make patriarchal adjustments in diverse social settings in China, including that of the wealthy and educated urban middle class, for a variety of material, ideological, and emotional reasons.[6] However, in the families described here, as in the case of the rural-to-urban migrant families in Shandong described by Andrew Kipnis (chap. 5), pragmatic, material considerations are instrumental in sustaining such expectations in ways that have to be associated with their conditions of existence. The man—in these cases, husband, son, and lover—becomes the pivot at the center of the woman's imagination of the requirements for her own material and emotional security.

At the same time, all three stories reveal a disjuncture between acknowledgment of the man as the imagined pillar of household security and the remunerative, caring, and emotional work of the women. The two elderly mothers aside, the three women featured in these family stories are all wage earners, contribute huge physical and emotional energy to everyday domestic tasks, and undertake the demanding emotional work of attending to their mothers-in-law's and daughters' needs. While neither Xiao Yan nor Young Gao's wife took much of an active part in our conversations in their husbands' presence—indeed sometimes when Xiao Yan did, her husband told her not to interrupt—their activities and demeanor frequently suggested interests, opinions, and possible desires that were at odds with their deference to their husbands. Glimpses of aspirations for another kind of life emerged through Young Gao's wife's insistence on going to Tian'anmen during the protests of May and early June 1989. Similar glimpses emerged in a few brief comments Xiao Yan made one day, in her husband's presence, about a tourist trip she had made to Hong Kong a few years before.

Across their different ages and generations, the factors of poverty, material constraints and uncertainty, and poor education have been crucial in the accommodations of patriarchal arrangements discussed above. Distance from the formal structures of state employment and political organization, and rejection of the terms of the Party-state's language of power shaping the new "ruling class" (Guo and Sun 2002), sustained a space in which "traditional" ideas about gendered and generational attitudes toward patriarchal authority could survive, despite the appearance of huge changes in urban family life. The "privatization" of household and family life for many, maybe most, Dashalanr residents has done little to alter these ideas. With minimal pension or welfare benefits, the parameters of material support to which Meiling, Xiao Xi, and Xiao Yan had access were defined by their marital connections. The pragmatism in their choices on where to live and whom to marry was thus framed by the wider context of scarcity, the state's meager provision of welfare, and in recent years its aggressive commercial interest in pushing urban transformation. Over long decades, the accumulation of these factors urged a reassertion of the patrilocal household as the pivot of social support. Left to their own limited capacity and constantly threatened with relocation, these women were faced with the alternatives of dependence on patrilocal marriage or perpetual precariousness.

For their part, the two men described here, Young Gao and Zhao, both saw fulfillment of their patriarchal roles as core elements of their sense of being a good person. In Young Gao's case, this was articulated mainly through his distress at his failure to be a good son and husband, but it gave Zhao a strength and resoluteness that preserved his integrity in the face of his neighbors' disdain. If their devaluation of their wives—Zhao's silencing of his wife, Young Gao's complaints about his wife's domestic negligence— was not commensurate with their wives' everyday practice, it shored up their attachment to a notion of male authority as the core value of, and claim for, a social and family order denied them by the state.

Gail Hershatter has described how aged rural women repeatedly "assert the stability of their virtuous remembered selves across time," creating "continuity in the face of state inconstancy and familial neglect. They narrate a world full of hardship, indexing stubborn inequities that have yet to be recognized or addressed" (2011, 288). Along the same lines, the activities and values that Old Mrs. Gao and Meiling represent and sought recognition for center on accounts of having kept their families going in the face of conditions of extreme bitterness. Harking back to experiences of childhood suffering during the war-torn 1920s and 1930s, Old Mrs. Gao's story of constancy—to her mother, husband, and children—inversely mirrored her hardship. In Meiling's case, even if few of her neighbors cared to acknowledge her achievements, her constant reiteration of her determination and integrity—"I know I'm a good person"—contained an implicit call for recognition and compensation for the injustices of the world she found herself in. Claims to virtue indicated a sense of self-worth that was inseparable from deeply embedded gendered attachments to values of filiality and family obligation.

Patriarchy, therefore, appears as a recurring, if interrupted and paradoxical theme, featuring in both women's and men's practices, beliefs, and attitudes. As these three stories suggest, material and social circumstances and needs converged with a gendered sense of obligation, dignity, and integrity to sustain marriage as the pivot of patriarchal attachments and arrangements. Women in China have long exercised considerable power in domestic matters, in multiple ways, and through this, as many have argued (Judd 1994; Stafford 2009), in the wider world of social and political order. Evidence of their creative strength, hard work, and independence has long since replaced the trope of the victim of an oppressive feudal system. But in the case of the women of Dashalanr, continued investment in the structures of patriarchal authority and the trappings of patriarchal privilege are no less part of their understanding of family and social order and their claims for recognition, however much their practice might suggest otherwise. A patchy and reconfigured patriarchy thus continues at the same time that it is repeatedly questioned by practice.

NOTES

1   For a description of Dashalanr's conditions in the early aughts of the twenty-first century, inherited from the 1950s, see Zhu Mingde 2005, 213–17.

2   This paper draws on research I have been conducting since 2007 in Dashalanr, where I have been working in the Xuanwu District (now Western District) archives and collecting the oral histories of local residents, most of whom have lived in the neighborhood all their lives. I am hugely indebted to the late photographer Zhao Tielin and his assistant Huang Mingfang for introducing me to Dashalanr and its long-term residents.

3   According to the 2011 revision to China's Marriage Law, residential property is no longer to be jointly owned and divided equally in the event of divorce. Instead, whoever paid for the apartment or house is the legal owner and retains it in its entirety. Widely dubbed "the law that makes men laugh and women cry," the new ruling was presented as an attempt to reduce the inci-

dence of divorce, but its effect is to make many women vulnerable to patrilineal control.

4   I thank Gail Hershatter for this formulation.

5   These stories are reminders of Ellen Judd's (1994) argument that women's strength can be construed as a creative response to their subordination.

6   See Engebretsen, chapter 8; Jankowiak and Li, chapter 7; and Zavoretti, chapter 6.

PART 3

NEW TECHNOLOGIES, NEW INSTITUTIONS

CHAPTER TEN

TAKING PATRIARCHY OUT OF POSTPARTUM RECOVERY?

SUZANNE GOTTSCHANG

IMAGES of Kate, the Duchess of Cambridge, emerging from the hospital wearing a short dress and high heels only nine hours after giving birth on May 4, 2015, evoked envy and wonderment from observers around the world. China's blogs, websites, and news outlets, however, registered a different response.[1] How could the duchess violate so many of the taboos associated with postpartum recovery? Chinese women are expected to observe the long-standing tradition of "sitting the month" (*zuo yuezi*), a one-month period of postpartum rest and seclusion aimed at helping new mothers recover from the imbalances produced by childbirth. Contemporary sitting-the-month practices include staying indoors, resting in bed, and avoiding things like showering, drinking cold liquids, brushing teeth, or exposing oneself to breezes, especially cool ones. Chinese bloggers and news media, in commenting on Kate's postpartum appearance, went so far as to note the temperature in London that day: it was much too chilly and breezy to be safe for a new mother to walk out of the hospital in high heels.[2]

Not everyone in the Chinese blogosphere agrees with this view, but the debates surrounding Kate's postpartum behavior highlighted the continuing importance of sitting-the-month practices in contemporary China. While some bloggers went as far as to question the relevance of this "traditional" practice, most were concerned primarily with debating the relative merits of different ways of sitting the month. Particularly prominent in these debates were arguments about the need to develop a more "modern" and "scientific" approach to sitting the month. Should women sit the month using modern, scientific methods with the assistance of experts, or should they do it at home under the care of their mothers-in-law or, better still, their mothers? These debates are linked to recent technological and institutional developments in the context of China's increasingly medicalized and consumer-oriented society. Beginning in the late twentieth century, sitting-the-month centers or hotels have opened in China's major cities. These centers offer the opportunity to sit the month under the guidance of physicians and nurses, allowing new mothers to recover from childbirth away from the purview of their mothers-in-law and/or mothers. In addition to these centers, a new set of sitting-the-month services has emerged in the context of China's early twenty-first-century booming urban economy. These include sitting-the-month nurses and attendants who stay with new mothers in the home and sitting-the-month food delivery services that provide alternatives or additions to the typical practices supervised by older female kin.

These emergent sitting-the-month practices offer an opportunity to explore the reconfiguration of traditional patriarchal family structures and reproductive hierarchies. At a time when "traditional" birthing practices such as midwife-attended births and births outside the hospital have almost entirely faded and are dismissed as "backward," the persistence of sitting-the-month practices in urban China offers an opportunity to assess the extent to which modernist discourses and state policies promoting the medicalization of childbirth and women's bodies have challenged older reproductive hierarchies, including the power of elder mothers to manage the actions of younger mothers during the period of postpartum recovery. This chapter explores these changing patriarchal power relations in the family in the context of new developments in reproductive technologies such as sitting-the-month centers. The idea of "co-production" of technologies in a dynamic relationship to social institutions, identities, discourses, and practices makes this process visible (Jasanoff 2006). Co-production also reinforces how micro and macro levels of social analysis collapse if we attend to the fact that "the national or global constitutional orders we recognize and live by are constantly remade in innumerable, localized engagements; without this perpetual re-performance they might as well cease to exist" (Jasanoff 2006, 81). Bourdieu's (1977) concept of "official" (formal) and "practical" kinship also helps highlight how the strategies and technologies available to new mothers and their mothers-in-law and mothers in negotiating sitting the month can work to either reconfigure or maintain gender and generational hierarchies. Working together, these frameworks can help make clear how new and old versions of reproductive technologies like sitting the month can mediate power relations within the family.

My engagement with new developments in reproductive technologies and postpartum-recovery institutions in Reform era China goes back to fieldwork in a neighborhood general hospital in Beijing between 1994 and 1996. Subsequently, between 2004 and 2007, I undertook a follow-up fieldwork research project in two sitting-the-month centers in Shanghai. These materials refer to particular times and places, but when put together, they point to broader processes of transformation in sitting-the-month practices. Similar changes are occurring in other cities in China, but the shape of these transformations is diverse and takes a variety of manifestations as individuals and families navigate China's rapidly changing social, cultural, political, and economic landscape. This chapter also draws on materials collected online and in the context of short follow-up trips to China between 2007 and 2012.

SITTING THE MONTH IN HISTORICAL
AND CULTURAL CONTEXT

Typically supervised by mothers-in-law and/or mothers, numerous prohibitions and prescriptions grounded in traditional Chinese medical knowledge aim to help women and newborns recover from the dangerous imbalances of pregnancy and childbirth.[3] Sitting the month ideally restores balance in the woman's body and protects her and her infant and family during this vulnerable period. Although the rules vary over time and place, the most common prescriptions include no bathing, no hair washing, no leaving the house, and no eating of raw food or food with "cold" or chilling effects on the body and its organs. Instead, a mother should eat "heating" foods like sesame oil chicken or black-boned chicken. Women can also facilitate recovery by avoiding such activities as exercise, visiting others, weeping, sexual intercourse, and joining the family for meals.[4] Avoidance of bathing, drafts, excessive activity, and sexual intercourse, as well as eating a special diet, all aim to aid in restoring the woman's body after the rigors of pregnancy and childbirth. Seclusion from outsiders and family members protects new mothers and infants from disease and stress. The potential benefits of sitting the month also extend to women's long-term health, as the practice is seen to help new mothers prevent later chronic health problems such as back pain, arthritis, and headaches (Holroyd, Lopez, and Chan 2011). The importance of sitting the month in terms of long-term health protection was brought home to me by a Chinese friend who attributed the occasionally debilitating chronic back pain she suffered in 2010 to not sitting the month with her first child. She was married to an American and residing in the United States at the time, and her mother was not able to visit from China and assist with sitting the month.

Today urban Chinese women give birth in hospitals under the supervision of nurses and physicians. This shift to the hospital was initiated in the first half of the twentieth century and consolidated in the second half. Yet, long before the idea of hospital births came to be considered essential for protecting maternal and infant health, earlier Chinese medical traditions developed specialties in women's health (*fu ke*) and children's health (*er ke*) centered around the balance between the *yang* (male, active, hot) and the *yin* (female, passive, cold) in the female body. Charlotte Furth notes that in Qing dynasty China, "biological processes for women were based on an underlying exchange economy according to which women's vital blood is expended in the reproductive functions of menstruating, gestating, bearing and nursing children" (1987, 28; 1999, 92). Biological change was not benign. The blood of childbearing polluted the fetus, the mother, and her surroundings. In the Qing dynasty, ideas about pollution became a medical problem to be solved by physicians (Furth 1987, 29), and the dangers of gestation and childbirth became defined as health problems. Such health problems, however, were considered preventable. Medical routines and practices targeting mother and infant, such as proper disposal of the placenta, tonics, and ritual baths, were believed to protect both from disease (ibid.).

The practice of sitting the month was shaped by these developments. Furth suggests that it was in the Qing dynasty that sitting the month became associated with a systemic body of medical procedures aimed at controlling female pollution and thus helping the infant and the family cast off the dangers associated with the maternal body. The logic defining the mother's body as dangerous or inimical to the development of the child as a member of the family coincides with the perception that women had potential power to undermine male interests in maintaining and strengthening the lineage (Furth 1987, 29). In a patrilineal and patrilocal marriage system, women's potential to disrupt the family derives from the fact that they married into and resided with their husbands' families and thus were outsiders who might threaten family solidarity by prioritizing the interests of their husbands to the exclusion of larger family interests. On the one hand, as a wife, a woman remained outside her husband's family. On the other, as a mother, she was necessary not only for literally producing the next generation but also for overseeing the moral development of her young child, yet the emotional ties she built over time were also seen to bind her son more closely to her than to his father's family (M. Wolf 1972). Women in this context were often depicted as ambiguous subjects (i.e., subjects that were both inside and outside, pure and impure, virtuous and malicious), and medical developments during the Qing dynasty only reinforced these patrilineal ideologies. For Qing doctors, sitting the month was not just about taking care of individuals (the mother and the infant); it was also about protecting the interests of the patrilineal family and protecting everyone from the dangers of female pollution. Sitting the month was an important time for remedying some of the dangers and consequences of childbirth, but beyond this period of immediate recovery, future possibilities of producing descendants rested on the well-being of women.

The practice of sitting the month in the age of hospitals, nurses, and physicians continues to be shaped by patrilineal ideologies and family models, but new mothers now need to deal with the additional challenges of a nuclear family based on conjugal love (Jankowiak and Li, chap. 7) and nurture of the precious only child. New mothers are expected to return to full activity soon after childbirth, to contribute their wages to the household while taking care of family life. Regaining a pre-pregnancy body shape as rapidly as possible figures prominently in contemporary expectations. Popular magazines, books, websites, and advertising uphold this imperative as essential to performing the duties of motherhood. Diet and exercise are promoted as the most scientific and modern ways of rapidly losing the weight gained during pregnancy. Some of these recommendations seem extreme—beginning to do sit-ups and straight-leg lifts two days after giving birth, for example (Lucia 2011). The importance of losing pregnancy weight is one of the first topics found on popular websites for new Chinese mothers. A webpage headline on PCLady suggests, "Capture this golden moment: start losing weight while sitting the month" (ibid.). The first sentence explains that losing weight can become one of the greatest nightmares for new mothers. Why does weight loss matter so much to women? This article's premise rests on the assumption that it is women's nature to wish to be beautiful (ibid.). It goes on to explain that weight loss after childbirth also restores a woman's confidence. In addition to these demands on their bodies, women are also receiving the message that they must manage all aspects of their postpartum recovery as part of their role as confident, modern mothers seeking the best for themselves and their children.

These new expectations may be viewed as consequences of a consumer-oriented culture in which women have become both consumer and object in shaping lives as mothers (Evans 1997, 1995; J. Yang 2011). They contrast with the priorities and experiences of sitting the month among earlier generations of women. For example, most women interviewed who came of age during the Mao years described sitting the month as a period when the body was restored to its pre-pregnancy state by eating well and resting rather than by dieting and exercising. Whether and how that generation of women was able to sit the month depended not only on whether they resided in a city or a village at the time of childbirth but also on whether political campaigns or agendas in their workplaces made it imperative for them to return to their jobs.[5] As a retired obstetrics nurse related to me in 1994: "When I gave birth to my son in 1960, I was able to fully rest for two weeks. But I got called back to the hospital to participate in political meetings. I did not think I could stay home." In sum, while specific expectations have changed, the future of the family continues to depend on a woman's bodily well-being after childbirth.

SITTING THE MONTH: HOSPITALS, EXPERTS, AND CONSUMER CULTURE

Sitting the month exhibits the malleability of all traditions—it is subject to change in relation to larger social contexts and negotiated by individuals in practice. Contemporary sitting-the-month practices are not just shaped by the consumer-oriented culture that began to form in the 1990s (Yan 2011; Evans 2010). In addition, state policies, including the Marriage Law, the Birth-Planning Policy, the privatization of housing, and economic reforms have also worked to reconfigure the relationship between the multigenerational patrilineal family, the nuclear family, and new mothers. In the context of these institutions, women's ideas and decisions about how best to employ the reproductive technologies of postpartum recovery help produce ideals and potentials for the development of a strong, confident mother who in turn will produce a healthy, conscientious granddaughter or grandson and capable citizen.

Maternal Health and Hospitals: Global Politics and Consumer Culture

Since the 1990s, national policies and programs ensure that all women, whether in rural or urban areas, give birth in hospitals under the care of physicians. In order to achieve this goal, new hospital facilities have been built or refurbished; midwives, who usually managed uncomplicated deliveries, have been either retrained as physicians or transferred to other positions; referral networks, especially in rural areas, have helped handle complicated cases or emergencies; and hospitals and pregnant women in rural areas have received subsidies for births in hospital settings. In sum, the state has "institutionalized childbirth" (Feng et al. 2011; Liu, Maloni, and Patrini 2012). China's commitment to institutionalizing childbirth is an aspect of its participation in the United Nations Millennium Development Goals. The fifth goal sought a 75 percent reduction in maternal mortality ratios around the world and increased access to reproductive health care by 2015 (Tang, Li, and Wu 2006). In terms of the population's well-being, China's efforts have paid off. Maternal deaths declined from 97 per 100,000 births in 1990 to 32 per 100,000 births in 2012 (WHO 2015). However, the consequences of institutionalizing and medicalizing childbirth extend beyond improved maternal mortality ratios. As increasing numbers of births occurred in hospital-based facilities, China also saw a parallel increase in the number of cesarean sections performed. The arrival of sitting-the-month centers in cities in China in the twenty-first century thus may be seen as an outgrowth of the increasingly biomedical and surgical approach to childbirth.

While state policies focus on universal hospital births, established urban hospitals and new stand-alone maternity hospitals now offer a variety of services that personalize the birth experience. Emphasizing privacy and individualized attention, these units provide amenities ranging from private labor and delivery suites, food delivery from local restaurants, five-star-hotel-type suites with kitchens, luxury transport to and from the hospital, and, in one hospital, a medical butler service.[6] The cost to give birth in these facilities ranges from ¥8,000 (US$1,300) at a Shanghai district-level hospital's VIP obstetrics department to more than ¥90,000 (US$14,750) at international or joint venture hospitals.[7] Wealthy Chinese and international patients as well as those with moderate incomes avail themselves of these services. Many families believe they should spare no expense to ensure the arrival of a healthy, intelligent child. These centers extend the logic of institutionalization and commodification of childbirth in China, for if successful and safe childbirth requires biomedical supervision, postpartum recovery, an equally vulnerable time, might be best undertaken in a specialized sitting-the-month center.

Sitting the Month, Science, Expert Knowledge, and the Single Child

The questions and concerns about the use of scientific methods for sitting the month raised by the Duchess of Cambridge's appearance outside the hospital in May 2015 are part of broader discussions in Chinese online forums and websites. These discussions stem from two critical developments that intensified in the 1990s and continue to the present: the centrality of the application of scientific knowledge in China's modernization project begun under Deng Xiaoping, and the shift in population policy from emphasizing adherence to the Birth-Planning Policy and reducing the quantity of the population to improving its quality (*suzhi*). Translated into policies and practices, the medical and scientific management of pregnancy, childbirth, and infant care is reinforced in government-sponsored prenatal and parenting courses and in popular media, including websites, popular books, and news outlets. From preconception to childhood, the message from these outlets is that mothers are responsible for the quality of their children and require expert advice and guidance if they are to succeed (Gottschang 2001; J. Zhu 2010).

Unlike direct policies like the Birth-Planning Policy, the use of expert knowledge, whether by the state or by the community, works more indirectly so that individuals learn how to govern themselves in ways that intersect with state interests (see Greenhalgh and Winckler 2005; see also Klein, chap. 11 in this volume). In the context of ensuring the production of a high-quality child, mothers also matter. Their bodies, their knowledge, and their capacities shape the course of rearing a child. Thus a "scientific" postpartum recuperation becomes central to the project of producing a high-quality child. Recently, online resources have also come to form an alternative venue for those seeking expert advice and support for sitting the month. Consulting any of China's popular search engines such as Sohu or Baidu for information on sitting the month yields thousands of sites. For example, a search on Sohu brings up websites from Chinese content providers such as PCBaby, which offers articles addressing various aspects of sitting the month including weight loss, tips for recovery from cesarean sections, and "traditional" recipes for the recovering mother. This expansion of online sources on sitting the month may be seen as yet another instance of expert knowledge reinstitutionalizing a "traditional" practice in a new context, but it may also be seen as an increasingly important resource for new mothers as they negotiate their postpartum recoveries with their female kin.[8]

The recent availability of expert knowledge online and in print to help guide urban women as they sit the month might reflect China's increasingly consumer-oriented culture. Yet together with the state's medicalization of childbirth and the constant pressure for women to produce highly intelligent and capable future citizens, these forces work to coproduce more flexible possibilities for sitting the month in twenty-first-century China. Such possibilities then present new ways for new mothers to sidestep or negotiate the authority of the experiences and knowledge of their own mothers.

Looking at how women manage the tradition of sitting the month over time makes visible the workings of co-production and negotiations of practical and official kinship relations. As they anticipate and then experience sitting the month, women bring together knowledge and technology from their mothers' generation and from their own. In doing so, they seek ways of balancing enduring patriarchal expectations with their own practical concerns with health. Much as Harriet Evans (chap. 9), Elisabeth Engebretsen (chap. 8), and Roberta Zavoretti (chap. 6) show us, echoes of filial piety arise as women wish to maintain good relations with their elder kin while recovering, while at the same time they seek to balance the logics of consumer culture, science, modernity, and the emerging nuclear family. Their reflections on this process, from about 1990 to the present, offer insight into how women choose their own paths from a welter of shifting and sometimes contradictory messages about motherhood and its duties. Together, these points in time help illuminate the elastic nature of patriarchal kinship and reproductive hierarchies in the face of rapid social change.

Sitting the Month in 1990s China

As Yang Huizhi, a twenty-six-year-old factory worker told me in 1996: "Giving birth is very tiring. Sitting the month is a time when you should rest your body and protect it against illness and infection."[9] Huizhi's observation was shared by all thirty women in my study sample. No one questioned the vulnerability of the postpartum body or the necessity of a monthlong recovery. We had extensive discussions about the postpartum period and sitting the month, and all thirty women said that they knew about sitting the month primarily from their mothers or mothers-in-law.[10] Most frequently mentioned was the necessity of rest for a new mother. All stressed that childbirth exhausts a woman's body and makes her vulnerable to illness.

Still, some parts of sitting the month were irritating to the young mothers. The prescription that elicited the most concern were the prohibitions against showering, washing hair, and brushing teeth. Wu Qiuping's response was typical: "Impossible!" (Bu keneng!). A young factory worker, she believed that not showering was a backward practice that did not suit modern, urban lifestyles. "I plan on visiting a friend's house nearby if my mother-in-law does not allow me to shower," she explained. Often, as women told me about this practice, they also admitted that they would absolutely refuse to follow this restriction. By contrast, many women accepted prohibitions that amounted to rejecting modern practices: twenty-one, for example, mentioned that watching television or reading at this time could cause eyestrain or vision problems in the future.

Dietary prescriptions were accepted as a routine part of recovery, and these meshed with long-standing ideas about body and balance (Su 1997). Food is important in many facets of health maintenance in China (Farquhar 2002), but the kinds of foods believed necessary after birth were contested, as Qiuping's narrative shows:

> I know that you should drink fresh chicken blood when sitting the month. The blood helps strengthen the body after birth. My mother-in-law said that she drank blood after each of her births and recovered her health quickly. Today, she is strong and healthy. . . . I do not think drinking fresh chicken blood is a good idea. . . . I am going to try one of the tonics made from black boned chicken blood that you can buy in the stores. You know these? They are very popular. . . . I just think that this tonic might be better than the traditional practice of drinking chicken blood.

Wu Qiuping readily replaced a home remedy with a commodity, a signal that consumerism had entered the equation. However, her willingness to consume a product made from the same essential ingredient as that recommended by her mother-in-law reflects how such practices might be mediated between the generations. Many women in my study planned strategies for dealing with customs their senior female kin wished to impose. Qiuping's decision illustrates how practical kinship operates, as she simultaneously manages her health and works to preserve the cultural ideal of kinship by using a product that acknowledges her mother-in-law's knowledge and authority.

Li Yurong, a twenty-four-year-old office worker, saw problems and benefits when accepting help from female kin:

> Sitting the month was difficult. My mother-in-law made at least three meat dishes every day, and I do not like to eat meat. . . .
> My mother-in-law told me that I needed to eat meat because my body was cold after the birth. She told me I would get sick if I did not eat meat and if I did not protect myself from winds. . . . I did bathe, but I did not take any showers. I washed my hair only once a week, and even then, my mother-in-law told me I would get sick. I told her that I would get sick from not being clean. . . .

The baby was fine; my mother-in-law helped me a lot with him. She would feed him and let me sleep. . . . Now that this time is finished, I feel prepared to go back to work.

These comments show how a new mother could navigate the recovery period drawing on both modern sensibilities and traditional knowledge while relying on a mother-in-law to help care for herself and her infant. Yurong's appreciation of the respite her mother-in-law provided by caring for her infant, along with her feeling that she was prepared to return to work, did not mean that she felt obligated to follow her mother-in-law's precise instructions. Moreover, Yurong did not internalize any fear that avoiding many of the customs of sitting the month would cause problems in her relationship with her mother-in-law. Her perspective resonates with Hong Zhang's findings (chap. 12) that filial piety and the obligations of the younger generation to their seniors can exhibit the qualities of more interdependent rather than hierarchical relationships.

While women figured out ways of maintaining an acceptable level of cleanliness, difficulties arose around food and eating habits. In fact, the women I interviewed during the first forty-two days postpartum almost all mentioned conflict over food and their mothers' or mothers-in-law's authoritative knowledge about appropriate eating.[11] Some, like Yurong—who expressed frustration with her mother in-law's insistence that she eat meat in order to regain her health even though she did not like meat—felt overwhelmed by the types of food they were asked to consume. For others, their concern centered on eating the proper foods and losing weight.[12] In most cases, women complained that they were being required to eat too much. One woman told me that her mother-in-law made her eat chicken for the first seven days after she came home from the hospital: "chicken soup, chicken wings, roast chicken, stewed chicken—every day I ate chicken." Yang Huizhi's retired mother lived with her and her husband and forced her to eat tofu every day: "My mother knows that I don't like tofu very much, but every day during the month she would make a dish with it. If I would not eat it, she would serve it again later." In this instance, a mother and daughter locked horns over desires and acceptable practices that were clearly in conflict; the daughter refused to eat the tofu and the mother recycled it for the next meal. Its constant presence at meals resulted in Huizhi capitulating and eating a food she disliked. Perhaps the insistence on and resistance to eating the tofu could continue as it did because these women were mother and daughter. While seniority and authority are embodied in the mother's actions, her daughter may have felt more comfortable resisting food from her own mother for longer than she might have with a mother-in-law. Negotiating kinship relations not customarily represented as central to the Chinese patrilineal family thus might produce reactions that still represent a power difference in terms of seniority and yet incorporate the intimacy of the uterine family (M. Wolf 1972). Finally, at stake for both generations of women was the well-being of both mother and infant. In navigating between the authority and knowledge of the senior generation and those of new mothers, the interdependent nature of this recovery process remained central (J. Zhu 2010).

Sitting-the-Month Centers: The Future of Tradition?

A November 7, 2001, article in China's official Party newspaper, *People's Daily*, proclaimed "Chinese Mothers Give Up Traditional Childbearing Beliefs." It described Zhejiang as home to several hospitals that provide services to women during the first postpartum month, declaring that these centers offer "professional, scientific, and personalized instructions to young mothers during their period of 'confinement.'" The article makes clear that the technologies and knowledge that served earlier generations of women might not aid women of the twenty-first century: "To the older generation of Chinese, toothbrushing, showering, exposing oneself to wind, and eating certain foods are all taboo during the one-month confinement after a woman gives birth. Today, however, more young mothers in coastal Zhejiang are putting aside these misconceptions and spending their puerperium [postpartum] month in the hospital" (*People's Daily* 2001).

In addition to being in air-conditioned, clean rooms with televisions, a new mother can exercise under a physician's supervision to regain her former slim figure at an earlier date. The hospitals also provide new parents with training on promoting their infant's mental and physical development using "scientific" methods. The article explains how these hospitals fill an important need for young couples as they confront the traditions of their parents alongside their own more science-oriented views on reproduction and infancy.

Moving the tradition of sitting the month outside the home and the purview of senior female kin comes at a price. For example, by 2014, families in Zhengzhou, the capital of Henan in central China, could expect to pay an average of ¥10,000; Shanghai families could pay as little as ¥15,350 for the month, with some five-star-level centers charging more than ¥122,800. Despite the costs, centers are fully booked and have waiting lists.[13] With an average per capita disposable annual income (2013) of ¥26,995 for urban residents, a monthlong stay at a maternity hotel represents a substantial financial investment for a family (Yanlin Wang 2014).

The characterization of these centers in the *People's Daily* (2001) article mentioned above echoed the women I met in 2004 and 2007 who gave their reasons for choosing to spend their recovery outside the home. Li Xia, a twenty-six-year-old new mother recovering at the Bright Futures sitting-the-month center in 2004 explained:

> I followed all of the recommendations and requirements of my doctor during pregnancy to make sure my child was healthy and intelligent. One day, I realized that I needed to consider how best to recover and care for my baby too. I was so focused on the pregnancy that I had not thought too much about after! I wanted to make sure that we could use the most up-to-date scientific and medical methods to recover, so I found out about these sitting-the-month centers from my doctors. My mother-in-law is a smart, capable woman, but her ideas about sitting the month seemed old-fashioned.

Wang Fang, a twenty-seven-year-old administrator for a joint venture company in Shanghai, offered similar reasons:

> I am not sure that the traditional ways were useful or good for women, except for resting. Of course the body is depleted from childbirth and needs to recover. But these other methods, they seem like mostly superstitions. I wanted to be able to rest fully after childbirth, and my mother supported the idea of me stay-ing in a sitting-the-month center. When she gave birth, all she wanted was to rest, but she did not. . . . Her own mother was dead, and her mother-in-law had health problems. . . . My mother is very strong and healthy, and she did not get the chance to rest, and she did not follow the rules for sitting the month. Here, I get plenty of rest in a peaceful environment while the nurses take care of me and my son, and they use modern medicine and hygienic practices—so I don't worry about anything either.

In addition to seeking modern scientific and medical institutions for their recovery, the concerns registered by these women about older women's "traditional" or "old-fashioned" beliefs were shared by the twelve women I interviewed in 2004 and 2007. By removing themselves from the spaces of the home, these women hoped to eliminate negotiations about how best to sit the month. Wang Yuqing, an office worker from Shanghai, explained in 2007:

> My mother-in-law and mother are very strong, capable women, and they were very helpful during pregnancy; they did not interfere too much. If the doctor told me to do something, then they agreed that this advice was best followed. But sitting the month—aiya! I knew that they would think they were the experts and I would have little say about anything. I worried that there would be conflict among us and that since I would be tired after the birth, it would be difficult for me to manage them and rest and care for my baby. My husband agreed. So I heard about these types of centers at the hospital. I asked my mother and mother-in-law to help me find one that was hygienic, had a good reputation, and offered good care for me and the baby. This way, they participated in the decision and could not complain too much if they thought the whole thing was a bad idea!

Including senior female kin in the decision-making process worked as a strategy for preventing bad feelings between generations. Three other women I spoke to also mentioned that their mothers or mothers-in-law helped choose the sitting-the-month center. New mothers, then, drew on the expertise and knowledge of their mothers or mothers-in-law in selecting the venue, a space where other aspects of their expertise would not be welcome. In doing so, these women began forging a new equilibrium in their generational relationships.

Efforts to balance the needs and interests of younger and older generations of women at the sitting-the-month center were reflected in the guest rooms. On a tour of the Bright Futures Center, I noted that each room contained two twin beds. Director Ye informed me that husbands as well as mothers-in-law or mothers often stayed in the rooms, "but they are forbidden to interfere or change the foods, regimens, or activities for women during their stay." I asked if the center had difficulties enforcing this policy, and she laughingly replied: "Almost all older women try at least once or twice to smuggle in a special soup or a chicken dish, or they try to convince their daughters not to follow some of the practices of the center. But our nurses and staff make clear that such interference will not be tolerated." In this instance, medical personnel bypass new mothers and exert authority in managing the older generation.

Most of the new mothers I met at Bright Futures and Gold Month said that their husbands and their mothers stayed with them at different points during their monthlong recovery.[14] Zhang Lihua explained that her mother stayed during the week and her husband came for the weekend: "It is less lonely for me here with my mother or my husband staying." When I asked why she chose such a center, Lihua replied: "This is the most modern method for regaining my strength and health. I believe that there are some aspects of traditional ways of sitting the month that are helpful, because it would not continue to be so important if it was not effective. But I am not able to know which methods are best and which are not—an expert in such matters, like a physician, knows much more."

Another new mother, Wang Anyu, believed that the center offered the most modern and safest means of recovering from childbirth, but she also missed the comforts and familiarity of home. She was happy to have her mother and husband take turns staying with her, because they made her feel more comfortable with living in an unfamiliar setting. Women's belief in the recovery process offered by the centers and their longing for the familiarity of home could work to coproduce a new type of role for the two generations. Whether it is keeping their daughters or daughters-in-law company or helping to locate the best possible center for sitting the month, the contours of the official kinship role of senior female kin as authorities in the family might be maintained in these practices.

Compromise between generations could also come about because sitting-the-month centers draw on the principles of traditional Chinese medicine to aid women's recovery. From serving diets based on these principles, to protecting women from unnecessary drafts, to limiting visitors, to caring for infants—the routines of the center represented an amalgam of old and new. Shi Li, a twenty-seven-year-old office manager, commented on how traditional foods and practices assuaged her mother's concerns about sitting the month at the Gold Month center: "My mother believes that some of the traditions of sitting the month are not negotiable, especially eating the proper foods to help the body heal. She was not worried once she knew that all the foods here are prepared using the methods of traditional Chinese medicine." Other women echoed these comments. Sitting-the-month centers that used the practices and principles of traditional Chinese medicine in their recovery regimens then provided another opportunity for new mothers to navigate the reproductive hierarchies of the family. The effort required of new mothers and their families to purchase and use modern biomedical and traditional technologies for postpartum recovery and the attempts of senior female kin to remain part of their daughters' or daughters-in-law's recovery in the spaces of these centers illustrate how the management of reproduction in contemporary China continues in a dynamic relation between practical and official forms of kinship.

． ． ．

In a 2009 overview of childbirth in China, Harvey and Buckley argue that the state project to modernize the nation by using modern science and medicine, and by rejecting traditions and customs, brought about the medicalization of childbirth for most women in China (2009, 57). Regarding sitting the month, they state: "To the extent that *zuo yuezi* persists, it does so largely because of its interconnectedness with the role of elderly mothers who, because of their age, have the authority to override the salient modernistic discourse and instead impose traditional customs to control the younger women's actions during this month" (64). Their conclusion rests on an assumption that such a long-standing custom persists because of the traditional authority of senior female kin in a multigenerational patrilineal household.

The persistence of sitting-the-month practices in contemporary China is not a product of unchanging gendered generational hierarchies but is negotiated between new mothers and their mothers or mothers-in-law, whether this is done in the home or in a center. Young women in the 1990s relied on their knowledge and modern sensibilities about which aspects of sitting the month might be avoided or revised without compromising recovery from childbirth. They used a range of strategies, from minimally sitting the month to eating distasteful foods to substituting a more hygienic, modern form of traditional remedies such as chicken blood to manage the process. In the twenty-first century, new mothers are opting to recover in sitting-the-month centers using new technologies of postpartum recovery managed by modern medical authorities. At first glance, this usage of modern biomedical technologies and traditional Chinese medicine appears to be a strategy aimed at erasing the authoritative role played by senior female kin in the process of postpartum recovery, but this may not be the case. By opting to recover in sitting-the-month centers under the supervision of nurses and physicians, new mothers are not rejecting the foundations of the knowledge and authority of their mothers and mothers-in-law. Members of the senior generation kept their daughters company in a space outside the comforts and familiarity of home by maintaining a regular presence at the centers. In both instances, technology and knowledge worked dynamically to reinforce and reconfigure structures of authority and power regulating the relations between older and younger women in the family.

SUZANNE GOTTSCHANG

NOTES

This chapter owes its evolution from a conference paper to Stevan Harrell's and Gonçalo Santos's unfailing editorial assistance. Francesca Bray, Henrike Donner, and two anonymous reviewers also provided helpful insights and direction.

1   See Julie Makenin, "British Princess's Debut Produces Postpartum Shock and Awe in China," May 7, 2015, and Fan Yiying, "Sitting the Month: Gift or Torture?" May 11, 2015, *What's on Weibo*, www.whatsonweibo.com/sitting-the-month/ (accessed June 12, 2015).

2   Makenin, "British Princess's Debut," and Fan, "Sitting the Month," *What's on Weibo*, www.whatsonweibo.com/sitting-the-month/ (accessed June 12, 2015).

3   Ahern 1975; Furth 1987; M. Wolf 1972; Topley 1974; Pillsbury 1978; R. Watson 1985; Santos 2004; S. Sanna Chen 2012. According to Chinese medical and ritual traditions, women's bodies are said to be particularly "polluting" and vulnerable to winds and cold during the period of pregnancy and childbirth. As to newborns, their souls are only very loosely attached to their bodies, so they are still very vulnerable beings. In this context, the aim of sitting the month was to counter the ill effects of birth pollutants and to prevent infant soul loss.

4   S. Sanna Chen 2012; Pillsbury 1978, 13; Liu, Maloni, and Patrini 2012.

5   In more contemporary contexts, Santos (chap. 4) finds that in rural Northern Guangdong, women must return to work as soon as possible, leaving their infants in the care of paternal grandparents.

6   Shanghai Red Leaf International Women's Hospital offers medical butler services that handle logistics for patients; see Redleaf Hospital, "Postpartum Services," http://www.redleafhospital.com/index/department/id/5 (accessed July 18, 2015).

7   These prices refer only to labor and delivery and the hospital stay. Prenatal care is paid for separately. For prices in 2014, see *Shanghai Expat*, www.expat-medicare.com/content/giving-birth-shanghai (accessed June 30, 2015).

8   See J. Zhu 2010.

9   All names, personal and institutional, are pseudonyms.

10   See also Holroyd, Lopez, and Chan 2011.

11   See J. Zhu, 2010 for a discussion on how mothers and pregnant daughters manage their conflicting ideas about nutrition during pregnancy.

12   Conflicts about body shape may also manifest in relationships between mothers-in-law and daughters-in-law (Santos, pers. comm., 2013). Santos notes that in rural Guangdong, a mother-in-law described her frustration with her son who married a slender young woman, a body type associated by her peers and her husband with youth and urban life. The mother-in-law worried that the young woman's slimness meant that she would not be strong enough to help with farming and would have difficulties bearing children. In fact, the senior

woman's concerns were confirmed when the young woman had a difficult childbirth, and yet, while sitting the month, the new mother sought to regain her pre-pregnancy slim body shape.

13   See Zhao Dan, "Yuezi zhongxin zuo yuezi zui gui ershi wan" (Most expensive sitting-the-month centers now ¥200,000), May 24, 2014, *Dongfang ribao*, http://wenku.baidu.com/view/a7adbb4e4431b90d6d85c713.html (accessed June 2015), and "Health Center Gears Up to Pamper New Moms," *China Daily*, February 14, 2007, http://english1.china.org.cn/english/health/200081.htm (accessed March, 18, 2013).

14   It may be notable that only one woman's mother-in-law stayed with her, but my sample is much too small to generalize.

CHAPTER ELEVEN

ASSISTED REPRODUCTIVE TECHNOLOGIES, SPERM DONATION, AND BIOLOGICAL KINSHIP

A Recent Chinese Media Debate

KERSTIN KLEIN

I N 1988, only ten years after the birth of the world's first baby conceived through in vitro fertilization (IVF) in England, China reported the birth of its first baby conceived from IVF and embryo transfer. This marked the beginning of China's intensive involvement with assisted reproductive technologies (ARTs), which are methods to achieve pregnancy by artificial or partially artificial means.[1] A lot of work has been done in anthropology and science and technology studies on the impact of ARTs in different national and cultural contexts. Some of this work has focused on the specificities of national social, cultural, legal, and ethical responses to ARTs (e.g., Inhorn and Van Balen 2002; Strathern 1992) including those in China.[2] These debates over ARTs in China are playing an important role in the reexamination of traditional notions of patrilineal kinship.

The development of ARTs in China is unique in that its rise coincides with the biopolitical setting of a mandatory policy limiting couples to one child.[3] Between the 1960s and 1980s, China experienced one of the most rapid and impressive declines in fertility ever recorded in a national population (Riley 2004), beginning even before the policy was implemented nationwide in 1979. The total fertility rate went down from six children per woman in the late 1960s to just over two children in the early 1980s (ibid.). Little more than two decades into the Birth-Planning Policy, the fifth census of China's National Bureau of Statistics in 2000 reported that the total fertility rate had further dropped to 1.22 (OECD 2010), but the result was deemed implausible due to an underreporting of births and was estimated as more likely to be below 1.5 (Cai 2013).

Since 2000, there has been a shift from a "Leninist" approach toward a more "neoliberal" approach to birth planning, as Greenhalgh and Winckler (2005) have pointed out. This is a gradual shift from Maoist mobilizational and Stalinist bureaucratic approaches of population control to comprehensive reform under Jiang Zemin, which sought to limit direct control by the state in favor of more indirect governance through the market and legal system and by communities, families, and individuals themselves. A range of new institutions now supplements the work of the Population Planning Commission, including other state bodies, overseas development agencies, commercial enterprises, and independent professionals who advertise products and provide services and advice. The state also allowed limited, grassroots nongovernmental organizations and village self-government to promote voluntary compliance with population policy targets. The new "softer" approaches, along with preexisting "harder" methods of direct control, indicate that the state succeeded to some extent in creating "self-regulating" subjects "whose interests, desires, and choices align with those of the neoliberal market and state" (ibid., 244), for example, by delaying pregnancy, using contraception, or opting for abortion.[4]

In this new biopolitical context of neoliberal population control and greater self-regulation by Chinese citizens, there emerged a new concern around infertility. Before the Birth-Planning Policy, population growth and reproduction were regarded as abundant in China (Handwerker 2002), but since the population became something that has to be controlled and fiercely limited, there has been a growing perception that infertility is on the increase. The Chinese media generally report that the infertility rate was only 3 percent twenty years ago and is now 12.5 percent (*People's Daily* 2012b; *South China Morning Post* 2013). According to the Chinese Population Association's "Investigative Report into the Current State of Infertility in China," released during the China International Summit Forum on Infertility in 2009, at least 40 million couples were estimated to have difficulties in having children or were actually infertile, putting the infertility rate at 12.5 percent for all couples between twenty-five to thirty years of age (*South China Morning Post* 2009). In the absence of national time series statistics, it is difficult to know whether infertility is actually on the rise, or whether there is merely an increased perception of crisis when infertility occurs, but it is unlikely that the actual rate of infertility could have risen that much.

In any society, ARTs and the donation of embryos and gametes (eggs and sperm) are strongly influenced by sociological environments and national policies. Many concerns surrounding these issues are unique to China, where traditional beliefs about biological patriliny are being called into question by the exigencies of reproduction in a situation of low fertility and perceived or real increase in infertility. In this situation, people are slowly developing new ideas about what is important in kinship and descent, including rethinking the meaning of both biological and social patriliny, one of the key components of Chinese patriarchy.

In 2012, the sudden death of a sperm donor in Wuhan triggered a public discussion on the dangers of the practice of sperm donation. This discussion revealed a number of cultural biases against sperm donation, leading to a national media debate about ARTs and the shortage of donors to China's numerous human sperm banks.[5]

CULTURAL AND SOCIAL FACTORS OF INFERTILITY AND REPRODUCTION IN CHINA

In traditional Chinese thinking, patrilineal kinship is viewed as sacred, and much emphasis is placed on the spiritual connectedness between ancestors and their patrilineal descendants. The tie of descent is of utmost concern to a family (Liao, Dessein, and Pennings 2010). Especially in rural areas of China, many people still adhere to traditional values about reproduction and the family. It is held to be a man's greatest obligation to provide his family line with at least one heir, a male child who is able to continue the tradition of ancestor worship and to contribute at least one son to the patriline in his turn (Bray 2008). Equally, it has been seen to be the woman's duty to bear sons for her husband in order to carry on his family line.

Qiu Renzong (2002), a bioethicist prominent in the discourse on IVF and stem cell research in China, has noted that ancestor worship and patrilineal descent are more important than individual identity. Filial piety is a central principle of Chinese tradition, and procreation has been an important aspect of filial piety for thousands of years (ibid.). Childlessness was a failure of filial duty to parents and ancestors (Heng 2009). Hence China's history is full of examples of how alternative techniques of reproduction were used to bypass infertility or to get hold of additional children, in particular if a couple was unable to bear a son. Such reproductive techniques included adoption of (extra) sons from agnates or even from strangers (when it often resembled purchase more than adoption), uxorilocal marriage of daughters, adoption of daughters who were then married uxorilocally, or taking concubines when a wife had not produced an heir.[6] That such practices were widespread in premodern China suggests that traditional notions of patrilineal descent were not based only on biological principles (*qi*) but also on socio-legal considerations (Bray 2008). Only the strictest interpretations of Confucian tradition prohibited child adoption among close relatives belonging to the same patrilineal clan or extended family and sharing the same surname (J. Watson 1975a), but even then, exceptions were sometimes allowed. Beginning in the 1990s, the practice of adoption came under the Birth-Planning Policy, making it very difficult for couples with children to adopt, either from close relatives (Mosher 2006) or from orphanages (Johnson 2004). Until 1999, the law allowed adoption only for couples who were both childless and over the age of thirty-five. In 1999, the law was amended to permit adoption from orphanages for couples over thirty years of age with or without birth children, but adoption outside orphanages still requires that parents be childless.

In this new era of strict birth planning and intensive regulation, adoption from strangers has become a more widely accepted strategy for both childless and reproductive couples who may have lost an only child to accidents, disease, or other causes or who want to complete their families. According to Weiguo Zhang (2006a), adoption is a strategy not only for reaching the ideal family size but also for achieving the ideal sex composition among children. For instance, a couple who already has a girl will use adoption to add a boy, but more families are also seeking to adopt girls. Today, there is in fact a major shift in the roles of sons and daughters,[7] and of men and women generally. Chinese people value daughters more highly than ever before (Johnson 2004), and as Lihong Shi discusses in chapter 2, in rural Northeast China a growing number of couples prefer to have a singleton daughter because increasing numbers of sons have failed in their roles as providers of adequate support for their elders. Today, there are fewer children (especially sons) available for adoption than there were before the Birth-Planning Policy. In this sense, it seems that the Birth-Planning Policy and the perception that infertility is on the rise have mutually reinforced each other. When there were extra children available, infertility was also a problem, but there were other ways of dealing with it. The paradox of the situation is that while the regime has actively tried to limit fertility, it has also limited the earlier alternatives for dealing with infertility.

Given the strong cultural emphasis on reproduction and on continuing the patriline, and given the shortage of children available for adoption or for marrying in, ARTs have become salient. At a time when at least the perception of infertility has gone up, ARTs take on a new cultural importance. They offer new alternative ways of dealing with infertility. For some couples, treatment with ARTs is not biologically possible without the involvement of donors. Sperm donation and cryopreservation serve as remedies for the lack of male gametes in infertile couples and satisfy the male partner's desire to have a child, despite the absence of a biological, or "ancestral," link. Babies born with the aid of ARTs help to prevent the social stigma of childlessness (Handwerker 1998), but involvement of a third party (the donor) disrupts the biological link between the father and his offspring. Consequently, ARTs are highly controversial in China. It can be argued that adoption of donated embryos left over from IVF treatment would be the same as non-agnatic child adoption, because both types of adoption imply that the child is not biologically related to his or her social parents. However, while child adoption has always been accommodated in China, embryo donation and embryo adoption are strictly banned (Klein 2010).

REGULATION OF ARTS, GAMETE DONATION, AND SPERM BANKS IN CHINA

Since ARTs became available in China in the early 1990s, the number of government-approved and government-licensed fertility clinics offering IVF services to infertile married couples has surpassed one hundred. Rapid growth of ARTs services has created a huge demand for donor sperm. About 10 percent of infertile couples reportedly turn to a sperm bank for help (*Shanghai Daily* 2005). There are approximately thirty reproductive centers in China that are qualified to offer artificial insemination with donor sperm treatments (Ping et al. 2011, 647), but all are facing the same problem, a shortage of sperm donors. In large cities like Beijing, Shanghai, Nanjing, and Guangzhou, more than ten thousand couples hope to undergo artificial insemination with donor sperm as soon as possible (Gong et al. 2009, 645), but long waiting lists and waits of up to two years cause some infertile couples to give up on their plans (Ping et al. 2011, 647). China's first human sperm bank, at Xiangya Reproduction and Genetics Hospital in Hunan, was built in 1981; it was also the first to be licensed by the Ministry of Health in 2001. Each province is entitled to have only one sperm bank. China's fourteenth sperm bank was opened in Hebei in January 2012, and the seventeenth in Sichuan in 2013 (*China Daily* 2013b).

The donation of gametes (eggs and sperm) is a lawful act that has been regulated by the Ministry of Health (National Health and Family Planning Commission since 2013) under a series of legal regulations and official directives for human assisted reproductive technologies and sperm banks since 2001 (MOH 2001a, 2001b, 2001c, 2003). The standard protocol requires that all sperm banks be closely monitored and administered by both central and local health authorities. The Ministry of Health issued decree no. 44 in 2006, on the regulation of medically assisted human reproduction techniques and accreditation of human sperm banks (MOH 2006b), which stipulates that the license of every infertility center has to be renewed every two years. If requirements are not met, the service is suspended.

Egg (oocyte) donation is seen as less of a problem than sperm donation or even child adoption, because it "only" entails a loss of genetic connectedness to the mother, not to the father (Heng 2009).[8] According to Ministry of Health regulations covering ARTs and accreditation of human sperm banks (MOH 2006b), only women who undergo IVF or intracytoplasmic sperm injection qualify as egg donors, and oocyte donation is permitted only if the patient has twenty or more mature oocytes.[9] Of these, at least fifteen must be retained for the patient's own use, for insemination by her husband's or a donor's sperm, and the extra oocytes are cryopreserved. If the patients become pregnant and have healthy live births, they are allowed to donate their remaining cryopreserved eggs to other infertile couples. Such extremely stringent regulations have led to a severe shortage of available donor oocytes and long waiting lists for prospective donor egg recipients at all fertility clinics in China. At the same time, egg banks do not yet exist in China, but ARTs professionals have urged the government to adopt regulations so that egg banks can be officially opened (People's Daily 2013).

Sperm donation is a more sensitive issue, because the biological father provides the relevant genetic or patrilineal link. The guidelines for ARTs and human sperm banks stipulate that only men between the ages of twenty-two and forty-five years are eligible to donate (MOH 2001, 2003). A donor's health records and sperm quality must meet strict requirements. The guidelines further stipulate that ARTs cannot be provided to single women or unmarried or same-sex couples, and also that a donor can impregnate only up to five married women via artificial insemination or IVF. His sperm cannot be used again when one of the recipients becomes pregnant. Medical institutions are required to maintain confidentiality for all persons who are involved in ARTs, including donors, who are guaranteed anonymity. Neither the offspring nor the receiving couple can obtain a sperm or egg donor's identity. Due to the emphasis on patrilineal bloodlines, which has the potential to make a donor child difficult to accept (Qiu 2002), most Chinese couples respect anonymity, as it goes hand in hand with the secrecy rule (Liao, Dessein, and Pennings 2010). When the act of conception via donor is kept secret, the child will also never ask for his or her genetic father's name.[10]

Nevertheless, demand for donor sperm exists, in spite of the continuing cultural bias toward biological patrilineal continuity. This is not very surprising in light of previous attitudes toward adoption. Today, as in earlier times, the emphasis on biological connection and patrilineality clearly does not have the same significance as the desire for a child, even if patrilineal continuity in the biological sense is possible only with genetically linked male offspring. As Chinese citizens have become more aware of ARTs, many clinics have also experienced a rise in patients seeking treatment for "infertility," when in fact they are hoping for sex selection with the aim of having a boy. There are no estimates for the sex ratio of ARTs babies, but sex-selective abortion has been banned since 2003, when the Ministry of Health's revised ARTs regulations went into effect, stating that "any identification of the sex of a fetus with no medical purpose and abortions based on gender preferences are strictly prohibited."

SPERM DONATION AND THE NATIONAL SHORTAGE OF SPERM DONORS REPORTED IN THE MEDIA

In 2012, the death of a thirty-five-year-old doctoral student in the city of Wuhan who had made his fourth donation at the local university's sperm bank received great exposure and brought the issue of sperm donation to the center of attention (*China Daily* 2012b).[11] The case prompted the head of Guangdong's family planning commission to appear on a local radio program, telling Chinese men that "donating your sperm is healthy. . . . It won't hurt you or kill you" (*China Daily* 2012a). The unusual plea from an official representative of the state signified that the government had been forced to step into a burgeoning crisis, which led to a surge of media reports on the issue of sperm donation and the national shortage of sperm donors. Newspapers have debated this more broadly, looking at national culture and the individual motives of donors, recipients, and those opposing sperm donation.

The shortage of sperm donors is generally attributed to China's patrilineal kinship tradition and the fear of having unknown offspring. Indeed, many Chinese men have been found to believe that allowing unknown women to conceive children using their sperm defies traditional values regarding child rearing and family responsibility. A student at Wuhan University of Technology, for instance, admitted, "I can't bear the thought that I might someday meet my offspring, whom I wouldn't even know" (*China Daily* 2012a). It is also true, however, that preserving the kinship line is not a significant individual value, compared to the worry that others (in particular, family and friends) could find out that an infertile couple had used sperm donation to help them conceive. A graduate student in Beijing told journalists that he kept his donation a secret, fearing that his family "might kill me for letting a stranger use the precious family seed" (*China Daily* 2010). A student in Shanghai who distributed several hundred leaflets in his dormitory informing residents about sperm donation and calling for donors reported that he had "yet received no feedback" (*Global Times* 2012a). He explained this by suggesting that many fear losing face and that becoming a sperm donor would hinder their chances of getting girlfriends.

In all cities, sperm banks are therefore struggling to find sufficient donors to meet the demands of local fertility clinics. At the same time, the number of men who are willing to become sperm donors has also been growing in recent years. For instance, Guangdong's sperm bank saw an increase of almost 100 percent (to more than nine hundred donors) in 2010 compared to past averages (*China Daily* 2011a). Beijing's sperm bank, which is run by the National Research Institute of Family Planning, used to receive an average of only two visitors a day in 2010, but staff members have begun to see an increase in numbers (*China Daily* 2010).

Chinese men who choose to become sperm donors have stated that their motivation is to help couples who are infertile to conceive a child. For instance, a university student told journalists, "I'll just be glad if I can help a childless couple" (*China Daily* 2010). A thirty-four-year-old civil servant in Shanxi decided to become a sperm donor because his brother had became infertile after a car accident, a condition that eventually led to a divorce (*China Daily* 2013d). He believed that if his brother and sister-in-law had known about the service offered by sperm banks, the divorce could probably have been prevented. Nevertheless, he kept the donation a secret from his wife, as he was not sure if she would have accepted his action in the prevailing sociocultural environment in China.

The value of patrilineal descent has also been interpreted in a reverse way by this very student, who added, "Actually, I should thank them for continuing my family line" (*China Daily* 2010). This is interesting, because unlike the above-mentioned students who refuse to donate, this donor offers a new idea about what it means to continue the family line. In this interpretation, what matters is not so much the social acknowledgment and upbringing of the child, or even knowing who or where the "offspring" are, but the "biological" fact that part of the man's social obligation has been fulfilled and a biologically connected paternal family line is continued in posterity. The strictest Confucian views demanded combined biological and social generational (spiritual-ancestral) continuity, while the less strict ones would allow social continuity in the absence of biological continuity when the combination was not possible. However, there has never been celebration, promotion, or even approval of biological continuity in the absence of social continuity. Selling a son or daughter, for instance, was a shameful matter and was to be undertaken only when a couple had too many and were desperately in need of the income.

Although the numbers of sperm donors may have gone up gradually in recent years, there is still a striking gap between the supply of and demand for donor sperm. The media have reported that Chinese sperm bank staff do not credit this imbalance only to cultural prejudices against sperm donation but also blame the decline in sperm quality on excessively strict government guidelines. Two-thirds of the semen collected over a decade by Shanghai's human sperm bank was found to be of insufficient quality, a doctor told journalists (*China Daily* 2013f). It is generally believed that changing lifestyles—including long hours of sitting at computers, stress, irregular sleep schedules, and increasing substance abuse—as well as pollution are the main causes for a decline in the quality of Chinese sperm. The director of Shanghai's sperm bank was also quoted as saying that between 2003 and 2005, only four hundred of more than two thousand applicants met the physical eligibility criteria for becoming sperm donors and that "more than 60% washed out due to sperm quality" (Shanghai Daily 2005). Thus, the above-mentioned student in Shanghai who helped the local sperm bank by encouraging sperm donation among his classmates was surprised to find out that he did not qualify as a sperm donor and that only three out of ten students from his university were deemed eligible donors (*Global Times* 2012a). A similar picture also emerges from Hubei, where 1,672 men applied to become sperm donors in 2011, and only 233 met the strict eligibility criteria (*China Daily* 2012a).

A study of sperm donations in four major Chinese sperm banks between January 2003 and December 2009 came to similar conclusions regarding the sperm donation applications. Ping et al. (2011) found that out of 19,471 prospective donors, only 6,467 (33.2 percent) men qualified and were recruited as donors. The main reasons for non-recruitment were found to be semen parameters below the required threshold (in 55 percent, or 10,709 out of the 19,471 applicants) or a positive test for sexually transmitted diseases (in 7.9 percent, or 1,538). The stringent screening guidelines and high semen-quality requirements apparently are a more significant factor in the lack of donors than sociocultural prejudices against sperm donation.

In their study, Ping et al. (2011) also found that college students constitute the largest occupational group (92.7 percent, or 18,049), and that only a small percentage consisted of office workers or trade and medical professionals. The majority of donors were also unmarried (95.2 percent, or 18,536), and 99.1 percent (19,296) did not have children. This agrees with newspaper reports, according to which university students compose more than 50 percent of sperm donors in Beijing, up to 70 percent in Shanghai, 85 percent in Shandong (*China Daily* 2010), and 95 percent in Guangdong (*China Daily* 2011a). Given the large number of student donors, university campuses have become the primary recruitment sites for local sperm banks. Some sperm banks have built successful collaborations with student unions to promote sperm donation (*China Daily* 2012a). According to the director of Guangdong's sperm bank, "student union members normally talk to students one-on-one in private about sperm donation, which works for us, although it takes time" (*China Daily* 2011a). In the past, the bank also tried to promote its services by distributing posters and leaflets but found that this was not effective. Sometimes students also work as recruiters for sperm banks by trying to advertise sperm donation in their dormitories and among classmates. However, sperm banks also use other platforms. The director of Shanghai's sperm bank, for instance, has appeared on local radio programs and also gives lectures at the city's Fudan and Tongji Universities in order to increase awareness (*China Daily* 2012a). Such activities have proved to be more successful, as several hundred students usually contact the sperm bank after such a campaign.

Among those who qualify as sperm donors, some change their minds when they discover that it can take up to ten months or longer to complete the entire process of having semen samples declared eligible for donation. After visiting the sperm bank three times for initial tests, donors need to undergo blood screening. As a complete donation sample consists of 50 milliliters of semen, and an average ejaculation consists of 2–6 milliliters, donors are required to make ten to fifteen visits at intervals of at least five to seven days, with a final visit six months after the last collection to undergo a final HIV test. Sperm banks usually reimburse between ¥200 (US$30) and ¥300 (US$50) for each visit and give out a large bonus payment after completion of the final blood test.[12] In Shanghai, the payment for sperm donors in 2012 was reported to have gone up from ¥4,000 to ¥5,000 (*Global Times* 2012a), which was slightly above the average monthly income in that city (*China Daily* 2011b). The ministerial guidelines for ARTs and human sperm banks (MOH 2001, 2003) prohibit the buying and selling of human gametes, though, and medical staff therefore insist that the cash handouts are not incentive payments but compensation for making the donation. The director of the Guangdong sperm bank thus told the media that it "doesn't mean they are selling sperm" but that the sperm bank is "providing meals and transport fees and compensation for loss of working time" (*China Daily* 2011a).

As for the motives of donors, the director finds that "most regard the donation as an act of charity to help those needing artificial insemination." A graduate student in Beijing noted that the cash incentive was not the only reason that he became a sperm donor, but he also said that the payment of ¥3,500 "was very attractive." A twenty-two-year-old university student in Shanxi also did not want people to think that he had sold his sperm (*China Daily* 2013d). Although he was paid thousands of yuan, a considerable amount of money for a student, he objected to misrepresenting his actual intention, which was to help infertile couples. Unlike many other men who keep their decision to donate a secret, he had a modern and open-minded girlfriend who encouraged the idea and accompanied him to the sperm bank.

Some Chinese sperm banks, including the Jiangsu bank in Nanjing, do not stop accepting donation applications from working men because of concerns about the quality of their samples. There is no science behind it, but the director of Nanjing's sperm bank explains that this problem is the result of lifestyle, because "working males are usually under excessive pressure and many have bad habits, including drinking, which negatively affects their sperm" (*Global Times* 2012a). Less than 20 percent of the sperm donated by office, or so-called white-collar, workers was found to qualify, as the sperm bank told journalists shortly after, in contrast to more than 40 percent of the sperm donated by college students (*China Daily* 2013g).

China's first and largest sperm bank, the Reproductive and Genetic Hospital in Changsha, Hunan, has more than 100,000 samples of semen stored in its facility (*China Daily* 2013c) and provides sperm to twenty-three cities and other provinces. This sperm bank has chosen a more conservative approach to recruiting donors and prefers to keep everything private, including the advertising, as the director does not think that "Chinese people are open enough to accept advertising for sperm banks in magazines or on television because it is still a very sensitive topic" (*China Daily* 2010). Sperm banks in bigger cities like Shanghai are more inclined to experiment with advertising and use wider platforms, including social media, to appeal to more men, in particular the younger generation of blog and social-networking site users. Hangzhou's sperm bank, for example, posted on its official Sina Weibo site that it would offer a maximum bonus of ¥6,000 to sperm donors, stirring up a lot of debate online (*China Daily* 2013e). Setting up blogs on popular Chinese websites has become another common strategy many sperm banks use to reach the male public. Such tools offer the advantage of engaging directly with large numbers of Internet users and provide those who are considering sperm donation the opportunity to ask about the services and get other sexual health advice.

Nevertheless, ARTs are still suspect, and their use often remains a secret. For example, a married couple in Jiangsu whose child was born in 2005 knew nothing about the donor, except that he was twenty-five years old at the time of donation and had facial features similar to the husband's, stated that the donation was "a secret that we'll have to keep from everyone, including our daughter, until the day we die" (*China Daily* 2013a). Yet the demand for donor sperm is so high and the waits in licensed clinics so long that the media have also reported that an unregulated online black market of sperm donations has appeared in response to the sperm crisis. In this black market, males offer "to donate their sperm directly" to infertile couples, and customers and donors match up on their own and arrange for the "donation," either through self-performed artificial insemination with donor sperm or by actual intercourse (*Global Times* 2012b). Infertile couples may join such groups in order to avoid the long waits at licensed fertility centers. In the black market, however, sperm quality is not verified by laboratory tests but instead is suggested by vivid descriptions of the success enjoyed by numerous other couples, nor are any formal health checks required (*China Daily* 2012a). The risk of infection with sexually transmitted diseases, including the possibility that these volunteers may have HIV, therefore represents a dark and risky side to the black market's appeal of cheaper costs and shorter waiting times.

FINAL OBSERVATIONS

Attitudes toward choices in ARTs vary greatly in China. Sperm donation may no longer be taboo in China, as the *Global Times*—a Beijing-based conservative daily under the auspices of the major state-owned *People's Daily*—pronounced in 2012 (*Global Times* 2012a), but sperm banks in the country are still facing the difficult situation that many still perceive donating sperm as a shameful act. Traditional Chinese culture frowned on masturbation, and pseudo-scientific theories and mysticism in the past called for men to retain their vital essence (Ellis and Ho 1982).[13] But despite the heavy traditional baggage, many members of the younger generation are now somewhat more at ease with the practice, such as one man who said that "what I need to do for it is not difficult" (*China Daily* 2010). As Chinese men are more willing to become sperm donors, and vastly growing numbers of couples also accept the use of a sperm donor to fulfill their reproductive wishes, both donors and receiving couples have started to accept what traditionally would have been seen as a rupture of their patriline. In this new climate, many couples and individual donors endeavor to make their own decisions, even if they are up against established cultural values and family expectations. Nevertheless, they still face a shortage of sperm donors.

To a large extent, the sperm crisis is attributable to a lack of education and public debate about sperm donation. Many men feel embarrassed because of their lack of knowledge and because there is too little debate on the subject. In the past few years, sperm donation has been steadily rising, but the number of donors is still nowhere close to sufficient. The irony is that people who take part in such debates (in China as well as in the West) often imagine that the beliefs and practices of earlier times were a lot less flexible than historical and ethnographic sources show they actually were. It was only the strictest of Confucians who thought ARTs were unacceptable. The current view of "tradition" is essentially an anachronistic one, based more in popular ideas of genetics than in historical reports of lived Confucian tradition.

The recent debate in Chinese newspapers about the national shortage of sperm donors has been surprisingly open-minded, with much emphasis on the growing number of men who choose to become sperm donors and their motivations. More of such debate would help resolve the contradiction between the still-prevalent cultural values about reproduction and the reality that, under the Birth-Planning Policy, adoption is not always an option for couples who want children and are unable to conceive naturally. In many other parts of the world, ARTs such as donor conception and surrogate motherhood also have forced a rethinking of what relatedness means when procreation includes more than one father or mother (Bray 2008; Strathern 1992), and this has often been a difficult process requiring campaigns and lengthy public debates.

Medical professionals in the ARTs sector in China have also given different reasons for the Chinese sperm crisis and the long waiting lists for donor-assisted conception in licensed ARTs clinics: overly strict government guidelines for ARTs and the quality of human sperm. For Ping et al. (2011), the primary factor is the high semen-quality threshold in China. Semen parameters are three times higher than those defined for healthy males by the World Health Organization, and consequently almost 50 percent of applicants are regularly disqualified. Other detrimental aspects of the guidelines are the ban on donations from men over forty-five years of age and from homosexuals. For the director of the country's largest sperm bank in Hunan, limiting sperm donation from an individual donor to a maximum of five women is also a "waste of resources" (*China Daily* 2010). She argues that the chance of marriage between offspring from the same donor is already extremely slim when provided to five women in a population of only 3 million and that "for a country of 1.3 billion people, one man's sperm could safely be provided to at least 10 women." The director of Guangdong's sperm bank agrees, suggesting that if China is to seriously address the sperm donor crisis, the ratio between donors and women trying to conceive through donation needs to change (Nanfang 2012).

It is also noteworthy that biological connectedness to the mother has taken on a new meaning in the context of ARTs. According to the director of Shanghai's sperm bank, many couples value ARTs over adoption, because a child conceived with the aid of a sperm donor "at least gets the mother's DNA" (*Global Times* 2012a). This implies not only that kinship ideology is changing toward a more liberal way of thinking but also that ARTs bring about a more bilateral view of kinship in which biological connectedness to the birth mother is deemed important and a significant replacement for paternal connectedness when this is not an option. When having offspring matters more than a child's biological connectedness to the father's ancestral line, and when biological connectedness to the mother's line becomes important (and a new kinship value in its own right), the patriline—as one aspect of the persistence of patriarchy in China—is on the decline.

NOTES

I thank Stevan Harrell and Gonçalo Santos for their invaluable comments during the process of revising my conference paper into a book chapter.

1   ARTs also include intracytoplasmic sperm injection, cryopreservation, cytoplasmic transfer, pre-implantation genetic diagnosis, and artificial insemination.

2   Greenhalgh and Winckler 2005; Handwerker 1998, 2002; Klein 2010; Qiu 2002.

3   In actuality, this one-child quota applies only to the Han majority living in cities. Han families living in rural areas are allowed to have two children if the first-born child is a girl.

4   Harrell et al. (2011) propose a more nuanced comparative analysis for the rural-urban divide.

5   Much of the material in this chapter is analysis of public discourse about sperm donation, particularly that appearing in major Chinese newspapers, primarily the national English-language newspaper *China Daily*, with occasional references to others. *China Daily* is run by the Chinese government

and is an example of the large, mainstream, state-owned news outlets over which the Chinese government still has the most control (L. Chen 2013); it is generally regarded as one of the most reliable and authoritative newspapers in China. It is published and distributed in most cities in 150 countries and regions outside China and therefore does not only influence domestic readers but also functions as a window onto China for the public abroad.

6   Bray 2008; Wolf and Huang 1980; Waltner 1990; R. Watson 1985; J. Watson 1980.

7   Shi, chapter 2; Obendiek, chapter 3; Zhang, chapter 12.

8   According to this rationale, sperm donation normally should be banned just like embryo donation and adoption—because it also conflicts with traditional Chinese kinship culture. The fact that it is not banned implies that the rationale for banning embryo donation may be a different one, possibly to create an unprecedented surplus of leftover IVF embryos in the global stem cell research race (Klein 2010).

9   It is rather uncommon to find IVF or intracytoplasmic sperm injection patients with twenty or more mature oocytes (and even then, not all such patients are willing to share their excess oocytes with another patient). With few exceptions, this can be achieved only through extremely high dosages of ovary-stimulating hormones, which are regularly used in China (Klein 2010) but increase the risk of complications from ovarian hyperstimulation syndrome.

10   The rule of anonymity is comparable to the traditional feeling that if one adopts a son from a non-agnate, it is best to adopt one from far away, because that way the child will have great difficulties finding his biological parents (Wolf and Huang 1980).

11   The donor's father sued the school for more than ¥4,000,000.

12   In the United States, the screening process is similar and takes from eight weeks to six months, depending on the sperm bank.

13   Semen (*jingzi*), which shares one character with the Chinese word for "essence" or vitality (*jinghua*), traditionally has been believed to contain the very life force of a man. Once all *jing* has been expended, it was believed that the body dies, and although *jing* can be lost in many ways, this most notably occurs through the loss of body fluids. Semen, it was therefore believed, must be retained as much as possible, and donating one's sperm would be equivalent to giving away one's life force.

CHAPTER TWELVE

RECALIBRATING FILIAL PIETY

Realigning the State, Family, and Market Interests in China

HONG ZHANG

C HINESE family size, structure, and power relations have undergone enormous transformations as a consequence of Mao's socialist revolution from 1949 to 1978 and post-Mao reform from 1978 to the present. However, filial piety, understood as adult children's duty to support aged parents, has remained a core cultural value and patriarchal principle that still serves as a moral compass for the intergenerational contract in Chinese families. While the combined impacts of the Birth-Planning Policy, population mobility, and the rise of empty-nest households have lately raised concerns about the erosion of traditional family support systems for elder care in China, the same demographic and social forces are also at work to heighten the importance of intergenerational bonds and have led to new responses from the state, family, and market that may give new life to the long-standing notion and practice of filial piety in contemporary China.

Government policy and programs, my ethnographic research in both rural and urban settings, and the mission statements of an emerging elder-care industry all reveal how filial piety is recalibrated as a cultural asset that the state, family, and market can use to redefine and even realign their shared stake in old-age security and elder care. The state has adopted a two-pronged approach to old-age security, setting up a national pension system and making a renewed effort to codify and promote the filial obligation. At the same time, demographic and socioeconomic change have affected the intergenerational bond as well as filial expectations and practices. In this context of state-led market reform and the transition to a consumer-based society, an entirely new "elder-care industry" has developed, giving rise to what can be called a "commodification" of filial piety.

THE STATE FACTOR: FROM PENSION OVERHAUL
TO PROMOTING FILIAL VIRTUES

Mao's socialist revolution had paradoxical effects on the traditional family system.[1] On the one hand, parental authority based on patriarchal power and family resource control was severely weakened by collectivization of family patrimony and ideological attacks on ancestor worship and parental arranged marriage. On the other hand, collectivization in the countryside, restrictions on rural-to-urban migration, and the pension system that came with state employment in the cities not only provided a measure of socialist safety net for the elderly but also facilitated the delivery of parental care by keeping adult children physically close to their parents.

Rebuilding a National Social Security System

China's post-Mao market reform, however, has dismantled the collective-based welfare system and pursued a market-based economic policy that loosened restrictions on migration and emphasized individual and family responsibility for old-age support. This complete reversal of Mao's collective and state welfare system generated enormous uncertainties over old-age support for urban and rural families alike, but its impact on the livelihood and filial support of rural elderly in the first two decades of market-driven reform was particularly devastating. In his study of Xiajia Village in Heilongjiang in the 1990s, Yan noted a rise in parental abuse and abandonment after decollectivization (Yan 2003). In a Hubei village in the mid-1990s and early aughts, I witnessed frequent family disputes over parental support and witnessed a trend of aging parents living alone and taking care of themselves (H. Zhang 2004, 2009). In urban China, however, while market reform eliminated lifetime employment and other work-unit welfare benefits, the pension system for urban retirees remains (Davis-Friedmann 1991, 112–13). This urban pension system affords a moderate measure of old-age security for urban retirees, and since the early aughts, the Chinese government has sought to establish a uniform old-age insurance system that contains *dibao* (minimal income support) for all urban elderly residents, including those who were not in the workforce and who were previously excluded from the pension plan (PRC White Paper 2006). According to a 2010 survey conducted in seven provinces, 78.88 percent of urban residents age sixty-five and older have their own sources of income, mostly from their pensions or spouses' pensions, 6.11 percent get *dibao* from the municipal government, and only 15.01 percent of urban elderly depend on their adult children for financial support (Y. Wang 2012).[2]

In the first two decades of reform, prioritization of GDP growth and an urban-centered development model caused stagnation of the rural economy and widening of the rural-urban income gap. Since 2002, the Chinese government has attempted to address the imbalance between urban and rural development and introduced a series of pro-rural policies such as the New Rural Co-operative Medical System (Xin Nong He) (NRCMS) in 2003,[3] removal of agricultural taxes and levies in 2005, and the New Rural Old-Age Insurance (Xinxing Nongcun Yanglao Baoxian) (NROAI) pilot program in 2009.[4] These new measures, although still in their early stages and evolving, seem to have already had some tangible effects on the economic burden of rural families with regard to parental support. In my trip in 2010 to the Hubei village where I had conducted research in the mid-1990s and early aughts, I witnessed some improvement in intergenerational relations and the well-being of rural elderly.

Mr. Wei's story is a case in point. When I first met him in 1993–94, he was seventy-two years old and full of bitterness about how old people were being discarded by both their children and the state in the wake of decollectivization. He had two sons but chose to live separately due to family conflicts. He said he had already accumulated an entire bottle of sleeping pills and would end his own life if he became too sick to provide for his own care. In my subsequent trips to the village between 2000 and 2003, he was still in despair about the deteriorating life of the rural elderly and told me about several more cases of elderly parents committing suicide in the village. He said that his own days were numbered, as he now suffered from prostatitis and did not want to get any treatment for fear of burdening his sons with mounting medical bills. However, in 2010, eighty-nine-year-old Mr. Wei was not only reasonably healthy but in a happy and relaxed mood. He told me that he was still alive today because of the "filial" actions of his two sons. Mr. Wei had decided to end his life in 2005 when his prostatitis worsened, but his sons intervened and took him to the county hospital, where he underwent a successful operation and fully recovered. Mr. Wei's younger son told me that he and his brother literally had to "kidnap" their father and take him to the hospital by car, as Mr. Wei insisted that he had lived long enough and there was no point wasting money on him. He agreed to be treated only when his son told him that his hospital fees would be "mostly" covered by the NRCMS. In fact, NRCMS covered only 30 percent of Mr. Wei's surgery and hospital charges, and his two sons and one daughter shared the rest of the cost.

My impression of improving intergenerational relations was validated by the village Party secretary, who told me that family disputes over parental support had indeed declined in the village in the past few years, after villagers had seen their incomes increase following the removal of the agricultural tax and levies in 2005 and after implementation of the NRCMS and NROAI. The reimbursement coverage of the NRCMS expanded from 30 percent in 2003 to 70 percent in 2010. But the most pivotal event for rural families seems to be the NROAI, introduced in 2010, which gives a monthly pension of ¥55 (US$9) to anyone over the age of sixty. Although the NROAI pension of ¥55 is meager in comparison to average monthly pensions of ¥1,000–3,000 for urban retirees, many rural elderly still regard it as a significant departure from the first two decades of reform when they felt totally abandoned by the state and feared that they would be a burden to their adult children. The Party secretary also told me that when the first NROAI pension was given out in this village in 2008,[5] many people in their seventies and eighties were in disbelief—they had never received or expected to receive any money from the state in their lifetime. Mr. Wei, who had had only despairing words to say about the livelihood of rural elderly in the 1990s and early aughts, now said that his relationship with his sons had improved in recent years and that the NRCMS and more recently the NROAI did offer rural elderly a sense of relief and hope for the future.

Legislating Parental Support and Promoting Filial Virtues

Parental support was codified in the 1950 Marriage Law, but in the Mao era there was little need for legal recourse, since both the urban work-unit system and the rural collective could effectively prevent potential negligence of parental support. In 1996, China passed the Law of the People's Republic of China on the Protection of the Rights and Interests of the Elderly (the Elder Law). Chapter 2 of the Elder Law explicitly states, "The elderly shall be provided for mainly by their families," and it outlines specific legal obligations of family members, including providing financial support, medical expenses, and housing; as well as no interference from adult children in parents' decisions on divorce, remarriage, or post-remarriage life.

While the intent of the Elder Law was to protect the well-being and rights of the elderly, in reality the law was marred by problems of enforcement and strained intergenerational relations even further when parents had to sue their children for old-age support. At the time the law was implemented,

China was undergoing deep structural market reform that not only led to large-scale layoffs at state enterprises but also sent health-care and educational costs skyrocketing. Job competition and life pressures have forced many adult children to choose between paying for their only child's education and providing elder care and covering medical costs for their aging parents. As a result, despite the 1996 Elder Law, there have been increasing incidences of parental neglect and abandonment—dead parents in empty-nest homes unnoticed for days, sick parents dumped in hospitals while family members simply disappeared, and, most disturbing, a sharp increase in both urban and rural elder suicides.[6] Indeed, there is widespread fear that the competitive market economy and rapid urbanization and modernization will lead to the final demise of the filial tradition.

It is perhaps in recognition of this rising public fear that the Chinese state initiated a series of high-profile campaigns attempting to revive Confucian virtues of filial piety. In 2004, seven central government branches cosponsored a nationwide educational campaign advocating "respecting, loving, and helping senior citizens" (*zunlao, ailao, zhulao*) with the goal of finding and publicizing new "filial exemplars." This "filial exemplars campaign" would culminate with an award conference every other year in Beijing, where ten people would be given the title Chinese Exemplar of Filiality and Respect for the Elderly (Zhonghua Xiaoqin Jinglao Kaimo), fifty to sixty people would receive Honorable Mention (Zhonghua Xiaoqin Jinglao Timing Jiang), and more than two thousand people would be awarded the title Chinese Filial and Respecting the Elderly Star (Zhonghua Xiaoqin Jinglao Zhi Xing). The new filial exemplars include not only children devoted to parental care but also private citizens who volunteered their time and effort to caring for seniors, entrepreneurs who donated money to build elder-care facilities, and government officials who prioritized work on behalf of the elderly. Like the *Classic of Filial Piety*, the new filial exemplars' stories would be written into elementary and middle-school textbooks (Li Weiwei 2005).

Beginning in 2010, another nationwide official campaign designated every October as Respect the Elders Month (Jinglao Yue), connecting with the tradition of Double Ninth Holiday (Chongyang Jie) as a day for showing respect for elders.[7] Five main themes would be emphasized: mobilizing those in all walks of life to visit and show concern for the elderly, encouraging volunteers to provide companionship or do chores for the elderly, strengthening elder rights protection, organizing various recreational events for the elderly, and increasing publicity about the challenges of population aging in order to mobilize the whole society to help and show respect for the elderly (National Committee on Aging 2011).

In August 2012, the All-China Federation of Women and the National Committee on Aging published new guidelines for modern filial standards modeled on the Twenty-Four Paragons of Filial Piety from the Yuan dynasty, the New Twenty-Four [Exemplars of] Filial Piety (Xin Ershisi Xiao). The new filial standards include teaching parents how to surf the Internet, buying suitable insurance for parents, taking parents for regular health checkups, visiting parents regularly, listening to parents telling stories of the past, taking parents on vacation, and encouraging widowed parents to remarry. These new filial guidelines were met with criticism, cynicism, and even amusement from the public. Some argue that the government should put more effort into building a better social safety net for the elderly rather than exhorting families to follow the new filial guidelines, others find the guidelines suitable only for urban middle-class families but out of reach for millions of rural migrants, and still others point out that the new standards are not coercive but are reminders for youth to strengthen relationships with their parents and practice filial piety in their own flexible ways (Wang Yiqing 2012; *People's Daily* 2012a).

At the end of 2012, the regime implemented an amendment to the Elder Law, often dubbed the "visit home often law" (*chang huijia kankan fa*) because it contains a new article requiring adult children to visit their parents "regularly." This new law has ignited intense public debate on the well-being of the elderly and parental support in contemporary China. While many welcome the move and see it as encouraging the whole society to pay more attention to and care for the elderly, others argue that job-related migration and the work pressures of modern life have made it difficult for adult children to keep in close contact with and provide care for their parents.

On the whole, there is little disagreement with the general sentiment that adult children still have filial duties and that these need to be reemphasized in the current atmosphere of rampant consumerism. Two recent national surveys show that more than 80 percent of respondents from twenty to eighty years of age agreed that children should be filial and have an obligation to support parents (Y. Li 2010; Liu 2012). By reviving filial virtues, the state can both ease some public fears about the decline of filial piety and gain legitimacy by officially endorsing and bolstering the filial tradition.

CHANGING FAMILY STRUCTURE, THE RISING CARE BURDEN, AND MODIFIED FILIAL EXPECTATIONS

New demographic realities have also put further strains on the traditional family-based system of elder care. Chinese household size has continuously decreased in the past three decades—the average household size was 4.41 people in 1982 and dropped to 3.96 in 1990, 3.44 in 2000, and 3.10 in 2010. China's market reform has given rise to massive migration of the rural young to major urban centers. As a result, more and more aging parents are living in "left-behind" (*liushou*) or empty-nest households. Yan Qingchun, deputy director of the National Committee on Aging, observes that "living in a 'left-behind' or 'empty-nest' household has become a new norm for the Chinese elderly," and "the proportion of elderly living in 'empty nests' in urban areas went from 42 percent in 2000 to 54 percent in 2010, and the proportion of their rural counterparts went from 37.9 percent in 2000 to 45.6 percent in 2010" (Xie Liangbing 2013). This trend will intensify in the near future, as the first generation of parents who were subject to China's Birth-Planning Policy reaches old age. According to Xu and Feng's survey, more than 66 percent of singletons live separately from their parents (Xu and Feng 2011). In the meantime, more and more people live to an advanced age and need long-term care. However, China still has not developed any social programs for long-term care, and the responsibility and costs fall largely on family members.

There are, however, also new signs that intergenerational relations are being renegotiated and filial practices reinterpreted in order to confront and cope with new demographic and socioeconomic challenges. In rural Northern Guangdong, Gonçalo Santos (chap. 4) notes the widespread practice of "surrogate parenting" arrangements, in which grandparents take total care of grandchildren so that the grandchildren's parents can earn money in the city. My recent ethnographic studies in both rural and urban China have revealed three new phenomena: gender-neutral intergenerational relations, modified filial expectations, and a shift from traditional dependent elder care (*yilai yanglao*) to intergenerational independence and interdependence.

Gender Equity and the Filial Role of Daughters

Mao's socialist revolution after 1949 somewhat weakened the son-centered family system of filial responsibility, as the redistributive and collective economy undermined patriarchal authority and women were able to join the labor force and earn income. Studies have shown that daughters could be filial to their natal families in various forms.[8] But until recently a daughter's filial role was mostly optional and marginal—giving parents spending money, providing emotional support by visiting parents, or offering temporary caregiving when parents were sick—until China's Birth-Planning Policy made the daughter's filial role essential and obligatory for many families.

Among urban families with singleton daughters, this change is obvious, but even among multi-sibling families in rural China, daughters are assuming a greater role and obligation. In my longitudinal study of the village in Hubei, I noticed that middle-aged parents who had no more than two children due to the Birth-Planning Policy made deliberate efforts to both cultivate emotional bonds with their daughters and invest in their daughters' future. These parents emphasized to me that with only one son and one daughter, both children were equally important to them; some parents even claimed that daughters were more reliable and filial than sons. As a result, a new marriage pattern dubbed "bilateral marriages" (*liangbian dianli*), which mandates a daughter's filial obligation to her natal parents, has quickly gained momentum in this area, rising from 25 percent of such marriages in 2002 to more than 80 percent in 2010.[9]

In my 2012 research on caregiving by adult children in Beijing and Shanghai, I also found that daughters played an active role in providing long-term care for their parents, and in some families, daughters would be willed an equal or greater share of their parents' assets when they contributed to parental caregiving. For example, Ms. Zhao was born in 1954 and has four brothers and five sisters, all of whom have contributed care to their parents. The parents had a courtyard house in Beijing with ten rooms, and each sibling inherited one room. Ms. Zhou in Shanghai was the youngest of three siblings, with an elder sister and an elder brother. She was given the largest share of their parents' property, as she lives with their widowed mother, who suffers from dementia, and is her main caretaker. In other words, the patriarchal tradition of emphasizing the son's importance for parental support has been revised in contemporary China, and some parents not only have begun to recognize the importance of a daughter's filial role but also actively seek to secure their daughters' filial obligations, whether through financing their daughters' marriages or through willing them equal or greater shares of parental assets.

Filial Expectations Modified and Redefined

My recent interviews with elderly parents in Beijing and Shanghai also revealed that even though these parents are either living in empty-nest households and providing their own care or seeking other nonfamilial forms of elder care through institutions or paid home care, they are reluctant to blame their adult children for being unfilial. The new dominant discourse on elder care from the parents' point of view is "not to become a burden on" or "not to become an obstacle that holds back" their children (*tuo zinü de houtui*). One could argue that this new discourse shows the decline or even reversal of the filial tradition, but one could also argue that Chinese parents genuinely believe that it is unrealistic to depend on the traditional filial practice to meet their needs in light of new societal and demographic realities. My interviews with urban Chinese parents gave the impression that they see the discourse of "not becoming a burden" on their children as a "modern" way of life, and while some have to accept it out of necessity, others embrace it very willingly. To these parents, filial virtues and intergenerational ties are still important but can be expressed in different ways, not exclusively in the traditional filial mode, as shown in the following two case studies collected in 2012.

Mr. Yang, a Beijing native, was an eighty-five-year-old widower. He had one son and two daughters, all of whom lived in Beijing. He used to live with his son's family, but in 2011, after his wife passed away, he decided to live in a neighborhood-run elder home. He had a monthly pension of ¥3,000, enough to cover the cost of ¥1,800 at this elder home. He told me that his son was busy at work, and he did not want to become a burden on him and his family, so he made the decision to live in the elder home. Mr. Yang was in reasonably good health and was very enthusiastic about the various group recreational activities offered by this elder home such as tai chi, singing, and handicrafts. His three children took turns visiting him once a week, so he still maintained frequent contact with them. Mr. Yang was very happy with the current arrangement and was even proud of the fact that he used his own pension to pay for his elder-care needs and did not burden his children financially or physically.

Ms. Wan and her husband had worked and lived in Beijing for more than fifty-five years and were seventy-seven and eighty-three years old. Both were healthy and retired, with a combined pension of more than ¥8,000 a month. But as they aged, and with their only son living far away in Europe, the couple decided in 2011 to move to Shanghai to be closer to her siblings and their families. Since Ms. Wan did not have housing in Shanghai, she and her husband now live in a residential home, not far from Ms. Wan's elder brother's family. When I asked Ms. Wan if she would consider moving to Europe to live with her son's family, she said that she and her husband did travel to Europe twice to see their son, but they did not want to live there and burden their son with elder care because their son is a chief engineer for a German auto company and is busy with his career and family life.

Ms. Wan's case can be seen as a harbinger of a future awaiting China's one-child parents. They want the best education and career for their only child, even though it can mean that the child will study, work, and live far away from home, often in a foreign country. Most middle-aged parents of singletons whom I interviewed indicated that emotional connection is more important than financial support or physical care and that children do not have to live with parents in order to be filial; regular phone calls or visits home can be seen as filial. A recent study on institutional care and the changing perception of "filial piety" also shows that even placing elders in institutions can be considered filial when adult children are unable to provide physical care but have made efforts to find good-quality facilities and help with paying the cost for their parents (Zhan, Feng, and Luo 2008). Clearly, many Chinese families still value filial virtue highly, but its practices are redefined and reconfigured in such a way that the intergenerational obligation is maintained and remains meaningful even though parents and their adult children do not live together.

From Traditional Dependent Elder Care to Intergenerational Independence and Interdependence

Recent socioeconomic changes have led not only to new familial arrangements but also to new attitudes and beliefs about the proper relationship between the generations, one that includes both the feasible independence of the older generation and a more balanced reciprocity between the older generation and its children. Several strategies exist for achieving this new interdependence.

First, there is a growing belief among parents that the best guarantee for their future old-age support is their own financial independence. This is more achievable for urban parents, who have pensions after retirement. Even in rural China, saving for future old-age support has become a common practice among young and middle-aged parents. In my 2010 research trip to the same Hubei village, I learned that enrollment in the NROAI had reached 100 percent among working adults under the age of sixty, who were paying a monthly premium for the pension, which they can withdraw only after turning sixty. The Party secretary told me that when the NROAI was first piloted in this local area in 2008, there was already a demand for the program and the village cadres did not even need to mobilize and persuade villagers to participate. More and more rural parents knew that they would depend on themselves for their future old-age support, since so many young people were leaving the village to find employment and opportunities in urban areas.

Second, small family size resulting from China's Birth-Planning Policy also allows parents to better invest in their children's future and maintain a closer intergenerational bond, as there is less competition for parental resources. These parents are eager to become grandparents and are ready to offer child care. But at the same time, they also want to make sure that their grandparenting is not free and will not compromise their own sources of income (cf. Santos, chap. 4). The recent rise of what I call "outsourcing grandparenting" in Zhongshan is a case in point. Villager Cao turned fifty in 2010 and had only two daughters, the elder one born in 1982 and the younger one in 1988. In 2000, his elder daughter went to Zhejiang to work in a textile factory, where she met her future husband, who came from Hunan. During the New Year break of 2005, the couple returned to Zhongshan to marry uxorilocally, since the bride had no male sibling and the groom had a younger brother. They returned to Zhejiang to work after the wedding, but in 2006, the wife returned to Zhongshan to give birth to a son and stayed home to care for him until he was one year old. Then she went back to Zhejiang to work, leaving her son in the care of her natal parents. When her son turned two, her parents sent him to a local kindergarten about four miles away. A truck would pick him and other local children up around nine in the morning and bring them back to the village at four in the afternoon. The monthly kindergarten fee was ¥100, and it was paid with the money the boy's mother sent home. Villager Cao told me that his daughter and son-in-law were earning good cash incomes (¥1,700–2,000 each per month) and he wanted to support the young couple by taking care of their son. But he and his wife did not want grandparenting to consume all their time and energy (see Santos, chap. 4), so they sent their grandson to a kindergarten, giving them time to work in the fields. This trend of outsourcing grandparenting was fairly recent, starting around 2007, when privately run rural kindergartens became popular as a way of meeting the needs of two working-age generations.

Third, urban midlife retired parents have adopted a "horizontal or peer-aging strategy" to cope with the consequences of three decades of the universal one-child policy in urban China. Urban parents born in the 1950s and 1960s are under intense pressure to invest heavily in their only children's education and career success since their children are their "only hope" (Fong 2004). By 2010, these parents began to enter retirement age. In my 2011 and 2012 research trips to Beijing and Shanghai, I interviewed more than forty such parents. Although most of them will face an empty-nest future in their old age, they do not moan about the doomsday of a bleak lonely future awaiting them. Instead, these parents are extremely proactive in forging, enlarging, and reconnecting a social network of mutual support and peer-aging activities among their age cohort. Many told me that their lives are busier and more fulfilling because they now have the time to do what they like or even pick up new hobbies.

Ms. Hao, for example, was born in 1955 and worked in a state-owned department store from the time she returned from being sent down to the countryside in 1978 until she retired at age fifty in 2005. She had one son, born in 1983, who had a job but was not married yet. I first met Ms. Hao in 2009 in a community center where she took lessons on modeling with a group of seven or eight retired women of her age. I saw Ms. Hao again in the summer of 2012, when she told me that her weekly schedule was full with new activities since I had last seen her: folk dancing on Mondays, square dancing on Tuesday and Wednesday afternoons, modeling on Wednesday and Thursday mornings, and ballroom dancing on Fridays. She told me that having such a busy schedule not only kept her body healthy and fit but allowed her to make new friends as well as renew ties with old ones. In her modeling practice, she met new female friends who shared her interest, and every Wednesday afternoon, she would spend two and half hours square dancing with her sent-down-youth buddies.

I went with Ms. Hao to her square dance on a Wednesday afternoon, met her square-dancing friends, and had a group discussion with them. Many of them shared stories similar to Ms. Hao's—a busy retirement life with a variety of recreational activities scheduled throughout the week. Some of Ms. Hao's square-dancing friends had recently become grandparents, but they emphasized that while they helped their sons or daughters with child care when they could, every Wednesday from 2:30 pm to 5:00 pm was the time for them to have a good time with their sent-down-youth friends. They told me that they cherished the time they had been together as sent-down youth and were occasionally nostalgic about the collective and idealistic spirit of those years. Now that they were retired and their only children were grown up, they and their sent-down friends with similar experiences could reunite. They emphasized that the traditional filial-care model is no longer feasible with so many families having only one child, nor is it desirable, as modern life is already busy and competitive for young people, and caring for parents would add many pressures for the younger generation. So as parents, the best they can do is to keep themselves healthy and active as long as possible so that their only child need not worry about them. From talking to these midlife parents and others, the consensus seems to be that intergenerational reciprocity is important, but it can be best achieved when older and younger generations have independent lives and do not get in each other's way.

In the current mix of macroeconomic and demographic shifts, and with the government's blessing, an entire elder-care industry (*yanglao qiye*) has emerged, rapidly expanded, and gained more momentum in the past three decades. The main selling point for this new elder-care industry is often the cultural tradition of filial piety.

The Emergence of Paid Household Services for Elder Care

In urban China, market reform has spurred the emergence of a household service industry (*jiazheng fuwu*) for child care, household chores, and elder care. In all major Chinese cities, household service companies (*jiazheng gongsi*) have sprung up, offering a wide array of self-paid household services. The government has encouraged the growth of this service sector, since it provides employment for rural migrants and middle-aged laid-off urban workers while meeting diverse needs of urban families. One key pitch for the elder-care service is that it helps busy urban adults fulfill their filial duty. Hiring a live-in caregiver or a paid helper for elder care has become a common option when family members are not available to provide care. In 2008, a national TV program explained how a Chinese businessman hired three highly paid home aides to care for his aged mother. Although this filial son was unable to provide daily care for his mother, paying for high-quality care left him "with no regret when his mother eventually passed away in peace and with dignity" (Sheying Chen 2009, 174). Although this extreme case of "paid filial piety" is out of reach for the majority of urban families, there has been an increasing trend of urban families turning to paid elder-care services since the 1990s. Charlotte Ikels notes that the proportion of elder support delivered solely by family members dropped sharply from 86.5 percent in 1987 to 48.1 percent in 1998, but at the same time the proportion of older people receiving some form of paid help increased from 3.8 percent in 1987 to 25 percent in 1998 (Ikels 2004b), a trend that has certainly accelerated since that time.

Boom in Fee-Based Institutional Care

In Mao-era China, institutional care was set up only for those elderly who were childless and had no source of income. This institutional care was also called "welfare" care, since it was free of charge for those who met the criteria. Until the 1980s, institutional care was viewed with both ambivalence and fear because it had a reputation as a solution for the destitute elderly who had no family members to care for them. Since the 1990s, as China further pushed for market reform, state-run welfare homes began to face budget cuts and were required to become financially self-sufficient by finding other sources of funding (Shang 2001). As a way of generating revenue, state-run welfare homes began to charge fees for those elderly who did not qualify for free care but were willing and able to pay for residential care. At the same time, the government also encouraged street neighborhood committees and the private sector to set up fee-based elder homes both as a new growth area for the economy and to meet the increasing elder-care need. As a result, fee-based elder homes have grown exponentially in the past two decades in major Chinese cities. However, residential care is not without controversy and still carries the stigma of parents being deserted by their children (H. Zhang 2006).

To mitigate this public anxiety, many elder homes promote residential care by appealing to the cultural value of filial piety, as some typical mission statements for elder homes show: "Fulfilling Chinese sons' and daughters' filial duty and relieving worries for millions of families" (Ti Zhonghua ernü jinxiao, wei qianwan jiating jieyou), "Fulfilling the filial duties of sons and daughters, alleviating worries for empty-nest elderly" (Ti tianxia ernü jinxiao, wei kongwo laoren fenyou), and "Help the elderly resolve difficulties, fulfill the filial duty of sons and daughters" (Bang shishang laoren jienan, ti tianxia ernü xingxiao). In other words, residential care is repackaged as a way of both helping busy and career-oriented children fulfill their filial duty by purchasing care at elder homes and helping parents and families reconcile the moral dilemma posed by modern, competitive life by purchasing a solution to their elder-care needs.

Commercial Elder-Care Insurance: A New, Fast-Growing Industry

China is still in the early stage of developing a national social security system, and as mentioned earlier, the pension system for the rural population started only in 2010 and is still very limited. Moreover, the Chinese government has emphasized that China has "become old before getting rich" (*wei fu xian lao*). On the one hand, as a country with only a mid-range per capita income,[10] it does not have the resources or the time to build a comprehensive old-age social security system for a rapidly aging population. On the other hand, China's market reform and rapid economic growth have given rise to a growing middle class with strong purchasing power. The combination of an underdeveloped social security system and a rising middle class with more disposable income has given great impetus to the fast growth of commercial insurance companies in China. With families mostly shouldering elder-care costs and the continuing cultural expectations of filial piety, insurance companies see a potential market niche in elder-care insurance. They target adults in their thirties and forties, urging them to buy various commercial insurance products for their parents as a modern form of showing filial piety. Eye-catching phrases touting filial virtues are often seen in TV commercials, on billboards, and in online advertisements: "Elderly's Insurance, Children's Filial Piety" (Laonian ren baoxian, ernü de xiaoxin), "Buy insurance to show filial piety" (Mai baoxian biao xiaoxin), "Mother's Day is coming, purchase insurance to express gratitude to your mother" (Muqin Jie daolai, song fen baoxian huibao mama), "Do your filial act early, don't forget to buy insurance for your parents" (Jinxiao yao chenzao, buyao wangji gei fumu mai baoxian).

In an advertisement headlined "How to buy insurance for parents? The true filial piety lies in ensuring a healthy life for parents" (Zhongguo Ping'an 2012), China Ping'an, one of China's largest commercial insurance companies, promotes its Health Insurance for the Elderly (Laonian ren jiankang baoxian) plan in this advertisement: "Filial piety is a traditional virtue of our Chinese nation. Securing a healthy life for parents is the children's obligation. As long as one has a loving heart for parents, we believe it is not a very difficult task to decide how to buy an elder-care insurance policy. As for which elder-care insurance to buy, some experts suggest 'Health Insurance for the Elderly' from China Ping'an Insurance. This insurance is a healthcare plan designed especially for the elderly."

As a business model, commodification of filial piety and elder-care services may provide families with a new means of performing their filial duty and providing parental support. This business model may have enormous growth potential as China's first generation of one-child-policy parents are beginning to enter their sixties in the millions, and many adult children of single-child families may not live with or even live in the same geographic area as their parents. The Chinese government also encourages the development of a paid elder-care industry and old-age insurance as a new growth engine for the country's economy. However, the commercialization of filial virtue and parental care also presents a huge social risk and moral dilemma. As a consequence of the development of its market economy in the past thirty years, China has witnessed a rapid spike in income inequality, with one study from the University of Michigan showing China's Gini coefficient reaching .55, putting China among the world's worst in income inequality. Paid filial virtue and parental care may enable families with good financial resources to achieve better elder care, but for those families who are financially distressed, especially rural families, their inability to purchase paid elder care or old-age insurance could potentially implicate them as somehow morally lacking in terms of fulfilling their filial obligation.

• • •

In this new realignment of state, family, and market interests, what has emerged is a "modernized filial piety" that not only reinvigorates the filial tradition in a new form but also spawns new practices. Ideologically, the new formulation of filial piety is no longer associated with the traditional notion of "subordination of the young to parental authority," but is modified and re-embraced as compatible with the changing times. In practice, this new filial piety emphasizes both generational interdependence and independence, underscores a parent-child relationship that is reciprocal rather than hierarchical, and demonstrates a more gender-egalitarian stance in which both sons and daughters are important. In essence, filial piety in its modern form gains new currency in China as it simultaneously solidifies the cultural value of family obligation and frees family members to pursue and adapt flexible filial forms and practices in accordance with family situations and inclinations.

In its modern form, this new filial piety is appealing to the state, because it not only carries on the cultural tradition but also helps stabilize the family and society at large. It is also appealing to parents and children alike. Parents feel that they are neither being abandoned by their children nor becoming a burden to them, while children feel that they can pursue their careers and personal lives without compromising their filial obligations. The beneficial effect of filial piety for the business and elder-care industry is only going to increase in the years to come as China's population ages and the need for diversified and innovative elder-care services grows exponentially. However, China is a developing country with a high level of income inequality, and the commercialization of filial obligation may further increase social disparity and distress for many families who are already struggling financially in a highly competitive and consumer-oriented society.

NOTES

1   Davis-Friedmann 1991; Ikels 2006; Whyte 2003, 2004.
2   The same report shows a sharp contrast in sources of income for the rural elderly sixty-five years and older: only 9.27 percent had pensions, 24.6 percent

still had to work to support themselves, and more than 55.56 percent depend on their children.

3   According to the document issued by the Ministry of Health in 2006, the NRCMS began as a pilot program in 2003 with the goal of reaching 40 percent of rural counties by 2006, 60 percent by 2007, and all rural areas by 2008. See MOH 2006a.

4   In the NROAI, rural residents sixty years and older would get a monthly pension of ¥55, while those younger than sixty must pay premiums for fifteen years in order to receive full pensions after the age of sixty. The NROAI was piloted in a few selected rural counties in 2008 and expanded to 23 percent of rural counties in China by the end of 2010 (Xinhua 2011).

5   Zhongxiang County in Hubei, in which Zhongshan Village is located, was among the first rural counties selected to pilot the NROAI in 2008. The pilot program for NROAI in Zhongxiang was hugely successful, with the participation rate reaching 99.2 percent by 2011, and a national conference on the NROAI was held in Zhongxiang on October 27 and 28, 2011. See F. Yang 2011.

6   The study by Jing et al. (2011) shows the urban elderly's suicide rate was higher in 2000–2009 than in 1990–99, with the highest rate in 2005, and that suicide rates among rural elderly were three times higher than for urban elderly during the same period. Chen's study on suicides among rural elderly shows a relatively stable rate of suicides from 1980 to 1994 and a sharp spike between 1995 and 2008 (Chen Bofeng 2009; Dahe News 2007).

7   The Double Ninth is the ninth day of the ninth lunar month, which usually falls in October in the Gregorian calendar.

8   Miller 2004; Shi 2009; Whyte and Xu 2003; Yan 2003.

9   H. Zhang 2005, 2007a, 2007b.

10   According to the CIA World Factbook, China ranked 122 behind Peru (110) and Cuba (116) in GDP per capita in 2010. https://www.cia.gov/library/publications/resources/the-world-factbook/rankorder/2004rank.html

GLOSSARY

Note: All terms are standard Chinese (Mandarin), except for Cantonese terms indicated by [C].

a-gung leung-gung-po wa-si [C] 阿公两公婆话事 (paternal) grandfather and his wife call the shots
a-me [C] 阿嬷 [standard Cantonese pronunciation, a-ma] mother, also ma-ma, 妈妈

bang 帮 help
bangmang 帮忙 help
bu fu zeren 不负责人 do not take responsibility
bu keneng 不可能 impossible
bu nan 不男 not manly
bu nü 不女 not feminine

chaiqian 拆迁 demolish [housing] and move [people]
chang huijia kankan fa 常回家看看法 "Go home to see [them] often law"
changbaiban 常白班 permanent daytime shift
chengzhongcun ren 城中村人 people in "villages in the middle of cities"
Chongyang Jie 重阳节 Double Ninth Holiday

da nanzi zhuyi 大男子主义 male chauvinism, machismo
da zayua 大杂院 big courtyard with multiple families
danwei 单位 [work] unit
Dashalanr 大栅栏 neighborhood in Beijing
di suzhi 低素质 low-quality [person]
dibao 低保 guaranteed minimum [income]

er ke 儿科 pediatrics

fangchan zheng 房产证 housing [ownership] certificate

fu ke 妇科 gynecology

funü 妇女 woman

funü jiefang 妇女解放 women's liberation

fuquan zhi 父权制 patriarchal system; also jiazhang zhi 家长制

fuquan zhi 夫权制 husband's power system

ganhuo 干活 do work; to labor

ganqing 感情 emotional closeness

gongzuo 工作 work, formal employment

guanggun 光棍 bachelor

guigei erzi 归给儿子 revert to the son

hai keyi 还可以 not bad, acceptable

haizi wenti 孩子问题 the question of children

hetong 合同 contract

hongbao 红包 "red envelope," gift of cash

Huining 会宁 county in Gansu

hukou 户口 household registration [system]

hunqing gongsi 婚庆公司 wedding company

hutong 胡同 lane or alley in Beijing

Jihua Shengyu Zhengce 计划生育政策 Birth-planning Policy, "one-child policy"

jihuang [North China dialect] 饥荒 debt

jiahun 假婚 fake marriage

jiashu 家属 family members

jiazhang zhi 家长制 patriarchy

jiazheng fuwu 家政服务 "household management service," housework

jiazheng gongsi 家政公司 housework company

jiazu 家族 lineage or clan

jin 斤 a unit of weight, about 600 grams before 1949, now 500 grams

jing 精 semen

jinghua 精华 vital essence

jinglao yue 敬老月 respect-the-elders month

jingzi 精子 semen

kaifa qu 开发区 development district

kaifang 开放 open, liberal

kailang 开朗 pleasant, convivial

kuai 块 colloquial term for yuan 元 (unit of currency)

lala 拉拉 lesbian

lao guniang 老姑娘 old maid

laogong 老公 husband or boyfriend

laopo 老婆 wife or girlfriend

lei si le 累死了 dead tired

liang 两 unit of weight, one-sixteenth of a jin 斤 before 1949, now one-tenth of a jin

liangbian dianli 两边典礼 bilateral [wedding] ceremony

liushou ertong 留守儿童 left-behind child[ren]

lou-baan [C] 老闆 boss

lou-ma [C] 老媽 "old mother," [usually paternal] grandmother, term used to show affection and respect

lou-sai [C] 老细 boss; also si-tau 事头

luan 乱 chaotic, mixed up

lunban 轮班 rotating shifts

mei shi zhao shi 没事找事 make a fuss over nothing

men dang hu dui 门当户对 "doors lining up opposite each other," a marriage between families of equal status

mian chao huangtu bei chao tian 面朝黄土背朝天 facing the yellow earth with backs to the sky

nainai 奶奶 [usually paternal] grandmother

nannü pingdeng 男女平等 males and females equal, gender equality

nei 内 inside, interior

nongcun hunli chengli ban 农村婚礼城里办 a rural[-style] wedding held in a city

nüxing 女性 woman, female

nüxing zhuyi 女性主义 feminism

nüxingzhuyi yundong 女性主义运动 feminist movement

pa erzi 怕儿子 fearing a son

pan erzi 盼儿子 wishing for a son

peifu 佩服 respect, look up to

pinjin 聘金 bridewealth, brideprice

pojia 婆家 [a woman's] marital family

putong hua 普通话 standard Chinese language (Mandarin)

qi 气 breath, motive force, vitality

renqing 人情 human feelings

sai-man-jai [C] 细蚊子 "little mosquitoes," children

sheng nü 剩女 leftover woman

sifang qian 私房钱 a woman's private money, not belonging to her husband's household

si-tau [C] 事头 boss

suzhi 素质 quality [of a person]

suzhi jiaoyu 素质教育 "quality education"; all-round education

tianjing diyi 天经地义 "The way of Heaven and the principle of earth," immutable or unquestionable principle of existence

tongku 痛苦 bitterness, hardship, pain

tongqi 同妻 wife of a gay man

tongxue 同学 classmate

tongyangxi 童养媳 a bride raised in her prospective husband's household from childhood

tongzhi 同志 gay (homosexual) (originally "comrade")

tuo zinü de houtui 拖子女的后腿 "pull the children's back legs," hold back your children

wei fu xian lao 未富先老 old before it is rich [said of a country or society]

weisheng guanyuan 卫生官员 "sanitary official," janitor or garbage collector

Xin Ershisi Xiao 新二十四孝 New Twenty-Four [Exemplars of] Filial Piety

xinghun 形婚 "form marriage," short for xingshi hunyin

xingshi hunyin 形式婚姻 "form marriage," fake marriage, marriage in name only (usually between a lesbian and a gay man)

xingxhi hunyin ba 形式婚姻吧 fake marriage bar

xinxing nongcun yanglao baoxian 新型农村养老保险 new-style rural old-age insurance

Xuanwu 宣武 former district of Beijing

yali 压力 pressure, stress

yang 养 nurture

yanglao qiye 养老企业 elder-care company

yat chi sat juk chin gu han [C] 一次失足千古恨 one wrong step can cause a thousand regrets

yeye 爷爷 [usually paternal] grandfather

yilai yanglao 依赖养老 dependent elder care

yiye qing 一夜情 one-night stand

Yingde 英德 municipality in Northern Guangdong

you wenhua de ren 有文化的人 educated people

yuk-san-chin [C] 肉身钱 "corporeal body money," bridewealth, brideprice

zeren 责任 responsibility

zha you 榨油 press oil

zhen 真 genuine

zhi yao ren hao 只要人好 as long as the person is good

zhichi 支持 support

Zhonghua Xiaoqin Jinglao Kaimo 中华孝亲敬老楷模 Chinese Exemplar of Filiality and Respect for the Elderly

Zhonghua Xiaoqin Jinglao Timing Jiang 中华孝亲敬老提名奖 Chinese Filial and Respecting the Elderly Honorable Mention

Zhonghua Xiaoqin Jinglao Zhi Xing 中华孝亲敬老之星 Chinese Filial and Respecting the Elderly Star

Zouping 邹平 municipality in Shandong

zunlao, ailao, zhulao 尊老, 爱老, 助老 respect the elders, love the elders, help the elders

zuo laodong 做劳动 do physical labor

zuo shi 做事 do things

zuo yuezi 坐月子 sit the month

zuo yuezi 作月子 do the month: spend a month recovering from childbirth

REFERENCES

ACWF (All China Women's Federation). 2013. "Woguo nongcun liushou ertong, chengxiang liudong ertong zhuangkuang yanjiu baogao" [Research report on the situation of left-behind children and migrant children in the Chinese countryside]. Zhongguo Funü Xinwen [China Women's News]. http://acwf.people. com.cn/n/2013/0510/c99013–21437965.html. Accessed February 6, 2016.

Ahern, Emily Martin. 1973. *The Cult of the Dead in a Chinese Village*. Stanford: Stanford University Press.

———. 1975. "The Power and Pollution of Chinese Women." In Margery Wolf and Roxanne Witke, eds., *Women in Chinese Society*, 193–214. Stanford: Stanford University Press.

Aijmer, Göran, and Virgil Ho. 2000. *Cantonese Society in a Time of Change*. Hong Kong: Chinese University Press.

Attané, Isabel. 2012. "Being a Woman in China Today: A Demography of Gender." *China Perspectives* 4: 5–15.

Attias-Donfut, Claudine, and Martine Segalen. 2002. "The Construction of Grandparenthood." *Current Sociology* 50: 281–94.

Bai, Limin. 2006. "Graduate Unemployment: Dilemmas and Challenges in China's Movement to Mass Higher Education." *China Quarterly* 185 (March): 128–44.

Baker, Hugh D. R. 1968. *A Chinese Village: Sheung Shui*. Hong Kong: Hong Kong University Press.

———. 1979. *Chinese Family and Kinship*. London: Macmillan.

Bao Wei, Aiguo Ma, Limei Mao, Jianqiang Lai, Mei Xiao, Guoqiang Sun, Yingying Ouyang, Shuang Wu, Wei Yang, Nanping Wang, Yanting Zhao, Juan Fu, and Liegang Liu. 2010. "Diet and Lifestyle Interventions in Postpartum Women in China: Study Design and Rationale of a Multicenter Randomized Controlled Trial." *BMC Public Health* 10: 103. doi:10.1186/1471–2458–10–103.

Barclay, Katie. 2011. *Love, Intimacy and Power: Marriage and Patriarchy in Scotland, 1650–1850*. Manchester: Manchester University Press.

Barlow, Tani. 1991. "Theorizing Woman: *Funü, Guojia, Jiating* (Chinese Woman, Chinese State, Chinese Family)." *Genders* 10: 132–60.

———. 1994. "Politics and Protocols of Funü: (Un)making National Woman." In Christina K. Gilmartin, Gail Hershatter, and Lisa Rofel, eds., *Engendering China: Women, Culture and the State*. Cambridge, MA: Harvard University Press.

———. 2004. *The Question of Women in Chinese Feminism*. Durham, NC: Duke University Press.

Beck, Ulrich, and Elisabeth Beck-Gernsheim. 2002. *Individualization: Institutionalized Individualism and Its Social and Political Consequences*. London: Sage.

Beck, Ulrich, Anthony Giddens, and Scott Lash. 1994. *Reflexive Modernization: Politics, Tradition and Aesthetics in the Modern Social Order*. Stanford: Stanford University Press.

Beijing Shi Bianzuan Weiyuanhui [Beijing Municipal Compilation Committee], ed. 2000. *Beijing zhi, shizheng juan, fangdichan zhi* [Beijing annals, volume on municipal administration, property annals]. Beijing: Beijing Publishing House.

Bellah, Robert, Richard Madsen, William Sullivan, Ann Swidler, and Steve Tipton. 1985. *Habits of the Heart: Individualism and Commitment in American Life*. Berkeley: University of California Press.

Bijker, Wiebe E. 2010. "How Is Technology Made? That Is the Question!" *Cambridge Journal of Economics* 34 (1): 63–76.

Bogel, Katherine. 2001. *Hooking Up*. New York: New York University Press.

Bossen, Laurel. 2002. *Chinese Women and Rural Development: Sixty Years of Change in Lu Village, Yunnan*. Lanham, MD: Rowman & Littlefield.

Bott, Elizabeth, 1957. *Family and Social Network*. London: Tavistock Publications.

Bourdieu, Pierre. 1977. *Outline of a Theory of Practice*. New York: Cambridge University Press.

———. 1990. *The Logic of Practice*. Cambridge: Polity.

Brandtstädter, Susanne. 2003. "The Moral Economy of Kinship and Property in Southern China." In Chris Hann, ed., *The Postsocialist Agrarian Question: Property Relations and the Rural Condition*, 419–40. Münster: LIT.

Brandtstädter, Susanne, and Gonçalo D. Santos, eds. 2009. *Chinese Kinship: Contemporary Anthropological Perspectives*. London: Routledge.

Bray, Francesca. 1997. *Technology and Gender: Fabrics of Power in Late Imperial China*. Berkeley: University of California Press.

———. 2009. "Becoming a Mother in Late Imperial China: Maternal Doubles and the Ambiguities of Fertility." In Susanne Brandtstädter and Gonçalo D. Santos, eds., *Chinese Kinship: Contemporary Anthropological Perspectives*, 181–203. London: Routledge.

———. 2013. *Technology, Gender and History in Imperial China: Great Transformations Reconsidered*. New York: Routledge.

Brown, Melissa J. 2004. *Is Taiwan Chinese? The Impact of Culture, Power, and Migration on Changing Identities*. Berkeley: University of California Press.

———. 2007. "Ethnic Identity, Cultural Variation and Processes of Change: Rethinking the Insights of Standardization and Orthopraxy." *Modern China* 33 (1): 91–124.

Brown, Melissa J., Laurel Bossen, Hill Gates, and Damian Satterthwaite-Phillips. 2012. "Marriage Mobility and Footbinding in Pre-1949 Rural China." *Journal of Asian Studies* 71 (4): 1035–1067.

Brown, Melissa J., and Marcus W. Feldman. 2009. "Sociocultural Epistasis and Cultural Exaptation in Footbinding, Marriage Form, and Religious Practices in Early 20th-Century Taiwan." *Proceedings of the National Academy of Sciences USA* 106 (52): 22139–22144.

Brown, Melissa J., and Damian Satterthwaite-Phillips. 2016. "Economic Correlates of Footbinding: Implications for Women and Economic Development." Unpublished manuscript.

Buck, John Lossing. 1937. *Land Utilization in China*. 3 vols. Nanking: University of Nanking.

Burger, Richard. 2012. *Behind the Red Door: Sex in China*. London: Farshaw Books.

Buss, David M. 2007. "The Evolution of Human Mating." *Acta Psychological Sinica* 39 (3): 502–12.

Butler, Judith, and Joan Scott. 1992. *Feminists Theorize the Political*. New York: Routledge.

Butler, Judith, and Elizabeth Weed, eds. 2011. *The Question of Gender: Joan W. Scott's Critical Feminism*. Bloomington: Indiana University Press.

Cai, Yong. 2013. "China's New Demographic Reality: Learning from the 2010 Census." *Population and Development Review* 39 (3): 371–96.

Caldwell, John C. 1982. *Theory of Fertility Decline*. New York: Academic Press.

———. 2005. "On Net Intergenerational Wealth Flows: An Update." *Population and Development Review* 31 (4): 721–40.

Callister, Lynn Clark. 2006. "Doing the Month: Chinese Postpartum Practices." *American Journal of Maternal and Child Nursing* 31 (6): 390.

Cancian, Francesca. 1985. *Love in America: Gender and Self Development*. Cambridge: Cambridge University Press

Chan, Anita, Richard Madsen, and Jonathan Unger. 2009. *Chen Village: Revolution to Globalization*. Berkeley: University of California Press.

Chan, Kam Wing. 2009. "The Chinese *Hukou* System at 50." *Eurasian Geography and Economics* 50 (2): 197–221.

Chang, Leslie T. 2008. *Factory Girls: From Village to City in a Changing China*. New York: Spiegel & Grau.

Chen Bofeng. 2009. "Daiji Guanxi Biandong yu Laonianren Zisha—dui Hubei Jingshan Nongcun de Shizheng Yanjiu" [Changes in intergenerational relations and elderly suicides—an empirical study in rural Jingshan, Hubei]. *Sociological Research* 2009 (4).

Chen Feinian and Liu Guangya. 2012. "The Health Implications of Grandparents Caring for Grandchildren in China." *Journals of Gerontology Series B: Psychological Sciences and Social Sciences* 67 (1): 99–112.

Chen, Lily. 2013. "Could or Should? The Changing Modality of Authority in the *China Daily*." *Journal of the British Association for Chinese Studies* 2: 51–85.

Chen Meixuan. 2013. *"Eating Huaqiao" and the Left Behind: The Moral Socio-economic Consequences of the Return of Overseas Chinese to a South China Village.* PhD diss., University College London, Department of Anthropology.

Chen, S. Sanna. 2012. *Zuo Yue Zi Sitting the Month in Taiwan: Implications for Intergenerational Relations.* PhD diss., Case Western Reserve University, Department of Anthropology.

Chen, Sheying. 2009. "Aging with Chinese Characteristics: A Public Policy Perspective." *Ageing International* 34: 172–88.

Cheng Y. M., W. Yuan, W. D. Lan, W. M. Zhang, T. Y. Wang, and Y. Wang. 2003. "A Study of Factors Associated with Caesarean Section Rates in Beijing, Shanghai and Chengdu." *Chinese Journal of Epidemiology* 24: 893–96.

Cherlin, Andrew. 1978. "Remarriage as an Incomplete Institution." *American Journal of Sociology* 84: 634–50.

———. 2004. "The Deinstitutionalization of American Marriage." *Journal of Marriage and Family* 66: 848–61.

China Daily. 2010. "Sperm Shortage Breeds Frustration." November 15.

———. 2011a. "College Students Ease Lack of Sperm Donations." March 21.

———. 2011b. "China's 2011 Average Salaries Revealed." July 6.

———. 2012a. "Sperm Banks Reach Out for Donors amid Supply Shortage." May 16.

———. 2012b. "Father Files Suit in Sperm Donor's Death." June 20.

———. 2013a. "Banking on Sperm." January 20.

———. 2013b. "Sichuan Gets Its First Sperm Bank." January 16.

———. 2013c. "China's Largest Sperm Bank Produces 40,000 Tube Babies." January 21.

———. 2013d. "Sperm Donors Recount Their Experience." January 21.

———. 2013e. "Sperm Bank Offers High Bonuses for Donors." May 7.

———. 2013f. "Pollution Blamed for Worsening Sperm Quality." November 6.

———. 2013g. "Quality of Donated Sperm Is Low, Sperm Bank Says." November 7.

Chiu, Joanna. 2013. "China's Fake Gay Marriages." *Daily Beast*, April 19. www.thedailybeast.com/articles/2013/04/19/china-s-fake-gay-marriages.html. Accessed August 2, 2015.

Cho, John (Song Pae). 2009. "'The Wedding Banquet' Revisited: 'Contract Marriages' between Korean Gays and Lesbians." *Anthropological Quarterly* 82 (2): 401–22.

Cho, Sumi, Kimberlé Williams Crenshaw, and Leslie McCall. 2013. "Toward a Field of Intersectionality Studies: Theory, Applications, and Praxis." *Signs* 38 (4): 785–810.

Chu, Godwin C., and Yen-an Chü. 1993. *The Great Wall in Ruins: Communication and Cultural Change in China.* Albany: State University of New York Press.

Chu, Junhong. 2001. "Prenatal Sex Determination and Sex-Selective Abortion in Rural Central China." *Population and Development Review* 27 (2): 259–81.

Chung, Him, and Jonathan Unger. 2013. "The Guangdong Model of Urbanisation: Collective Village Land and the Making of a New Middle Class." *China Perspectives* 2013 (3): 33–41.

Cohen, Myron L. 1976. *House United, House Divided: The Chinese Family in Taiwan.* New York: Columbia University Press.

Cohen, Philip N., and Wang Feng. 2009. "Market and Gender Pay Equity: Have Chinese Reforms Narrowed the Gap?" In Deborah S. Davis and Wang Feng, eds., *Creating Wealth and Poverty in Postsocialist China,* 37–53. Stanford: Stanford University Press.

Collier, Jane F. 1997. *From Duty to Desire: Remaking Families in a Spanish Village.* Princeton, NJ: Princeton University Press.

Cong Zhen and Merril Silverstein. 2012. "Custodial Grandparents and Intergenerational Support in Rural China." In Kalyani K. Mehta and Leng Leng Thang, eds., *Experiencing Grandparenthood: An Asian Perspective,* 109–28. Dordrecht and New York: Springer.

Cowan, Ruth S. 1983. *More Work for Mother: The Ironies of Household Technology from the Open Hearth to the Microwave.* New York: Basic Books.

Cowgill, Donald O., and Lowell D. Holmes, eds. 1972. *Aging and Modernization.* New York: Appleton-Century-Crofts.

Croll, Elisabeth. 1981. *The Politics of Marriage in Contemporary China.* Cambridge: Cambridge University Press.

———. 2000. *Endangered Daughters: Discrimination and Development in Asia.* London: Routledge.

———. 2006a. *China's New Consumers: Social Development and Domestic Demand.* London: Routledge.

———. 2006b. "The Intergenerational Contract in the Changing Asian Family." *Oxford Development Studies* 34 (4): 473–91.

Dahe News. 2007. "Bufen diaocha yiqi laoren shijian" [A partial investigation of incidents of elder abandonment]. January 15. www.dahe.cn/xwzx/rdtj/jdt/t20070115_805876.htm. Accessed August 5, 2015.

Davis, Deborah. 2000. "Introduction: A Revolution in Consumption." In Deborah Davis, ed., *The Consumer Revolution in Urban China,* 1–22. Berkeley: University of California Press.

———. 2006. "When a House Becomes His Home." In Wenfang Tang and Burkart Holzner, eds., *Social Change in Contemporary China: C.K. Yang and the Concept of Institutional Diffusion.* Pittsburgh, PA: University of Pittsburgh.

———. 2014. "On the Limits of Personal Autonomy: PRC Law and the Institution of Marriage." In Deborah S. Davis and Sara L. Friedman, eds., *Wives, Husbands and Lovers: Marriage and Sexuality in Hong Kong, Taiwan, and Urban China,* 41–61. Stanford: Stanford University Press.

Davis, Deborah, and Sara L. Friedman, eds. 2014. *Wives, Husbands, and Lovers: Marriage and Sexuality in Hong Kong, Taiwan, and Urban China.* Stanford: Stanford University Press.

Davis, Deborah, and Stevan Harrell, eds. 1993. *Chinese Families in the Post-Mao Era.* Berkeley: University of California Press.

Davis-Friedmann, Deborah. 1983. *Long Lives: Chinese Elderly and the Communist Revolution*. Stanford: Stanford University Press.

———. 1991. *Long Lives: Chinese Elderly and the Communist Revolution*. Expanded ed. Stanford: Stanford University Press.

Davison, Nicola. 2011. "Gay Marriage with Chinese Characteristics." *Slate*, February 9. www.slate.com/articles/news_and_politics/dispatches/2011/02/gay_marriage_with_chinese_characteristics.html. Accessed August 2, 2015.

de Brauw, Alan, Qiang Li, Chengfang Liu, Scott Rozelle, and Linxiu Zhang. 2008. "Feminization of Agriculture in China? Myths Surrounding Women's Participation in Farming." *China Quarterly* 194: 327–48.

Deng Yunxue. 2012. *Gender in Factory Life: An Ethnographic Study of Migrant Workers in Shenzhen Foxconn*. M.Phil thesis, Applied Sciences, The Hong Kong Polytechnic University.

Diamant, Neil J. 2000. *Revolutionizing the Family: Politics, Love, and Divorce in Urban and Rural China, 1949–1968*. Berkeley: University of California Press.

Diamond, Norma. 1975. "Collectivization, Kinship, and the Status of Women in Rural China." *Bulletin of the Concerned Asian Scholars* 7 (1): 25–32.

Ding, Min, and Jie Xu. 2015. *The Chinese Way*. New York: Routledge.

Dong, Guoli, and Yanqing Xie. 2013. "Metaphorical Imagination and Reconstruction of the Term of Family: The Practice of State Power in China since 1949." *China Studies* [Beijing] 17: 109–37.

Dong Jinquan, Yao Cheng, Liu Qun, Zhang Lijun, Zhang Nannan, Chen Qun, and Guan Chao. 2011. "Dangdai qingniande ze'ou biaozhun jiqi xingbie chayi: Dui 1255 zezheng hun guanggao de neirong fenxi" [The standards of choosing spouses and gender differences among contemporary youth based on the content analysis of 1,255 marriage ads]. *Journal of the Shanxi College for Youth Administration* [Shanxi Qingnian Guanli Ganbu Xueyuan xuebao] (2): 7–11.

Dosser, Dave, John Balswick, and Carol Halverson. 1986. "Male Inexpressiveness and Relationships." *Journal of Social and Personal Relationships* 3: 241–58.

Du Fenglian and Xiao-yuan Dong. 2010. "Women's Labor Force Participation and Childcare Choices in Urban China during the Economic Transition." Working Paper 2010–04. University of Winnipeg, Department of Economics.

Du, Shanshan. 2002. *Chopsticks Only Work in Pairs: Gender Unity and Gender Equality among the Lahu of Southwest China*. New York: Columbia University Press.

Du, Shanshan, and Ya-chen Chen. 2011. *Women and Gender in Contemporary Chinese Societies: Beyond Han Patriarchy*. Lanham, MD: Lexington Books.

Duara, Prasenjit. 2000. "Of Authenticity and Woman: Personal Narratives of Middle Class Women in Modern China." In Wen-Hsin Yeh, ed., *Becoming Chinese: Passages to Modernity and Beyond*, 342–64. Berkeley: University of California Press.

Duncombe, Jean, and Dennis Marsden. 1993. "Love and Intimacy: The Gender Division of Emotion and `Emotion Work': A Neglected Aspect of Sociological Discussion of Heterosexual Relationships." *Sociology* 27 (2): 221–41.

Ebrey, Patricia Buckley, and Rubie S. Watson. 1991. *Marriage and Inequality in Chinese Society*. Berkeley: University of California Press.

Editors, LCB. 2013. "Baby Business: China's Maternity Hotels Expand at Home and Abroad." http://learnchinesebusiness.com/2013/04/13/baby-business-chinas-maternity-hotels-expand-at-home-and-abroad/. Accessed August 2, 2015.

Ellis, Denise, and M.S. Ho. 1982. "Attitudes of Chinese Women towards Sexuality and Birth Control." *Canadian Nurse* 78 (3): 28–31.

Engebretsen, Elisabeth L. 2009. "Intimate Practices, Conjugal Ideals: Affective Ties and Relationship Strategies among *Lala* (Lesbian) Women in Contemporary Beijing." *Sexuality Research & Social Policy: Journal of NSRC* 6 (3): 3–14.

———. 2014. *Queer Women in Urban China: An Ethnography*. New York: Routledge.

Engels, Friedrich. (1884) 1972. *The Origin of the Family, Private Property and the State*. New York: International Publishers.

Evans, Harriet. 1995. "Defining Difference: The Scientific Construction of Gender and Sexuality in the People's Republic of China." *Signs* 20 (2): 357–406.

———. 1997. *Women and Sexuality in China: Dominant Discourses of Sexuality and Gender since 1949*. Cambridge: Polity Press.

———. 2008. *The Subject of Gender: Daughters and Mothers in Urban China*. Lanham, MD: Rowman & Littlefield.

———. 2010. "The Gender of Communication: Changing Expectations of Mothers and Daughters in Urban China." *China Quarterly* 204: 980–1000.

Eyferth, Jacob. 2009. *Eating Rice from Bamboo Roots: The Social History of a Community of Handicraft Papermakers in Rural Sichuan, 1920–2000*. Cambridge, MA: Harvard University Asia Center.

———. 2012. "Women's Work and the Politics of Homespun in Socialist China, 1949–1980." *International Review of Social History* 57 (3): 365–91.

Faircloth, Charlotte, Diane M. Hoffman, and Linda L. Layne, eds. 2013. *Parenting in Global Perspective: Negotiating Ideologies of Kinship, Self and Politics*. New York: Routledge.

Fang, I-chieh. 2013. "The Girls Who Are Keen to Get Married." In Charles Stafford, ed., *Ordinary Ethics in China*. London: Bloomsbury.

Farquhar, Judith. 2002. *Appetites: Food and Sex in Post-Socialist China*. Durham, NC: Duke University Press.

Farrer, James. 2014. "Love, Sex, and Commitment: Delinking Premarital Intimacy from Marriage in Urban China." In Deborah S. Davis and Sara L. Friedman, eds., *Wives, Husbands, and Lovers: Marriage and Sexuality in Hong Kong, Taiwan, and Urban China*, 62–96. Stanford: Stanford University Press.

Farrer, James, and Sun Zhongxin. 2003. "Extramarital Love in Shanghai." *China Journal*, no. 50: 1–36.

Feng Nailin. 2011. *Zhongguo 2010 nian renkou pucha ziliao* [Materials from the 2010 population census of the People's Republic of China]. Beijing: China Statistics Press. http://tongji.oversea.cnki.net.offcampus.lib.washington.edu/npccen/EngNavi/YearBook.aspx?id=N2012060678&floor=1.

Feng, Xing Lin, Sufang Guo, David Hipgrave, Jun Zhu, Lingli Zhang, Li Song, Qing Yang, Yan Guo, and Carine Ronsmans. 2011. "China's Facility-Based Birth Strategy and Neonatal Mortality: A Population-Based Epidemiological Study." *Lancet* 378 (9801): 1493–1500.

Feuchtwang, Stephan. 2002. "Remnants of Revolution in China." In Chris M. Hann, ed., *Postsocialism: Ideals, Ideologies and Practices in Eurasia*, 196–200. London and New York: Routledge.

Fielde, Adele M. 1884. *Pagoda Shadows: Studies from Life in China*. Boston: W.G. Corthell.

Fincher, Leta Hong. 2014. *Leftover Women: The Resurgence of Gender Inequality in China*. London: Zed Books.

Firestone, Shulamith. 1970. *The Dialectic of Sex: The Case for Feminist Revolution*. New York: William Morrow.

Fong, Vanessa. 2002. "China's One-Child Policy and the Empowerment of Urban Daughters." *American Anthropologist* 104 (4): 1098–1109.

———. 2004. *Only Hope: Coming of Age under China's One-Child Policy*. Stanford: Stanford University Press.

———. 2007. "Parent-Child Communication Problems and the Perceived Inadequacies of Chinese Only Children." *Ethos* 35 (1): 85–127.

Freedman, Maurice. 1958. *Lineage Organization in Southeastern China*. London: Athlone Press.

———. 1966. *Chinese Lineage and Society*. London: Athlone Press.

———. 1979. *The Study of Chinese Society*. Edited by G. William Skinner. Stanford: Stanford University Press.

Fu Xiaoxing and Zhang Kecheng. 2013. "Zai yinxing 'hun' yu zhidu hun de bianjie youzou: Zhongguo nan tongxinglian qunti de hunyin xingtai fenxi" [Straddling the borders of implicit "marriage" and institutional marriage: An analysis of marriage patterns of the Chinese gay male population]. *Huanan Shifan Daxue xuebao* [Journal of South China Normal University, Social Science ed.] 205 (6): 22–30.

Furedi, Frank. 2002. *Paranoid Parenting: Why Ignoring the Experts May Be Best for Your Child*. Chicago: Chicago Review Press.

Furth, Charlotte. 1987. "Concepts of Pregnancy, Childbirth and Infancy in Ch'ing Dynasty China." *Journal of Asian Studies* 46 (1): 7–36.

———. 1999. *A Flourishing Yin: Gender in China's Medical History 960–1665*. Berkeley: University of California Press.

Gaetano, Arianne M. 2004. "Filial Daughters, Modern Women: Migrant Domestic Workers in Post-Mao Beijing." In Arianne Gaetano and Tamara Jacka, eds., *On the Move: Women in Rural-to-Urban Migration in Contemporary China*, 41–79. New York: Columbia University Press.

Gaetano, Arianne M., and Tamara Jacka. 2004. *On the Move: Women in Rural-to-Urban Migration in Contemporary China*. New York: Columbia University Press.

Gates, Hill. 1987. "Money for the Gods." *Modern China* 13(3): 259–77.

———. 1996. *China's Motor: A Thousand Years of Petty Capitalism*. Ithaca, NY: Cornell University Press.

———. 2001. "Footloose in Fujian: Economic Correlates of Footbinding." *Comparative Studies in Society and History* 43 (1): 130–48.

———. 2015. *Footbinding and Women's Labor in Sichuan*. London and New York: Routledge.

Giddens, Anthony. 1991. *Modernity and Self-identity: Self and Society in the Late Modern Age*. Stanford: Stanford University Press.

———. 1992. *The Transformation of Intimacy: Sexuality, Love, and Eroticism in Modern Societies*. Cambridge: Polity Press.

———. 1999. *Runaway World: How Globalization Is Reshaping Our Lives*. London: Profile Books.

Global Times. 2012a. "Higher Standards from Banks and Growing Infertility Triggers Donor Sperm Drought." May 28.

———. 2012b. "Sperm Black Market." October 10.

Glosser, Susan L. 2003. *Chinese Visions of Family and State, 1915–1953*. Berkeley: University of California Press.

Godelier, Maurice. 2012. *The Metamorphoses of Kinship*. London: Verso.

Goh, Esther. 2011. *China's One-Child Policy and Multiple Caregiving: Raising Little Suns in Xiamen*. New York: Routledge.

Gong, D., Y. L. Liu, Z. Zheng, Y. F. Tian, and Z. Li. 2009. "An Overview on Ethical Issues about Sperm Donation." *Asian Journal of Andrology* 11: 645–52

Goode, William. 1963. *World Revolution and Family Patterns*. New York: Free Press.

Goodman, David. 2008. *The New Rich in China: Future Rulers, Present Lives*. New York: Routledge.

Goody, Esther N. 1982. *Parenthood and Social Reproduction: Fostering and Occupational Roles in West Africa*. Cambridge: Cambridge University Press.

Goody, Jack. 1973. "Bridewealth and Dowry in Africa and Eurasia." In Jack Goody and Stanley J. Tambiah, eds., *Bridewealth and Dowry*, 1–47. Cambridge: Cambridge University Press.

———. 1990. *The Oriental, the Ancient and the Primitive: Systems of Marriage and the Family in the Pre-industrial Societies of Eurasia*. Cambridge: Cambridge University Press.

Gottschang, Suzanne Z. 2001. "The Consuming Mother: Infant Feeding and the Feminine Body in Urban China." In Nancy Chen, Constance Clark, Suzanne Gottschang, and Lyn Jeffrey, eds., *China Urban: Ethnographies of Contemporary Culture*, 89–103. Durham, NC: Duke University Press.

———. 2007. "Maternal Bodies, Breast-Feeding, and Consumer Desire in Urban China." *Medical Anthropology Quarterly* 21: 64–80.

Graeber, David. 2001. *Toward an Anthropological Theory of Value: The False Coin of Our Own Dreams*. New York: Palgrave.

Gramsci, Antonio. 1971. *Selections from the Prison Notebooks.* Edited and translated by Quintin Hoare and Geoffrey Nowell Smith. London: Lawrence and Wishart.

Greenhalgh, Susan. 1994. "Controlling Births and Bodies in Village China." *American Ethnologist* 21 (1): 1–30.

———. 1988. "Fertility as Mobility: Sinic Transitions." *Population and Development Review* 14 (4): 629–74.

———. 2010. *Cultivating Global Citizens: Population in the Rise of China.* Cambridge, MA: Harvard University Press.

———. 2013. "Patriarchal Demographics? China's Sex Ratio Reconsidered." *Population and Development Review* 38 (supplement): 130–49.

Greenhalgh, Susan, and Edwin A. Winckler. 2005. *Governing China's Population: From Leninist to Neoliberal Biopolitics.* Stanford: Stanford University Press.

Guang Lei and Fanming Kong. 2010. "Rural Prejudice and Gender Discrimination in China's Urban Job Market." In Martin King Whyte, ed., *One Country, Two Societies: Rural-Urban Inequality in Contemporary China,* 241–64. Cambridge, MA: Harvard University Press.

Guilmoto, Christophe Z., and Qiang Ren. 2011. "Socio-economic Differentials in Birth Masculinity in China." *Development and Change* 42 (5): 1269–96.

Guo Yuhua. 2001. "Daiji guanxi zhong de gongping luoji jiqi bianqian: Dui Hebei nongcun yanglao shijian de fenxi" [The logic of fairness and its change in intergenerational relations: An analysis of cases of elderly support in rural Hebei]. *Zhongguo xueshu* [Chinese scholarship] 4: 221–54.

Guo Yuhua and Sun Liping. 2002. *Suku: Yi zhong nongmin guojia guannian xingcheng de zhongjie jizhi* [Pouring out grievances: A mediated mechanism for the shaping of peasants' idea of the state]. *Zhongguo xueshu* 4: 130–57.

Guttman, Matthew G. 1996. *The Meanings of Macho: Being a Man in Mexico.* Berkeley: University of California Press.

Hamilton, Gary G. 1990. "Patriarchy, Patrimonialism, and Filial Piety: A Comparison of China and Western Europe." *British Journal of Sociology* 41 (1): 82–104.

Han, Hua, Benjamin Gertsen, Stevan Harrell, He Wenting, Rachel Wall, Wang Chi, Wang Jianxiong, Wang Shuo, and Yao Shishi. 2009. *Dahua's Wedding: Marriage, Migration, and Social Change in Southwest China.* Ethnographic film, privately distributed.

Handwerker, Lisa. 1998. "The Consequences of Modernity for Childless Women in China: Medicalization and Resistance." In Margaret M. Lock and Patricia A. Kaufert, eds., *Pragmatic Women and Body Politics,* 178–206. Cambridge: Cambridge University Press.

———. 2002. "The Politics of Making Modern Babies in China: Reproductive Technologies and the 'New' Eugenics." In Marcia Claire Inhorn and Frank Van Balen, eds., *Infertility around the Globe: New Thinking on Childlessness, Gender, and Reproductive Technologies,* 178–205. Berkeley: University of California Press.

Hansen, Mette Halskov. 2014. *Educating the Chinese Individual: Life in a Rural Boarding School.* Seattle: University of Washington Press.

Harrell, Stevan. 1981. "Growing Old in Rural Taiwan." In Pamela T. Amoss and Stevan Harrell, eds., *Other Ways of Growing Old*, 193–210. Stanford: Stanford University Press.

———. 1982. *Ploughshare Village: Culture and Context in Taiwan*. Seattle: University of Washington Press.

———. 1985. "The Rich Get Children: Segmentation, Stratification, and Population in Three Zhejiang Lineages." In Susan B. Hanley and Arthur P. Wolf, eds., *Family and Population in East Asian History*, 81–109. Stanford: Stanford University Press.

———. 1997. *Human Families*. Boulder, CO: Westview Press.

———. 2013. "Orthodoxy, Resistance and the Family in Chinese Art." In J. Silbergeld and D.C.Y. Ching, eds. *The Family Model in Chinese Art and Culture*, 71–90. Princeton, NJ: Princeton University Press.

Harrell, Stevan, and Sara A. Dickey. 1985. "Dowry Systems in Complex Societies." *Ethnology* 24 (2): 105–20.

Harrell, Stevan, Wang Yuesheng, Han Hua, Gonçalo D. Santos, and Zhou Yingying. 2011. "Fertility Decline in Rural China: A Comparative Analysis." *Journal of Family History* 36 (1): 15–36.

Harvey, David. 1989. *The Condition of Postmodernity: An Inquiry into the Origins of Social Change*. Oxford: Blackwell.

Harvey, Travis Anna, and Lila Buckley. 2009. "Childbirth in China." In Helen Selain, ed., *Childbirth across Cultures*. New York: Springer.

Hays, Sharon. 1996. *The Cultural Contradictions of Motherhood*. New Haven: Yale University Press.

Heng, Boon Chin. 2007. "Growing Surplus of Frozen Embryos in China Offers Opportunities for the Development of Human Embryonic Stem Cell Banks." *Regenerative Medicine* 2 (6): 873–74.

———. 2009. "Stringent Regulation of Oocyte Donation in China." *Human Reproduction* 24 (1): 14–16.

Hershatter, Gail. 2002. "The Gender of Memory: Rural Chinese Women and the 1950s." *Signs* 28 (1): 43–72.

———. 2007. *Women in China's Long Twentieth Century*. Berkeley: University of California Press.

———. 2011. *The Gender of Memory: Rural Women and China's Collective Past*. Berkeley: University of California Press.

Hildebrandt, Timothy. 2011. "Same-Sex Marriage in China? The Strategic Promulgation of a Progressive Policy and Its Impact on LGBT Activism." *Review of International Studies* 37 (3): 1313–33.

Holroyd, Eleanor, Violeta Lopez, and Sally Wai-Chi Chan. 2011. "Negotiating 'Doing the Month': An Ethnographic Study Examining the Postnatal Practice of Two Generations of Chinese Women." *Nursing Health Science* 13 (1): 47–52.

Hsing, You-tien. 2010. *The Great Urban Transformation: Politics of Land and Property in China*. Oxford: Oxford University Press.

Hsiung, Ping-chun. 1996. *Living Rooms as Factories: Class, Gender, and the Satellite Factory System in Taiwan*. Philadelphia: Temple University Press.

Hsu, Francis L. K. 1948. *Under the Ancestors' Shadow: Chinese Culture and Personality*. London: Routledge.

Huang, Philip C.C. 1990. *The Peasant Family and Rural Development in the Yangzi Delta, 1350–1988*. Stanford: Stanford University Press.

———. 2002. "Development or Involution in Eighteenth-Century Britain and China? A Review of Kenneth Pomeranz's *The Great Divergence: China, Europe, and the Making of the Modern World Economy*." *Journal of Asian Studies* 61 (2): 501–38.

Ikels, Charlotte. 1990. "The Resolution of Inter-generational Conflict." *Modern China* 16 (4): 379–406.

———. 1993. "Settling Accounts: The Intergenerational Contract in an Age of Reform." In Deborah Davis and Stevan Harrell, eds., *Chinese Families in the Post-Mao Era*. Berkeley: University of California Press.

———. 2004a. *Filial Piety: Practice and Discourse in Contemporary East Asia*. Stanford: Stanford University Press.

———. 2004b. "The Impact of Housing Policy on China's Urban Elderly." *Journal of Urban Anthropology* 33 (2–4): 321–55.

———. 2006. "Economic Reform and Intergenerational Relationships in China." *Oxford Development Studies* 34 (4): 388–400.

Inhorn, Marcia Claire, and Frank Van Balen, eds. 2002. *Infertility around the Globe: New Thinking on Childlessness, Gender, and Reproductive Technologies*. Berkeley: University of California Press.

Jacka, Tamara. 1997. *Women's Work in Rural China: Change and Continuity in an Era of Reform*. Cambridge: Cambridge University Press.

Jankowiak, William. 1993. *Sex, Death and Hierarchy in a Chinese City*. New York: Columbia University Press.

Jankowiak, William, and Xuan Li. 2014. "The Decline of the Chauvinistic Model of Chinese Masculinity: A Research Report." *Chinese Sociological Review* 46 (4): 3–18.

Jankowiak, William, Yifei Shen, Cancan Wang, Shiyu Yao, and Shelly Vorsche. 2015. "Investigating Love's Universal Attributes: A Research Report." *Cross-Cultural Research* 49 (4): 422–36.

Jasanoff, Sheila. 2006. *States of Knowledge: The Co-production of Science and the Social Order*. New York: Routledge.

Jaschok, Maria, and Suzanne Miers, eds. 1994. *Women and Chinese Patriarchy: Submission, Servitude, and Escape*. Hong Kong: Hong Kong University Press; London: Zed Books.

Jiang, Quanbao, and Jesús J. Sánchez-Barricarte. 2012. "Bride Price in China: The Obstacle to 'Bare Branches' Seeking Marriage." *History of the Family* 17 (1): 2–15.

Jing, Jun, ed. 2000. *Feeding China's Little Emperors: Food, Children, and Social Change*. Stanford: Stanford University Press.

Jing Jun, Zhang Jie, and Wu Xueya. 2011. "Zhongguo chengshi laonianren zisha wenti fenxi" [Suicide among elderly people in urban China]. *Population Research* 35 (3): 84–96.

Johnson, Kay Ann. 1983. *Women, the Family, and Peasant Revolution in China.* Chicago: University of Chicago Press.

———. 1996. "The Politics of the Revival of Infant Abandonment in China, with Special Reference to Hunan." *Population and Development Review* 22 (1): 77–98.

———. 2004. *Wanting a Daughter, Needing a Son: Abandonment, Adoption and Orphanage Care in China.* Saint Paul, MN: Yeong & Yeong Book Company.

Jones, Charles. 2001. "Law, Patriarchies, and State Formation in England and Postcolonial Hong Kong." *Journal of Law and Society* 28 (2): 265–89.

Judd, Ellen. 1989. "Niangjia: Chinese Women and Their Natal Families." *Journal of Asian Studies* 43 (3): 525–44.

———. 1994. *Gender and Power in Rural North China.* Stanford: Stanford University Press.

———. 2009. "Families We Create: Women's Kinship in Rural China as Spatialized Practice." In Susanne Brandstädter and Gonçalo D. Santos, eds., *Chinese Kinship: Contemporary Anthropological Perspectives,* 29–47. London: Routledge.

Kam, Lucetta Y. L. 2012. *Shanghai Lalas: Female* Tongzhi *Communities and Politics in Urban China.* Hong Kong: Hong Kong University Press.

Kandiyoti, Deniz. 1988. "Bargaining with Patriarchy." *Gender and Society* 2, no. 3: 274–90.

———. 1998. "Gender, Power and Contestation: Rethinking Bargaining with Patriarchy." In C. Jackson and R. Pearson, eds., *Feminist Visions of Development: Gender Analysis and Policy,* 135–39. London: Routledge.

Kipnis, Andrew B. 1996. "The Language of Gifts: Managing Guanxi in a North China Village." *Modern China* 22 (3): 285–314.

———. 1997. *Producing Guanxi: Sentiment, Self, and Subculture in a North China Village.* Durham, NC: Duke University Press.

———. 2001. "The Disturbing Educational Discipline of 'Peasants.'" *China Journal* 46: 1–24.

———. 2009. "Education and the Governing of Child-Centred Relatedness." In Susanne Brandstädter and Gonçalo Santos, eds., *Chinese Kinship: Contemporary Anthropological Perspectives,* 204–22. London: Routledge.

———. 2011a. "Chinese-Nation-Building as, Instead of, and Before Globalization." *ProtoSociology* 28: 25–47.

———. 2011b. *Governing Educational Desire: Culture, Politics and Schooling in China.* Chicago: University of Chicago Press.

———. 2012a. "Constructing Commonality: Standardization and Modernization in Chinese Nation-Building." *Journal of Asian Studies* 71 (3): 731–55.

———. 2012b. "Introduction: Chinese Modernity and the Individual Psyche." In Andrew B. Kipnis, ed., *Chinese Modernity and the Individual Psyche,* 1–18. New York: Palgrave Macmillan.

———. 2012c. "Private Lessons and National Formations: National Hierarchy and the Individual Psyche in the Marketing of Educational Programs." In Andrew B. Kipnis, ed., *Chinese Modernity and the Individual Psyche*, 187–202. New York: Palgrave Macmillan.

———. 2016. *From Village to City: Social Transformation in a Chinese County Seat.* Berkeley: University of California Press.

Klein, Kerstin. 2010. "Illiberal Biopolitics and 'Embryonic Life': The Governance of Human Embryonic Stem Cell Research in China." In John Yorke, ed., *The Right to Life and the Value of Life: Orientations in Law, Politics and Ethics*, 399–421. Farnham, UK: Ashgate Publishing.

Kloet, Jeroen de. 2008. *China with a Cut: Globalization, Urban Youth and Popular Culture.* Amsterdam: Amsterdam University Press.

Ko, Dorothy. 2005. *Cinderella's Sisters: A Revisionist History of Footbinding.* Berkeley: University of California Press.

Kong, Travis S. K. 2011. *Chinese Male Homosexualities: Memba, Tongzhi, and Golden Boy.* London: Routledge.

Ku, Hok Bun. 2003. *Moral Politics in a South Chinese Village: Responsibility, Reciprocity, and Resistance.* Lanham, MD: Rowman & Littlefield.

Lavely, William, and Ronald Freedman. 1990. "The Origins of the Chinese Fertility Decline." *Demography* 27 (3): 357–67.

Li Peilin. 2006. *Hexie shehui shijiang* [Ten lectures on harmonious society]. Beijing: Shehui Kexue Wenxian Chubanshe.

Li Weiwei. 2005. "Zhonghua Xiaoqin Jinglao Shi Da Kaimo pingchu" [Ten Great Chinese Exemplars of Filiality and Respect for the Elderly chosen]. Xinhuanet, January 8. www.dahe.cn/xwzx/rdtj/jdt/t20070115_805876.htm. Accessed August 5, 2015.

Li, Xuan. 2014. "Parental Power-Prestige and the Effects of Paternal versus Maternal Acceptance on the Psychological Adjustment of Chinese Adolescents." *Cross-Cultural Research* 48 (3): 223–30.

Li, Xuan, and Michael E. Lamb. 2012. "Fathers in Chinese Culture: From Stern Disciplinarians to Involved Parents." In David W. Shwalb, Barbara J. Shwalb, and Michael E. Lamb, eds., *Fathers in Cultural Context*, 15–41. New York: Routledge/Taylor & Francis.

Li Yifei et al. 2015. *Zhongguo liushou ertong xinling zhuangkuang baipishu (2015 nian)* [White paper on the mental condition of China's left-behind children (year 2015)]. White paper, Shangxue Lushang Ertong Xinling Guan'ai Zhongxin [On the Road to School Center for the Mental Care of Children], Beijing.

Li Yinhe. 2010. *Wu chengshi jiating jiegou yu jiating guanxi diaocha baogao* [Report on five-city survey on family structure and family relationship]. Beijing: Chinese Academy of Social Science (CASS) Five-City Research Project.

Liao, Junhong, Bart Dessein, and Guido Pennings. 2010. "The Ethical Debate on Donor Insemination in China." *Reproductive Biomedicine Online* 20 (7): 895–902.

Liu, Lige, Xiaoyi Jin, Melissa J. Brown, and Marcus W. Feldman. 2014. "Male Marriage Squeeze and Inter-provincial Marriage in Central China: Evidence from Anhui." *Journal of Contemporary China* 23 (86): 351–371. doi:10.1080/10670564. 2013.832541.

Liu, Wenrong. 2012. "Xiaodao shuailuo? Chengnian zinü zhichi fumu de guannian, xingwei, jiqi yingxiang yinsu" [Decline of filial piety? Concepts, behaviors and impact factors of adult children on parental support]. *Zhongguo qingnian* 2012 (2): 22–32.

Liu, Yajiun, Guanghui Li , Yi Chen , Xin Wang , Yan Ruan , Liying Zou , and Weiyuan Zhang. 2014. "A Descriptive Analysis of the Indications for Caesarean Section in Mainland China." *BMC Pregnancy and Childbirth*. doi:10.1186/ s12884–014–0410–2, www.biomedcentral.com/1471–2393/14/410.

Liu, Yan Qun, Judith A. Maloni, and Marcia A. Patrini. 2012. "Effect of Postpartum Practices of Doing the Month on Women's Physical and Mental Health." *Biological Research for Nursing* 16 (1): 55–63.

Lomoro, O. A., J. E. Ehiris, X. Qian, and S. L. Tang. 2002. "Mothers' Perspectives on the Quality of Postpartum Care in Central Shanghai, China." *International Journal for Quality in Health Care* 14 (5): 393–401.

Lucia. 2011. "Zhuazhu huangjinqi: Cong zuo yuezi kaishi jianfei" [Capture this golden moment: Start losing weight while sitting the month]. PC Lady.com.cn, http://fitness.pclady.com.cn/jf/medicine/1102/658912.html. Accessed March 2012.

Mao Zedong. 1966. *Quotations from Chairman Mao Tse-tung*. Bilingual ed.. Beijing: Foreign Languages Press.

Marshall, Tara C. 2008. "Cultural Differences in Intimacy: The Influence of Gender-Role Ideology and Individualism—Collectivism." *Journal of Social and Personal Relationships*, 25: 1434–1694.

Mathews, Gordon. 2014. "Being a Man in a Straitened Japan: The View from Twenty Years Later." In Satsuki Kawano, Glenda Roberts, and Susan Orpett Long, eds., *Capturing Contemporary Japan: Differentiation and Uncertainty*, 60–80. Honolulu: University of Hawai'i Press.

Mauss, Marcel. (1924) 1990. *The Gift: Forms and Functions of Exchange in Archaic Societies*. New York: Norton.

May, Shannon. 2010. "Bridging Divides and Breaking Homes: Young Women's Lifecycle Labor Mobility as a Family Managerial Strategy." *China Quarterly* 204: 899–920.

McLanahan, Sara, Irwin Garfinkel, Ron Mincy, and Elisabeth Donahue. 2002. *The Future of Children: Fragile Families*. Princeton, NJ: Princeton University Press.

Mead, Margaret, and Martha Wolfenstein, eds. 1955. *Childhood in Contemporary Cultures*. Chicago: University of Chicago Press.

Miège, Pierre. 2009. "'In My Opinion, Most *Tongzhi* Are Dutiful Sons': Community, Social Norms, and Construction of Identity among Young Homosexuals in Hefei, Anhui Province." *China Perspectives* 2009 (1): 40–53.

Miller, Eric. 2004. "Filial Daughters, Filial Sons: Comparisons from Rural North China." In Charlotte Ikels, ed., *Filial Piety: Practice and Discourse in Contemporary East Asia*, 34–52. Stanford: Stanford University Press.

Millet, Kate. 1969. *Sexual Politics*. New York: Doubleday.

Minter, Adam. 2014. "China Needs Millions of Brides ASAP." *Bloomberg View*, December 25. http://www.bloombergview.com/articles/2014–12–25/ china-needs-millions-of-brides-asap.

Mitchell, Juliet. 1971. *Woman's Estate*. London: Penguin.

MOH (Ministry of Health). 2001a. "Renlei fuzhu shengzhi jishu guanli banfa" [Regulations for the administration of human-assisted reproductive technology]. Issued on February 20. National Health and Family Planning Commission of the People's Republic of China. http://www.moh.gov.cn/mohzcfgs/ s3576/200804/29614.shtml. Accessed February 6, 2016.

———. 2001b. "Renlei jingzi ku guanli banfa" [Regulations for the administration of sperm banks]. Issued on February 20. National Health and Family Planning Commission of the People's Republic of China. http://www.moh.gov.cn/ mohzcfgs/pgz/200804/29615.shtml. Accessed February 6, 2016.

———. 2001c. "Weishengbu guanyu fabu renlei fuzhu shengzhi jishu he renlei jingzi ku xiangguan jishu guifan, biaozhun ji lunli yuanze de tongzhi" [Notice from the Ministry of Health concerning the norms, standards, and ethical principles of ART and sperm banks]. Issued on May 14. Wenfa wang [Legal inquiry web]. http://www.51wf.com/law/1117610.html. Accessed February 6, 2016.

———. 2003. "Weishengbu Guanyu Xiuding Renlei Fuzhu Shengzhi Jishu he Renlei Jingzi Ku Xiangguan Jishu Guifan, Jiben Biaozhun, he Lunli Yuanze de Tongzhi" [Notice from the Ministry of Health concerning the revision of the norms, standards, and ethical principles of ART and sperm banks]. Issued on September 30. National Health and Family Planning Commission of the People's Republic of China. http://www.nhfpc.gov.cn/qjjys/s3581/200805/ f69a925d55b44be2a9b4ada7fcdec835.shtml. Accessed February 6, 2016.

———. 2006a. "Guanyu jiakuai cujin xinxing nongcun hezuo yiliao shidian gongzuo de tongzhi" [Directive on speeding up and promoting the task of rural experimental areas for the new-style rural cooperative health insurance]. Xinhuanet. Issued on January 10, 2016. http://news.xinhuanet.com/politics/2006–01/19/ content_4071514.htm.

———. 2006b. "Weishengbu guanyu yinfa renlei buzhu shengzhi jishu yu renlei jingzi ku jiaoyan shishi xize de tongzhi" [Decree no. 44, on the regulation of human clinical-assisted reproduction technologies and accreditation of human sperm banks]. Issued on February 7. Zhongguo Qiye Jicheng. www.jincao.com/ fa/10/law10.145.htm. Accessed February 4, 2016.

Moore, Henrietta. 1994. *A Passion for Difference*. Cambridge: Polity Press.

Morgan, Lewis Henry. 1877. *Ancient Society*. Marxists Internet Archive. www .marxists.org/reference/archive/morgan-lewis/ancient-society/ch24.htm.

Mosher, Steven W. 2006. "China's One-Child Policy: Twenty-Five Years Later." *Human Life Review* 32: 76–101.

Murphy, Rachel. 2003. "Fertility and Distorted Sex Ratios in a Rural Chinese County: Culture, State, and Policy." *Population and Development Review* 29 (4): 595–626.

Nanfang. 2012. "Guangdong Sperm Bank Faces Severe Donor Shortage." May 31. Nanfang.com. http://www.thenanfang.com/blog/guangdong-sperm-bank-faces-severe-donor-shortage. Accessed January 17, 2014.

National Bureau of the Census. n.d. "Census Data." http://data.stats.gov.cn. Accessed August 5, 2015.

National Committee on Aging. 2011. "Quanguo 'Jinglao Yue' huodong jianjie" [Brief introduction to National Elder Respect Month.] http://www.cncaprc.gov.cn/contents/82/23476.html. Accessed February 4, 2016.

Nie Mao, Li Lei, and Li Huajun. 2008. *Shangcun: Zhongguo nongcun liushou ertong yousilu* [Injured Village: Reflections on the troubled thoughts of Chinese rural left-behind children]. Beijing: Renmin ribao chubanshe.

Obendiek, Helena. 2016a. *"Changing Fate": Educational Mobility and Family Support in Rural Northwest China.* Münster: LIT.

———. 2016b. "Rural Family Background, Higher Education and Marriage Negotiations." *Modern Asian Studies* 50 (4).

OECD (Organization for Economic Co-operation and Development). 2010. *OECD Economic Surveys: China 2010.* Vol. 6. www.ingentaconnect.com/content/oecd/03766438/2010/00002010/00000006/1010061e.

Ortner, Sherry B. 1972. "Is Female to Male as Nature Is to Culture?" *Feminist Studies* 1 (2): 5–31.

———. 1990. "Gender Hegemonies." *Cultural Critique* 14: 35–80.

———. 1996. *Making Gender: The Politics and Erotics of Culture.* Boston: Beacon Press.

———. 2006. *Anthropology and Social Theory: Culture, Power, and the Acting Subject.* Durham, NC: Duke University Press.

Ortner, Sherry B., and Harriet Whitehead, eds. 1981. *Sexual Meanings: The Cultural Construction of Gender and Sexuality.* New York: Cambridge University Press.

Osburg, John. 2013. *Anxious Wealth: Money and Morality among China's New Rich.* Stanford: Stanford University Press.

Oxfeld, Ellen. 2010. *Drink Water, but Remember the Source: Moral Discourse in a Chinese Village.* Berkeley: University of California Press.

Palmer, Michael. 2007. "The Transformation of Family Law in Post-Deng China: Marriage, Divorce and Reproduction." *China Quarterly* 191: 675–95.

Parrish, William L., and Martin King Whyte. 1978. *Village and Family in Contemporary China.* Chicago: University of Chicago Press.

Patil, Vrushali. 2013. "From Patriarchy to Intersectionality: A Transnational Feminist Assessment of How Far We've Really Come." *Signs* 38 (4): 847–67.

People's Daily. 2001. "Chinese Mothers Give Up Traditional Childbearing Beliefs." Zhongguo Wang [China.org]. http://www.china.org.cn/english/SO-e/21710. htm. Accessed February 6, 2016, .

———. 2012a. "Toushi Xin Ershisi Xiao: Chule zinü nuli, shehui zhengce ying geng wanbei" [Thoroughly examine the New Twenty-Four Exemplars of Filial Piety: In addition to the efforts of sons and daughters, social policy should also be more complete]. September 13. Zhongguo Xinwenwang [Chinanews.com]. http://www.chinanews.com/sh/2012/09–13/4179357_2.shtml. Accessed February 6, 2016.

———. 2012b. "Increasing infertility concerns Chinese couples." December 19. *People's Daily Online.* http://en.people.cn/90782/8062966.html. Accessed March 7, 2016

———. 2013. "Experts Push for Egg Banks to Combat Illegal Trading." May 29. *People's Daily Online.* http://en.people.cn/90882/8258933.html. Accessed March 7, 2016.

Pillsbury, Barbara L. 1978. "'Doing the Month': Confinement and Convalescence of Chinese Women after Childbirth." *Social Science and Medicine* 12 (1B): 11–22.

Ping, Ping, Wen-Bing Zhu, Xin-Zong Zhang, Yu-Shan Li, Quan-Xian Wang, Xiao-Rong Cao, Yong Liu, Hui-Li Dai, Yi-Ran Huang, and Zheng Li. 2011. "Sperm Donation and Its Application in China: A 7-Year Multicenter Retrospective Study." *Asian Journal of Andrology* 13 (4): 644–48.

Pomeranz, Kenneth. 2000. *The Great Divergence: Europe, China, and the Making of the Modern World Economy.* Princeton, NJ: Princeton University Press.

———. 2003. "Women's Work, Family, and Economic Development in Europe and East Asia: Long-Term Trajectories and Contemporary Comparisons." In Giovanni Arrighi, Takeshi Hameshita, and Mark Selden, eds., *The Resurgence of East Asia: 500, 150 and 50 Year Perspectives,* 124–72. New York: Routledge.

Potter, Jack M. 1968. *Capitalism and the Chinese Peasant: Social and Economic Change in a Hong Kong Village.* Berkeley: University of California Press.

Potter, Jack M., and Sulamith H. Potter. 1990. *China's Peasants: The Anthropology of a Revolution.* Cambridge: Cambridge University Press.

PRC White Paper. 2006. "The Development of China's Undertakings for the Aged." *China Daily,* December 12. http://www.chinadaily.com.cn/china/2006–12/12/content_756690.htm. Accessed February 6, 2016.

Pun Ngai. 2005. *Made in China: Women Factory Workers in a Global Workplace.* Durham, NC: Duke University Press.

———. 2012. "Gender and Class: Women's Working Lives in a Dormitory Labor Regime in China." *International Labour and Working Class History* 81: 178–81.

Qiu Renzong. 2002. "Sociocultural Dimensions of Infertility and Assisted Reproduction in the Far East." In Effy Vayena, Patrick J. Rowe, and P. David Griffin, eds., *Current Practices and Controversies in Assisted Reproduction: Report of a WHO Meeting on "Medical, Ethical, and Social Aspects of Assisted Reproduction,"* 75–80. Geneva: WHO.

Quinn, Naomi. 1996. "Culture and Contradiction: The Case of Americans Reasoning about Marriage." *Ethos* 24 (3): 391–425.

Raposza, Kenneth. 2014. "In China, Rich Population Growth Beats World Average." *Forbes*, June 14. www.forbes.com/sites/kenrapoza/2014/06/20/in-china-rich-population-growth-beats-world-average/. Accessed August 5, 2015.

Riley, Nancy E., ed. 2004. "China's Population: New Trends and Challenges." *Population Bulletin* 59 (2): 1–36.

Rofel, Lisa. 1999. *Other Modernities: Gendered Yearnings in China after Socialism.* Berkeley: University of California Press.

———. 2012. "Grassroots Activism: Non-normative Sexual Politics in Post-socialist China." In Wanning Sun and Yingjie Guo, eds., *Unequal China: The Political Economy and Cultural Politics of Inequality in China*, 154–67. New York: Routledge.

Rogers, Susan Carol. 1975. "Female Forms of Power and the Myth of Male Dominance: A Model of Female/Male Interaction in Peasant Society." *American Ethnologist* 2 (4): 727–56.

Rosaldo, Michelle Z. 1974. "Woman, Culture, and Society: A Theoretical Overview." In Michelle Z. Rosaldo and Louise Lamphere, eds., *Woman, Culture, and Society*, 17–42. Stanford: Stanford University Press.

Sahlins, Marshall D. 1978. "On the Sociology of Primitive Exchange." In Marshall D. Sahlins, *Stone Age Economics*, 185–276. Chicago: Aldine-Atherton.

Salaff, Janet. (1981) 1995. *Working Daughters of Hong Kong: Filial Piety or Power in the Family?* London: Cambridge University Press.

Sanday, Peggy Reeves. 1981. *Female Power and Male Dominance: On the Origins of Sexual Inequality.* Cambridge: Cambridge University Press.

Sanders, Douglas. 2012. "Same-Sex Marriage: An Old and New Issue in Asia." Paper presented at the Ninth Asian Law Institute Conference "Law: An Asian Identity?" May 31–June 1, 2012. Cited by permission of author.

Santos, Gonçalo D. 2004. *The Process of Kinship and Identity in a Cantonese Lineage Village in Southeastern China.* PhD diss., Department of Anthropology, ISCTE–Lisbon University Institute.

———. 2006. "The Anthropology of Chinese Kinship: A Critical Overview." *European Journal of East Asian Studies* 5 (2): 275–333.

———. 2008. "On 'Same-Year Siblings' in Rural South China." *Journal of the Royal Anthropological Institute* 14 (3): 535–53.

———. 2009. "The 'Stove-Family' and the Process of Kinship in Rural South China." In Susanne Brandtstädter and Gonçalo D. Santos, eds., *Chinese Kinship: Contemporary Anthropological Perspectives*, 112–36. London: Routledge.

———. 2011. "Rethinking the Green Revolution in South China: Technological Materialities and Human-Environment Relations." *East Asian Science, Technology, and Society: An Interdisciplinary Journal* 5 (4): 477–502.

———. 2013. "Technologies of Ethical Imagination." In Charles Stafford, ed., *Ordinary Ethics in China*, 194–221. London: Bloomsbury.

———. Forthcoming. "On Intimate Choices and Troubles in Rural South China." *Modern Asian Studies* 50 (2).

Santos, Gonçalo D., and Aurora Donzelli. 2009. "Rice Intimacies: Reflections on the 'House' in Upland Sulawesi and South China." *Archiv für Völkerkunde*, 57–58: 37–64.

Sargeson, Sally. 2012. "Why Women Own Less and Why It Matters More in China's Urban Transformation." *China Perspectives* 2012 (4): 35–42.

Sargeson, Sally, and Yu Song. 2010. "Land Expropriation and the Gender Politics of Citizenship in the Urban Frontier." *China Journal* 64: 19–45.

Schlegel, Alice. 1977. *Sexual Stratification: A Cross-Cultural View.* New York: Columbia University Press.

Schweitzer, Peter P. 2000. "Introduction." In Peter P. Schweitzer, ed., *Dividends of Kinship: Meanings and Uses of Social Relatedness*, 1–32. London: Routledge.

Sechiyama, Kaku. 2013. *Patriarchy in East Asia: A Comparative Sociology of Gender.* Leiden: Brill.

Shanghai Daily. 2005. "Shanghai Sperm Bank Seeking Deposits." August 23.

Shen Yifei. 2011. "China in the 'Post-patriarchal Era.'" *Chinese Sociology and Anthropology* 43 (4): 5–23.

———. 2013. *Geti Jiating iFamily: Zhongguo chengshi xiandaihua jincheng zhong de geti jiating yu guojia* [iFamily: The individual, the family, and the state in the process of modernization in modern China]. Shanghai: Shanghai Sanlian Shudian.

Shi, Lihong. 2009. "'Little Quilted Vests to Warm Parents' Hearts': Redefining Gendered Performance of Filial Piety in Rural Northeastern China." *China Quarterly* 198: 348–63.

———. 2011. "'The Wife Is the Boss': Sex-Ratio Imbalance and Young Women's Empowerment in Marriage in Rural Northeast China." In Shanshan Du and Ya-Chen Chen, eds., *Women and Gender in Contemporary Chinese Societies: Beyond Han Patriarchy*, 89–108. New York: Lexington Books.

———. 2014. "Micro-blogs, Online Forums, and the Birth-Control Policy: Social Media and the Politics of Reproduction in China." *Culture, Medicine and Psychiatry* 38 (1): 115–32.

Silverstein, Merril, Cong Zhen, and Li Shuzhuo. 2006. "Intergenerational Transfers and Living Arrangements of Older People in Rural China: Consequences for Psychological Well-Being." *Journal of Gerontology: Social Sciences* 61 (5): S256–66.

———. 2007. "Grandparents Who Care for Their Grandchildren in Rural China: Benefactors and Beneficiaries." In Ian G. Cook and Jason L. Powell, eds., *New Perspectives on China and Aging*, 49–71. New York: Nova Science Publishers.

Siu, Helen F. 1993. "Reconstituting Dowry and Brideprice in South China." In Deborah Davis and Stevan Harrell, eds., *Chinese Families in the Post-Mao Era*, 165–88. Berkeley: University of California Press.

Siu, Helen F., and Wing-hoi Chan. 2010. "Introduction." In Helen F. Siu, ed., *Mer-*

chants' Daughters: Women, Commerce, and Regional Culture in South China, 1–22. Hong Kong: Hong Kong University Press.

Skinner, G. William. 2002. "Family and Reproduction in East Asia: China, Korea, and Japan Compared." The Sir Edward Youde Memorial Lecture, University of Hong Kong, October 8. Unpublished manuscript.

Sommer, Matthew. 2000. *Sex, Law, and Society in Late Imperial China*. Stanford: Stanford University Press.

———. 2009. "Qingdai xianyade maiqi anjian shenpan: Yi 272 jian Baxian, Nanbu yu Baodixian anzi wei lizheng" [The adjudication of wife-selling in Qing county courts: 272 cases from Ba, Nanbu, and Baodi Counties]. Translated by Lin Wenkai. In Qiu Pengsheng and Chen Xiyuan, eds., *Ming Qing falü yunzuo zhongde quanli yu wenhua* [Power and culture in Ming–Qing law], 345–95. Taipei: Lianjing chuban gongsi.

South China Morning Post. 2009. "Infertility Epidemic Stalks the Mainland's One-Child Generation." October 7.

———. 2013. "Pollutants' Effect on Infertility Rates in China to Be Examined." September 4.

Stacey, Judith. 1983. *Patriarchy and Socialist Revolution in China*. Berkeley: University of California Press.

Stafford, Charles. 2000. "Chinese Patriliny and the Cycles of Yang and Laiwang." In Janet Carson, ed., *Cultures of Relatedness: New Approaches to the Study of Kinship*, 35–54. Cambridge: Cambridge University Press.

———. 2009. "Actually Existing Chinese Matriarchy." In Susanne Brandtstädter and Gonçalo D. Santos, eds., *Chinese Kinship: Contemporary Anthropological Perspectives*, 137–53. London: Routledge.

Stockman, Norman, Norman Bonney, and Sheng Xuewen. 1995. *Women's Work in East and West: The Dual Burden of Employment and Family Life.* New York: M.E. Sharpe.

Strand, David. 1989. *Rickshaw Beijing: City People and Politics in the 1920s.* Berkeley: University of California Press.

Strathern, Marilyn. 1992. *Reproducing the Future: Essays on Anthropology, Kinship and the New Reproductive Technologies.* Manchester: Manchester University Press.

Su Haiying. 1997. "Popo zhu de 'dingxin dan'—sanxia hanzu funü zuoyuezi xingwei de renleixue diaocha" [Mother-in-law's "tranquilizing egg": An anthropological investigation into the practices of sitting the month of Han women in the Three Gorges area]. *Xinan Minzu Xueyuan xuebao* [Journal of Southwest Institute for Nationalities].

Swartz, Teresa T. 2009. "Intergenerational Family Relations in Adulthood: Patterns, Variations, and Implications in the Contemporary United States." *Annual Review of Sociology* 25: 191–212.

Symons, Donald. 1979. *The Evolution of Human Sexuality.* Oxford: University of Oxford Press.

Tambiah, Stanley. 2009. "Bridewealth and Dowry Revisited: The Position of Women in Sub-Saharan Africa and North India." *Current Anthropology* 30 (4): 413–35.

Tang, Shenglan, Xiaoyan Li, and Zhuochun Wu. 2006. "Rising Cesarean Delivery Rate in Primiparous Women in Urban China: Evidence from Three Nationwide Household Health Surveys." *American Journal of Obstetrics and Gynecology* 195 (6): 1527–32.

Tang, Wenfang, and William Parish. 2000. *Chinese Urban Life under Reform*. Cambridge: Cambridge University Press.

Tatlow, Didi. K. 2012. "Chinese Law Could Make Divorced Women Homeless." *New York Times*, September 7. www.nytimes.com/2011/09/08/world/asia/08iht-letter08.html?pagewanted=all&_r=0. Accessed August 2, 2015.

Thatcher, Margaret. 1987. Interview with *Women's Own* magazine. October 31. Brian Deer: Selected Investigations & Journalism. http://briandeer.com/social/thatcher-society.htm.

Thøgersen, Stig, and Anru Ni. 2008. "'He Is He, and I Am I': Individual and Collective among China's Rural Elderly." *European Journal of East Asian Studies* 7 (1): 11–37.

To, Sandy. 2015. *China's Leftover Women: Late Marriage amongst Professional Women and Its Consequences*. New York: Routledge.

Tomba, Luigi. 2012. "Awakening the God of Earth: Land, Place and Class in Urbanizing Guangdong." In Beatriz Carrillo and David S. G. Goodman, eds., *China's Peasants and Workers: Changing Class Identities*, 40–61. Cheltenham, UK: Edward Elgar.

Topley, Marjorie. 1974. "Cosmic Antagonism: A Mother Child Syndrome." In Arthur P. Wolf, ed., *Religion and Ritual in Chinese Society*, 233–51. Stanford: Stanford University Press.

Tran, Lisa. 2015. *Concubines in Court: Marriage and Monogamy in Twentieth Century China*. Lanham, MD: Rowman & Littlefield.

Tucker, Robert C. 1978. *The Marx-Engels Reader*. New York: W.W. Norton.

Veblen, Thorstein. 1899 (1934). *The Theory of the Leisure Class*. New York: Penguin Books.

Valentine, Gill. 2007. "Theorizing and Researching Intersectionality: A Challenge for Feminist Geography." *Professional Geographer* 59 (1): 10–21.

Walby, Silvia. 1990. *Theorising Patriarchy*. Oxford: Basil Blackwell.

———. 1997. *Gender Transformations*. London: Routledge.

———. 2011. *The Future of Feminism*. London: Polity.

Wallis, Cara. 2011. "Mobile Phones without Guarantees: The Promises of Technology and the Contingencies of Culture." *New Media and Society* 13 (3): 471–85.

Waltner, Ann B. 1990. *Getting an Heir: Adoption and the Construction of Kinship in Late Imperial China*. Honolulu: University of Hawai'i Press.

Wang, Danyu. 2004. "Ritualistic Coresidence and the Weakening of Filial Practice in Rural China." In Charlotte Ikels, ed., *Filial Piety: Practice and Discourse in Contemporary East Asia*, 16–33. Stanford: Stanford University Press.

Wang, Xiaoli, Yan Wang, Sui Zanzhou, Jun Wang, and Jinlan Wang. 2008. "A Population-Based Survey of Women's Traditional Postpartum Behaviours in Northern China." *Midwifery* 24 (2): 238–45.

Wang Yanlin. 2014. "Per Capita Income Grows 8.1% in 2013." *Shanghai Daily*, February 25. http://www.shanghaidaily.com/business/economy/Per-capita-income-grows-81-in-2013/shdaily.shtml. Accessed February 6, 2016.

Wang, Yingyi. 2015. *Cooperative Marriage: A "Fake Marriage" or a New Intimate Alliance?* MPhil diss., The University of Hong Kong. http://hub.hku.hk/handle/10722/208607. Accessed August 2, 2015.

Wang Yiqing. 2012. "Filial Piety Does Not Need a Code." *China Daily*, August 31. www.chinadaily.com.cn/cndy/2012–08/31/content_15722710.htm. Accessed August 5, 2015.

Wang Yuesheng. 2012. *Chengxiang yanglao zhong de jiating daiji guanxi yanjiu* [Research on intergenerational relations in urban and rural Chinese households]. *Kaifang Shidai* 2012 (2): 114.

Wasserstrom, Jeffrey. 1984. "Resistance to the One-Child Family." *Modern China* 10 (3): 345–74.

Watson, James L. 1975a. "Agnates and Outsiders: Adoption in a Chinese Lineage." *Man* 10 (2): 293–306.

———. 1975b. *Emigration and the Chinese Lineage: The Mans in Hong Kong and London*. Berkeley: University of California Press.

———. 1980. "Transactions in People: The Chinese Market in Slaves, Servants and Heirs." In James L. Watson, ed., *Asian and African Systems of Slavery*, 223–50. Berkeley: University of California Press.

Watson, Rubie S. 1985. *Inequality among Brothers: Class and Kinship in South China*. Cambridge: Cambridge University Press.

———. 1991. "Afterword: Marriage and Gender Inequality." In Rubie S. Watson and Patricia Buckley Ebrey, eds., *Marriage and Inequality in Chinese Society*, 347–68. Berkeley: University of California Press.

———. 2004a "Chinese Bridal Laments: The Claims of a Dutiful Daughter." In James L. Watson and Rubie S. Watson, *Village Life in Hong Kong: Politics, Gender, and Ritual in the New Territories*, 221–50. Hong Kong: The Chinese University Press.

———. 2004b. "The Named and the Nameless: Gender and Person in Chinese Society." In James L. Watson and Rubie S. Watson, *Village Life in Hong Kong: Politics, Gender, and Ritual in the New Territories*, 199–220. Hong Kong: The Chinese University Press.

———. 2004c. "Wives, Concubines, and Maids: Servitude and Kinship in the Hong Kong Region, 1900–1940." In James L. Watson and Rubie S. Watson, *Village Life in Hong Kong: Politics, Gender, and Ritual in the New Territories*, 169–98. Hong Kong: The Chinese University Press.

———. 2013. "Chinese Patriarchy: Past, Present, Future." Keynote lecture delivered at the international conference "Is Chinese Patriarchy Over? The Decline and

Transformation of a System of Social Support," Max Planck Institute for Social Anthropology, Halle (Saale).

Weber, Max. 1978. *Economy and Society: An Outline of Interpretive Sociology.* Berkeley: University of California Press.

Wei, Yanning. 2016. *From Migrant Children to Left-Behind Children: A Study of China's Rural-Urban Dual Structure.* PhD diss., Department of Geography, University of Washington.

Weitman, Sasha. 1973. "Intimacies: Notes toward a Theory of Social Inclusion and Exclusion." In Arnold Birenbaum and Edgar Sagarin, eds., *People in Places: The Sociology of the Familiar,* 217–38. New York: Praeger.

White, Tyrene. 2006. *China's Longest Campaign: Birth Planning in the People's Republic, 1949–2005.* Ithaca, NY: Cornell University Press.

Whyte, Martin K. 1997. "The Rate of Filial Obligations in Urban China." *China Journal* 38: 1–31.

———, ed. 2003. *China's Revolutions and Intergenerational Relations.* Ann Arbor: Center for Chinese Studies, The University of Michigan.

———. 2004. "Filial Obligations in Chinese Families: Paradoxes of Modernization." In Charlotte Ikels, ed., *Filial Piety: Practice and Discourse in Contemporary East Asia.* Stanford: Stanford University Press.

Whyte, Martin K., and William L. Parrish. 1984. *Urban Life in Contemporary China.* Chicago: University of Chicago Press.

Whyte, Martin K., and Qin Xu. 2003. "Support for Aging Parents from Daughters versus Sons." In Martin K. Whyte, ed., *China's Revolutions and Intergenerational Relations,* 167–95. Ann Arbor: Center for Chinese Studies, The University of Michigan.

Wolf, Arthur P. 1995. *Sexual Attraction and Childhood Association: A Chinese Brief for Edward Westermarck.* Stanford: Stanford University Press.

———. 2005. "Europe and China: Two Kinds of Patriarchy." In Theo Engelen and Arthur P. Wolf, eds., *Marriage and the Family in Eurasia: Perspectives on the Hajnal Hypothesis,* 215–41. Amsterdam: Aksant.

Wolf, Arthur P., and Chieh-shan Huang. 1980. *Marriage and Adoption in China, 1845–1945.* Stanford: Stanford University Press.

Wolf, Margery. 1968. *The House of Lim: A Study of a Chinese Farm Family.* Englewood Cliffs, NJ: Prentice-Hall.

———. 1972. *Women and the Family in Rural Taiwan.* Stanford: Stanford University Press.

———. 1985. *Revolution Postponed: Women in Contemporary China.* Stanford: Stanford University Press.

WHO (World Health Organization). 2015. "Global Health Observatory Data: Maternal Mortality: Country Profiles." www.who.int/gho/maternal_health/countries/en/#C.

Wu Liangyong. 1999. *Rehabilitating the Old City of Beijing: A Project in the Ju'er Hutong Neighbourhood.* Vancouver: University of British Columbia Press.

Xie Liangbing. 2013. "Yanglao zhi Jiong" [The predicament of elder care]. *Jingji guancha*. www.eeo.com.cn/2013/0219/240119.shtml. Accessed August 5, 2015.

Xinhua. 2011. "New Old-Age Pension Promises Dignified Life for Seniors in China's Rural Areas." *China Daily*, January 3. www.chinadaily.com.cn/business/2011–01/03/content_11787946.htm. Accessed August 5, 2015.

Xu Jun and Feng Xiaotian. 2011. "Woguo diyidai dushengzinu de yanglao wenti yanjiu" [Research on problems of elder care for our country's first generation of single children]. *Renkou yu jingji* [Population and economics], no. 5: 55–62.

Yan, Hairong. 2008. *New Masters, New Servants: Migration, Development, and Women Workers in China*. Durham, NC: Duke University Press.

Yan, Junhao, Guoning Huang, Yingpu Sun, Xiaoming Zhao, Shiling Chen, Shuhua Zou, Cuifang Hao, Song Quan, and Zi-jiang Chen. 2011. "Birth Defects after Assisted Reproductive Technologies in China: Analysis of 15,405 Offspring in Seven Centers (2004–2008)." *Fertility and Sterility* 95 (1): 458–60.

Yan, Yunxiang. 1996. *The Flow of Gifts: Reciprocity and Social Networks in a Chinese Village*. Stanford: Stanford University Press.

———. 1997. "The Triumph of Conjugality: Structural Transformation of Family Relations in a Chinese Village." *Ethnology* 36 (3): 191–212.

———. 2003. *Private Life under Socialism: Love, Intimacy, and Family Change in a Chinese Village, 1949–1999*. Stanford: Stanford University Press.

———. 2006. "Girl Power: Young Women and the Waning of Patriarchy in Rural North China." *Ethnology* 45, no. 2 (Spring 2006): 105–23.

———. 2009. *The Individualization of Chinese Society*. Oxford: Berg.

———. 2010. "The Chinese Path to Individualization." *British Journal of Sociology* 61 (3): 489–512.

———. 2011. "The Individualization of the Family in Rural China." *Boundary 2* 38 (1): 203–29.

Yang, Fuchun. 2011. "Quanguo xin nongbao gongzuo jingyan jiaoliuhui zai Zhongxiang zhaokai" [National work experience exchange conference on implementing NROAI is held in Zhongxiang]. *Hubei ribao* [Hubei daily], October 30. http://www.people.com.cn/h/2011/1030/c25408–2669163039.html. Accessed February 4, 2016.

Yang, Jie. 2011. "Nennu and Shunu: Gender, Body Politics and the Beauty Economy in China." *Signs* 36 (2): 333–57.

Yang, Lien-Sheng. 1957. "The Concept of *Pao* as a Basis for Social Relations in China." In John K. Fairbank, ed., *Chinese Thought and Institutions*, 291–309. Chicago: University of Chicago Press.

Yang, Martin C. 1945. *A Chinese Village: Taitou, Shantung Province*. New York: Columbia University Press.

Yau Ching. 2010. "Dreaming of Normal while Sleeping with Impossible: Introduction." In Yau Ching, ed., *As Normal as Possible: Negotiating Sexuality and Gender in Mainland China and Hong Kong*, 1–14. Hong Kong: Hong Kong University Press.

Yiu, Derek. 2012. "Wives of Gay Men Speak Out about 'Tragic Lives.'" *Gaystarnews*, February 24. www.gaystarnews.com/article/wives-gay-men-china-speak-out-about-%E2%80%98tragic-lives%E2%80%99. Accessed August 2, 2015.

Yun Shouqin. 2007. *Huining jiaoyu 600 nian* [600 years of education in Huining]. Baiyin, Gansu: Gansu Press.

Zhan, Heying Jenny, Xiaotian Feng, and Baozhen Luo. 2008. "Placing Elderly Parents in Institutions in Urban China: A Reinterpretation of Filial Piety." *Research on Aging* 30 (5): 537–71.

Zhang, Hong. 2004. "'Living Alone' and the Rural Elderly: Strategy and Agency in Post-Mao Rural China." In Charlotte Ikels, ed., *Filial Piety: Practice and Discourse in Contemporary East Asia*, 63–87. Stanford: Stanford University Press.

———. 2005. "Bracing for an Uncertain Future: A Case Study of New Coping Strategies for Rural Parents under China's Birth Control Policy." *China Journal* (54): 53–76.

———. 2006. "Family Care or Residential Care? The Moral and Practical Dilemmas Facing the Elderly in Urban China." *Asian Anthropology* 5 (1): 57–83.

———. 2007a. "China's New Rural Daughters Coming of Age: Downsizing the Family and Firing Up Earning Power in the New Economy." *Signs* 32 (3): 671–98.

———. 2007b. "From Resisting to Embracing? The One-Child Policy: Explaining New Fertility Trends in a Chinese Village." *China Quarterly* 192: 855–75.

———. 2009. "The New Realities of Aging in Contemporary China: Coping with the Decline of Family Care." In Jay Sokolovsky, ed., *Cultural Context of Aging: World-Wide Perspective*, 196–215. 3rd ed. Westport, CT: Greenwood Publishing Group.

Zhang, Jun. 2014. "Urban Middle-Class Understandings of the Term 'Patriarchy' (*Fuquanzhi / Jiazhangzhi*) in Contemporary China: A Guangzhou Survey." Manuscript.

———. 2016. "(Extended) Family Car, Filial Consumer-Citizens: Becoming Properly Middle-Class in Post-Socialist South China." *Modern China* 42 (1). doi.10.1177/0097700416645138.

Zhang, Jun, and Peidong Sun. 2014. "'When Are You Going to Get Married?' Parental Matchmaking and Middle-Class Women in Contemporary Urban China." In Deborah S. Davis and Sara L. Friedman, eds., *Wives, Husbands, and Lovers: Marriage and Sexuality in Hong Kong, Taiwan, and Urban China*, 118–45. Stanford: Stanford University Press.

Zhang, Li. 2010. *In Search of Paradise: Middle-Class Living in a Chinese Metropolis*. Ithaca, NY: Cornell University Press.

Zhang, Weiguo. 2006a. "Child Adoption in Contemporary Rural China." *Journal of Family Issues* 27 (3): 301–40.

———. 2006b. "Who Adopts Girls and Why? Domestic Adoption of Female Children in Contemporary Rural China." *China Journal* 56: 63–82.

Zhao, Gracie Ming. 2003. "Trafficking of Women for Marriage in China: Policy and Practice." *Criminology and Criminal Justice* 3 (1): 83–102. doi:10.1177/1466802503003001457.

Zhongguo Ping'an. 2012. "Zenyang gei fumu mai yanglao baoxian? Baozhang fumu de jiankiang shenghuo cai shi zhenzhengde xiaoshun" [How to buy insurance for parents? The true filial piety lies in ensuring a healthy life for parents]. Zhongguo Ping'an Shangcheng [China Ping'an Market]. http://baoxian.pingan.com/baoxiananli/yiwaixiananli/1355107042961.shtml. Accessed August 5, 2015.

Zhu, Jianfeng. 2010. "Mothering Expectant Mothers: Consumption, Production and Two Motherhoods in China." *Ethos* 38 (4): 406–21.

Zhu Mingde, ed. 2005. *Beijing chengqu jiaoluo diaocha* [Investigation of urban corners in Beijing]. Beijing: Shehui Kexue Chubanshe.

Zhu, Xiaoyang. 2014. *Topography and Political Economy in Rural China: The Story of Xiaocun*. Singapore: World Scientific.

Zuo, Jiping. 2009. "Rethinking Family Patriarchy and Women's Positions in Presocialist China." *Journal of Marriage and Family* 71 (3): 542–57.

CONTRIBUTORS

Melissa J. Brown is managing editor of the *Harvard Journal of Asiatic Studies*. Her published works include "Adoption Does Not Increase the Risk of Mortality among Taiwanese Girls in a Longitudinal Analysis" (*PLOS One*, 2015), "Marriage Mobility and Footbinding in Pre-1949 Rural China" (*Journal of Asian Studies*, 2012), and *Is Taiwan Chinese? The Impact of Culture, Power, and Migration on Changing Identities* (University of California Press, 2004). Her ongoing research examines the relations among kinship, gender, and economics in China, as well as marriage, identity, and adoption in Taiwan.

Elisabeth L. Engebretsen is a senior lecturer at the Centre for Gender Research, University of Oslo, Norway. She is the author of the monograph *Queer Women in Urban China: An Ethnography* (Routledge, 2014), which was awarded the 2014 Ruth Benedict Book Prize Honorable Mention from the Association for Queer Anthropology, American Anthropological Association; and coeditor of *Queer/Tongzhi China: New Perspectives on Research, Activism, and Media Cultures* (NIAS Press, 2015).

Harriet Evans is professor of Chinese cultural studies and director of the Contemporary China Centre, University of Westminster. Her research interests include gender, sexuality, and women's lives in modern and contemporary China, the transformation of urban life since the mid-twentieth century, and visual culture of the Maoist era. She is the author of *Women and Sexuality: Dominant Discourses of Female Sexuality and Gender since 1949* (1997), *The Subject of Gender: Daughters and Mothers in Urban China*, (2008), and coeditor of *Picturing Power in China: Posters of the Cultural Revolution* (1999) and *Gender in Flux: Agency and Its Limits in Contemporary China* (2011). She is currently completing an oral history of Dashalanr, a poor neighborhood in central Beijing, and leads the three-year Conflicts in Cultural Value project funded by the Leverhulme Trust, which investigates local, private heritage initiatives in southwestern China.

Suzanne Gottschang is a medical anthropologist with research interests in public health, reproduction, and policy in China. In addition to ongoing work on motherhood, infant feeding, and health policy in China, her research interests extend to the practice of traditional Chinese veterinary medicine in the United States and China and the intersection of design and anthropology. An associate professor at Smith College, she holds a doctorate in anthropology and a master's degree in public health. She was an An Wang postdoctoral fellow at Harvard University and a visiting scholar at China's Academy of Preventive Medicine.

Stevan Harrell is professor of anthropology, professor of environmental and forest sciences, adjunct professor of Chinese, and adjunct curator of Asian ethnology in the Burke Museum at the University of Washington. His works in the field of Chinese family, kinship, demography, and gender include *Chinese Families in the Post-Mao Era*, coedited with Deborah Davis (University of California Press, 1993), the edited volume *Chinese Historical Microdemography* (University of California Press, 1996), and *Human Families* (Westview Press, 1997). Most of his current research is on human-environment relations.

William Jankowiak is professor of anthropology, University of Nevada, Las Vegas. He is the author of more than 110 scientific papers and seven books (four edited) that range in subject matter from urban China, to the Mormon polygamous family, to drugs, foods, and labor, to romantic love around the globe. The Canadian Supreme Court is using his research on Mormon polygamous family life in its deliberations on whether a Canadian polygynous community is a legitimate, albeit alternative, lifestyle. In 2011, he hosted the eight-part series *Rites of Passion* for the History Channel. His first book on China, *Sex, Death and Hierarchy in a Chinese City* (Columbia University Press), is in its fifth printing. He is currently preparing a book manuscript restudy of Hohhot, *City Days, City Nights: The Individual in Chinese Society*, for Columbia University Press.

Andrew B. Kipnis is professor of anthropology in the School of Culture, History and Language at the Australian National University. His latest book is *From Village to City: Social Transformation in a Chinese County Seat*

(University of California Press, 2016). He is the author of five other books and for ten years was the editor of *The China Journal.*

Kerstin Klein is an independent scholar who received her PhD from the London School of Economics and Political Science. Her thesis looked at the biopolitics of human embryonic stem cell research in China. She then worked as a clinical researcher in sexual health at the Homerton University Hospital NHS Foundation Trust and, subsequently, at Barts Health NHS Trust in London. Her publications have contributed to the understanding of debates and political processes around regenerative and reproductive medicine in China.

Xuan Li holds a PhD from the Department of Psychology, University of Cambridge. Her work focuses on parent-child interaction in rural and urban families in contemporary China and involves both qualitative and quantitative approaches. She is particularly interested in parenthood (especially fatherhood), child and youth development, and everyday family practices against the backdrop of China's recent social transformations.

Helena Obendiek manages the East Asia program at Konstanz University of Applied Sciences and is a research associate at the Max Planck Institute for Social Anthropology in Halle, Germany. She has done field research in Gansu and Xinjiang Autonomous Region. She is the author of *The Tarim Basin Carpet: A Tradition in Transition* (China Heritage Arts Foundation, 1997). Currently she is completing a book about her research in rural Gansu, *"Changing Fate": Education, Poverty and Family Support in Rural China.*

Gonçalo Santos is an assistant professor at the University of Hong Kong. He was previously an LSE Fellow in Anthropology at the London School of Economics (2007–11) and a senior research fellow at the Max Planck Institute for Social Anthropology (2011–13). He is the author of various peer-reviewed articles on contemporary China and is coeditor of *Chinese Kinship* (Routledge, 2009). He is also coeditor of a special issue on love, marriage, and intimate citizenship in China and India (*Modern Asian Studies*, 2016). He is currently completing a monograph on love, family relations, and everyday ethics in contemporary China.

Lihong Shi is an assistant professor in the Department of Anthropology at Case Western Reserve University. Her research focuses on reproductive politics and family and gender relations in China, particularly reproductive choice and family change under China's birth-planning policy and the demographic and sociopolitical consequences of the policy.

Roberta Zavoretti is a social anthropologist and the author of the forthcoming book *Making Place, Making Class: An Ethnographic Inquiry into the Limits of China's "Rural to Urban Migrant" Paradigm*. She was educated in Venice (Ca' Foscari) and London (SOAS) and currently works as a research fellow at the Max Planck Institute for Social Anthropology in Halle (Saale), Germany; her research project looks at marriage and class mobility in contemporary mainland China.

Hong Zhang received her PhD in anthropology from Columbia University and is currently an associate professor of East Asian studies at Colby College, Maine. Her research interests include population aging and changing family structure, rural family life and marriage patterns, labor migration, emerging elder-care patterns, and the politics of satire and humor in contemporary China. She has published essays and peer-reviewed articles on these topics in *Signs, China Quarterly, China Journal, Journal of Contemporary China, Asia Anthropology,* and *Journal of Long Term Home Health Care.*

INDEX

breastfeeding, 101

bridal agency, 55

brideprice. *See* bridewealth

bridewealth, 17, 25, 43–45, 54, 57n12, 66–69, 71, 72n10, 107–8; cost of, 67, 87, 136; negotiation of, 68–69, 71. *See also* dowry; marriage; wedding

Brown, Melissa, 13, 17, 22, 26, 28, 94

Buckley, Lisa, 216

Cancian, Francesca, 158

capitalism, 39, 41, 46, 55, 95, 106, 125, 165

care. *See* child care; elder care

cell phones, 48, 54, 116

cesarean section, 207–8. *See also* childbirth

chastity, 134, 137, 150. *See also* virginity

Chengdu, 152

chengzhongcun ren (villagers-in-the-city), 114, 116, 123–28

child brides, 185

child care, 14, 17, 19–20, 24, 26, 29, 43, 45–46, 53, 56, 60, 64, 77, 79, 92, 94–95, 98–99, 102, 122, 124, 126, 140, 142, 144, 215; cost of, 93, 103–4; "4-2-1" pattern, 100; by grandparents, 3, 22, 93, 98, 100–101, 103–4, 106–7, 118–20, 138–39, 211, 240, 244–45; paid, 100, 246; public child-care support, 93–94, 106; of sons, 121; and *yang* (nurture), 140, 142. *See also* "grandparenting outsourcing"

child rearing, 14, 20, 93–94, 99–100, 106, 225; cost of, 62

childbearing, 30, 131, 137, 165, 178, 204, 212

childbirth, 98, 101, 165, 201–9, 213, 216; medicalization/institutionalization of, 202, 207–8, 216; national policy on, 206

childlessness, 168, 223, 226, 246

Chinese Communist Party (CCP), 3, 14–16, 27, 39, 45, 56, 74, 96, 113, 124, 127, 186, 189, 192, 196, 237, 243; revolution, 18, 107. *See also* policy of party state

Chinese New Year. *See* Spring Festival

Chinese Population Association, 220

Cho, John (Song Pae), 171

class, 4, 9, 10–11, 18–19, 25, 31, 34, 127, 130, 136, 159, 164–66, 169, 179; emergence of distinctive, 146; and homosexuality, 179; middle class, 15, 18, 23, 67, 93, 140, 143, 172, 177, 195, 239, 247; "ruling class," 196; under-class, 183; working class, 152, 159–60

clubs (nightclubs), 133–34

collectivization, 16–17, 45, 235. *See also* decollectivization

college. *See* education

coming out, 173–74, 177–78

commercialization, 8; of filial piety, 248–49

commodification: of childbirth, 207; of filial piety, 235, 246, 248; of women, 71

concubines, 221

Confucian: and neo-Confucian principles, 5, 40; philosophy, 11, 13, 74, 80, 194, 222, 226, 230, 238

conjugal: family, 93, 106, 154; happiness, 47; income, 50, 82; interaction, 159; life, 65; love/intimacy, 147, 149, 158, 205; pressures, 166; property, 32, 175; ties, 4–5, 19, 93, 131, 157. *See also* marriage

conjugality, triumph of, 5, 106

consumer culture, 206, 209

"consumer revolution," 62

consumerism, 210, 239

contraception, 60, 220

contract marriage (*xinghun*). *See* marriage

coproduction of technologies, 202

co-residence with parents, 82, 86

Elder Law, 237–39

emigration, 132–34

emotional: bond between parents and children, 20–22, 79–81, 87–88, 167, 169–70, 194, 204, 243; bond between parents and daughters, 26, 83, 241; chastity, 150; companionship, 182; dependence, 147, 155, 161; egalitarianism, 147, 151, 155, 157, 160; intimacy, 14, 30–32, 65, 114, 152–56, 158–59, 162; managers, women as, 156, 160; pressure, 170, 179; responsibility to self, 161; support, 65, 81, 240; work, 142, 156, 195

emotions, 19–20, 29–31, 65, 80, 147–49, 151, 164, 171–2, 176, 180, 185; and "helping," 39, 56; and middle generation, 159

employment, 60, 63, 76, 78, 84–85, 98, 116, 124, 172–73, 177, 184, 186, 188–89, 192, 194, 196, 235, 243, 246; graduate, 84–85; lifetime, 235; market, 87; temporary and informal, 184. *See also* labor

empowerment: through education, 88–89; of middle generation, 106; of women, 67, 71, 74, 83

Engebretsen, Elisabeth, 22, 29, 209

Engels, Friedrich, 7–9, 15–16, 32, 94

ethics, 80, 148, 150, 162, 182, 187, 195

Europe, 33, 133, 169, 242

Evans, Harriet, 21–22, 26, 29, 209

examinations, 83

expert: analysis, 93, 101; knowledge, 207–8

factory work. *See* labor, factory

family: extended, 16, 19, 20, 23, 105, 121, 125, 127, 152, 156, 222; multigenerational patrilineal, 206; nuclear, 5, 15–16, 18–19, 22, 33, 54, 60, 121–22, 152, 205–6, 209; size, 12, 20, 24, 94, 222, 234, 239–40, 243; structure, 11,

234, 239–40. *See also* household

farming, 42–43, 63, 75–76, 99, 103–4, 117–18, 121, 124–28; and feminization, 118; income from, 128; in "premodern" communities, 125; of vegetables for sale, 96, 98, 101, 103. *See also* labor: rural/agricultural; villagers-in-the-city

"fearing a son" (*pa erzi*), 63, 70

feelings (*ganqing*), 81. *See also* emotions

feminism, 9–10, 33–34, 35n19, 129, 165; second wave, 9, 129; third wave, 9, 130; and women's liberation, 144n1

fenjia (dividing the household), 126–27

fertility, 15, 20–22, 24–25, 90n6; clinics, 223–26, 230–31; decline in, 20–22, 24, 74, 76, 82, 88, 97, 219, 221–22

Fielde, Adele, 42

"filial exemplars," 21, 238–39

filial piety, 3, 7–8, 13, 20–23, 26, 50, 54, 59, 62–66, 70–71, 74–75, 79, 83, 95, 102, 105, 108, 131–32, 136, 140, 142, 165, 169, 171, 173, 176, 187–89, 191–95, 197, 209, 211, 221, 234, 236, 238–40, 242–243, 246–49; codification of, 21, 237, 239; commodification of, 21, 235, 246, 248–49; decline of, 64, 66, 102, 238, 242; and homosexuality, 178; and insurance plans, 3, 20–21, 239, 247–49; "modernized," 88, 249; policy to promote, 238; and role of daughters, 7, 50, 59, 65, 70–71, 74, 83, 95, 108, 240–241

finances: and savings, 66; separation of, 60, 173; son as burden on, 62, 66, 68–70. *See also* bank accounts

financial support, 62–66, 68, 75–79, 82–83, 85, 87–89, 153, 236–37, 243; of sons' weddings, 69–70

food preparation, 64. *See also* sitting the month

footbinding, 14, 41–42

Foshan, 96–97

Friedman, Sara, 6, 19, 21
funerals, 13
Furth, Charlotte, 204
Fuzhou, 42

gambling, 189
ganqing (feelings), 81
Gansu, 24–26, 62, 74–75, 114, 121
Gates, Hill, 41
gay: activists, 163–64, 173, 179; compartmentalization of personal life, 164–65, 170, 172; marriage, 163, 165; men's wives (*tongqi*), 164; *xinghun* (lesbian-gay contract marriage), 163–74, 176–80, 180n2. *See also* courtship; homosexuality; lesbian; marriage
gender: axis of patriarchy, 11, 13, 16, 18–20, 23, 26–27, 32, 56n1, 71, 164; and the Chinese Communist Party, 14–15; conformity, 168, 172–73, 176; dualist system of, 177; equality/ inequality, 4, 9–10, 13–17, 27, 29, 30–34, 35n19, 53, 56, 94, 131, 147, 165, 171, 176–77, 179, 240, 249; relations, 4–7, 14, 27, 31, 70, 75, 88, 108, 115, 171; roles, 19, 24, 188
generation. *See* intergenerational
generational axis of patriarchy, 11, 16, 18–20, 22–24, 26–27, 32–33, 71, 164
genetics, 224–25, 231
Giddens, Anthony, 5
gifts, 12, 25, 48, 51, 53, 57n12, 71, 80, 88, 108, 174
Gini coefficient, 248
"girl power," 55, 71
global: capital, 39, 46, 55, 95, 108; modernity, 106, 165, 176–77, 180
globalization, 4–5, 7, 18, 106, 164
Gottschang, Suzanne, 23
"grandparenting outsourcing," 105, 244
Great Leap Forward, 17
Greenhalgh, Susan, 220

Guangdong, 3, 22, 24, 26, 47, 61, 91, 94–95, 97, 100, 106, 108, 225–26, 228, 232, 240
guanggun (bare branches, i.e., men unable to find a wife), 170. *See also* bachelors
Guangzhou, 91, 95–97, 101, 223
guanxi (social relationship), 27, 84
guigei erzi (revert to the son), 63
Guttman, Matthew, 156

Hainan, 25
Han (ethnic group), 27, 34n1, 41, 46, 232n3
handicraft, 41–43, 45, 242
Hangzhou, 229
harmony: of family, 131, 144, 152, 154–55; of society, 165, 178
Harrell, Stevan, 4, 30, 122–23
Harvey, Travis Anna, 216
Hebei, 121, 223
Heilongjiang, 5, 71, 235
"helping" (*bang*), 39–47, 49–51, 56, 94
Henan, 121, 212
Hershatter, Gail, 196
Herzfeld, Michael, 26
heteronormativity, 29, 164, 166, 172, 176–78
hierarchy: filial, 176, 211, 249; gender and generational, 3–5, 10–14, 17, 32–33, 178, 202, 216; reproductive, 209, 215
high socialism, 74
HIV. *See* sexually transmitted diseases
Hohhot, 30, 147, 149, 152–53, 157–58, 161
home. *See* housing
homophobia, 178–79
homosexual: communities, 146; sperm donation, 231
homosexuality: and reproductive technologies, 231, 224; visibility of, 165, 178–80. *See also* courtship; gay; lesbian; marriage

Hong Kong, 196
hongbao (red envelope), 113
hospital, 70, 92, 132, 139, 186, 201–7, 211–12, 214, 223, 229, 236–38
house building/renovation, 25, 67, 69, 81, 96, 98; cost of, 67
household, 8, 13, 24, 28–29, 54, 60, 96, 99, 114–15, 117–27, 130–32, 142, 144, 152, 182–83, 185, 188, 194–96, 205, 239; as gendered space, 94; empty-nest, 234, 238, 240–41, 244, 246; gendered division of labor, 28, 53, 143, 152; "helping," *See* "helping"; *hukou* (household registration), 17, 76, 170, 172; items and furniture, 67; patrilineal, 17, 19, 24, 216; politics, 129; power relations, 131; privatization of, 196, 206; service industry, 246; size, 239–40; viricentric, 118–19, 124; women's economic contribution to, 39, 42–45. *See also* dividing the household
housewife, 188
housewifization, 29
housework, 7, 17, 28, 45–46, 63–65, 144, 157, 195, 246
housing: company-provided, 116–17; in Dashalanr, 183, 187; demolition, 187; and inheritance, 63, 77, 88, 132, 187, 241; investment in, 120; living arrangements, 42–44, 60, 63, 65, 138–39, 142, 152, 168, 173, 195; "mansions," 96, 98; market privatization, 136, 206; and marriage, 25, 31–32, 49, 67–69, 78–79, 84, 86–89, 113–14, 136, 143, 168, 171, 175, 197n3; options, 117; ownership, 118, 131, 146; purchase, 78–79, 84, 86–87, 89, 114, 117, 120–21, 131, 136–37, 139–40, 143–44, 153; reform, 16, 136; rental, 121, 123–24, 137, 140; subsidized, 116, 121, 123–24, 128n3; support for elderly, 237. *See also* house building/renovation

Huang, Philip, 41
Hubei, 25–26, 45, 227, 235–36, 241, 243
Huining, 75–81, 83–85
hukou (household registration), 17, 76, 170, 172
Hunan, 42, 51, 223, 229, 232, 244
hunqing gongsi (wedding ceremony company), 113–14
hutong (lane or alley in Beijing), 183–84

Ikels, Charlotte, 246
income, 12, 15, 44, 50–54, 62–63, 66, 75–76, 82, 87, 89, 95, 99–102, 116, 118, 123, 125, 127–28, 171, 207, 212, 227–28, 237, 240, 244, 246–48; *dibao* (minimum income support), 235–36; disposable, 248; and gender, 15, 44, 50–53, 95, 99, 101–2, 106, 118, 152, 186, 240; increase in, 116; inequality of, 53, 248–49; of migrant workers, 19, 48–53, 117; of older generation from children, 103; pooling, 120, 131, 142; rural-urban gap in, 236. *See also* bank accounts; breadwinner; finances; remittance (of income)
individualism, 5, 32, 147, 151–52, 164, 169–70
individualization of Chinese society, 5–6, 18, 32–33, 108, 165
industrialization, 4, 31, 74, 116
infertility, 3, 20, 25, 220–26, 229–30. *See also* fertility
inheritance, 63, 77, 79, 88, 128, 132, 241; patrilineal (patrimony), 8, 12, 14–15, 19, 109, 124–25, 130, 187, 235
Inner Mongolia Autonomous Region, 147, 151
"innovators," 154
institutionalization, 5–6, 39, 45, 207
institutions (social), 5–6, 9, 11–13, 15, 18–20, 148, 152, 156, 182, 202, 206,

labor (cont'd)

45; professional, 142; "reeducation through labor," 189; retail, 123; rural/agricultural, 17, 41–42, 44–46, 60; shift, 118, 120, 122, 139; wage, 22, 46, 48–50, 72n5, 76, 96, 128. *See also* farming; housework; migration

land: allocation, 118, 125–27; appropriation, 114, 123, 127, 128n4; leasing, 96; ownership, 43–44, 63, 127; and patriarchy, 8, 24; rights, 117–18, 127. *See also* farming

Lanzhou, 75, 83–85

lawsuits, 64

"left behind": children (*liushou ertong*), 22, 92–93, 98, 101; parents, 238, 240

"leftover women" (*sheng nü*), 170

lesbian: activists, 163–64, 173, 179; compartmentalization of personal life, 164–65, 170, 172, 174, 178; marriage, 163, 165, 168; pressure on, 167–68, 171; *xinghun* (lesbian-gay contract marriage), 163–74, 176–80, 180n2. *See also* courtship; gay; homosexuality; marriage

Li, Xuan, 16, 30–31

liangbian dianli (bilateral [wedding] ceremony), 241

Liaoning, 3, 26, 60–61, 97

Lijia Village, 60–71

lineage organization, 12–13, 96, 119

"little emperor," 100

"little mosquitoes" (*sai-man-jai*, children), 22, 91–92, 100, 102

liushou ertong ("left behind" children), 22, 92–93, 98, 101

longevity, 18, 108

lou-baan (the boss), 102

lou-sai. See lou-baan

love, 16, 18, 23, 29, 65, 67–68, 84, 102, 108, 146, 148–61, 169, 190; expressions of, 159; language of, 147; in marriage, 16, 31, 146–47, 151, 155, 160–61, 174, 205; same-sex, 178, 180. *See also* affection; emotions; marriage; romance

machismo (*dananzi*), 135

"mansions." *See* housing

Mao Zedong, 41, 95, 235, 240

Maoist: era, 4, 7, 14–19, 21, 27, 29–31, 39, 42, 45–46, 94, 96, 106–7, 205, 234–35, 237, 240, 246; approach to population control, 220; model of wife and mother, 143; strategy, 94

market-based economic policy, 235, 238

market reforms, 4, 76, 105, 234–35, 238, 240, 246–47. *See also* Reform era

marriage, 3–4, 6–7, 15–19, 22, 25–26, 29–32, 40, 43–44, 47, 49, 54, 58n20, 65–69, 71, 78–79, 82, 84–85, 87–89, 97–98, 103, 108, 125, 127, 131–37, 139–44, 146–50, 154–71, 173–75, 177–180, 183, 185, 190, 194, 196–97, 204, 232, 237, 241; age for women, 132, 143, 170; among elderly, 237; arranged, 153, 235; "bilateral," 241; and conjugal love, 16, 31, 146–47, 151, 155, 160–61, 174, 205; deinstitutionalization of, 6, 19, 27–28, 34n6; and development of self, 147; "dutiful spouse" model of, 152–54, 159–60; "emotionally egalitarian" model of, 147, 149–50, 154–57, 165; fake (*jiahun*), 3, 29, 163, 178, 180n2; impact of education on, 82; impact on remittance, 50–53; local marriage customs, 95; mobility, 44, 46; negotiation, 71, 87; pressure, 163–64, 166, 168–70, 174–75, 179; regulations, 87; and relationship with property, 117, 128, 134, 136, 139, 143; same-sex, 164, 169, 179; uxorilocal, 125, 221, 244; virilocal, 7, 17, 19, 95, 107, 120; *xinghun* (lesbian-gay contract marriage), 163–74, 176–80, 180n2. *See also* bridewealth; courtship; patrilocality; wedding